I WILL BRING YOU HOME

Songs of Prayer, Stories of Faith

REFLECTIONS ON 40 YEARS OF LITURGICAL COMPOSITION

I WILL BRING YOU HOME

Songs of Prayer, Stories of Faith

REFLECTIONS ON 40 YEARS OF LITURGICAL COMPOSITION

DAVID HAAS

GIA PUBLICATIONS, INC.
CHICAGO

G-9617

Published by GIA Publications, Inc.
7404 South Mason Avenue
Chicago, IL 60638
www.giamusic.com

Art Direction and Design: Andrew Schultz
Also available in Kindle/E-Book format
A CD of selected songs is also available: *I Will Bring You Home*
CD-1041

ISBN: 978-1-62277-284-1

For Alec Harris

TABLE OF CONTENTS

TABLE OF CONTENTS

TABLE OF CONTENTS

TABLE OF CONTENTS

TABLE OF CONTENTS

POSTLUDES

FOREWORD

In our parish's weekly printed worship bulletin, used primarily for listing hymnal numbers and supplemental music, we often devote available remaining space to telling the story of one of the hymns being sung that day. It's been pleasantly surprising to experience the frequency of comments from folks who enjoy learning the story behind some of the songs we sing. In this book, David Haas tells the back story of a significant cross-section of his forty years of creative output. Hymns and songs that worshippers have come to cherish. But there's so much more.

Everyone who knows David, knows that he is always eager to engage in the lively art of conversation. And he writes here in a conversational style so that you almost hear his voice as you read. The tone of this book is that of fireside chat; a group of friends gathered with him in which someone asks, "David, tell us about how you came to write *Blest Are They*, and the story pours forth. The details are rich, and often there is a touch of humor, often a bit self-deprecating.

While this book may be considered a collection of memoirs, I think it to be more of an autobiography—the story of one's life. Yes, it's all about creating music for the community of believers at worship, but that *is* David's life. Being a composer of sacred song is not what he does, it is what he is. It's his vocation. He lives this passion every day. It permeates his being more than any other composer I have personally known. David Haas is pastoral musician, composer, lyricist, preacher, liturgist, missionary; he is consumed with zeal for the word of God—forever paraphrasing that word in song; he cares, cares about everyone, with special focus on youth and those marginalized by society as well as by the Church.

If you know David, you will feast on the tales he tells herein. If "David Haas" is mostly a name that you have encountered appended to a musical score, be prepared to make a new friend.

Robert J. Batastini
Vice President / Senior Editor emeritus
GIA Publications, Inc.

TESTIMONIES

I Will Bring You Home begins as a story of over 100 musical compositions, mostly liturgical, of David Haas, song-writer and educator. David uses his consummate story-telling skills to detail how the music came about. This book becomes a charming autobiography of David's life, and more interestingly, of David's faith. It reveals his love for his parents and his wide range of friends and serves as a thank-you for those who assisted him in composing and performing his works. It reveals both the heights of his success and depths of his doubts. I Will Bring You Home also serves as a contribution to the history of the post Vatican II era, a unique period of composition in the history of Catholic music. But, for believers it shows how revelation works through the very human and messy at times process of musical composition. "Faith becoming music is part of the process of the Word becoming Flesh" (Joseph Ratzinger/Pope Benedict XVI). David Haas has risked telling how his faith has become music and therefore, gifted us with a rich meditation of how the Words become flesh. A must-read for pastoral musicians, *I Will Bring You Home* serves as a guide for young composers, a course in theology for Christian believers ... and for his friends and fans, a chance to relive precious moments in history.

Rev. Virgil C. Funk
President Emeritus, National Association of Pastoral Musicians

David—the one that slung Goliath—and became King by some squeamish deeds—gets credit for the hymns we know as the Psalms. Many of the Prophets up to and including Jesus, and down to our own day, knew those lyrics from memory and did not need to reference them when they quoted them. Comes here another David, who has given us tunes and poetry that are so ingrained in our hearts and heads that we cannot recall when or where we first heard them, but can finish all the verses of our favorites without need of a hymnal. How did these happen? Why are they so much a part of our prayer and praise? David of the Haas family here lets us know. In sharing his prompts and inspirations, may we be energized again for deepening our intimacy with Jesus, and for engaging with one another in bringing the Gospel home.

Rev. Raymond B. Kemp
Georgetown University
Washington DC

I WILL BRING YOU HOME

Whether it be a birth, a baptism, a death, a funeral or a special moment in-between, to be an "eye witness" is to occupy a privileged place. This unique vantage point draws one into the very heart of an experience with all of its vulnerability and creativity. I have been an eye witness and active participant to almost all of the 40 years of life and work and faith described by David in these pages. David invited me to be part of the recording team from almost the beginning and I knew these pieces had to be put in service of God's people in worship and mission. I witnessed the impact of this vital sung prayer in communities where I served and in conferences and workshops where I presented. And from decades of my experience, I have witnessed the stories of God's people coming alive, through joy and sorrow, because David shared his gifts of story, music, text and faith. It is impossible to imagine our Church 50 years after the council without 40 years of David's compositions so faithfully shared. Thank you David. I sure am glad I was on the planet at the same time you were!

Bonnie Faber
Voice Teacher and Pastoral Musician
Minneapolis, Minnesota

Many years ago the liturgical pioneer Msgr. John (Jack) Egan proclaimed in one of his talks: "Liturgy and Social Justice are two sides of the same coin. You cannot have one without the other." Of all the liturgical composers I know, there is no one whose music embodies this philosophy more than David Haas. You will find this tethering in these pages. We, the Church, are in debt to him for his magnificent body of work, which has brought the Spirit of Vatican II into the homes of our hearts and places of worship.

Ray Repp
Pioneer Liturgical Composer
Palm Springs, California

As a Protestant, I am a fairly late-comer to the David Haas fan club. I only truly encountered his work when serving on the committee to select hymns for *Glory to God*, the most recent hymnal of the Presbyterian Church (USA). Immediately, I was drawn to his poignant melodies that help the wisdom of scripture sink deeply into the heart. "Blest Are They," his setting of the Beatitudes, stood at the top of my list whenever people would ask, "What are your favorite pieces in the new hymnal?" Those who have a longer familiarity with David's body of work will be enchanted to meet old friends in this volume: both the songs they have sung for years, and the people with and for whom they were written. I was equally enchanted to make new friends, encountering many pieces I had not yet sung, and being so taken by their stories that I had to rush to find recordings so I could listen while I read about them. In addition to these musical delights, I found intellectual stimulation from David's insights into the liturgical composer's craft, and spiritual sustenance from his meditations on the many passages of scripture he has woven into music. This is a collection of stories to savor at so many levels; I plan to keep it on my bedside table as a devotional aid, to help sing me to sleep at night, and wake me refreshed in the morning.

Mary Louise Bringle
Hymn Text Writer; Professor of Philosophy and Religion
Brevard College, Brevard, North Carolina

I first met David decades ago at various liturgical and religious education conventions. His voice was inspirational, his music fresh and accessible. The many lyric poems collected here and the accompanying stories of their birth reveal a gifted, faith-filled composer whose songs have enriched Catholic liturgy. On several occasions I had the pleasure of meeting David's late parents, both of whom were musicians and educators. In them I clearly saw the origin of David's many gifts, and perhaps the reason his lyrics often contain the word "home." This work provides a human context for sacred symbols. What a gift.

Jack Miffleton
Pioneer Liturgical Composer, Musician and Educator
San Fransisco, California

I was and continue to be, the lucky recipient of David's first song born in the wee hours of the morning from a very special gift he didn't even know he had. Blessed are we that he would treasure his gift for all these years to come—listen to it, make it his journey and share it with the rest of us. Throughout my life his music has been key in reminding me of God's presence. I have been living in Rome for many years now, and I'm surrounded by churches. They are beautiful and *maestoso*. Yet, it is in my car or in my kitchen listening to David's songs when my heart swells, pushing me toward goodness and reminding me that I am not alone—precisely what I felt on the day of my First Communion, sitting on my living room floor surrounded by people who loved me—with David telling and singing me to "look to the sun." Good on you, David. Good on you.

Maria "Mimi" Infante
Rome, Italy

In this marvelous and gigantic story, David Haas shares his own journey as a child of God as it unfolded in his music over the past forty years. With generous praise for his colleagues in liturgical and catechetical ministries, David helps us all see with clear eyes how God speaks to us in prayer as we sing the psalms, canticles, and texts of our faith tradition. Continuing the tradition we have known since ancient times, David presents us here with a midrash-like introduction to these sung prayers. This is a story book and one that I would like to put into the hands of every leader in the church today to help us all recall, as he wrote in one of his songs, that "All of us, all are beloved of God."

Bill Huebsch
Author, Catechist, Adjunct faculty at the Institute for Pastoral Studies
Loyola University of Chicago

I WILL BRING YOU HOME

It is said that stories are the glue that holds people together—relationships, groups and communities, and Church. If so, then songs are one of the strongest ways to both tell a story and draw people into the story as they learn the words and the melodies together. David's book does both! He shares with us the experiences, people and places that gave birth to many of the songs he has given to us to sing as we journey. In doing so, he gives us glimpses into the people—Good News in the flesh —and how they taught, preached and stirred the Spirit to work with him in creating his music. It is delightful! Woven into the text is a side-ways autobiography laced with thanksgiving for all the people who have walked with him, and theology learned along the way. Read—listen to the music, sing along and together let us bless the Lord, and make music as minstrels of the word of God in our flesh now. Experience the old saying: To sing is to pray twice—as we magnify our God who is the music of the universe—our one song. Thanks, David, for your sharing your gifts with us again.

Megan McKenna
Author, Storyteller and Theologian
Albuquerque, New Mexico

Our memories often hold the real treasures of our life journey. It's why the act of remembering—what we call "anamnesis" when we celebrate Eucharist—is such an important part of the liturgy. It's an act of great generosity that David Haas has allowed us a glimpse into his life as a composer and shared with us the stories behind songs that we've come to know and love. Many of these pieces have been our companions as we've offered thanks, wept in sadness, cried out in joy, sought consolation, asked for mercy and reached out in hope. In this, David's songs have attached themselves to some of our most treasured life moments as well. I'm so very grateful for his music in my journey of faith and for his willingness to share these stories with us. They are stories not just about his songs but about a man who has tried to be faithful to the gift that's been given to him to use for our sake.

Dan Schutte
Liturgical Composer; Original member of the "St. Louis Jesuits"
Composer-in-Residence, University of San Fransisco

Philosophers of symbolism tell us that two things are required for something to be a true religious work of art: It must be sufficiently beautiful, be classified as art, and it must issue forth from an authentic religious experience. Nobody doubts the beauty of the songs that David Haas has written over the course of forty years. Now, in this warm, personal memoir, David shares many of the rich experiences that helped give birth to those songs. His music and his lyrics speak for themselves, outside of the intimate context that inspired them, but they will be more meaningful after reading the stories of their birth. A good read for everyone, and a must read for anyone involved in church music.

Ronald Rolheiser, OMI
Author of "The Holy Longing"
President, Oblate School of Theology, San Antonio, Texas

In a post Vatican II liturgical world and in the midst of a mid-twentieth century "hymn explosion," some composers became well-known for their musical craft, others for their text-writing, and still others for their pastoral voice. Few managed to weave all three of those into a career spanning more than forty years. With multiple selections included in Presbyterian, United Methodist, Lutheran, and Baptist hymnals (to name just a few), the importance and influence of David's compositions reaches much farther than the Roman Catholic Church and will continue to shape people's faith into the future. He is leaving a legacy of congregational song, and this glimpse into his story is a gift to all those who have been nurtured by the pastoral ministry of David Haas.

Brian Hehn
Director of The Center for Congregational Song
of The Hymn Society in the United States and Canada
Dallas, Texas

"My life is at the service of the gospel. God has given me this gift of grace." This antiphon from the Liturgy of the Hours reminds me of David. His life speaks, no, sings the reality of these words. What a volume of work David has given us in his forty years of liturgical ministry. His music accompanies us on every step of our Christian journey, giving us voice, expressing what is in our heart in times of joy and in times of sadness. His songs accompany us, helping us to walk the liturgical year in prayerful beauty. Thank you, David, for this wonderful musing on such a rich creative life.

Sr. Suzanne Toolan, RSM
Liturgical Composer; Resident Liturgist and Taizé Prayer Leader for the Mercy Center
Burlingame, California

Although in the introduction of this book David refers to himself as "merely a very tiny footnote in the overall remarkable story of contemporary liturgical music since the Second Vatican Council," I would maintain that he is more so, one large footprint in the liturgical music scene. And just as footprints tell us where we've been, they also hint of the direction we're headed. So it is with David's music these past forty years. Read through the lyrics of this amazing collection, but enjoy the stories tied to the songs. They can help us appreciate the joys (and sometimes the pains) that went into composing the music we have grown to love and appreciate.

Gary Ault
Pioneer Liturgical Composer; Original member of "The Dameans"
New Orleans, Louisiana

David draws us into currents of hope. When he sings, he is a man caught up, a man in flow. When he sings, he becomes the song he is singing. And his singing makes him brave. He speaks the truth as he sees it, not looking over his shoulder for approval and disapproval. Whenever I sing his songs, hope flows through me and makes me brave. David has given us the gift of himself.

Sister Helen Prejean, CSJ
Author of "Dead Man Walking"

I WILL BRING YOU HOME

I remember being in college when I first heard David's music. His songs sounded so fresh and engaging to me. They seemed to embody a faith that was absolute—a faith that was wholly alive! What's more, singing David's songs was to enter into that faith. And you know, after all these years, that is still the case. His music has become a language for prayer. It has an immediately recognizable character: its clothing is lyricism, the kind that obligates the voice to sing; its substance, love. Just as the great composers of art song masterfully wove poetry with notes, David has lifted the poetry of prayer with melodies that soar then settle in the place where Spirit lives. David's music has forever enriched, enlivened, strengthened, and incarnated the prayer of all God's people. And now, with the sharing of the stories contained in these pages, his songs will once again sing in our hearts, and we will be blessed because of it.

William Gokelman
Composer, Arranger; Professor and Chair of the Department of Music
University of the Incarnate Word
San Antonio, Texas

I've known David a lifetime. Oh, how I remember his wonderful Mother conducting the church choir, with what I always determined was the most radiant smile God ever planted on a face and his Dad at the organ, always bigger than life, playing with such gusto as his arms and legs worked just as hard as his fingers did on the keyboard. Although David was five years older than me, we grew up together in the same neighborhood and church family that will always be home to the both of us. From the time he wrote his first song, "Mimi's Song" for my sister's First Communion, till the most recent songs "off the press," he has and will always be someone I've been lucky to call mentor, teacher and treasured friend. The other day I was going through some old papers and I came across a scribbled copy of "We Are Called" in David's hand on manuscript paper before it was ever published. God gave me a front row seat to David's life and career and because of that I have spent many years as a music minister and liturgist myself. Almost all the scripture I know by heart is because it was first shaped and cemented there by David's incredible gift of translating and giving life to God's spoken word. Not only has the word been the primary focus of David's lifetime, but also the expression of God's very thoughts into beautiful, prayerful melodies that often pop up in our heads in moments of great joy and deep pain. I am so glad that those of you holding this book in your hands are able to have a peek into what I have known for a long time, that God somehow chose David to be a window, allowing us a better way to God's heart and most profound love for us.

Lisa Driscoll
Director of Music, Holy Family Parish
Caledonia, Michigan

For the past 40 years, David Haas' amazing passion, vision and innovative spirit has enhanced and enriched the liturgical prayer of the Church. His presence, music and song resounds in the halls and walls of Churches and Dioceses across the United States and beyond. Year after year his generous and willing spirit is felt throughout the Los Angeles Religious Education Congress weekend. The birthing of this extraordinary "liturgical music memoir" gives testimony to David's creative and imaginative genius. Everything has a story, and it is significant that his focus on the story behind the song touches the heart with profound wisdom. As the songs are broken open by the story, readers are ushered into new depths of appreciation and inspiration. He is truly gift and blessing to thousands.

Sr. Edith Prendergast, RC
Former Director, Office of Religious Education
Archdiocese of Los Angeles

For as long as we have been singing, we have been singing David's music. His songs have been part of Hangad's repertoire since the very beginning—one of the first songs we learned and recorded together was "Now We Remain." Our homegrown composers here in the Philippines were influenced by his music, and after years of serving in this ministry, we find that we still go back to his music, again and again. We cannot exactly pinpoint why his songs stay with us, but perhaps it is in singing and praying them that we find our own prayers, our own voice. David' songs have a personal and prayerful quality, and this has resonated deeply with Hangad. Imagine our surprise when we finally had the opportunity to meet and sing with him during his visit to the Philippines in 2016! It was, and continues to be, a true meeting of minds and hearts. It was if we had known him all of our lives, and in a way, that is true, and continues to be the case! As long as we have been singing, we have been singing David's music. The music and stories contained in this book are such a blessing, from a true friend.

Mariel de Jesus
Hangad Music Ministry
Manila, Philippines

Our faith is given words in many ways—through catechesis within the community, through the formal study of theology, through the prayer of and with the church, and through the words we sing. When the words are married to music which enhances the words, we have more than either words or music alone, we have "deep words" that enter into our very being and stay with us. David's songs (words and music) have been part of my ongoing formation as an adult Christian for years and when both sought out of the memory banks or arising unbidden, they give coherence to the Spirit's yearnings. We are called to be the hands and feet and voice of Christ in the world— thanks be to God for David who gives us so many rich ways to name that call, and to, in turn, praise God for these gifts: "be the air we breathe, the voice we speak..."

The Rev. Dr. Lizette Larson-Miller
Huron-Lawson Professor, Huron University College
London, Ontario

In his comments on "Creating God," David notes the non-Roman Catholic hymn writers that he occasionally draws upon for texts. There are Lutheran, Presbyterian, Anglican, United Church of Christ, and Methodist poets on the list. It may be that as a Mennonite, I am the furthest afield in terms of liturgical commonality with David's own tradition. It is a mark of his ecumenical curiosity and engagement that he consistently seeks out words that sing the Biblical themes that all Christians share, despite the genuine differences that divide us. That ecumenical road runs two directions, of

I WILL BRING YOU HOME

course. David's music has had a profound influence on Mennonite worship since its relatively late introduction into our canon. "Holy is Your Name," "You Are Mine," and "Prayer for Peace" have emerged as heart songs for our congregations so rapidly and deeply that for many, they now represent distinctly Mennonite songs! (And really, you have not heard a Haas song sung properly until you hear a Mennonite congregation singing it in full harmony.) It was a dream-come-true for me when David first composed a tune for one of my texts, and I continue to be delighted by the way he illuminates my words. I am honored to have a few of our collaborations included in this book. I thank God for David, and I look forward to many more years of shared labor.

Adam M. L. Tice
Hymn Text Writer, Pastor; Editor, The Hymn
Goshen, Indiana

"We are called to act with justice, we are called to love tenderly, we are called to serve one another, and walk humbly with God." We are familiar with the words from Micah but singing them reaches my heart and soul and they become prayer. For me this is the gift of David and his music. Whether they be words of scripture or poetry born of his own life experience, they touch my very being. David and I are from the same town—in fact only a small grove of trees separated our back yards. We attended the same church and "made music together" in the folk group and as cantors. I have been blest to share his journey of life and song. In concert and workshops and in church communities, David continues to share this message, touching our individual life experiences when we sing and pray. My favorite memory is David calling to say "I've just finished a song. Will you listen?" And as we sat together on my piano bench, in song I was reminded that God is a God of love, hope, and forgiveness, of joy and lament; a God who shares my laughter and tears, who is "the song that I'm singing" and a "God of second chances." Thanks David, for your gift of song and friendship.

Jo Infante
Bridgeport, Michigan

As a co-host of the Open Your Hymnal podcast, I have seen how curious people are to learn the stories about the songs we sing. This heartfelt effort by David gives us a candid, and refreshingly honest glimpse into the inspirations, processes, and intentions behind his most beloved songs. Through his music and teaching, David has had a part in forming the faith of millions—this anthology continues this work, providing deeper context and reflection to songs many of us know by heart.

Zack Stachowski
Liturgical Composer; Co-host, "Open Your Hymnal,"
Director of Music, St. Ignatius of Loyola Parish
Ijamsville, Maryland

Very few people have labored with more dedication for the sung prayer of the church than David Haas. Presenting, performing, organizing, writing—and of course, composing—David has been a non-stop force of energy for a cause he passionately believes in. The face of the Church is different because of him. The songs on the lips and in the hearts of Christians are different because of him. I first encountered David when he presented to campus ministry musicians at Saint John's University and the College of Saint Benedict in the 1980s when I was an undergrad. I was moved to tears by the power of his witness. It came full circle when Saint John's Abbey and University presented him (along with Marty Haugen and Fr. Michael Joncas) our highest honor, the Pax Christi award in 2017. I am honored to write these words of testimony to affirm David's work, and to recommend this important collection looking back on this work. These reflections will be inspirational for so many people who have been touched by the life and work of David Haas.

Fr. Anthony Ruff, O.S.B.
Associate Professor of Theology; Coordinator of the "Pray Tell" Blog
St. John's Abbey and University; Collegeville, Minnesota

David's incredible gift of music has been the soundtrack of my life! Each song invokes vibrant memories of different times, places, and events. To read about the experiences and events surrounding these compositions just makes each one all the more special! In this collection David has given us all an intimate look at the stories behind some of his greatest songs. These songs have brought so many of us Catholics through terrible times of grief and tragedy, as well as helped us to celebrate when we've rejoiced with great abandon! Many of David's songs have touched us in profound ways and brought us ever closer to God. What a gift! As St. Augustine said, "Singing is for the one who loves," and David's music has helped so many faith communities to love God and each other a little deeper, a little stronger, and so very prayerfully. After reading this collection, these songs will be even further ingrained in all our hearts and memories for years to come. Thank you, David, for opening up these stories for all of us to hear!

Lisa Cressy
Director of Liturgy, Saint Ambrose of Woodbury
Woodbury, Minnesota

Ask me to name a handful of liturgical composers whose music inspired me to enter this field of ministry, and David Haas most definitely would be on that short list. After graduating from a music conservatory where I concentrated in classical composition, I quickly entered the seminary and began to compose music for our liturgies. But I needed to "re-learn" the craft from composing music for the sake of the concert hall to composing music for the sake of worship . . . and then one day, we sang Blest Are They! I'll never forget my first impression: "This is accessible," I thought to myself, "I could sing this . . . I want to sing this!" That remains my impression 30 years later. Whenever I hear David's music I cannot not sing aloud. When composers create works of art, they do more than share their music: they share their stories and we get a glimpse of their souls. This is what makes I Will Bring You Home a welcomed resource as it provides us with more in depth details of the stories behind the songs of a great composer. So thank you, David, for inspiring generations of pastoral musicians and for allowing us to glimpse your soul!

Fr. Ricky Manalo, CSP
Liturgical Composer
San Fransisco, California

I WILL BRING YOU HOME

In this book David invites us to take a heart-warming and soul-enriching journey through the personal life stories behind his music – the songs which has formed us among the many steps and chapters of our spiritual journeys. It's a journey well worth taking.

Deacon James Knipper
Publisher and CEO, Clear Faith Publishing
Princeton, New Jersey

For forty years, the music of David Haas has been a vehicle of prayer for people throughout the world. These texts and melodies have provided solace, comfort, and celebration for countless people. I Will Bring You Home is a journey through these forty years of inspiration and creativity. In this collection of reflections and the accompanying CD, David shares how each song was brought into the world, created from scripture and the depth of human experience. Knowing the stories behind the songs brings us to a deeper level as we pray these pieces with our choirs, our assemblies, and in our individual prayer. In my experience as a choir director, I know that sharing the background of a song's origin with the choir or with a cantor brings an energy to the singing and deeper level of prayer. Listen, read, pray, and be filled with God's healing love and grace as David takes us on a journey through these decades of sung prayers and stories of faith.

Andrea Goodrich
Director of Music for the Apple Valley Catholic Collaborative
Parishes of St. Elizabeth of Hungary, Acton, Massachusetts and St. Isidore,
Stow, Massachusetts

Born into a family of such surpassing musical interests that he and his siblings, as he has said, spent most of their childhood in concerts, recitals, lessons, and lots of rehearsals, David Haas became an internationally renowned Catholic composer, musician, minister, and teacher. It is no exaggeration to say that his music is played and sung around the world, in thousands of churches and dozens of languages and faith traditions. He is an accomplished author, teacher, and pastoral minister, but today we pay particular honor to the way in which he shaped his capacious musical talents and shared them with the world; his work has elevated hearts, shivered souls, and gathered millions of people together in song. That is great and holy work, and that is why the University of Portland today confers the degree Doctor of Humane Letters, HONORIS CAUSA, on David Haas, of Eagan, Minnesota.

On the Occasion of its One-Hundred-and Thirteenth Commencement Exercises
May 3, 2015
The University of Portland; Portland, Oregon

INTRODUCTION

With the exception of writing "Mimi's Song" while in the ninth grade, I composed my very first "liturgical song" in the summer of 1977. As I am writing these words, I realize that I have been composing liturgical music for forty years. A trembling thought. When I began work on this project I was not conscious of the amount of time that has passed by—that it comes on the 40-year anniversary is entirely coincidental. I have also come to realize that I have composed literally *hundreds* of songs, hymns, psalms, acclamations, litanies, ostinatos and other musical offerings for sung prayer. I am certain that in the minds of a lot of people, that this has been far too many. I look back on the pieces that I have penned over the years and admit with regret that I did not allow some of them to "cook" a bit longer than I did before publishing and recording them; or that I did not toss them into the trash bin altogether. But, one cannot go back and undo such things, and I guess I have to come to peace with it all.

I am humbled and grateful that I have been able to be a vessel for bringing to life music that has empowered people to pray and deepen their spiritual journey. The titles that I have chosen to reflect upon here represent the span of these 40 years, and for these stories and reflections I have chosen 127 songs, hymns, and psalm settings; 6 complete mass settings; 2 major resources of responsorial psalms; and 3 pieces that are not mine, but renderings of songs that have become very important to me over the years.

We know that the primary vocation of the liturgical composer is not to write music for themselves. Liturgical composers create music for the people of God, as a resource for communal prayer for the celebration of the liturgy (primarily, the Eucharist), as well as for the sacraments, funerals, and other rituals for the church. What we are creating, is *sung prayer* for others, *not* inspirational tunes for our own self-satisfaction or status. To place this in perspective, whenever I am asked, *whom* do I write for, or for what instruments or type of choir do I write for, I answer: "I compose music for a musically untrained congregation." The gathered assembly is *always* the primary minister of music in communal worship. Knowing this, I have gone back and forth wondering whether writing such a book as this was even a good idea.

However, no one could have never predicted, many years ago after the beginnings of the liturgical renewal, that the music that emerged, originally created for the liturgy, would also find its way into other corners of the Christian life for so many. Who would have thought at the outset of the Second Vatican Council that people would one day listen to this music in their cars, or on their electronic portable devices or while taking a walk, or at parish meetings or other gatherings in people's homes, where groups gather around the piano and sing their favorite "church songs"? For me, and for most of my liturgical composer colleagues, our primary intention is to, yes, compose music for the liturgy. But we have discovered that much of this music has "ministered," evangelized, and served as prayer *outside of the ritual experience* as well, stretching in my view, our understanding of the pastoral judgment so beautifully articulated in the US Bishops' 2007 statement, *Sing to the Lord.*

More and more over the years, people have wanted to know more about some of my liturgical compositions. I often get asked questions like: Where did this song come from? What "inspired" you to write this piece? What was your intent? Why did that particular scripture passage "speak" to you and cry out to you for music? Did you yourself have an interesting experience that led you to compose it? Did someone commission you to write this piece, and why? What are the liturgical needs that you have tried to respond to in your writing? What kind of liturgical music do you think we need these days? Is this a favorite psalm of yours? What is it like to collaborate with other composers? Who were your mentors? What is your musical background? These and so many other questions have become more frequent; so much so that when I have addressed these questions and shared stories about some of these songs, someone will often say, "you should write a book including some of these stories." So here you go.

As I have already shared, I wrote "Mimi's Song" while in the ninth grade (1972). I have included it here among my reflections. It is not really a liturgical song, but it *is* a song born out of faith, so I thought it was important to share its story here as well. It was 5 years later that I wrote my first so-called *liturgical* song, "My Lord and My God," and now 40 years later have only recently finished writing "I Will Walk with You." The stories of these two songs are shared in this book as well. I find it interesting that the first liturgical song I ever wrote quotes the apostle Thomas in his confession of faith, and that the most recent song of mine speaks about how God is still making the walk with us and remains present to us in all our "empty places." It makes for a nice set of bookends, I think.

It was quite a journey to put this liturgical music "memoir" together. Given the sheer volume of songs I have written over the years, how to choose? GIA has produced four different "Best of" CDs over the years, and they have done well, so it seemed like a good idea to include those songs and stories in this book. There are also a number of other songs that have emerged as favorites for many parishes, friends, and others over the years. Finally, there are some personal favorites I have put in for mostly selfish reasons, whether or not they are the favorites of others. I also sought out pieces that may not be that well-known or that have been "successful," but they hold some interesting stories, memories, and circumstances that brought them to life, or they raise issues that have become important to me.

I also wanted to archive a handful of my earliest pieces. In particular, I feature here three different songs from my very first, self-produced recording, *I Am Yours Today* (songs that go back to 1977-1979). These pieces are mostly forgotten, and so I wanted to resuscitate them a bit. I also have two brand new compositions that I just finished this last year ("What Can I Leave Behind?" and "I Will Walk with You"), and so I similarly wanted to shine some light on these "newbies." I also decided to include three songs that are not actually my compositions, but songs that I truly love or have arranged; songs that I have shared at concerts, retreats, and workshops (the African-American Spiritual, "Steal Away," Joe Wise's "Take All the Lost Home," and a traditional shaker song, "Gospel Kindred"). I will also share some thoughts and opinions about some of the interesting trends and developments that have occurred over the years in the cause and craft of "contemporary" music for the liturgy.

I need to remind everyone—and myself—that I and my compositions are merely a very tiny footnote in the overall remarkable story of contemporary liturgical music. I stand on the shoulders of the brave pioneers who courageously put themselves out there and gave us those very first expressions of sung prayer after the explosion of Vatican II. My own first experience of this revolution was the songs and psalms of people like Ray Repp, Fr. Joseph Gelineau, Joe Wise, The Dameans, Fr. Lucien Deiss, Jack Miffleton, Sr. Suzanne Toolan, Sebastian Temple, Fr. Clarence Rivers, Sr. Miriam Therese Winter, and Tom Parker. This music and what it represented literally changed my life during my years as a young boy and throughout my time as a teenager. I have no words to adequately express my thanks to God that I was alive and around during these initial years after the council. To get a more complete picture of what those groundbreaking times were like, my friend and fellow composer Ken Canedo has been doing a marvelous job of beginning to archive and share the story of these developments in the "contemporary" liturgical music scene, beginning with his first book, *Keep the Fire Burning: The Folk Mass Revolution* (that tells the story of the early beginnings of the "folk/guitar mass" movement in the 60's and into the 70's), and his most recent volume, *From Mountains High: Contemporary Catholic Music 1970-1985* (both are available from OCP Publications). I recommend both of these books for all who want to get inside a most fascinating and interesting story. I hope he and others keep adding more volumes to help us and those in the future to remember.

Later, during my mid-college years, I discovered the ground-breaking contributions of the St. Louis Jesuits as well as the wonderful hymns and song-prayers of Ed Gutfruend, Tim Schoenbachler, Alexander Peloquin, Carey Landry, Bernard Huijbers, Richard Proulx, and Tom Conry. It was these holy saints of God (and others) who provided the backdrop for me to discover that I might have a contribution to make myself, leading me to become closely connected with people like Michael Joncas and Marty Haugen, who were to become comrades in the cause and precious friends; along with mentors Fr. Jim Bessert; Sr. Roberta Kolasa, SJ; Sue Seid-Martin; and Rob Strusinski. All of this eventually brought me to my beginning days with GIA Publications—through the doors opened to me by Bob Batastini and Michael Cymbala, as well as Fr. Virgil Funk and those early stirrings of the *National Association of Pastoral Musicians* (NPM). They all had me at "hello."

In addition to the extraordinary blessings of working and partnering over the years with Michael and Marty—and in more recent years, the blessed grace of collaborating with Lori True—I have been the graced recipient of having associations over the years with dozens and dozens of liturgical composers, most specifically in collaborations and work with people such as Rob Glover; Dan Kantor; Leon Roberts; Kate Cuddy; Fr. Fran O'Brien; Bob Hurd; Joe Wise; Jeanne Cotter; Tom Franzak; Gary Daigle; Fr. John Foley, SJ; Bobby Fisher; David Clark Isele; Christopher Walker; Paul Inwood; Fr. Ricky Manalo, CSP; Dan Schutte; Fr. Christopher Willcock, SJ; Stephen Pishner; Donna Peña; Rory Cooney; Derek Campbell; Jesse Manibusan; Kathleen Harmon, SNDden; Tom Kendzia; Fr. Roc O'Connor, SJ; Jaime Cortez; Peter Kolar; Fr. Bob Dufford, SJ; Tony Alonso; Paul Tate; Zack Stachowski; and Michael Mangan. These are only a fraction of some amazingly gifted servants I have been able to collaborate with, learn from—all who have been a part of this marvelous musical and liturgical work of non-fiction. I have also been inspired to compose when I have discovered marvelous text-writing by poets such as Brian Wren, Timothy Dudley-Smith, Mary Louise Bringle, Adam Tice, Ruth Duck, Sylvia Dunstan, Jaroslav Vajda, Jeffrey Rowthorn, Shirley Erena Murray, and Fred Pratt Green. Most of the people named here have become good friends over the years who have played an important part in my many endeavors, and they are among those who hold many of the starring roles in the stories found here. You will also come to know the parishes and schools I have served in over the years in Michigan, Iowa and Minnesota. These communities of faith were the original birthing places of the bulk of much of the music dealt with in these pages, as well as my association with NPM and the *North American Forum on the Catechumenate*, the *Center for Ministry of the Diocese of Saginaw*, the *Los Angeles Religious Education Congress,* the *Big Island Liturgy and Arts Conference,* and *Music Ministry Alive!* I have been honored to have presented workshops, retreats and concerts in all 50 states; as well as many territories and numerous countries in many different parts of the world. Much of the music addressed here was born from these travels. So many stories. So much to be grateful for. Several of the people and places named throughout this book may not mean much to many who read through these pages, but they are important to me and I believe they deserve to be included, as they are in most cases, a central part of the stories. The liturgical music that I have composed over the years did not happen in a vacuum, and so I give a shout out to many beautiful saints who have been in the mix of it all.

The titles and texts of the songs that I have chosen and the stories/reflections for each are ordered here alphabetically. For each song, hymn, psalm, mass setting or resource, the story/reflection is preceded with background information: you will find specific CD/recording /MP3 information, and the catalog number is provided for the individual printed edition, as well as the source of each of the texts. Recorded versions of all of these pieces can be accessed through the download options and various recordings that you may or may not have. However, I have chosen 15 selections from this collection to include together in an actual physical CD under the same title, *I Will Bring You Home.* You can find the complete listing of the songs found on the CD in Appendix 3 at the end of the book.

I hope that those who read through these reflections will find them interesting and enjoyable. I also hope that these stories and reflections will expand any appreciation that people may have for certain compositions, or provide insight as to what was in my wacky brain when I created them, possibly—and hopefully—provoking some discussions. They might even bring some songs to your attention that you may not had any interest in before. If anyone is disappointed that I did not include "this song" or "that song," then for that I apologize. Next time you see me, ask me about them.

As already said, it was quite the trip down "amnesia" lane to go through these compositions, as most of them triggered amazing memories that have been locked up inside of me for many years. It was fun to do, rewarding to remember, and has been a true experience of gratitude and thankfulness to God. Enjoy the ride.

Soli Deo Gloria!

David Haas
November 26, 2017 / Solemnity of Christ the King
Eagan, Minnesota

MUSIC & STORIES

CD
MP3
Music

Living Spirit, Holy Fire; Do Not Be Afraid, I Am with You
X-7164a
G-7164

A FUTURE WITH HOPE

Music: David Haas
Text: Based on
Jeremiah 29:11-14
(alt. DH)

I know the plans I have for you,
not for harm, but for your good,
to give you a future, a future with hope.

Then when you come and call upon me,
when you pray, I will hear you;
when you search for me, you will find me there.

If you will seek me with all your heart,
I will be there, you will find me.
I will gather you, and bring you home.

When you feel lost, I will guide you,
I am with you, true to my promise;
when you call to me, I will bring you back.

Most Christians have their favorite passages from the Bible, and I am no different in that regard. One of the greatest seismic changes that rose out of the Second Vatican Council was the opening up of the scriptures for Catholics. Many of my Protestant friends are baffled by this, but Catholics of my age and older were often discouraged from reading the Bible. I remember one time hearing a Catholic say in referencing Protestants, "they may have the Bible, but we got the Mass." We have come a long way from those days and those attitudes, with the explosion of biblical scholarship among Catholic theologians, and with the ongoing popularity of Bible study groups, scripture courses, and published resources that bring the word of God closer to the average Catholic. I love studying scripture, and I give thanks to God for people like

I WILL BRING YOU HOME

Fr. Bill Taylor back home in Michigan, and my dear friend and colleague Art Zannoni (he was my Hebrew Scriptures professor in college), and of course Michael Joncas, for opening up to me the richness in biblical studies. Now I devour every book I can come across by scholars such as Marcus Borg; Sandra Schneiders; N.T. Wright; Dominic Crossan; Fr. Raymond Brown, SS; Sr. Barbara Reid, OP; Fr. Eugene LaVerdiere, SSS; and Walter Brueggemann. The more I study scripture, the more I hunger for more. If it were up to me, every liturgical composer would be required to take a core curriculum of scripture classes alongside music theory and the study of liturgy and the sacraments.

I have many favorite passages from scripture. A number of these come from the Psalter and the Gospels. But one of the most treasured scripture passages for me is Jeremiah 29:11-14, which is the source text for "A Future with Hope." In addition to being a cornerstone text for my own spiritual life, I have found that these verses, which so strongly profess God's fidelity and promise in the midst of the journey of life, speak on a deep pastoral level for young people, especially those of high school and college age.

But the same is true for all of us, regardless of our age—our lives are often inflicted with deep anxiety and worry filled with issues of discernment and concerns about the future. In 1996 I composed a poetic hymn based on this section of Jeremiah, titled "You Will Find Me in Your Heart," where I intentionally paraphrased these verses to be yoked together with the tune of an old English lullaby, "Golden Slumbers" (no, not the version by the Beatles on "Abbey Road," but they are the same words). At the time I felt as though these words contained a message where we could be "rocked to sleep," so to speak, with the hope that is announced.

That version never really took hold for many people, so in 2007 (over ten years later), I wanted to give it another try with this setting. Here I chose to encase this message musically as an anthem of faith and confidence—a song of hope that would proclaim more than mere comfort in difficult times, but also provide a vehicle of prayer and praise, proclaiming the fidelity and promise that God holds for all of us. As is the case with several other compositions of mine that I have written over the years, the quarter note "heart beat" pulse in the piano accompaniment that appears in this song is influenced by some of the pop-rock songs of my youth, especially "Hey Jude" and "Let it Be" by the Beatles, "She's Got a Way" by Billy Joel, "A Whiter Shade of Pale" and "Salty Dog" by Gary Brooker, and "Rocket Man" and "Tiny Dancer" by Elton John. I can't help it. I used to play these songs endlessly, late into the night at home when I was a teenager (often to the consternation of my parents), and the "feel" of these songs of that era (and others) seeped into my DNA. There is something about the steady and relentless pulse of these songs that provides a landscape and intensity for the wonderful melodies that accompany them. So "A Future with Hope" became a beneficiary—or a victim—of my love of that genre.

It is sad to me that these verses from Jeremiah do not appear anywhere in the Lectionary for Mass, or for any of our official sacraments and other rituals. There are so many occasions that this reading would serve well, especially for funerals (it was the first reading for my Father's funeral), celebrations of Confirmation, and for liturgies of the Sacrament of Reconciliation and Anointing of the Sick.

This reading and song has been a common theme for retreats that I have led, especially for young people, and I often use this song to punctuate the message. It is one thing to proclaim scripture from the ambo. But as powerful as that can be (especially when the lector proclaims it well), it is something even more provocative when the word of God is sung. "A Future with Hope" served as a favorite choice at the various *Music Ministry Alive!* institutes during its 19-year run, and so as I write this reflection I am holding close to my heart the 2000-plus young people who attended that program. I think of them and pray for all of them every time I lead this song at concerts alone, and especially when I sing it with Lori True. I hope these young ones—O my God, I forget that most of them are young adults now—are OK. I hope that they have come to experience this God who has great plans for us all, and who, when we seek God with all our heart, will seek us out, find us, and bring us home. (11.22.17)

CD
MP3
Music

God Is Here
X-6551a
G-6551

ALL IS READY

Music and Text: David Haas

Come, all you weary ones, who walk the journey;
Know you are welcome at the table of the Lord.
Come, bring your burdens here,
  find love and mercy.
With Christ before us, we gather as his friends!
All is ready, here and now; all are welcome here!

Come, all who struggle hard, all who are hopeful;
Know you are welcome at the table of the Lord.
Come, with your tired hearts, come,
  find new passion.
With Christ within us, we find new life again!
All is ready, here and now; all are welcome here!

Come, all you rich and poor,
  all who are challenged;
Know you are welcome at the table of the Lord.
Come, all who live in shame, we are your family.
With Christ beside us, we no longer are alone!
All is ready, here and now; all are welcome here!

Come, all you single ones, all who are married;
Know you are welcome at the table of the Lord.
Come, you who've lost your spouse,
  all who are lonely.
With Christ our brother,
  we are loved and made whole!
All is ready, here and now; all are welcome here!

Come, all you young and old, all male and female,
Know you are welcome at the table of the Lord.
Come, love of every kind, it does not matter.
With Christ all people are one in God's name!
All is ready, here and now; all are welcome here!

Come, all you anxious ones, who fear the future;
Know you are welcome at the table of the Lord.
Come, all from east and west, we stand together.
With Christ we rise now, to sing the reign of God!
All is ready, here and now; all are welcome!

Copyright © 1990 GIA Publications, Inc.

"All Is Ready" is the second part of a "ritual-unit" piece, a musical way of being intentional about not only gathering at the liturgy, but being equally intentional about hospitality and inclusion. This song was certainly influenced by Marty Haugen's hymn "All are Welcome" (which may prove to be one of the most important pieces of his great legacy), but it was also informed greatly by the writings of my good friend Bill Huebsch in his insights about "Whole Community Catechesis," in particular about honoring all of the different groupings of people that make up the Church: all should be welcomed, because Christ "welcomes all."

As is the case with Marty and his iconic hymn, many people have thanked me specifically for this piece of mine, because they appreciate that I am articulating—and singing—a welcome to those who often feel invisible in the Church, or not even considered—such as those who are single, those challenged both physically and psychologically, those who have experienced the loss of a spouse or someone dear to them, the young ones, those of diverse sexual orientations… The only downside of trying to be intentional about including these varied groups of people is that the hymn has six stanzas! Of course, there could have been more stanzas to include so many different groupings, but I had to stop!

In crafting the text, I chose not to utilize metaphorical images—I wanted it to be direct, concrete, and plain spoken. I wanted to name and, on behalf of Christ and the Church, make a direct invitation to people who so often feel locked out, or not seen. I wanted it to be an expression not only for those being invited, but for all of us "doing the inviting" in a clear and honest way.

I WILL BRING YOU HOME

In light of the nature of the text, other issues come to mind when reflecting on a piece such as this, with a text that is, to put it gently I guess—a bit outside the mainstream. First off, with this being a "gathering" hymn for celebrations of the Eucharist, some might wonder if such a text is problematic because it is not addressed to God, but rather, to the community, to each other. This is a discussion that liturgists often go back and forth with, and it is an important discussion. I would agree with some who caution us to remember that the liturgy is about worship. It is to be prayer and it is God who is to be praised. But the documents and guidelines that guide our liturgical celebration, such as *Sacrosanctam Concilium* (The Constitution on the Sacred Liturgy), the *General Instruction on the Roman Missal* and other documents, place before us the vision and intention of liturgy as advancing "the glory of God and the sanctification of the faithful." So it seems to me (and it has to others) that such a text can serve as a vehicle for expressing the "sanctification" of the gathered assembly, with all of its diversity—naming each as holy—and thus, a most blessed reason to give glory to God.

Some people might ask why we have to sing texts that sound "political"—and of course I agree that we have to be careful about using the liturgy to advance narrow and specific causes. But the liturgy *is* political—it is about what Jim Wallis would call "God's politics": the politics of inclusion, of mercy and acceptance; the politics of equality and holiness as reflected in the Gospel; the politics, theology, and spirituality that affirms and celebrates that God walks with us—all of us—in both the joy and the terror of life.

Finally, the question for some worshippers is this: is what we are singing *true?* I have had certain people say to me that they simply cannot sing a hymn like this one, or Marty's "All Are Welcome," or the great Huijbers/Oosterhuis hymn "What is this Place," because we are part of a church where many are not "welcome" at all; certain forces in the church, sometime from those in leadership, have gone so far as to say quite deliberately that certain people are not worthy. In addition, for those who are not allowed to come to the table and share in communion— because they are not Catholic—a hymn like this would be painful and not honest for them to sing. I certainly honor and reverence the pain and difficulty that people experience and how a piece like this might trigger some of that pain even more deeply. But alongside of that, is the reality that *most* of the music we sing and pray with on Sunday—are we always (or ever) living our lives in consonance with the message not only contained in our song-prayers, but in the scriptures proclaimed and message preached? If we only sang songs at church that resonated with how we live our lives—we would not have many songs to sing at all.

As my friend and hymn text author Sr. Delores Dufner, OSB, states courageously in what is arguably her most well-known and prophetic text, we "sing a new Church into being." We sing not of what we have achieved, but for what are longing for. What is true, without question, is that we all belong to Christ, and this Christ welcomes us all. Without exception. No matter what. (11.16.17)

CD
MP3
Music

To Be Your Bread; Singing Assembly;
You Are Mine: The Best of David Haas, Vol. 2
X-17208
G-3583

ALLELUIA, SING!

Music and Text:
David Haas

Blessed be our God! Blessed be our God!
Joy of our hearts, source of all life and love!
God of heaven and earth!
God of heaven and earth!
Dwelling within, calling us all by name!
Alleluia, Sing! Alleluia, Sing!

Gift of love and peace! Gift of love and peace!
Jesus the Christ, Jesus, our hope and light!
A flame of faith in our hearts!
A flame of faith in our hearts!
Proclaiming the day, shining throughout the night!
Alleluia, Sing! Alleluia, Sing!

Come, O Spirit of Truth! Come, O Spirit of Truth!
Promise of hope, kindness and mercy!
Come and dwell in our hearts!
Come and dwell in our hearts!
Justice and peace, the kingdom of God in us!
Alleluia, Sing! Alleluia, Sing!

I have composed several songs about the Trinity over the years. This was the first one. I remember the attempts that my early catechism teachers made in attempting to explain to us this grand and divine "mystery." It always seemed to be expressed and explained in these kind of terms: "well, you know, the Trinity is a *mystery*." While it most certainly is, I know that over the years I keep trying to expand my understanding of what "mystery" is, and thus, deepen my understanding of the Trinity. Mystery is *not*, in my thinking, about delving in things that are deep, beyond our understanding, and as a result, matters that we should restrain ourselves from exploring. Throughout my life, I am called to prod and explore who these "three persons" are, and what they represent and make manifest in our lives.

So "Alleluia Sing!" was intended to be a celebration of this mystery, a celebration that delights and finds joy in that journey of exploration. This is why the 5/4 time signature and the dance-type rhythmic playfulness is the grounding musical motif for this song. This also is one my earliest attempts to be more poetic in examining this mystery. I remember a homilist preaching on Trinity Sunday, saying to us: "how do you celebrate and pray a doctrine?" That has stayed with me over the years, and this is my attempt to truly "celebrate and pray" this doctrine of our faith, especially in Catholicism.

I do not remember if at the time it was conscious for me or not, but somewhere in composing this text, I chose to sing about the "verbs" of this doctrine, rather than the "nouns," meaning that the reality of the Father (Creator), Son and Spirit in our lives are not just finite truths. The layers of the Trinity are active, engaging, and constantly moving about and doing their "work" in and on us. The first person of the Trinity is the "source of all life and love," always "dwelling within, calling us all by name" (remember, when we were baptized, the priest, our parents and Godparents claimed us for Christ and did so by signing us with the cross, using the Trinitarian formula).

Jesus, the Son of God, is the supreme "gift of love and peace," our "hope and light," and most vividly expressed in this verse, "a flame of faith." I have always seen as one the stirrings of the Holy Spirit as the energy and activity in us to be God made manifest in a world aching for the reign of God. The Spirit dwelling within you and me, is the active and seen "promise of hope, kindness and mercy," and claiming that God's "justice and peace" the kingdom of God—is to be seen in "us."

So, "Alleluia, Sing!" is a celebration of the "verb-ness" of God moving in our lives. Now that is a doctrine that I can not only believe in and own as central to my faith, but one that I—and hopefully, we—can celebrate, and sing and dance to! (11.10.17)

CD
MP3
Music

With You by My Side, Vol. 2: Confirmation;
Living Spirit, Holy Fire, Vol. 2
X-5818a
G5818

ANOINTED AND SEALED

Music and Text:
David Haas

Anointed and sealed, God, your love is revealed;
anointed and sealed, for the life of the world!
Anointed and sealed, God, all darkness is healed;
we are sent—called to serve!
We are sent—called to serve!

Formed by your life giving water;
touched by the fragrance of grace;
marked with your Spirit, we follow in love,
renewed by you here in this place!

Formed by your Word, we are list'ning;
touched by the hope that you bring;
marked with your Spirit, your story we share,
renewed in our joy, here we will sing!

Formed by the feast spread before us;
touched by the food that you bring;
marked with your Spirit, your presence is here,
renewed from this meal, here we will live!

Formed by the gift of God's people;
touched by a vision in sight;
marked with your Spirit, your mission is clear,
renewed to be children of light!

This is a song that was specifically composed for celebrations of the sacrament of Confirmation, either as a song to be sung during the actual anointing of the confirmandi, or as a song of thanksgiving to conclude the rite. Confirmation is really tough, and it is often referred to as a "sacrament in search of a theology." Pastoral practice varies from diocese to diocese, from parish to parish. Lively debates still continue regarding the proper age for those receiving this sacrament. Not to over-generalize, but while some argue for the sacrament to be restored in its proper place in the order of the three sacraments of initiation (Baptism, followed by Confirmation, all moving toward the Eucharist), others argue that it still is a sacrament for junior high or high school years, or a celebration of Catholic adulthood... The debates are still unresolved, and will probably continue for some time.

I talk about this more elsewhere in this book, but the deeper problem seems to be the notion that this sacrament is when the candidates "get the Spirit." My response to that always is, well, so does this mean they did not have the Spirit prior to this day? What about Baptism? For me, a healthier understanding is to acknowledge the presence of the Spirit, but to see it as perhaps, hidden, and needs to be released and revealed, as I state in the lyrics of the refrain: "Anointed and sealed, God your love is *revealed*."

In each of the verses I wanted to emphasize three movements. In verse one, the rite of Baptism: "Formed by your life-giving water." Verse two focuses on the presence of the word: "Formed by your Word, we are listening." It is the word of God that is the primary "text" or "curriculum" for this sacrament—for all sacraments actually. The third verse celebrates the Eucharist, recognizing that we are "Formed by the feast spread before us." Finally, I created a fourth verse, where I wanted to find a way to express that the most profound manifestation of Christ's presence is to be found in each other: "marked with your Spirit, your mission is clear, renewed to be children of light." The refrain attempts to fuse together the ritual action of anointing and the call to be disciples: "We are sent—called to serve!"

After the song was finished, I just did not feel I could bring vocally the energy that I was looking for, so I asked Lori True and Tony Alonso to sing the verses on the recording. The song is dedicated to Tony, and while he was already confirmed for some time when we recorded the piece, I felt that he truly was (and continues to be) someone who takes his initiation seriously, as a pastoral musician, as a liturgical composer, and as a teacher.

I am not sure if the piece has "taken off," so to speak, but composing it was a wonderful way for me to articulate what I have always believed about this sacrament, and continue to hold to this day. I hope that the love of the Spirit of God is "revealed" wherever and whenever this song is sung and prayed. (12.11.17)

CD
MP3
Music

As Water to the Thirsty; Blest Are They
X-39009
G-3502

AS WATER TO THE THIRSTY

Music: David Haas
Text:
Timothy Dudley-Smith

As water to the thirsty, as beauty to the eyes,
as strength that follows weakness,
   as truth instead of lies,
as song-time and springtime and summertime to be,
so is my Lord, my living Lord, so is my Lord to me.

Like calm in place of clamor,
   like peace that follows pain,
like meeting after parting, like sunshine after rain,
like moonlight and starlight, and sunlight on the sea,
so is my Lord, my living Lord, so is my Lord to me.

As sleep that follows fever, as gold instead of grey,
as freedom after bondage, as sunrise to the day,
as home to the traveler and all we long to see,
so is my Lord, my living Lord, so is my Lord to me.

I have been a fan of the hymn text poetry of Timothy Dudley-Smith (an Anglican Bishop from England, mind you) since my earliest days of composing. The first text of his that I put music to was his poem, "Chill of the Nightfall," which became the message of my Christmas song, "Song of the Stable." Setting this particular text, "As Water to the Thirsty" came soon afterward, being brought to my attention by Marty Haugen. Every word in this hymn is a treasure, holding a deep knowledge of the Bible in all of the images that are contained in each of the stanzas. These are as follows:

Stanza 1:
Line 1 Psalm 63:1
2 Psalm 27:4
3 Psalm 28:7
4 1 Thessalonians 1:9
5 Exodus 15:2
6 Song of Songs, Chapter 2

Stanza 2:
Line 1 Kings 19:11, 12
2 Hebrews 13:20
3 John 20:11-18
4 Revelation 1:16
5 & 6 Psalm 104: 2ion.

Stanza 3:
Line 1 Psalm 4:8
2 Matthew 17:2
3 Psalm 146:7
4 Revelation 1:16
5 & 6 Luke 16:11-24

What an amazing yoking together of both the Hebrew Scriptures and the New Testament, yes? The brilliant and seamless crafting of each stanza still stirs in me every time I sing this piece, which has been a staple part of my concerts ever since its creation.

While this hymn/song can be sung by an assembly, it seems in a lot of places to have fallen into the category of "meditation song" (dear Lord, how I hate that phrase, but I guess that is what it is). I remember being a young director of music at the parish—when I thought I knew everything, and was going to single-handedly save liturgy and music as we know it—and an elderly woman approaching me after mass one day and saying: "Oh David, I just love your voice. Whenever you sing, I don't want to sing along; I just want to sit back, close my eyes, and listen." At that moment, I should have simply said thank you. But no, I had to make the moment into a workshop opportunity. I proceeded to "instruct her" that she was not supposed to just listen, but to participate fully by singing with the congregation. I told her that the role of liturgical music is not for a solo singer to "strut," but to empower the singing of the people. She felt a bit startled, and walked away, a bit sadder than she was when she first came up to me. Right at that moment I realized how awful and potentially damaging my response was. Basically—while unintentional—I devalued and invalidated her experience. She was trying to communicate to me that she was touched, moved and yes, praying. And then I turned around and told her there was something wrong with her experience. While most certainly, the singing of the assembly is the primary motivation that we should have as leaders, especially cantors, I have come to learn that people are pulled into an experience of prayer and the presence of the holy in ways beyond our rules and principles. She taught me much by that interchange. My only regret is that it was quite a while after this that I learned this important message. I wish I had the opportunity to apologize to her, and to thank her for the gift of wisdom that she, unintentionally, gave to me. I have come to value such experience of people, and over the years "As Water to the Thirsty" has become a song for just this kind of meditation and reflection.

I remember the first time my Dad heard me sing this piece. It instantly became a favorite of his and remained at the top of his list throughout his entire life. I remember vividly him telling me that when he died, he wanted me to share this piece at his funeral. It remains one of the most sacred moments of my life when I sang this at the evening prayer on the Vigil of his funeral celebration. The last couple years of his life, my Dad suffered from Alzheimer's, and one of the most precious periods of time spent with my father as he approached his passing was the very night before he died. I was sitting alone with him in the hospital, and he was gasping to breathe even through his comatose state. I just held his hand, and while we could not communicate verbally with one another or look into each other's eyes, I felt his index finger moving up and down my hand, as if to tell me he was OK, and that he knew I was there. And that moment, the beginning of the third stanza came to mind, and became my prayer for my Dad at this moment: "As sleep that follows fever, as gold instead of grey …"

The next morning, my Dad breathed his last, and the rest of the stanza came true for him, and yes, for me. Robert Haas had lived his life as the traveler that Dudley-Smith speaks of here, and the greyness of his life most certainly turned to the gold that was the entirety of his being for me. In those final months when Dad's ability to communicate was becoming more and more difficult, he still shared his joyful disposition and exultant delight every time I came to visit him. I would walk into his room, and he would literally jump up and throw his arms in the air with a big smile, and give me a big hug. He always welcomed me like I was the Prodigal Son. Actually, I have been exactly that, very much so, quite often in my life. In those chapters and moments of my life and in these final precious times together when he greeted me so lavishly and lovingly, he reminded me about the father in Luke's story:

So he set off and went to his father.
But while he was still far off,
his father saw him and was filled with compassion;
he ran and put his arms around him and kissed him. (Luke 15: 20)

My Dad was always like *this* Dad—he always "ran and put his arms around" me throughout my life. And this is exactly how God is with all of us. God chooses not to punish us, and does not just stand back and observe when we turn our lives around and seek mercy—no, God is constantly *running toward us* with arms outstretched and joy pouring forth, wrapping and kissing us with supreme compassion. God, I miss my Dad so much, because I know now more than ever that his manner with me in all of the journeys of my life was always to run toward me, put his arms around me, and kiss me.

I feel him with me in a very intense way, every time I share and pray this song. Thank you, Timothy, for giving us this text, and for providing for my Dad the words he found to believe in the dream of resurrection that guided his life, most certainly his passing, and his lasting memory for myself, my family, and for all those who remember him. (11.19.17)

CD
MP3
Music

To Be Your Bread; Light and Peace
X-17213
G-3079

AT EVENING

Music: David Haas
Text: Fred Pratt Green

Now it is evening:
lights of the city
bid us remember
Christ is our light.
Many are lonely,
who will be neighbor?
Where there is caring
Christ is our light.

Now it is evening:
Little ones' sleeping
Bid us remember
Christ is our peace.
Some are neglected,
who will be neighbor?
Where there is caring
Christ is our peace.

Now it is evening:
Food on the table
bids us remember
Christ is our life.
Many are hungry,
who will be neighbor?
Where there is sharing
Christ is our life.

Now it is evening:
Here in our meeting
may we remember

Christ is our friend.
Some may be strangers,
who will be neighbor?
Where there's a welcome
Christ is our friend.

While I have memories of singing hymns when I was a young boy, my real love of hymnody came during my first two years of college at Central Michigan University, when I sang in the choir at an Episcopal church nearby. It was then that I came to understand hymn singing, not as "filler" or "travelling music" for the priest, but as an actual act of worship. My Protestant brothers and sisters have a deeper understanding of this. Catholics still see hymns for the most part, as "scene change music." "At Evening" was the very first composition of mine where I utilized a poetic hymn text by a skilled hymn text poet—in this case, Fred Pratt Green, most famous for his iconic text, "When in Our Music God is Glorified." In the early days of my friendship with my good friend, pastoral musician and composer colleague, Rob Glover, he gave me a book containing many hymn texts by Green, and I still have it on my shelf now. Its cover and pages are more than tattered, as I reference this resource often, and it was the beginning of exploring many text writers that included Green, as well as people like Timothy Dudley-Smith and Brian Wren.

After I composed the melody, the piece sat around for a while, and I remember sharing it with John Foley (one of the original St. Louis Jesuits, who composed some of the earliest compositions that deepened my call to be a liturgical composer myself). What followed was a wonderful conversation and sharing around the time of evening being a time to recollect and examine the different activities and thoughts of our day. Talking and sharing about this was new for me, as I had yet to discover and learn more about the Prayer of Examen. The relentless central question of this hymn, "who will be neighbor?" provides such an examination of conscience for all of us, if we pay attention while we are singing and praying this hymn.

I included "At Evening" as the concluding piece on my music collection/recording, *To Be Your Bread*, but it developed a deeper focus when I began to learn more about the official daily prayer of the Church, the Liturgy of the

I WILL BRING YOU HOME

Hours. My love for the Liturgy of the Hours was nurtured in me by Michael Joncas and Sue Seid-Martin, who was an important mentor to me while she was Director of Music and faculty member at the St. Paul Seminary School of Divinity (in St. Paul, Minnesota) in the 1980's. "At Evening" became a staple for this community at their Thursday evening "prayer at table" celebrations for many years. In 1985 I was invited to serve as composer-in-residence at the Divinity school to work with Sue and with Bonnie Faber, another dear friend and colleague, who was also employed there as their voice teacher, cantor director, and adjunct instructor. During that time (1985-1988) Sue asked me (in the manner of an offer I could not refuse!) to compose, for the community, complete and through-composed settings of both morning and evening prayer that would serve as the primary settings for their common daily prayer together.

These settings developed into the resource, *Light and Peace*. The recording featured the Divinity School Chorale (its membership included seminarians as well as female and male Divinity students and staff) conducted by Sue, with Bonnie as one of the primary cantors—her singing here is some of her best. I have wonderful memories of those recording sessions, but most of all, how the community there embraced and prayed these settings. "At Evening" will always raise up for me the memories of my time there, and also, the relationship of daily prayer with the call to service and discipleship. (11.10.17)

CD
MP3
Music

God is Everwhere
X-95920
G-8857

BE A BLESSING

**Music and Text
David Haas**

Be a blessing to yourselves,
be a blessing to the world,
for each other: a covenant of love.
Be a blessing with your heart,
be a blessing with your lives,
in communion with God.

Find love in the food and feed each other;
find love in the food of love and grace;
find love in the food
    of forgiveness and mercy;
Be a blessing, be a blessing!

Find love in the food and heal each other;
find love in the food of light and good;
find love in the food
    of new and fresh beginnings;
Be a blessing, be a blessing!

Find love in the food and serve each other;
find love in the food of faith and hope;
find love in the food
    of righteousness and justice;
Be a blessing, be a blessing!

In 2009 the people of St. Paul and Minneapolis lost both an icon and a saint, when Giovanna D'Agostino, a legendary restaurateur and cookbook author, more affectionately known as "Mama D," passed away. Every March 19 for over

I WILL BRING YOU HOME

40 years Mama D celebrated the feast day of St. Joseph (the patron saint of charity to the poor and revered to the Italian people) and would prepare and serve up a free meal to the poor and needy in the area. At times, as many as 3,500 people would show up at her restaurant and local churches as one among many ways to celebrate the St. Joseph day events.

This beloved matriarch of a prominent restaurant family was once asked to comment as to why she thought the breakdown of the family was becoming more and more prominent in our society. Her answer: "TV dinners. There's no love in the food." She had a philosophy that centered around food: "We've gotten too modern for own good. I don't believe in microwaving. There are too many chemicals in what we eat. We feed our garbage cans better than our stomachs." One of her sons once said, "she would scold you and feed you and tell you she loved you." When teaching about cooking, Mama D would always admonish that "you have find and put love into the food." Mama D was more than an Italian chef and larger-than-life personality. Her understanding of food as a response in love made her a theologian.

What Jesus did throughout his "meal ministry" (read the Gospel of Luke), culminating on the evening of the Last Supper, was to "find and put love into the food"—this was the blessing that he offered, and the blessing that we all have been called to offer and become. This is what we do at every celebration of the Eucharist. We "bless," and so "transubstantiate," the food into the presence of God's love, Jesus the Christ. We are called to share and become that very "Body and Blood of Christ" for each other.

When my friend and mentor to so many, Fr. John Forliti—a priest of the Archdiocese of St. Paul and Minneapolis and chaplain at Cretin-Derham Hall where I served for a while—celebrated his jubilee of 50 years in the priesthood, I composed this song for the anniversary liturgy. John was—and continues to be as of this writing—an amazing priest who has touched many lives for years as both a pastor and teacher, and also was a major influence nationally for the beginning movements in religious education after the advent of Vatican II. For me, he became a good friend and model for ministry.

He also happens to be a great Italian cook himself, and was a friend of Mama D. Throughout his priesthood he most certainly has found and "put love into the food." At every school liturgy, he would conclude by first telling the students how beautiful they were. Would that every priest and minister lavish our young people with such affirmation! But right after that, he would follow that message with an instruction to always "be a blessing" by their lives.

Fr. John's invitation and Mama D's theology of finding and putting "love in the food" provided all I needed to compose this song; it soon became our usual closing song at the masses at CDH. It has become a popular song for children as well.

The message rings true and for me, serves as a profound invitation. Simple. Direct. Love and blessing, always remembering to "find and put love in the food," or to define it in another way: hospitality. If you were to ask me to summarize the vocation of Mama D, I would say that she was a "grandmother" to everyone she came in contact with. I cannot think about Grandmothers without calling to mind my own Grandmother, Grandma Carrie (on my mother's side). My brother, sister and I, as well as my cousins, used to call her "Groovy Grandma," because she really was. Her grandchildren were her treasures, and she was the very first person I can remember, blessing me. She would always say to all of us, "Oh, bless your heart." Over the years this blessing and the words that were attached to it sunk deeply into my spiritual bloodstream. All these later I catch my help saying the same thing to the young people whom I get to work with. Grandmas are very special, as an eight-year-old shared so prophetically in a school assignment to define "hospitality." For her, the definition of hospitality was: Grandma.

Grandmothers are people who had no children of her own.
They do like other girls and boys.
A grandfather is a "man" grandmother.
He goes for walks with the boys,
and they talk about fishing and stuff like that.

Grandmothers do not have to do anything except "be there."
They are so old—they should never play hard or run.
They should slow down when they come by things
like pretty leaves or caterpillars.
They should never say "hurry up."

Grandmothers are usually fat;
but not too fat to tie your shoes.
They were glasses and funny underwear,
and they can even take their teeth and gums off!

Everyone should try to have a Grandmother,
especially if you don't have a TV.

I WILL BRING YOU HOME

Because they are the only ones among the grownups—
who have time.

Mama D, Grandma Carrie—these Grandmothers, these "ministers of hospitality" have taught me much. They are calling me and all of us to be good Grandmothers, to "be there" and "have time" to find and put love in the food, to see everything and everyone as a blessing. So my friends, join me in this high calling: be a blessing. (11.24.17)

CD
MP3
Music

Star Child; With You By My Side, Vol. 1:
Journey or Life; Give Me Jesus
X-80305
G-5211

BE BORN IN US TODAY

**Music and Text
David Haas**

Through the winter and the cold,
our faith can weaken and grow old;
so we ache to find a song of a God,
one to whom we can belong.
Instead of power shown as might,
a tiny baby is your light;
we find a child who sings the way,
come now, be born in us today.

Christmas comes and Christmas goes,
yet pain and violence sadly grow.
We cry and hurt, when will it end?
Is there a savior, a messiah whom you'll send?
We pray in hope, please hear our cry,
or is the story just a lie?
We need the child to show the way,
come now, be born in us today.

In this time of joy and cheer,
we find resentment, bound by fear;
called to be believe, but we are blind,
give us a reason, a lifeline we can find.
Poisoned by selfishness and hate,
how much longer must we wait?
This child brings life to our decay,
come now, be born in us today.

Give us a sign that you are real,
numb though we are, help us to feel.
There's only one gift that we need,

I WILL BRING YOU HOME

a manger, too, where all can come and feed.
We need to know we're not alone;
a place of safety, a home.
Although the cross is here to stay,
come now, be born in us today.

Christmas songs are challenging for composers because it is really difficult for any of them to break through. There are so many of them, and in the end it is the familiar carols and other popular songs that are still the most widely sung. It is even more difficult to create Christmas songs that speak to the challenges and the more shadow side of this time of year and the struggles that so many experience when the holidays come around. I really do believe that this is a time of year where many of us—understandably so—want to escape from the struggles of life, and so there is a desire to keep the message happy and upbeat. I get it.

But I wanted to push the envelope a bit, and this song (along with other Incarnation songs of mine like "Birthsong," "Will You Come and See the Light?" and "Summer Sun and Winter Skies") is one of my bolder attempts to do so.

I remember reading somewhere that the season of Christmas is one of the times of year where suicides rise. What a shock for me when first reading about this, but after a while, it began to set in as to why. Christmas, for so many, is too often a mixed bag of celebration and joy alongside the realities of sadness, loneliness—even despair. Any season of the year can be coercive and manipulative, because with them come expectations—and Christmastime is a time when we are expected to be happy, child-like, and filled with "Christmas cheer." But for so many this is far from being the case. I wanted to somehow address this truth, and to help us all to see that this "cheerful" season is for some a time of lament.

This brings to the surface one of those coercive strands that, while not intentional, limits and makes small the fuller understanding of what we call the "paschal mystery." Our embracing death and suffering is not reserved for the season of Lent. This time of the Incarnation (Advent-Christmas) is actually the beginning of the Paschal journey. The very birth of Jesus announces this truth from the get-go. If we read deeper into the infancy stories in Luke and Matthew, we certainly see the hope and expectation of birth, but we see it taking place in the midst of darkness, isolation, and fear.

Music & Stories BE BORN IN US TODAY

If Christmas—and our celebrations and prayer of this season—do not, in some way, address and accept the realities of pain and sadness taking place in and around this time of warmth and joy, then we are not truly embracing Christmas. We need to be attentive to those who are crying out, and yes, doing so in the midst of this season. This story is not limited to the sweet story of the birth of Jesus. In fact, it really was not as sweet as we so often make it out to be. Christmas is not the story of the manger as much as it is the story of birth coming to us in the midst of poverty, darkness, sadness, grief, fear and hopelessness. It is a story about restoring hope when it seems to be absent, re-igniting in us all the awareness that we too ache for a "manger … where all can come and feed."

When some people first heard the recording of this song, they were a bit startled and were not sure if they liked it. A couple people told me that it was too dark, too transparent, too negative—basically, for some it was quite the "downer." I admit that in seeking out the "mood" and sentiment of this song, I was channeling Elton John's "Someone Saved My Life Tonight," in terms of its raw "crying out." On the other hand, some have said that "Be Born in Us Today" is one of their favorite Christmas songs, specifically because of its vulnerable character. One friend told me that they like it "because it is true." I think that is why it is one of the songs of mine that is closest to my heart as well, because beyond trying to speak to the realities of pain and suffering for people in our various circles of life, it is my story as well: of doubt, of fear, of worry and anxiety. A story of hope that while the "cross is here to stay," it can be transformed into a tree more beautifully decorated, not with ornaments, lights and garland, but with the promise of new life for us all, that can "be born in us today" and every day. (11.10.17)

To Be Your Bread;
Glory to God: The Best of David Haas, Vol. 4
X-80305
G-5211

BE LIGHT FOR OUR EYES

Music and Text:
David Haas

Come and be light for our eyes;
be the air we breathe,
be the voice we speak!
Come, be the song we sing;
be the path we seek!

Your life was given; food for all people,
body and blood—new life in our midst!
Death is no longer, life is our future,
Jesus, Messiah; name of all names!

We hold your presence; risen forever!
Your name now names us: people of God!
Filled with your vision, people of mission,
healing, forgiving; light for the world!

Lead us to justice, light in the darkness;
singing, proclaiming Jesus is Lord!
Teach us to speak, and help us to listen
for when your truth and our dreams embrace!

This song was composed initially around two experiences. The first was my meeting the composer Bob Hurd and his music ministry ensemble, "Anawim," for the first time—I think it was the summer of 1981. They presented a showcase of Bob's newer songs at the regional convention for the National Association of Pastoral Musicians at Santa Clara University in California. I remember vividly as being the very first time I heard his song, "In the Breaking of the Bread." It blew me away.

After the event, I went up and introduced myself (I was not nationally published at the time). We all sat around and shared songs (the only real song that I had copies to share was my unpublished score of "We Have Been Told"), and it was a wonderful time. Almost instantly, I became not only good friends with Bob, but with some of other members of the group, which including Dominic MacAller and Barbara Bridge (now both published composers themselves). I was not only impressed with the wonderful blend of how they sang as an ensemble, but also inspired by their obvious love and care for each other. Their vocal sound was a tight web of harmonies so connected and well-tuned to each other, all laid upon an equally tight instrumental foundation. This song is dedicated to Bob and Anawim, and to this day, Bob, Dom, and Barbara have remained good friends and colleagues. We have worked together in many different settings, including the "Music Ministry Alive" program that I began in 1999. We often reminisce about that first meeting so many years ago, and smile in gratitude.

The other source that helped bring life to this song was reading Matthew Fox's book, *Original Blessing* for the first time, and being introduced to his concept of "Creation-Centered Spirituality"—how all of creation, the entire cosmos, was and is caught up in the glory of God, as light, breath, the earth, and the creative arts all come together in an act of praise and celebration of all that is human, with Jesus at the center.

Musically, the refrain was my attempt to borrow from what I heard from the vocal arrangements of Anawim (Bob's arranger for those early songs was the very talented Craig Kingsbury) and provide a similarly "tight" and accented sort of sound, musically presented in a pseudo-rock-and-roll kind of tune and arrangement. The text of the refrain grew out of my need to name Christ as the ongoing "original blessing" in a series of "be" statements: "... *be* light for our eyes, *be* the air we breathe, *be* the voice we speak... *be* the song we sing, *be* the path we seek."

The energy needed to continue on the verses, which embody a breathless, almost desperate crying out to the risen Christ—pleading for him to be true to the promises of God's presence in his divine and human person and at the same time challenging ourselves to be that same presence, that same blessing for others: "fill'd with your vision, people of mission, healing, forgiving ..." I know that this strategy has worked, because over the years many cantors have complained that there seems to be nowhere to breathe in these verses.

I have always liked this song. After it was finished, recorded and published, I was a bit nervous and wondered if it would catch on with people, and whether or not it would be too difficult: the various meter changes and shifts on the refrain, and the need for a cantor with monster breath control to get through the verses! But I have been pleasantly surprised over the years—people have told me they used it, and it has appeared in various hymnals as well. So I am grateful. My primary hope and prayer when looking back and reflecting on the message of this song is that I myself may become more and more the light, breath, voice, song, and path of Christ to all that I encounter in my life. (11.10.17)

CD
MP3
Music

Before I Was Born; Without Seeing You: The Best of David Haas, Vol. 3
X-44802
G-5182

BEFORE I WAS BORN

Music: David Haas
Text: Psalm 139
(alt. DH)

You made me, you formed me.
You kept me alive long before I was born.
You kept me alive long before I was born.

You have sought me out, and found me;
you know where I sit or stand.
You know the depths of my heart,
whenever I move or rest,
you find me wherever I am.
You find me wherever I am.

Before the word comes from my mouth,
you know what I want to say.
You come close to me,
you lay your hand upon me.
All of this is too much for me.
All of this is too much for me.

How can I ever hide from you?
Where can I run from you?
Above and below—you are there.
To the dawn or to the sea—you are there.
Your hand will guide my way.
Your hand will guide my way.

I WILL BRING YOU HOME

You have created ev'ry inch of me,
you have knit me to my mother's womb.
You have record of all my days,
long before they ever began.
How amazing your thoughts, O God.
How amazing your thoughts, O God.

"Before I was Born" became my second compositional visit with Psalm 139. Back in 1987 I composed "You've Searched Me," and there I approached this psalm of God's relentless presence through the lens of vulnerability and the fear of standing before a God who knows us so well. With this new setting, published in 2000, what rose out of my spiritual life at the time was truly a stance of total awe and, as a result, the need to surrender to this God who knows us better than we know ourselves.

In this particular version of Psalm 139, I wanted to emphasize that this "knowing" from God begins at our birth. I have never had any children of my own, but observing the experiences of many friends over the years who are parents, I continually find it to be an amazing miracle. When I have been in the presence of friends holding their newly born infants in their arms, I have often said, "how you can you stand it?" Many times the parents answer by simply looking me in the eyes and respond with, "I know." This was the exact answer I remember that my friend (and president of GIA Publications) Alec Harris offered when I asked him this very same question after his son, Gabriel, was born. Psalm 139 immediately came to mind, and so did "Before I Was Born" fairly soon after. It is dedicated to the celebration of his life. Gabriel is a grown young man now.

While it was not intended at all to become a "pro-life" theme song, many pro-life groups have chosen this song for use in liturgical celebrations and events that center on the amazing and profound gift of life. And that certainly makes me happy. But one of the things I love about Psalm 139, and which I tried hard to communicate with this text, is that it sings of a God who not only knows us before we are born but also rejoices in the moment of our birth and walks with us—however much we may get lost or try to hide—throughout the entirety of our lives. This was our prayer for Gabriel on the day of his birth, and it is our prayer for every child brought into this world: that God will be with them, and with us—helping us all to celebrate the blessedness and precious nature of their existence, in every moment, their whole life. For me and for many, this is what it means to be truly pro-life: to defend the life in the womb being born into the world, but also, to defend all that humanity encounters up until the day of their passing into God's embrace. (11.24.17)

CD
MP3
Music

I Will Bring You Home
X-102505
G-9036

THE BELOVED OF GOD

Music and Text
David Haas
inspired from
the writings of
Henri Nouwen

I am, I am the beloved of God.
All of us, all are beloved of God,
not for what we do,
but because of who God says we are.
We are the beloved of God.

You are my beloved child from the beginning
  and throughout all time.
On you, on you my favor rests.

I have called you each
  by name from the beginning
  and throughout all time.
You are mine and I am yours.

While I have always been a fan of the great spiritual writer, Fr. Henri Nouwen, his message and spiritual vision have become a particularly central force in my spiritual and prayer life as I grow older. As a result, his writings have been the medium for my own survival amidst many challenges and struggles. He died suddenly from a heart attack in 1996, without my having the chance to meet him. Even so, I have felt more and more, a real kinship with him. A colleague once described Henri as a "contemplative nervous wreck." I relate well to this image as similarly true in my own life, a truth that friends (and foes perhaps) would certainly agree with. Henri's integrity as a spiritual mentor was centered in the truth that he, as wise as he was, lived with much torment and anxiety, and we know that he battled with issues of self-esteem, loneliness, and deep depression. His humanity was his gospel, and all of humanity—Christian and non-Christian, young and old, rich and poor—was his parish. For those not familiar with Henri, his life story is one worth exploring, and his books are filled with great wisdom and insight. They are presented so plainly with a tremendous simplicity, as to hold something dear and common for all of us who seek to live the spiritual life more authentically. In recent years I have authored books and presented talks on how Henri's wisdom can be integrated not only in our own personal spiritual path, but how we can actually pray with his vision, communally, and at times, in liturgical settings. His legacy is eternal.

One of Henri's central themes is the fundamental stance that all of us, not only Jesus, are the "beloved" of God. To get inside this more deeply and concretely, I would encourage everyone to read his marvelous book, *Life of the Beloved*. It is his passionate conviction that just as God was, and continues to be, pleased with his son Jesus, God is also pleased and delighted in you and me, who are also adopted and holy daughters and sons.

I wanted to find a way where as a community in a communal prayer setting we could name and celebrate our belovedness in song. It's one thing to say or recite something like, "I am the beloved of God," something deeply important to us. But it is so much more powerful and more penetrating to the heart when we sing such sentiments. That is what I attempted to do here with this song.

Another event that wedded itself to this desire to sing about being the beloved of God was the news that I received in 2015 that I was to receive an Honorary Doctorate in Humane Letters from the University of Portland, in Oregon. I was absolutely blown away—I had no previous relationship with and had never before even visited the University of Portland, and I questioned whether or not I or my contributions were worthy for such an honor, especially since academia and I have had a turbulent history over the years. But I then I thought about how wonderful it was that a university would recognize liturgical music and liturgical composition as a holy vocation. I felt (and still do) that I was accepting this honor not just for myself and around anything that I may have contributed over the years, but also on behalf of all my liturgical composer friends and colleagues, and for the cause of quality liturgical song in our communities of faith.

I was so thrilled with anticipation of this experience that in response I offered to present an evening retreat for the young collegiate music ministers involved there and for the general public the same weekend. And in addition, I offered to compose something just for them as a way of acknowledging their affirmation of my vocation as a liturgical composer. They enthusiastically said yes, and so when I was thinking about the young liturgical musicians there that I would soon be meeting (and the many young liturgical musicians that I have advocated for over the years), this image of them needing at this time in their life to see themselves as God's works of art, of being the "beloved of God," rang strong in my heart. This doubly inspired my resolve to compose this song, dedicated to the University of Portland community. I was given an additional thrill when it was premiered at the Baccalaureate Mass for this event, led by an amazingly talented music ministry of students under the direction of their wonderful university campus minister for music, Maureen Briare.

The trip and experience there was additionally very special as Helen and I were accompanied by our dear friends Bonnie Faber, Bishop Remi de Roo (retired bishop of Victoria, British Columbia), Pearl Gervais, Fr. Jim Bessert, Mary Werner, Fr. Virgil Funk, Dr. Michael Connolly (from the faculty in Portland), and my uncle, Bill Haas, who was able to offer words of wisdom to me in the midst of my self-doubt in receiving such an honor. He shared with me—having a doctorate himself—that the trappings of the actual degree are not what is being recognized. He helped me understand that the university was doing more than just recognizing my body of work; it was honoring who I am—the beloved of God. All of us are the beloved of God, for God celebrates who we are; not what we do. To be "in Christ" is to welcome in God's way of seeing us—as God's choice. While we are sinners, we also need to recognize that there is nothing too disgusting, too heinous, too horrific or too "sinful" that will push God away.

May we never forget this: that you and I are as much a child of God as Jesus was and is. We are the beloved of God. (11.10.17)

CD

MP3
Music

To Be Your Bread; Come and Journey;
Blest Are They: The Best of David Haas, Vol. 1;
Walking by Faith; Glory Day: David Haas and
Friends in Concert; Give Me Jesus
X-39023
G-2958

BLEST ARE THEY

Music: David Haas
Text:
Matthew 5:3-12
(alt. DH)

Blest are they, the poor in spirit;
    theirs is the kingdom of God.
Blest are they, full of sorrow; they shall be consoled.

Rejoice and be glad!
Blessed are you, holy are you!
Rejoice and be glad!
Yours is the kingdom of God!

Blest are they, the lowly ones;
    they shall inherit the earth.
Blest are they, who hunger and thirst;
    they shall have their fill.

Blest are they, who show mercy;
    mercy shall be theirs.
Blest are they, the pure of heart; they shall see God!

Blest are they, who seek peace;
    they are the children of God.
Blest are they who suffer in faith;
    the glory of God is theirs.

Blest are you who suffer hate, all because of me.
Rejoice and be glad, yours is the kingdom:
    shine for all to see.

I WILL BRING YOU HOME

"Blest are They" is most certainly a blessing and gift from God. I really do not believe I had much of a hand in creating and composing this piece. Even if it sounds a little romantic and schmaltzy to say so (you, David? Never!), I can only say that it was a power greater than myself, steeped in gratitude, that brought this song-prayer to life.

During the years 1982-1985 I served as the Director of Music and Liturgy at St. Thomas Aquinas Church in St. Paul Park, Minnesota (Archdiocese of St. Paul and Minneapolis). It was during that time that my creative energies as a liturgical composer were being nurtured and sustained—centered in composing music for sung prayer for a particular worshipping faith community. During that time, I was able to discover and celebrate not only a liturgically vibrant community, but also a community authentically committed to discipleship. To this day, St. Thomas Aquinas continues to be such a place, a center of Gospel living.

During my time there the parish had a regular ongoing commitment to the Archdiocesan Loaves and Fishes program at the Dorothy Day Center in downtown St. Paul. (The center, sponsored by Catholic Charities, is still a growing and expanding center for ministry to the homeless.) Once or twice a month, members of the parish would go to the center, and prepare and serve a meal for the homeless who came to its doors. Christian hospitality was—and still is, for all involved with the Catholic Worker Movement that Dorothy Day began together with Peter Maurin—at the center of the St. Paul location and all similar sites that were and continue to be part of the Loaves and Fishes program. At that time, the center did not operate as a typical "soup kitchen." Rather, it was a place for the homeless and hungry to call home—a gathering place to dine and feast on God's goodness and in the midst of the Christian community, the Body of Christ.

At the center of Dorothy Day's vision, those who came for food were to be seen as Christ and be served with the utmost dignity. They were not to be seen as "street people" or vagabonds. They were to be seen—and reverenced—as "guests." That was the language that everyone who worked and volunteered at the enter utilized when these saints, these holy people of God, were with them in their midst at the Center.

The Loaves and Fishes coordinator from our parish at the time was my good friend, Barbara Colliander, who was also the chairperson of our parish liturgy committee. Barbara invited me to join the team of volunteers from St. Thomas Aquinas, and I remember still, to this day, what I experienced for myself on that first volunteer outing. I was brought to tears at how Barbara did more than just serve the meal to these who were mostly broken and destitute people. Her lavish manner and attitude of care, generosity, hospitality, and her honoring all who were there with greatest levels of dignity was something that truly touched my heart. I was humbled by what I saw in Barb's loving presence and attentiveness to each and every person who came through the doors. I learned so much from her that day. I learned that holiness streams forth from the most unlikely vessels—in this case, the poor ones who were surrounding us during the dinner hour.

That evening as I was driving home, the relentless mantra in my mind and heart was "Blessed are you! Holy are you!" This is how Christ sees the broken and poor. That is how Barbara saw them that evening. This is how I, from that point forward, was called to see, honor, and embrace the poor, in an ongoing invitation. All I could think of that evening was Jesus' Sermon on the Mount in the fifth chapter of Matthew's gospel.

When I got home, I almost literally ran to the piano; "Blest Are They" came pouring out of me. I could not write down the notes and words fast enough. The entire piece was written in about 10 minutes. This does not happen very often. Inspiration for liturgical composers and all creative people is not an everyday occurrence, not like this. Most of the liturgical compositions we composers create are practical offerings, "functional art." There is nothing wrong with this understanding—in fact, it is at the center of what we do. We compose not for ourselves but for the people of God and, in particular, in the context of liturgical prayer for the various ritual actions and moments that bubble up in our common prayer. In other words, we write to task.

"Blest Are They" was and is one of those few exceptions in that vocation. I was not planning at that point to compose a setting of the Beatitudes. Prior to this, that section of Matthew's gospel was for me too intimidating and too "huge." It was not at that time on my screen as something to try to set to music. But the experience at the St. Paul Dorothy Day Center that evening in the early '80s, did something to me, and the image of discipleship witnessed to me by my friend Barbara … well, all I can say is that I felt compelled and driven. And the song—actually the prayer—came rushing out. The only change in the setting came a couple of weeks after we sang it at the parish, and one of the members of the choir, my good friend Jim Waldo, suggested the F minor chord on the second half of the refrain. That made it better for sure. When it was recorded for To Be Your Bread, Michael Joncas said, "there is something missing. The refrain needs a descant." And so we took a break, and, right then and there in the studio, Michael went to the piano and came up with the descant that was published and that is now a part of most renderings of this song. We recorded it minutes later.

I WILL BRING YOU HOME

I have lots of memories around this piece. The first time it was shared with an audience beyond St. Thomas Aquinas parish was at the St. Paul and Minneapolis Archdiocesan "Faith Gathering" held at the old Minneapolis Auditorium. The Come and Journey event was both filmed and recorded, and became a live concert album and feature film with Michael and Marty Haugen. Soon after that, it became the centerpiece for a national event that Michael, Marty and I presented for the National Association of Pastoral Musicians' 1985 national convention in Cincinnati. The first time I went to Hawaii and was one of the presenters for what was then the Big Island Liturgy and Arts Conference at Malia Puka O Kalani (Mary, Gate of Heaven) Church in Hilo, the song was used as the actual gospel proclamation for the Feast of All Saints, with chanting and hula accompanying it.

I also remember the very first time I met and sang with the very talented John Angotti many years later at an NCEA (National Catholic Education Association) National Convention for a joint concert. Before we sang "Blest Are They," John thanked me publicly for composing the song and then proceeded to tell everyone in the audience that he remembered it being sung at his First Communion (I suddenly felt very old!). I am also humbled by the many different instrumental versions that have been recorded, especially by the likes of people like Paul Tate, Jeanne Cotter, Stephen Petrunak, Greg Papesh, and Tom Kendzia.

On September 16, 1987, it happened to be one of the communion songs for the Papal Mass with John Paul II at Dodger Stadium in Los Angeles. The video (you can find it on YouTube) shows the ever-wonderful Frank Brownstead—wearing his white gloves so that the gargantuan choir could see him—while conducting the piece with joy and gusto. To top it all off, one can see the Pope actually singing along on the refrain. I have heard and experienced many different arrangements, renditions, and "covers" of the song at numerous events not only in the United States, but in other countries around the world. It has been translated into so many languages, I cannot keep up with them.

In 1995, Michael Joncas, Marty Haugen and I were honored as a trio, in receiving the Distinguished Alumnus Award from the University of St. Thomas in St. Paul. We had all studied there at different times (never together, however). It was quite the elegant evening where many other awards were presented as well, and many "V.I.P.s" and other distinguished guests were in attendance. The three of us were asked to conclude the evening by sharing and leading three songs, one by the each of us. We began by singing Marty's "Gather Us In," followed by Michael's "On Eagle's Wings." The evening was to conclude with "Blest are

They." So I am at the piano, playing the introduction and I am assigned to sing the first verse ("Blest are they, the poor in spirit ..."), but when I opened my mouth, nothing came out! I completely forgot the first word, "blest" ...and the song came to a screeching halt. Everyone laughed, thank God. Talk about ADHD, which I did not know I had at the time. (Years later, after I was formally diagnosed, I remember feeling upset—and being far too serious about it, and while having lunch with Michael a few days later, I said to him: "Well Michael, I have some upsetting news to share. I just found out that I have ADHD." His response? "Well, yeah ..." Everyone seemed to know except me.)

I also remember a funny incident, where at an event somewhere, a middle-aged woman came up to me and said, "I just love 'Blest Are They.' Especially the words—how did you come up with them?"

I have to say, however, that at the top of the list of cherished memories of "Blest Are They" have been the several times I have been able to sing and lead it at the site of the Mount of Beatitudes in Israel. Truly moments of humility and gratitude. And of course, I still remember that night at the Dorothy Day Center, being in the midst of people at the margins, that provoked the song to be composed in the first place.

I continue to be grateful and humbled by how "Blest Are They" has served the prayer for so many people over the years. After all these years, I still conclude all of my parish concerts with "Blest Are They." People often ask me, "do you get tired of doing "Blest Are They" all the time?"

My answer: No way. (6/1/2016)

CD
MP3
Music

Where the River Flows
X-34910
G-4345

BOUND FOR LIFE AND FREEDOM

Music: HAUL AWAY JOE
(Irish Tradtional,
adapted by DH)
Text:
David Haas

O God of freedom, God of justice;
you, whose love is strong as death:
Away, come away! Come heal us now!
For you have walked our path of darkness,
you, who call us to new faith:
Away, come away! Come heal us now!

Away, come away!
We're bound for life and freedom!
Away, come away! Come heal us now!

So, come and free us from the terror
you have known with nailed hands:
Away, come away! Come heal us now!
And hear the screams of pain and anger,
you, who know our tears and blood:
Away, come away! Come heal us now!

Come, sing a song for all the voiceless,
speak for all who cannot speak:
Away, come away! Come heal us now!
And free the millions: shamed, imprisoned;
stand for us who've lost our name:
Away, come away! Come heal us now!

O, listen to the sound of suffering,
be the promise in our fear:
Away, come away! Come heal us now!
So, shatter strong the sin of hunger,

be for us the bread of hope:
Away, come away! Come heal us now!

My guitar teacher from my later high school years back in Bridgeport, Michigan, John Gilmour, introduced me to a large treasure of indigenous folk music, largely from Ireland and the British Isles, but from other lands as well. This music really pulled me in, and many of the songs I learned remain with me to this day. They are mostly in the public domain, and because these tunes are so singable, I have adapted many of them over the years and created liturgical lyrics for them (like "Onward to the Kingdom," "Singing Praise to God," "Song for the Journey," "Know that the Lord is Near," and "Holy Is Your Name," just to name a few). "Bound for Life and Freedom" takes it melody from an intense and rollicking working sea shanty, "Haul Away Joe." The original lyrics are indicative of this genre of music:

*When I was a little lad
and so my mother told me,
way, haul away, we'll haul away, Joe!
That if I did not kiss the gals
me lips would all grow moldy.
Way, haul away, we'll haul away, Joe!*

> *Way, haul away, the good ship is a-bolding,
> Way, haul away, we'll haul away, Joe!
> Way, haul away, the sheet is now unfolding,
> Way, haul away, we'll haul away, Joe!*

*King Louis was the king of France
before the revolution,
way, haul away, we'll haul away, Joe!
But then he got his head cut off
which spoiled his constitution,
way, haul away, we'll haul away, Joe!*

I WILL BRING YOU HOME

Way, haul away, we'll haul for better weather!
Way, haul away, we'll haul away, Joe!
Way haul away, we'll haul away together!
Way, haul away, we'll haul away, Joe!

The cook is in the galley boys,
making duff so handy,
way, haul away, we'll haul away, Joe!
The captain's in his cabin lads,
drinking wine and brandy,
way, haul away, we'll haul away, Joe!

Way, haul away, I'll sing to you of Nancy!
Way, haul away, we'll haul away, Joe!
Way, haul away, she's just my cut and fancy!
Way, haul away, we'll haul away, Joe!

Way, haul away, we'll haul for better weather!
Way, haul away, we'll haul away, Joe!
Way haul away, we'll haul away together
Way, haul away, we'll haul away, Joe!

Again, while this song is a bit of a sea shanty, it also has a lament-like quality to it, filled with fear and anxiety. The image of "haul away" stuck with me for many years, but as I grew older I sort of packed it away in my memory. Then much later, in 1994, I was looking to compose a strong, chant-like song of lament and crying out for the season of Lent. Somehow, "Haul Away Joe" came back to consciousness, and the image of the work team on the boat, to "way, haul away." I played around with this a bit, thinking about the conversion that the Lenten season calls us to, and I came up with an adaptation of the original lyric to go like this: "Away, come away." And instead of the sailors who will "haul for better weather," I thought about seekers who long for better "weather" in the life of faith, and so I adapted it to be, "We're bound for life and freedom." I realized too that I had to adapt the arrangement and approach. All of the versions of "Haul Away Joe" that I heard over the years featured guitars, mandolins, bodhran, and even banjo—all going at a very quick clip. Because I wanted this to be a lament, I decided to slow the tempo down quite a bit, and then eliminate the instruments and have it be a cappella with some very open harmonies.

When we recorded it for the *Where the River Flows* recording, I asked Pamela Warrick Smith, an amazing singer from the Bronx, New York, to lead it. When I was teaching her the song, she had some great ideas. An expert in the singing and story-telling of the chain-gang songs, she suggested bringing that intense, sort of "work-camp" feel to it. Her performance is amazing (also the fact that she has an amazing vocal range—you can hear it on the recording). Every once in a while I will hear of a parish that utilizes this song for the celebration of the Scrutinies during Lent, which is exactly as I originally conceived it.

Like the slaves from the south who headed north to freedom, we too, in our fear and terror-filled times need to move toward freedom. All of us, in some way, whether it is obvious to us or not, are in need to cry out from time to time in our lives, "bound for life and freedom." (12.11.17)

CD
MP3
Music

Where the River Flows
X-34909
G-4344

CAROL OF THE CHILD

**Music and Text
David Haas**

No eye has seen, nor ear has ever heard;
joy beyond joy, a message from God's Word!
Go and proclaim now to all the land,
the reign of our God is close at hand!
Look for the gift born to us in a stall!
For here a little child will lead us all!

From the sword, a plowshare will be found,
Nations will lay their weapons on the ground!
Peace once hidden is now in our sight:
People of God, come and walk in the light!
Welcome the gift born to us in a stall!
For here a little child will lead us all!

On that day all hate and war will end,
wolf and lamb will call each other "friend."
Flowers will bud forth, ready to bloom,
greeting the Lord, yes, soon, very soon!
Come see the gift born to us in a stall!
For here a little child will lead us all!

Say to all frightened hearts, our God is here!
Coming with strength for all who live in fear!
Healing the blind one and freeing the slave,
here comes your God, who is longing to save!
Honor the gift born to us in a stall!
For here a little child will lead us all!

Make straight the path, do not delay!
Come and prepare all people for God's way!

Every valley, mountain and hill,
every pure heart for God's love to fill!
Share the gift born to us in a stall!
For here a little child will lead us all!

This holy child will lead us all!

Copyright © 1995 GIA Publications, Inc.

This happens to be a favorite of my Advent-Christmas songs, and it is sort of a midrash reflection on the wonderful images from Isaiah that we hear during this time of the year. While working on the text—which I had for a long time before I was able to come up with a melody—I wanted a way to wed together the prophecies of the Hebrew Scriptures with the prophetic tradition of John the Baptist as we encounter him in the gospels. And since I am always looking for ways to bind the Incarnation to the Paschal Mystery of death and resurrection when I compose for Advent and Christmas, I decided to also sneak into the fourth stanza some connections to the Third, Fourth and Fifth Sundays of Lent in Year A (the cycle we employ when celebrating the RCIA rituals during Lent): "Healing the blind one and freeing the slave, here comes your God who is longing to save!"

Whenever I hear the recording of this piece on *Where the River Flows,* I smile when I hear a very, very young Melissa Cuddy (daughter of Kate Cuddy) singing the third verse. This was the very first time Melissa had ever sung in a recording studio, and as any parent could imagine, Kate was a nervous wreck. I remember sitting at the recording console in the control booth with Kate hiding along the side wall, while her daughter was rehearsing with the track. Now, Kate was a mess, but Melissa—she was just fine, working like a seasoned pro. When we "pushed the red button" to record—she nailed it with the very first take! Kate resumed breathing normally, and Melissa came in the control booth, with me exclaiming to her, "Mel, that was wonderful!" To which she responded, "hey, no problem." Suffice it to say, Melissa sang on many recordings of mine over the years after that, not to mention those of Marty Haugen and many other liturgical composers with GIA. Once a pro—always a pro. (12.11.17)

CD
MP3
Music

Star Child
X-47109
G-5215

CHILD OF JOY AND PEACE

Music:
David Haas
Text:
Shirley Erena Murray

Child of joy and peace, born to ev'ry race—
by your star, the wise will know you,
East and West their homage show you,
Look into your face, child of joy and peace.

Born among the poor on a stable floor,
cold and raw, you know our hunger,
weep our tears and cry our anger—
yet you tell us more, born among the poor.

Ev'ry child needs bread till the world is fed;
you give bread, your hands enable
all to gather round your table—
Christmas must be shared, ev'ry child needs bread.

Son of poverty, shame us till we see
self-concerned, how we deny you,
by our greed we crucify you
on a Christmas tree, Son of poverty.

This text by Shirley Erena Murray is one of the most profound Christmas hymn texts that I have ever come across, and creating music for these words was an honor and a most prayerful process and experience for me. I have yet to find a text—and there many wonderful contemporary Christmas texts—that so artfully blends together the divide between Christmas and our concern for the poor, and the blending together of the historical story and the present-day situation of our lives:

Born among the poor on a stable floor,
cold and raw, you know our hunger,
weep our tears and cry our anger—
yet you tell us more, born among the poor

Then Shirley presents a Eucharistic metaphor for the Christmas event, fusing together the Eucharistic table, and the empty tables of hungry children:

Ev'ry child needs bread till the world is fed;
you give bread, your hands enable
all to gather round your table—
Christmas must be shared, ev'ry child needs bread.

And finally, the integration of passion and death with Christmastime, and the new insight of two expressions of the "tree of life":

Son of poverty, shame us till we see
self-concerned, how we deny you,
by our greed we crucify you
on a Christmas tree, Son of poverty.

Not much more needs to be said about this song, this "carol," a prophetic alternative for celebrating what our contemporary culture insists should be "the most wonderful time of the year." Maybe we need to think a bit more about that. It just is not so for many. (12.11.17)

CD
MP3
Music

Table Songs, Vol. 1
X-26510
G-3658

CHILD OF MERCY

**Music and Text
David Haas**

Child of mercy, child of peace,
Jesus, Bread of life,
food to fill our longing.
Child or justice, child of light,
Jesus, Saving cup,
Emmanuel—God with us.

All who walk in darkness have seen a great light,
to those who dwell in fear, a light has shone!

A child is born to us, a son is given us,
upon his shoulder glory rests!

We name him
"Wonder-Counselor, hero, mighty God,"
the Holy One for ever: Prince of peace!

We proclaim good news to you,
great tidings of joy:
To you is born a savior, Christ the Lord!

Gloria in Excelsis Deo!

"Child of Mercy" was one of those songs that came out of a direct request from a dear friend. I had the privilege of serving as Composer in Residence for a while at St. Thomas the Apostle Church in Minneapolis in the late 1980's and into the early 1990's, where my friend of many years, Mary Werner, served as Director of Liturgy and Music (she is still serving there). I often helped out at the piano for various liturgical celebrations there. She came to me during the beginning of Advent one year and said, "David I want you to compose a communion song for us for Christmas." I was happy to do so, and immediately replied, of course. But then there was more attached to this commission: "Now, David, I want it to speak specifically about the Eucharistic meal and the Incarnation; and, I want it to sound 'Christmassy' (is that a word?), and, it has to be able to be sung immediately, as I do not want to rehearse it before hand with the people before the liturgy begins."

Now this was becoming a bit more of a daunting task. But I did not want to disappoint my good friend, and so I decided to meet the challenge head on.

Inspired by another good friend's composition, "Night of Silence" (Dan Kantor's piece that as the years go by seems to become almost as well-known as the carol it is paired with!), I sought to find a familiar Christmas melody that I could yoke together with a very simple refrain so the people could, as Mary had requested, connect with it on the first hearing.

So I went through all of my favorite Christmas carols, those known and beloved by most Christians. I first considered utilizing the refrain for "O Come, All Ye Faithful," but then abandoned that idea, because I was concerned that the phrase "O come let us adore him" would lead some to see the sharing of the Eucharist on Christmas as a call to benediction and adoration. The sharing of communion is not adoration, but again, sharing in the sacred meal. The communion time at Eucharist is a verb, something we do—it is not a noun.

Then, of course, "Silent Night" came to mind. But Dan Kantor had beat me to that one ("Night of Silence"), so I could not be a copycat, nor do it better. After consideration, I landed on one of my favorites, "Angels We Have Heard on High" and its marvelous "Gloria in Excelsis Deo" refrain. At first I thought I would compose the song as very upbeat and joyous, as the carol is a true explosion of praise and the glory of God. But at the time, I think I was still in the mentality that a communion song needed to be more gentle, more reflective. (I no longer subscribe to that single-minded attitude now in regards to the communion song, as I believe more and more that the "mood" —I hate that word when thinking about liturgical music, but I cannot think of a better image when speaking about this—should actually be more in the spirit of rejoicing.)

I first tried to find new words with the florid melody of this refrain, but every attempt seems contrived and forced. Then it came to me—what about a descant, one that could be sung by members of the choir while the assembly sang a Eucharistic refrain to a different melody that would match harmonically with the "Gloria in Excelsis" tune? In other words, as Dan did with his iconic piece—I would create what is called a quodlibet.

Having decided temporarily on this approach, my next issue was what to do with the melody, and more importantly, the text of the refrain? This song was to be sung for the first time on Christmas Eve and Christmas Day, with the hopes of being versatile enough for the entire season of Christmas. I began to look at the scriptures, and of course the lectionary provides the various infancy story narratives that are found in Luke and Matthew. The references to the Christ child, the appearance to the shepherds, the harkening back to the prophet Isaiah clearly determined the song's direction. I then thought about the Incarnation, the breaking forth of the presence of the Jesus in history, the strong metaphors and themes of peace and light, and realized that every time we gather around the table to give thanks and to share in this festival meal of Christ being made present, we are celebrating Emmanuel—"God with us." The story of birth and the Word made flesh is most assuredly the sustaining story of what the Eucharist is for us who believe. The song began to take shape. Rather quickly, actually. It seemed to be successful not only for Christmas Eve and Christmas Day at St. Thomas, but for the entire season.

When the song was first given a larger exposure at a showcase presentation that GIA sponsored at a NPM convention, I was at the piano, and Bob Batastini (who was then the Senior Editor for GIA) was conducting. After the first verse, when the full-throated sopranos sang the descant along with the communion refrain, Bob backed up (while still conducting) to whisper in my ear while I was still playing, "David, I think they like it." Then he began to giggle, and both my face and my heart smiled. Not because I necessarily thought that it would become a "big seller," but because it seemed to have been a true Christmas gift for pastoral musicians and hopefully, and more importantly, a gift that would keep on giving for the praying community.

There really is something about those old carol melodies, yes? I now wish I had composed more verses to help the piece sustain itself as a single communion song and to be more adaptable for other celebrations during the season. I still might do that. If any of you reading this want to give it a shot—go for it.

Thanks Mary, for pulling this piece out of me. I am not sure I would have come up with it otherwise. (9.28.17)

CD
MP3
Music

Who Calls You by Name, Vol. 2; Alive in Christ
Jesus; Glory to God: The Best of David Haas, Vol. 4
X-41609
G-4870

CHRIST IS RISEN! SHOUT HOSANNA!

Music:
David Haas
Text:
Brian Wren

Christ is risen! Shout Hosanna!
Celebrate this day of days!
Christ is risen! Hush in wonder:
All creation is amazed.
In the desert all surrounding,
See, a spreading tree has grown.
Healing leaves of grace abounding
bring a taste of love unknown.

Christ is risen! Raise your spirits
from the caverns of despair.
Walk with gladness in the morning.
See what love can do and dare.
Drink the wine of resurrection,
not a servant, but a friend,
Jesus is our strong companion.
Joy and peace shall never end.

Christ is risen! Earth and heaven
never more shall be the same.
Break the bread of new creation
where the world is still in pain.
Tell its grim, demonic chorus:
"Christ is risen! Get you gone!"
God the First and Last is with us.
Sing Hosanna every one!

I WILL BRING YOU HOME

I have always loved the traditional Easter hymns and I never tire of singing them: "Jesus Christ is Risen Today," "Christ the Lord is Risen Today," The Strife Is O'er," "O Sons and Daughters/O Filii et Filiae," "Sing with All the Saints in Glory," and one that truly plucks my heart strings, my father's favorite from years ago, "Alleluia, Let the Holy Anthem Rise."

Then there are some of the lesser known—but equally moving—Easter hymns such as "That Easter Day with Joy Was Bright," "Now the Green Blade Rises," "Resucitó," and "This is the Feast of Victory" by Richard Hillert, whom I came to know in the later years of his life.

Like composing new Christmas songs, creating new hymns and songs for Easter is difficult because of the favorites that still stand the test of time for worshippers. There have been however, some contemporary Easter hymns that have broken through; some of my favorites include "Up from the Earth" (Rory Cooney), "All Shall Be Well" (John Foley), "This is the Day of New Beginnings/Christ Is Alive" (Lori True), "I Have Seen the Lord" (Bob Hurd), "Song of the Empty Tomb" and "On the Journey to Emmaus" (both by Marty Haugen), and many of the popular Taizé chants, in particular "Laudate Dominum."

Alongside my "The Tomb Is Empty" (addressed elsewhere in this book), my setting of Brian Wren's strophic hymn text, "Christ Is Risen! Shout Hosanna!" is a favorite among my feeble attempts to compose Easter hymns. The images that pop out in Brian's words are nothing less than profound:

Hush in wonder: all creation is amazed …

Raise your spirits from the caverns of despair.
Walk with gladness in the morning
see what love can do and dare …

Break the bread of new creation
where the world is still in pain.
Tell its grim, demonic chorus:
"Christ is risen! Get you gone! …

It was a great experience crafting a tune to match up with these wonderful expressions. Soon after it was published, I heard from Brian with very affirming words about the tune. That made my day, for sure. To this day these words and images provide for me a freshness that just sings and booms out, "Easter!" I hope it does the same for all of the communities that celebrate when they sing this hymn. (11.24.17)

CD

MP3
Music

Who Calls You by Name, Vol. 1; Blest Are They:
The Best of David Haas, Vol. 1;
Alive in Christ Jesus; Give Me Jesus
X-41615
G-4873

CHRIST WILL BE YOUR LIGHT

Music: David Haas
Text: Ephesians 5:8-15; Revelation 21:5 (alt. DH)

Arise! Arise! Awake, rise up from the dead!
Christ will shine! Christ will be your light!
> Once you were lost in the darkness,
> now you are light in the Lord!
> Live out each day as God's children.
> Live now as children of light!

> Light shines forth every beauty,
> justice and truth are revealed!
> Seek the ways of the Lord.
> Seek the way of light!

> "I am the light of the world,
> I will make all things new!
> Follow and you will find life.
> Follow and live in the light!"

This song was composed for the first volume of the Christian Initiation resource, Who Calls You by Name, as a joy-filled response to the gospel story of the Man Born Blind (John 9:1-41), appointed for the Fourth Sunday of Lent in Year A.

Of course, the story is more than just about the healing of actual physical blindness. It is a story about achieving insight; seeing things in a brand-new way, having one's world turned upside down. For me, whenever I finally see something that I have been blinded to for a long time, the result is that I am shaken up and challenged to new responsibility to "live in the light," and to, as Jesus does, help "make all things new." Moving from being "lost in the darkness" to saying yes to the call to "follow and live in the light" always asks much of us. I wanted this song to somehow express the joy of this new invitation, but to also ignite a renewed call to give witness with integrity.

When I was composing this song, my composer-friend Christopher Walker came to mind, and so I dedicated it to him; those of us who know Chris know him to truly be an ignition switch of joy and energy. Thanks for that gift, Chris. There are not many who can keep up with my extroverted nature. In that way, you are most certainly, my brother. (11.24.17)

CD

MP3
Music

Come and Journey; You Are Mine:
The Best of David Haas, Vol. 2;
When Love Is Found
X-3745CD12
G-4082

COME AND JOURNEY WITH ME

**Music and Text
David Haas**

Come to the song, come to the dance.
Bring all you are, bring all you be.
Come with your voice, come with your heart.
Come and journey with me.

Come let the sun fill up your eyes.
Take the time to look around,
and love—just love—and walk with each other.
Come and journey with me.

Come and see, come and be.
Be all you are and all you can be,
and leave all behind and calm your mind.
Come and journey with me.

The popularity of this song has always been baffling to me. To be honest I thought it was, initially, a kind of "throw away" song. I remember exactly when I wrote it. While serving as the Director of Music and Liturgy at St. Thomas Aquinas Church in St. Paul Park, Minnesota (1982-1985)—I was sitting in the sacristy behind the sanctuary, just minutes before I was to present a solo liturgical music concert for the community there. I was fiddling around tuning and playing my guitar, when this little chord pattern came to me, and the line "come and journey with me," with a John Denver like yodel attached ... so I came up with these very simplistic lines: "come to the song, come to the dance, bring all you are ... come let the sun fill up your eyes ... leave all behind and calm your mind ... come and journey with me." Without writing them down at all, I went out to begin the concert, and decided right then and there I was going to begin with this right there on the spot. I invited the people to echo the last line of each verse. I did my little yodel in the middle of the song, and that was it.

I never thought this would catch on at all. I did it for a few more concerts and retreats here and there. I remember being very nervous to share it with Michael Joncas and Marty Haugen when we were throwing out ideas for music to include in a big concert we were soon going to present (which included a huge camera crew, and a portable studio parked outside in a Winnebago to record the event) at the old Minneapolis Auditorium in the fall of 1984. I remember saying to them both, something like "well, here is a little song, not sure it is any good." After singing the song they both encouraged it to be included. Later when we were working the final editing and mixing of the recording and film, Marty said, "we should call this project Come and Journey." So that is how it happened.

The yodeling during the song is so obviously influenced by my age and my love during those years of John Denver songs. I always loved his song, "Calypso" with that powerful yodel-like refrain, and so that is why and how it crept into "Come and Journey with Me." The published versions of the piece do not encourage the yodeling, but rather, this "bridge section" is presented as an instrumental interlude. But whenever I sing it at concerts I include the yodel, although as I get older, it becomes more difficult to pull off. I never really have seen this as a liturgical song, but I know many people have sung it for weddings, and it gets shared at retreats and other types of events. I even adapted it many years ago for one of my outgoing phone messages on my answering machine:

Please leave your name after the tone,
I'll call you back when I get home.
Leave the day and the time that you called:
Leave your message with me;
leave your message with me.

I know … you have permission to roll your eyes, and groan now. (11.10.17)

CD MP3 Music

Creating God
X-21307
G-3329

CREATING GOD

Music:
David Haas
Text:
Jeffrey Rowthorn

Creating God,
your fingers trace the bold designs
    of farthest space;
let sun and moon and stars and light
and what lies hidden praise your might.

Sustaining God,
your hands uphold earth's mysteries known
    or yet untold;
let water's fragile blend with air,
enabling life, proclaim our care.

Redeeming God,
your arms embrace all now despised
    for creed or race;
let peace, descending like a dove,
make known on earth your healing love.

Indwelling God,
your Gospel claims one family with
    a billion names;
let ev'ry life be touched by grace
until we praise you face to face.

"Creating God" is a text by Jeffrey Rowthorn that caught my attention because of all of the ways he captures the identity of God through verbs, which describe and engage us in the activities of God, the very things that God does with, through, and in us. I wanted to find a way to capture melodically and harmonically the mystery and awe that surrounds these "God activities," and that refuses to let up on the mystery. I do not know if I captured this, but that was the intent, especially on the third stanza with the tight dissonances I chose to employ in the choral writing.

This hymn became the choice for the title of the CD and music collection that includes it, and it was the cause of some controversy for some time because many people read wrongly into the title, thinking that it expressed a human arrogance implying that we, ourselves, "create" God. The mistake here is that they saw this as something *we* are doing, rather than understand that the verbs utilized are describing what *God* is doing. God is the one doing the *creating, sustaining, redeeming* and the *indwelling*, not us. But I understand now how the title standing on its own could cause such confusion.

This is such beautiful and provocative poetry. I wish I had the poetic gift to come up with phrases like "your fingers trace the bold designs of farthest space," "let water's fragile blend with air," "your arms embrace all now despised for creed or race," and "your Gospel claims one family with a billion names."

It might be interesting for some to know that Rowthorn, as well as many of the other contemporary hymn text writers whose poetry many Catholic liturgical composers set to music—like Mary Louise Bringle, Adam Tice, Brian Wren, Sylvia Dunstan, Shirley Erena Murray, Fred Pratt Green, Timothy Dudley-Smith, Jaroslav Vajda, and Ruth Duck—are all from Protestant worshipping traditions. It might also be interesting to know if texts like these are actually finding a common home with singing congregations in Roman Catholic communities. I am not alone among Roman Catholic composers in being attracted to these texts and exploring how they can be wedded with strong contemporary melodies. Roman Catholic composer colleagues of mine like Tony Alonso, Lori True, Dan Kantor, Michael Joncas, Marty Haugen (who is actually Lutheran, but many see him as a Catholic composer), Zack Stachowski, and others seek out these texts with enthusiasm. However, I wonder how many of these types of texts are generally sung at celebrations of Roman Catholic Eucharist in the average parish? The fact that Protestant communities have a stronger and more sustained tradition of hymn singing as ritual acts of prayer, as opposed to the far too common Roman Catholic practice (whether intentional or not) of seeing hymns as music to accompany processions, such as gathering and dismissal, might play a role in why this is the case. Could it be that Roman Catholic pastoral musicians feel they are more bound by liturgical rules and regulations around the words they sing, and that they are more hesitant to introduce text that is more challenging? I honestly do not know, but as a Roman Catholic liturgical composer, I would love to take part in more conversations and debates around the issues of text writing and the role of poetry amidst a liturgy largely dominated by ecclesiastical and biblical texts. I think it would be interesting.

Michael Joncas, who himself is a very fine poet as well as composer, has attempted to infuse this genre of text writing in his ongoing series of hymn texts with OCP Publications, which presently includes two volumes: *Within Our Hearts Be Born* and *We Contemplate the Mystery.* These two collections of hymn texts (and more are to come) are proposing a Roman Catholic implementation of the common Protestant practice of singing a "hymn of the day," that would correspond with the Lectionary readings for each Sunday. I hope this proposal will encourage more writing in this regard among Catholic composers. Let's keep the hymns—with provocative texts like this one—coming! (11.24.17)

Music	Year A:	G-8481
MP3		X-93100
Music	Year B:	G-8482
MP3		X-93200
Music	Year C:	G-8483
MP3		X-93300
	Christmas, Triduum, Solemnities & Other Celebrations	
Music		G-8480
MP3		X-93000

CRY OUT WITH JOY

All of the compositions in this resource were composed by David Haas; Kathleen Harmon, SNDden; Stephen Pishner; Paul Tate; and Lori True.

The Cry Out with Joy series started as a single small idea that very quickly grew into a much bigger project when Lori True and I sat down and began dreaming. Talking about it for a while and coming up with an initial plan, we brought in our wonderful friends and fellow composers Stephen Pishner; Sr. Kathleen Harmon, SNDden; and Paul Tate to be part of the project.

The idea was simple, yet unique—it had not been tried before. Other publishers had put out resources containing musical settings of the weekly appointed responsorial psalms; some of these resources also included Gospel Acclamations. But we wanted to develop a resource that would be more than that—a holistic collection of music for the entire Liturgy of the Word. In addition to psalm settings we chose to include Gospel Acclamations, musical renderings of the Universal Prayers (Prayers of the Faithful), and some additional catechetical background and prayers that the cantor could access for both their preparation and in their actual proclaiming of the sung prayer.

These people sitting around the table in a common cause were awesome, and this project was truly a collaboration in the sense of there being common expectations and guidelines as to how we were going to go about our task. Since this was going to be a huge project (four complete volumes—one for each of the liturgical lectionary cycles, and a fourth volume for ritual masses, solemnities and so forth), I had the task of dividing the compositional assignments among the five of us. Every single setting was to be vetted and critiqued by the other composers. Each of us had to leave our egos at the door, present our settings to the other four, receive feedback, and if needed, go back to the drawing board to make edits or revisions.

We also all agreed on the "template" for how the pieces were to be structured—meaning, we agreed that the refrains would be "metered," but that the verses would be in a tone-like chant, with the final measure of the verses metered in order to be more hospitable for the community to enter in on the refrain each time. No one style or genre was dictated, but an overall principle was that we wanted all of the entries to be keyboard centered with guitar chords provided. We also made a decision (although it was debated back and forth) that we would not compose any obbligato arrangements. Our common intention was that this would be a resource primarily for cantors and basic instrumental accompaniment, although choral harmonies appear on most of the refrains. As a result, GIA published an ancillary edition of choral refrains for each volume. The recording was to be much more of a demonstration recording, a resource for cantors to learn the settings that would be assigned for them to sing at their parish. In addition to an actual physical CD, all of the pieces would have these excerpts provided as digital MP3 downloads.

Having Sr. Kathleen in our company was such a gift—she is not only a fine liturgist, but she is also is a recognized expert of the psalms. It was though we were participants in a seminar. This deeply informed our writing, as we explored how to best communicate those insights and nuances musically. Paul Tate, with his master's degree in music theory, was unbelievably helpful in helping us tighten and polish our voice leading and part writing, and he provided great ideas for arrangements, in addition to his own beautiful compositions. Lori True has composed in this resource some very fresh musical settings of many refrains, and holds a particular passion and gift for Intercessory prayer, so we appointed her to be the sole composer of very beautiful and creative Universal Prayer settings. She also was the author of the cantor preparation prayers that appear for each liturgy. Stephen brought some very unique musical genres to the table—particularly his refreshing gospel-style melodies. He also had us all splitting our sides with laughter during many of the grueling work sessions we had throughout the process. Me? Well, I provided comic relief, and I served as the primary convener of the group and the liaison with GIA.

While it has only been a short time since all of the volumes have been made available, we are all so very proud of this project. I, in particular, feel that it is a testimony to true collaboration and dedication that we were able both to work together and improve the quality of our craft as composers, and still provide parishes with a new and helpful resource. I am most proud to have been a part of a project that is unique—there is nothing out there that is quite like it. God bless you, Lori, Paul, Sr. Kathleen and Stephen … it was quite a ride! (11.22.17)

CD
MP3
Music

Echo of Faith
X-50713
G-5669

DEATH NO MORE

Music and Text
David Haas

When time is over, when all pain is past,
when sin is broken, peace declared at last,
our dreams we'll sing, with hope sung unsurpassed:
Alleluia! Death no more! Alleluia!
Alleluia! Death no more! Alleluia!

Then we'll embrace those aching to be fed,
no longer slaves, but children loved instead,
the rocks will sing, and stones will turn to bread:
Alleluia! Death no more! Alleluia!
Alleluia! Death no more! Alleluia!

Born from the water, we can finally see,
with Christ we journey, bound for that same tree,
graves will be opened, all creation free:
Alleluia! Death no more! Alleluia!
Alleluia! Death no more! Alleluia!

People of hope, compassion as our guide,
to follow Jesus, we no longer hide,
proclaim we must, with faith we will abide:
Alleluia! Death no more! Alleluia!
Alleluia! Death no more! Alleluia!

We'll sing God's song, and rage against the night,
we'll find the music, strength to meet the fight,
together serve and witness to the light:
Alleluia! Death no more! Alleluia!
Alleluia! Death no more! Alleluia!

Over the past 40 years, by the grace of God, my music has placed me in some amazing situations where I have found myself in the presence of some real, living saints. One of those is Sr. Helen Prejean, whose life-long vocation of advocating the abolishment of the death penalty has awakened and inspired so many, most profoundly through her book (that became an academy award winning movie) *Dead Man Walking*. We met back in 2000 to collaborate on a couple of projects together, and I have been humbled to appear with her for some of her presentations. I was fortunate to interview her for a video program on the death penalty, titled "Death No More," and this hymn of the same name was composed intentionally for that project. We have remained friends over the years, and are able to see each other from time to time—her schedule is amazing. To say that Sr. Helen is an inspiration is more than an understatement. It does not come close to expressing the impact that she has had on me—not just on me, but on a church still learning to embrace its responsibility in helping awaken the world to the horrors of the death penalty and the deepening of the wounds that come with the destruction of life.

I remember the first conversation we had when we began to get to know one another. We were sitting in her apartment in New Orleans, and while she was familiar with my music (I heard that the "Song of the Body of Christ" was a favorite of hers), she wanted to know more, and anyone who has come to know Sr. Helen finds out very quickly that she does not beat around the bush. I remember her asking, "so David, what is it exactly that you do? I know you write all of this beautiful music, but what do you do in the midst of that?" I remember stammering a bit (if for nothing more, realizing that I was sitting with a living saint), and I stumbled around explaining to her that I travelled a lot presenting workshops, retreats and concerts. She kept prodding me: "what do you do during these events?" I explained further that I share my music, and that I assist pastoral musicians and liturgy planners in their skills as parish leaders of music and prayer; that I work with them on their musical abilities, their liturgical knowledge, and so forth. She would not let up: "and why, David, do you think that this is important?" Oh my goodness. She was not trying to criticize what I was doing or mock it in any way—she just really wanted to know! And I believe now (and I have teased her about it since then) she was challenging me to define and clarify my vocation. As we talked more and more, the layers continued to peel away, and I realize that all of my efforts and activities as a pastoral musician, liturgist, workshop leader and composer—these all need to have a clear grounding in faith, and an even clearer grounding in mission. She knew that I was aware of the mission, but she was helping me to express it in clearer terms—to get to the heart of the matter. Being in her presence, hearing her story, and being more attentive to the cause that she has committed her life to, helped me to put all of the efforts of good liturgy, quality music and sacramental practice into balance and to confront its relevance: What is good liturgy and quality music if it does not rub shoulders and walk alongside the angst of life, and the stories of the pain and suffering of God's people?

We pastoral musicians spend far too much time obsessing about vocal blend, recruiting choir members, buying hymnals, and being "liturgically correct" in our choices and practices. We are concerned too much of the time with trying to "get the people to sing," while forgetting to ask a more important question: "why should they?" What difference will singing make in the midst of unspeakable horror, like the senseless destruction of life and our compulsion for revenge? We are being called to "sing God's song, and rage against the night," to "find the music" so we can continually sing and announce God's great agenda, that has nothing to do with good liturgy and quality music, but rather: "death no more!" (12.3.17)

CD	**God Never Tires**
MP3	X-101006
Music	G-9488

DEDICATE YOURSELVES

Music: David Haas
Text:
Colossians 3:12-17
(alt. DH)

Holy and beloved, chosen:
Clothe yourselves with heartfelt mercy,
forgive as the Lord forgives
and, over all, put on love.
Dedicate yourselves to thankfulness.
Let the word of Christ dwell in you.
With psalms and hymns and songs,
give thanks and praise to God.

Bear with one another; forgive one another,
forgive as the Lord forgives you.
In wisdom made perfect,
admonish one another in love.

Whatever you do, in speech or in action,
do it in the name of Jesus.
Give thanks to God,
give thanks to God in Christ.

"Dedicate Yourselves" is a musical setting of Colossians 3:12-17, and it is one of those passages that I have always loved, especially because it is a wonderful instruction as to what the true nature of love is, if love is going to be activated and lived out in the way of Christ. If we were to truly examine and act on the attributes here, we could, seriously, transform how we are in relationship with each other. Consider just some of the qualities that are lined out here: "… forgive as the Lord forgives." A homily could be preached upon these few words alone; when we consider how lavishly forgiven we are—this is how we are to forgive one another. Other lines that jump out at me include "Over all, put on love," and my favorite line in the refrain, "Dedicate yourselves to thankfulness." The call to gratitude in all things is how we should attempt to greet every morning, every situation, every challenge, and every blessing that we receive. Phrase after phrase in these verses proclaim what is at the heart of our stance of love and care, for those we love intimately, and yes, for those for whom offering love is so very difficult to do.

I composed this song for the wedding of Zack Stachowski and Natalie Spehar, on October 10, 2015 in Annapolis, Maryland. I have known Zack ever since he was a young boy, and from a very early age, we all knew that he was a child prodigy; over the years he has grown into a true virtuoso violinist. I first got to know him through Stephen Petrunak at St. Blaise Church in Sterling Heights, Michigan, where Zack was born and grew up. He has matured into a true servant who is not only an incredibly talented musician (Oh, did I mention that he also plays the piano, guitar, and is a wonderful singer as well?), but one who understands the connection with the liturgy and pastoral care. Someone with Zack's level of talent could have pursued a career as a solo violinist or become a member of a major orchestra. But Zack has chosen to "dedicate" himself in thankfulness to God as a full time pastoral musician, music director, and more recently, as an emerging liturgical composer (also published by GIA Publications). In the summer of 2017 we collaborated on a project together for GIA titled, *God Never Tires*; "Dedicate Yourselves" is part of this collection. To collaborate with Zack on this was a true delight.

I believe Zack to be an ambassador representing the next creative generation of liturgical music—not only through his compositions, but through the many other ministerial initiatives he is involved with. He is the co-founder of the podcast series, "Open Your Hymnal," with his close friend, Matt Reichert. Zack—and Natalie (who happens to be magnificent musician in her own right)—have become a very precious part of my life, and it was an honor to compose this piece for them and to lead it at the wedding liturgy itself. God bless you, Zack and Natalie. You both have truly "dedicated yourselves" to sharing your gifts with the church and the world, with the full knowledge of the source that gave birth to them. (11.25.17)

CD
MP3
Music

Where the River Flows;
Glory Day: David Haas and Friends in Concert
X-34907
G-4342

DEEP DOWN I KNOW

**Music and Text
David Haas**

Deep down I know, I must thank God,
Oh, deep down I know, I must thank God!

Lost in the night, I feel the hand of God;
deep in my soul, I know God is near!
When I awake to greet the sweet morning,
I see the holy light shine before me!

My heart is glad, leaping for happiness;
my God will walk with me, and I'll never die,
for God will destroy the demons
    that haunt me;
forgiving with mercy—giving me peace!

Stand up, my friends,
    and feel the pow'r of God
stirring within you: answer the call!
Look all around you,
    and you'll see the face of God!
Bound to each other, we will be free!

My friend and colleague, Bob Piercy, died far too young—at the age of 52. During the 1990's up until his passing in 2011, Bob was a most joyful and intense presence for so many who worked pastorally and nationally in the areas of religious education, ministry with children, liturgy, as well as a deep commitment to social justice activism. Having worked as a professional dancer and actor in musical theatre in an earlier time of his life, he brought those skills and energy to ministry at both parish and national levels. Bob worked for many different ministry publishers over the years (Liturgy Training Publications, Resources for Christian Living, Living the Good News, The American Bible Society, and GIA Publications). His gift of humor was such that some of his storytelling would leave those of us who knew him laughing so hard that our sides hurt. I was able to collaborate with him over the years with workshops and other events, in particular on the *Walking by Faith* project we worked on together for what was then Brown-ROA (a religious education publisher, soon afterwards to become Harcourt Religion) and GIA.

This song is dedicated to Bob, because the explosive joy in this song was an attempt to embody the same sort of rejoicing that Bob lived throughout his entire life. Everything Bob did, said, taught, and danced, was so "deep." His eyes, his face, his entire being just radiated in everything he did. His lively extroversion was a font of so many happy times and experiences of church for so many.

With this song, I give thanks to Bob and others who were and are, like him. Deep down. (12.11.17)

CD
MP3
Music

As Water to the Thirsty; You Are Mine The Best of
David Haas, Vol 2; Who Calls You by Name, Vol. 1
X-17711
G-3338

DEEP WITHIN

Music: David Haas
Text:
Jeremiah 31:33,
Ezekiel 36:26,
Joel 2:12 (alt. DH)

Deep within I will plant my law,
not on stone, but in your heart.
Follow me, I will bring you back,
you will be my own, and I will be your God.

I will give you a new heart,
a new spirit within you
for I will be your strength.

Return to me, with all your heart,
and I will bring you back.

While I have lived in the twin city area of Minnesota now for most of my life, I grew up in Bridgeport, Michigan (near Saginaw, or even more familiar to many, right next to Frankenmuth), and I lived in Michigan until my mid-college years. With the exception of one year in Iowa, I have lived here in Minnesota ever since. But I still hold my Michigan roots very dear, and I still consider to this day the Saginaw Diocese to be my "spiritual home." I have returned there on a regular basis over the years to visit family and life-long friends, and have the honor to still be invited to share concerts, workshops and retreats throughout the diocese. Both of my parents are buried in the cemetery in Bridgeport.

For many years I was very connected to their diocesan lay ministry program and regularly helped to lead retreats for the Center for Lay Ministry there. During those years under the direction of Sr. Roberta Kolasa, SJ and Sr. Jo Gaugier, OP, the program initiated and nurtured a tremendous program that has been recognized nationally over the years as a model for the formation of lay people for ministry. During the years when both Bishop Francis Reh and

I WILL BRING YOU HOME

Bishop Ken Untener were leading the diocese, many were commissioned as lay ministers to take on major leadership roles in parishes. At the center of this program the candidates for lay ministry were expected to take part in regular retreat experiences, and I was fortunate to have been asked to return home and serve as retreat leader for many of these gatherings. This song came to life during one of our retreats while I was preparing to speak about the covenant relationship that God has with us. It is always much easier to "go to church," than to actually "be Church." The values of being the church, the Body of Christ, were very much the values and vision of Bishop Francis, Bishop Ken, and Roberta and Jo during those years.

When we travel through the Hebrew Scriptures (Old Testament), this theme of God's relationship with a people is constant, especially through the prophets. When we read, pray and study scripture, I have learned that we need to not only look at what is there; but also, what is not there. God's promise is always this: "I will be your God, and you will be my people." God never proclaims: "I will be your God, and you will be my series of individual and interpersonal relationships." We are to be a *people.* It is not about "me," no, it is about "we." In our spiritual lives and in our actions and beliefs as Christians, we spend the majority of time talking about and thinking about our personal relationship with God, and ask questions of ourselves like, "what is God's will for me?" But as a question, this one is neither biblical nor part of our Church tradition. Our faith, our journey, and our liturgy and prayer—is communal. The word "liturgy" in the original Greek, means "the work of the people." So, the song echoes the wisdom of the prophets (to be a prophet, by the way, in the biblical understanding, is not to be a fortune teller, but more correctly, a "spokesperson for God"): "you will be my own, and I will be your God."

We also spend a lot of energy making sure we follow the rules, obey church teaching, remain orthodox to doctrines, follow the rubrics, and be sure we line up with the directions of the institutional church. But again, as the prophets teach and as the song begins, the law of God is "not on stone, but in your hearts." The ultimate question of our faith should not be, "did we follow the rules?" It hopefully will be, "are we better Christians than before?"

This song is dedicated to my good friend, Pam Cole. She was a participant at the very retreat in Michigan when and where I composed this song. Pam has always understood that it is the latter question that needs to be held closest to our hearts. She served for many years in parish and diocesan ministry, and up until her recent retirement she gave herself so humbly for many years as the director of the East Side Soup Kitchen in Saginaw. While not a church-based center, their work and her inspiring leadership are most certainly, without question, centered in God's promise of hope for all people in the midst of tremendous poverty. It is in such struggles that community, "a people," is desperately needed to respond to the "least of these." Pam has shown all who have known her what this is about. She has lived her life with God's presence, "deep within" every day of her life. (11.10.17)

CD
MP3
Music

Where the River Flows; Give Me Jesus;
Do Not Be Afraid, I Am With You; I Will Live On
X-8-0314
G-4349

DO NOT LET YOUR HEARTS BE TROUBLED

Music:
David Haas
Text:
John 14:1-3, 6-7,
10-14 (alt. DH)

Do not let your hearts be troubled,
have faith in God and faith in me.
I will go forth to prepare a place you,
then I'll come back to take you with me,
that where I am, you may also be.

In God's house there are many places
for you alone to dwell in safety.
You know the way to where I'll lead you,
if you are lost, I will show the way.

I am the way, the truth and the life,
only through me can you know what I know.
If you knew me, you would see the vision,
if you see me, you see your God.

The words I speak are not only of myself,
it is your God who lives within me.
If you believe that your God and I are one,
I will provide when you call my name.

I have always loved this section from John's Gospel. As one who seems to be regularly "troubled" by so many things—I worry a lot and suffer from anxiety issues—the message of "do not let your hearts be troubled" in any context is comforting good news, indeed. The belief that there is something better waiting; that suffering is, in the wide view of things, temporary; that God is attentive to this and walking with us—all this is at the center of what it means to belong to God. It is the grounding for all of us who are called to serve our sisters and brothers.

Over the years when this gospel passage has come up in the Lectionary (Fifth Sunday of Easter, Year A) or when families have chosen this reading for the funeral of a loved one, I have often looked for a musical setting of this passage, but alas, I could never find one. So I composed this setting partially in response to that need. When I get asked the question about a particular piece and what moved or "inspired" me to write it, I remind people that liturgical composers usually do so out of a particular and genuine need. We compose liturgical music to serve the prayer of the people gathered for prayer; we create these settings so that the liturgy will be filled with sung prayer that responds to the word that is proclaimed and preached in our midst. In that sense, liturgical composition is more craft than inspiration. Certainly, many compositions have risen out of being "inspired," but at the center of what we liturgical composers do is the creation of music that will serve the liturgy and serve the people's prayer, regardless of the circumstances that call it forth. This is the case with "Do Not Let Your Hearts Be Troubled." This song was written, not consciously in response to a life-event, but by a pastoral musician (in this case, me) looking for a musical setting that would help this gospel proclamation more effectively come to life—a song-prayer that would advance God's word. One of my fondest memories of this song was being able to lead it at my mother's funeral. She was very specific that she wanted this song used. We did. It was a beautiful moment of prayer. I think of her quite a bit whenever I lead this song. Actually, as you could imagine, I think about her all the time, period!

Soon after the song was composed, a line from the refrain began to jump out at me: "I will go forth to prepare a place for you." I was working on this song during a time of very difficult transition in my life, and I was spending a lot of time with my good friend Dan Kantor. Dan and I are both alumni of University of St. Thomas, and we have known each other for years. In addition to him being an incredible musician, pianist and composer ("Night of Silence," anyone?), his primary livelihood over the years has been as a graphic designer and artist (he has designed many of my CD covers over the years). Now Dan, he really loves good food and good restaurants. So we used to go out to dinner together often at various different restaurants in the twin cities, most of which I had never been to or heard of, and we would talk and talk and talk. Dan has many wonderful qualities; one of them is that he is a great listener, very educated and wise about many things. I have learned much from him over the years.

I WILL BRING YOU HOME

During many of these long dinners and thought-provoking conversations, Dan and I shared our struggles with always looking forward beyond the present state of affairs, especially in times of challenge and worry about the future. I remember talking about trusting that there is always the promise of something new, different, and transformative—as long as we stay open and vigilant along the journey. While I was putting the final touches on this song, the phrase "I will go forth to prepare a place for you" brought Dan and the gift of his friendship to mind, which led to my dedicating the song to him. Dan's gift to me, in his friendship, was to walk with me, and to help create a space for me to enter into discernment. This is ultimately, what I hope this song helps us to do—*discern* the place and state where we find ourselves. And spiritual friendship is when someone walks with us into the unknown, helping us to open up in courage and nurture a new relationship with ourselves. "Do Not Let Your Hearts Be Troubled" is a musical celebration of discernment where we can choose new ways of living by letting God provide the direction.

So I give thanks to God for Dan, and so many other dear friends who have calmed my troubled heart throughout my life. Such calm and courage is offered to all of us. (11.10.17)

CD
MP3
Music

Who Calls You by Name, Vol. 2; Blest Are They:
The Best of David Haas, Vol. 1; Alive in Christ Jesus
X-34009
G-3655

DUST AND ASHES

Music: David Haas
Text: Brian Wren

Dust and ashes touch our face,
mark our failure and our falling.
Holy Spirit, come,
walk with us tomorrow,
take us as disciples,
washed and wakened by your calling.

Take us by the hand and lead us,
lead us through the desert sands,
bring us living water,
Holy Spirit, come.

Dust and ashes soil our hands—
greed of market, pride of nation.
Holy Spirit, come,
walk with us tomorrow,
as we pray and struggle
through the meshes of oppression.

Dust and ashes choke our tongue
in the wasteland of depression.
Holy Spirit, come,
walk with us tomorrow,
through all gloom and grieving
to the paths of resurrection.

I WILL BRING YOU HOME

While many Christians dread the season of Lent coming around each year, I happen to love its annual arrival—especially at the get-go, on Ash Wednesday with its call to conversion, so beautifully colored by the scriptures appointed for this day that precede the gospel reading:

"Even now, says the Lord,
return to me with your whole heart,
with fasting, weeping and mourning ...
return to the Lord ...
gracious and merciful is he,
slow to anger, rich in kindness ...
blow the trumpet in Zion,
proclaim a fast,
call an assembly;
Gather the people,
notify the congregation;
Assemble the elders,
gather the children ..." (From Joel 2:12-18)

"We are ambassadors for Christ ...
We implore you on behalf of Christ,
Be reconciled to God ...
Behold, now is a very acceptable time;
behold, now is the day of salvation." (From 2 Corinthians 5:20-6:2)

And the responsorial psalm, which actually, my friends, is the true second reading, that comes alive in this verse:

A clean heart create for me, O God,
and a steadfast spirit renew within me.
Cast me not out from your presence,
and your Holy Spirit take not from me. (Psalm 51:12-13

I have come to learn that the responsorial psalm is more than just a beautiful prayer-poem that gifts the liturgy on a spiritual and more metaphorical level. The psalm, in its role in the liturgy, serves as a "bridge" to understanding the gospel. The psalms are, yes, on the very lips of Christ (as he was an observant Jew), and these prayers were a part of his religious tradition. With that understanding, we look at this verse of the psalm, and find it to be cry for the presence of the Holy Spirit to come and dwell in our lives. Too often we reduce the Holy Spirit to nothing more than a vibrant image for the season of Pentecost—but the Spirit is at the heart of Lent, and on Ash Wednesday, this cry to the Spirit to be among us is intentional.

And so, when I came across this powerful text of Brian Wren, it was the first time that I felt a true musical possibility of celebrating the relationship of ashes and Spirit—a relationship at the heart of the *Rite of Christian Initiation of Adults*, as those seeking full initiation in the Church move into the final period of their journey to font and table. This time of inventory and examination is not only for the elect—those preparing to receive the Easter sacraments. No, it is the repeatable, relentless, and ongoing celebration of our coming to God with the entirety of ourselves, for renewal, conversion, and the cry for clean hearts. Such renewal comes from calling upon the Holy Spirit to dwell among us in the reality, the "dust and ashes" of our lives. During Lent we recognize that we need to be led through "the desert sands," but we do so with the full knowledge and hope of the "living water," so we cry out "Holy Spirit, come."

I purposely wanted to find a melody and arrangement that would truly promote the text, and not draw any overt musical attention away from it. It is hard to embody both "ashes" and "Spirit" musically without one or the other image being cheated, so to speak. When listening to the recording I get chills every time I hear it, and Bonnie Faber and Kevin Walsh (the two cantor soloists) totally brought to it their sense of the awe of this season—not to mention Bobby Fisher's masterful guitar playing, and Marty Haugen's unique re-creation of the Japanese Shakuhachi flute on the synthesizer.

During Lent we do not forget about the resurrection, and during Easter, we do not cast out the season of Lent and repentance that precedes the celebration of the empty tomb. Brian highlights this message powerfully throughout this text, particularly at the conclusion of the third verse, when the song cries out to the Spirit to walk with us "through all gloom and grieving to the path of resurrection." Now, why could I not have thought of that line? (11.20.17)

CD
MP3
Music

God Has Done Marvelous Things;
Glory Day: David Haas and Friends in Concert
X-80510
G-4735

E NA LIMA HANA

(THE WORKING HANDS)

**Music and Text
for Refrain:
David Haas and
Joe Camacho
Music and text
for Verses:
David Haas**

E Na Lima Hana, E Malama Aina;
Meke Kino, Meka Puu'wai.

Translation:
*With our working hands,
we care for and nurture the land,
the body, and the heart.*

With our hands, we press onward to the plow.
Never turning back,
　　we face the myst'ry far beyond.
With our hands,
　　we will shape each other stories.
We will write the vision down;
　　never tire until it's done.

With our hands,
　　we will put our weapons down.
We will care for the earth;
we will speak a word of peace.
With our hands, we will wash each other's feet.
We will break the bread of justice;
　　we will share the cup of dreams.

With our hands,
　　we'll reach out to one another.
We will touch and heal each other;
　　we will dry each other's tears.
With our hands,
　　we will work to build the promise;

for our God will be our strength,
and like the eagle we will fly.

Throughout this book I speak often of the wonderful experiences I have had in Hawaii over the years, being a presenter at many Big Island Liturgy and Arts Conferences (BILAC), but even more so, my connection to the Malia Puka O Kalani (Mary, Gate of Heaven) parish community in Hilo. What was so unique about the BILAC event from its inception up until only a few years ago, was that the conference was centered in the day to day life of the wonderful people of this community, placed in the center of native Hawaiian homelands, in a village named *Keaukaha.*

While the conference was an event for people throughout all of the Hawaiian Islands and beyond, the theme each year was always developed from the people of Malia, from the vision of their pastor Fr. George DeCosta. For many years, several of us visiting composers would be asked to compose a theme song that would express and celebrate this theme, to be used not only for the conference but for many of their parish celebrations throughout the year. I was honored to have been chosen to compose the theme song for their 1995 conference, with the theme, "E Na Lima Hana: The Working Hands."

As was the case for my "Song of the Body of Christ" (composed a few years earlier), I wanted to find a simple melody that could be sung almost immediately, so again I looked for a tune that came from the Islands. Attending a hula competition the year before, I remember hearing this haunting melody. I tried to discover the actual source of the tune, but I was not successful. I changed it ever so slightly, and that became the melody, with my friend from Malia, Joe Camacho, helping me to come up with the right Hawaiian phrases for the refrain.

The melody and words for the verses are my own, building upon the grounding proclamation that Fr. George had created around the theme. This image of our "working hands" is so powerful. It challenges us to move from the "right" way of doing the ritual, towards embracing the discipleship that the entire liturgy calls for, so pointedly phrased in the words leading up to the Eucharistic Prayer when in the receiving of both the bread and wine we are asked to offer the "fruit of the earth" and the "fruit of the vine" as the "*work of human hands.*" With these hands, as the Hawaiian text translates, we are to "care for and nurture the land, the body, and the heart." (11.24.17)

Star Child
X-80307
G-5219

THE ENCOUNTER

Music: David Haas
Text:
Jaroslav J. Vajda
("Where Shepherds
Lately Knelt," with
additional text from
"Silent Night")

Where shepherds lately knelt,
    and kept the angel's word,
I come in half-belief, a pilgrim strangely stirred;
but there is room and welcome there for me.

In that unlikely place I find him as they said:
sweet new born Babe, how frail!
    And in a manger bed:
a still small Voice to cry one day for me.

How should I not have known Isaiah would be there,
his prophecies fulfilled?
    With pounding heart, I stare:
a Child, a Son, the Prince of Peace—for me.

    Silent Night, Holy Night,
      Silent Night, Holy Night.
    All is calm, all is bright.

Can I, will I forget how Love was born
and burned its way into my heart—unasked,
unforced, unearned,
to die, to live, and not alone for me?

When I stumbled on this powerful Christmas proclamation-poem by Jaroslav Vajda, I was totally taken in by its power, and as the text states, I was "in half-belief" that someone could find within themselves such a fresh announcement of the Incarnation. It is impossible to cite individual phrases that speak stronger than others, because I believe every word here is packed with prophecy, providing an exemplary fusing together of the mystery of Christ's birth and the destiny of his passion and death. I knew that I had to take a stab at finding a way to present this poem in a musical way.

Because the words are so dense and thick with imagery and meaning, I did not want the melody to overwhelm the message, so I first came up with a rhythmic device in the piano arrangement. The constancy of the eighth-note movement in the accompaniment was intended to create a sense of anticipation and excitement. I decided to purposely create a melody that would not be particularly memorable. The influence of the brilliant Broadway composer Stephen Sondheim was brought to bear; I love how he speaks about how in theatre, the music should always help elevate the plot and tell the story. The same could be said about the charge to compose liturgical music. While I am miles away from coming close to Sondheim's gift in doing this, I gave allegiance to his stance and purposely chose a repeatable, almost relentless five note unison phrase that would hopefully help each line of text build upon the previous one, to again, create a sense of dramatic proclamation. After I finished the piece, I wanted to somehow tie the astonishing announcement of Christ's birth with a traditional and familiar recall, and so as an interlude between the third and final stanza, I placed a fragment of "Silent Night" into the scene of the story.

"The Encounter" eventually became part of the *Star Child* CD and music collection that was released just before Christmas 1991; it features not only some of my original music, but also songs by Lori True, Dan Kantor, Grayson Warren Brown, and John Foley. The collection also includes some very unique and interesting arrangements of traditional carols that forced me to stretch myself as an arranger, such as some "out there" arrangements of "Ding! Dong! Merrily on High" (the instrumental interlude was deliberately influenced by the Beach Boys—I am not kidding) and an adaptation of "I Saw Three Ships" titled "Christmas Day." This project was one where I wanted the CD to be of the highest quality in both performance and in production, so it would have appeal not only as a series of individual Advent and Christmas songs for liturgy but also provide people with a good listening experience. From this standpoint, I believe this CD to be among the best I have ever released—in no small part due to the tremendous musicianship and artistry of my fellow singers on the recording: Lori True, Kate Cuddy, David Fischer, Jim Waldo and Tom Franzak. They were just awesome on this project; they really cared about the music and thought of it as their own. The same is true for the amazing instrumentalists that you hear, people like Bobby Fisher, Stephen Petrunak, Dik Hedlund, Kenni Holmen, Eileen Bird, Tom Franzak, Bruce Kurnow, Gordy Knudtson, and others. An extra perk for me personally was that I got to play the harpsichord on one of the tracks.

Accompanying the rollout of the CD, most of the people mentioned here joined me on a six city "tour" where we shared not only the music, but our love and care for one another and for the season. What a wonderful memory. One of the best Christmas gifts I have ever received. (11.25.17)

CD
MP3
Music

Table Songs, Vol. 1
X-26516
G-3702

FAITH, HOPE AND LOVE

Music:
David Haas
Text:
1 Corinthians
13:13; 1 John 4:7
(alt. DH)

Faith, hope and love, let these endure among you;
and the greatest of these is love.
The greatest of these is love.

Come, let us love, for love is of God,
in God alone will love be our truth!

Come, let us love, for love is of God,
and we will become God's own children!

Come, let us love, for love is of God,
and we shall see our God, who first loved us!

This song was composed as a request from my friend Barbara Conley Waldmiller to write a song for her wedding liturgy. She and Ken specifically asked for a communion song, and so thinking about the sacrament of marriage and the ritual of communion sharing, I very quickly thought of the image of "faith, hope, and love." I was intimidated for many years to consider composing a song around this powerful and beloved phrase because of the centrality of its message, but also because I had been in love for quite some time with Alexander Peloquin's gorgeous "Faith, Hope and Love" from his *Lyric Liturgy.* I could not imagine my composing anything near to the beauty of his version.

Still, this text kept ringing in my head, so I decided to accept the fact that I would not be able to create anything nearly as beautiful, and went to work. As a nod to Peloquin, I decided to give the piece a thick SATB choral texture like his version, even though we did not have a big choir on the day of Barb and Ken's wedding. So Barb and Ken—it was a wonderful honor to lead the music on your wedding day. Know that you helped me to finally muster up the courage to put these biblical passages to music. While I am certainly not Peloquin, I hope this song has spoken to you both—and so many others—as you celebrate the gift of married love. (11.24.17)

CD
MP3
Music

Psalms for the Church Year, Vol. 3;
Without Seeing You: The Best of David Haas, Vol. 3
X-80517
G-4262

THE FRAGRANCE OF CHRIST

Music: David Haas
Text: Psalm 138;
The Rite of
Dedication of a
New Church

Lord, may our prayer rise like incense in your sight,
may this place be filled with the fragrance of Christ.

I will thank you, Lord, with all of my heart,
you have heard the words of my mouth.
In the presence of the Lord I will bless you,
I will adore before your holy temple.

I will thank you, Lord,
 for your faithfulness and love,
beyond all my hopes and dreams.
On the day that I called you answered;
you gave life to the strength of my soul.

All who live on earth shall give you thanks
when they hear the words of your voice.
And all shall sing of your ways:
"How great is the glory of God!"

This is an example of a composition that was composed to a specific task, in response to a commission from what was at the time a relatively new parish community, St. Thomas the Apostle Church in Naperville, Illinois. Anne Mueser, their music director, asked me to compose a piece to accompany the ritual actions of the anointing and incensation of the altar and the walls for the dedication of their new worship space. The text was a yoking of one of the prayers in the dedication ritual together with Psalm 138 (one of the suggested texts from the ritual for this moment in the liturgy). I have experienced this piece used for this specific ritual moment for both the dedication of a brand-new church, and also for the dedication of a renovated space.

This refrain, obviously, is explicitly "Christ" centered; to broaden the song's usefulness, I also created two alternative refrain texts for when the psalm is utilized as either a responsorial psalm at Eucharist, or for the celebration of Morning Prayer (Psalm 138 is found in the texts for morning prayer in the Divine Office). In addition to the first refrain originally being intended for use at the rite of dedication, it also would work as a psalm choice for evening prayer (vespers).

I had no idea at the time that this piece would have the staying power it has seemed to demonstrate over the years, nor that my friend Kate Cuddy would eventually become the Director of Music and Liturgy there at St. Thomas several years later. I always think of this wonderful parish community when I hear this psalm at a liturgical celebration, and I continually give thanks for the "fragrance of Christ," the scent of holiness that should fill all of our spaces—and our hearts—when we gather to pray. (11.20.17)

CD
MP3
Music

As Water to the Thirsty; Creating God;
Mass of Light
X-17704
G-3109

GLORY TO GOD
from MASS OF LIGHT

Music: David Haas
Text: The Roman Missal, 1973

The year was 1984, during the time I was serving as the Director of Music and Liturgy at St. Thomas Aquinas parish in St. Paul Park, Minnesota. The event that was being planned and anticipated was the 100th Anniversary celebration of the parish on the feast day of St Thomas Aquinas, January 28. The task (which I imposed on myself), was to compose a piece for the liturgical celebration, with the presider and homilist being our archbishop at the time, Archbishop John Roach (Archdiocese of St. Paul and Minneapolis).

The parish was blessed with many gifted instrumentalists and singers from its various ensembles, and we also had some fine cantors, so I was not concerned about its presentation. I *was* concerned about the quality of the composition, and whether or not I would be able to get it written in time for us to rehearse it properly before the celebration took place! I knew that I wanted the piece to be a liturgical song, sung by the assembly, since our community loved to sing. I had no interest in writing a choir anthem and I also quickly abandoned the idea of trying to compose something around some of the writings of St. Thomas Aquinas. I mean, after all, how do you beat *Pange Lingua?*

For reasons that I cannot remember, I thought it would be good to compose a setting of the Glory to God (Gloria) for the occasion. So I went to work. My musical influences were many; I am classically trained, but I have always been an eclectic in terms of musical taste and am, among other things, a fan of both Elton John and Billy Joel. Because Jeanne Cotter was going to be the pianist for the celebration (those of you who know her are aware of her amazing piano skills), I chose to write something that would be very pianistic in nature, in a "pop" style; I wanted something that could hold a strong and attractive melody and at the same time be easy for people to pick up, especially since there was no time to rehearse it with the people beforehand. Once I knew what I wanted to write, the piece came quickly; I remember writing it in one sitting, in less than a half hour. (Got lucky, I guess.) It was very well received. I conducted the choir, brass and other instruments; Jeanne was amazing on the piano; Kathy Rustin was wonderful as the cantor in leading the people, and the people sang like crazy. In fact, before the final blessing, Archbishop Roach mentioned how much he appreciated the good music for the celebration, and singled out the fact that he really liked the Glory to God—so much so, he made a point to find me after the liturgy was over to tell me that he thought it was the best Gloria he had ever experienced. Wow.

People at various parishes throughout the Archdiocese heard about it, asked for copies, and also found success in singing it. I had not yet attached this to a Mass setting; this was before I had yet composed any mass settings at all. I admit I was intimidated by Marty's *Mass of Creation*. It was so good and so "right." So while it was not yet part an entire mass, I published and recorded this Gloria as part of the *As Water to the Thirsty* collection in 1987.

Not long after it was published, I received a call from Ken Mervine, the Director of Music at St. Ann's Church in Raritan, New Jersey, who commissioned me to compose a mass setting for their parish. Because they had a priest who was a good singer, he also wanted me to include in this mass a sung setting of what was then Eucharistic Prayer IV. I decided then that this Glory to God would be part of this new setting, to be called *Mass of Light*, which was published and recorded in 1989.

I am grateful and very appreciative for so many who have over the years, shared their affirmation about this setting of the Gloria. Thanks to Jeanne for adding some spice and color to the rhythmic piano arrangement that I started with, one that many pianists see as a true challenge of their keyboard "chops." Thanks especially to the people of St. Thomas Aquinas. May the "glory" be, ultimately, to God alone. (11.10.17)

CD
MP3
Music

A Changed Heart;
Do Not Be Afraid, I Am With You
X-82210
G-7730

GOD, GRANT THIS SUFFERING SOUL RELEASE

Music: David Haas
Text: Adam Tice

God, give your faithful servant peace;
you have inspired the final breath.
You grant the suffering soul release,
free from earth's pain in timely death.

Into your open hands receive
this spirit, for the body dies.
Grant us the grace to fully grieve
as we now loose our former ties.

God, help us all complete this race,
to live so when our course is run,
when we at last reach your embrace,
we too will hear you say, "Well done."

I wrote this musical setting of Adam Tice's text when my Dad was entering the most painful chapter of his struggle with Alzheimer's, as he inched toward his death. Those who knew him would agree with me that he was one of the most positive and joyful people I ever knew, and that is why it was so painful for me— not so much for him, but for me and my family to watch—to see him become more diminished with his memory and in his ability to communicate. Adam's words, and the tune I created around them, became a prayer for me while I and the members of my family were on the path of the long goodbye. Dad remained joyful to the end for the most part. I am so grateful for that. I still miss him so much. (11.25.17)

CD

MP3 Music

God Has Done Marvelous Things;
Glory Day: David Haas and Friends in Concert;
Without Seeing You: The Best of David Haas, Vol. 3
X-80520
G-4731

GOD HAS DONE MARVELOUS THINGS

Music: David Haas
Text:
Herbert Brokering

Earth and all stars! Loud rushing planets:
 Sing to the Lord a new song!
O, victory! Loud shouting army:
 Sing to the Lord a new song!

God has done marvelous things!
I too, I too sing praises with a new song!
God has done marvelous things!
I too, I too sing praises with a new song!

Hail, wind, and rain! Loud blowing snowstorm:
 Sing to the Lord a new song!
Flowers and trees! Loud rustling dry leaves:
 Sing to the Lord a new song!

Trumpet and pipes! Loud clashing cymbals:
 Sing to the Lord a new song!
Harp, lute, and lyre! Loud humming cellos:
 Sing to the Lord a new song!

Engines and steel! Loud pounding hammers:
 Sing to the Lord a new song!
Limestone and beams! Loud building workers:
 Sing to the Lord new song!

Classrooms and labs! Loud boiling test tubes:
 Sing to the Lord a new song!
Athlete and band! Loud cheering people:
 Sing to the Lord a new song!

> Knowledge and truth! Loud sounding wisdom:
> Sing to the Lord a new song!
> Daughter and son! Loud praying members: S
> ing to the Lord a new song!

I have always gotten a kick out of this text, having seen it in various Lutheran hymnals over the years. In Lutheran circles, this hymn has apparently been received with mixed reactions; I do not know how that has developed, increased, or diminished over the years. Either way, I love it, if for nothing more than how Herbert Brokering had the courage to break out, explore, and boldly put forward the possibilities for new sources in offering praise to God. All creation, all people, all of the elements—even amidst some of the most unlikely places—are called upon to offer praise.

As a text writer myself I have always wondered what creative storehouse or muse triggered Herbert to come up with the word "loud" as a repetitive binding force in this song— not to mention the images of "rushing planets," "blowing snowstorms," "humming cellos," "engines and steel," "pounding hammers," "loud boiling test tubes," … my goodness!

Thanks to the generosity of the original publisher and copyright holder, Augsburg Press, I was able to bring this text to life musically and have it become the title song for the wonderful collaboration that I was to be a part of with Leon Roberts in 1997. When we all sang it in the studio, it felt like we were part of a prayer-meeting! The Spirit really took over when we were in the circle that night singing this hymn. You can sense it when you listen to the track. The instrumentalists made some very creative additions (thanks to Marty Haugen in particular), and the soloists are just awesome. In addition to my singing the opening two verses, you will hear tremendous "musical proclamations" for the rest, from Lori True, David Fischer, Yolande Bruce, and Fr. Ray East. If you watch the video of the *Glory Day* concert that I did around the same time, you will see a marvelously choreographed interpretation of the song danced by Bob Piercy, Donna Anderle, Jean Bross-Judge and Joe Camacho—along with a marvelous ensemble of young people.

Ed Harris, the founding president of GIA Publications, really liked it when I played it for the staff there for the first time. Ed, this is why the song is dedicated to you.

I simply love the wonderful imagination that is packed into this text. I am not sure how many people have chosen this piece for their celebrations, but for me, I will always smile when I think of it, especially with the original group of singers and players who found in the words that Herbert created, and the music that I came up with, some really "marvelous things." (11.24.17)

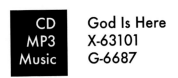

CD
MP3
Music

God Is Here
X-63101
G-6687

GOD IS HERE

**Music and Text:
David Haas**

Why do you stare at the skies up above
while your hearts are broken and looking for love?
Don't get lost in the things of the past,
but believe in the promise of a truth that will last.

God is here, God is here,
one thing I know: God is here!
God is here, God is here,
one thing I know: God is here!

Why do you dwell on what's happen'd before?
Release all that burdens you; open the door.
The future we reach toward is not found in the sky,
for the reign of God's glory will never die!

Here in this place, with the gifts that we bring,
the Body of Christ is found—our reason to sing!
In our coming and going, in ev'ry day,
God's presence is stirring here proclaiming the way!

With our strengths and our talents,
in our weakness and fear;
in joy and in sorrow, God's healing is near.
In growth and in faith, in the darkness of sin,
a new hope is present here where love can begin!

The church that we ache
for can be found in this place,
in our working for justice; in the presence of grace.
For we are God's people, all holy and strong;
to serve is our mission, with Christ as our song!

I WILL BRING YOU HOME

Why do you seek the living among the dead?
Jesus is risen, friends, just as he said.
All things are made new, true to God's Word;
it's beginning right here, right now,
        haven't you heard?

This song, especially the phrase "one thing I know: God is here," was inspired initially by a homily Fr. Paul Jaroszeski, pastor of my parish of St. Cecilia's in St. Paul, preached on the celebration of Ascension in 2003. I am always captivated by the first reading for Year A, taken from the Acts of the Apostles (Acts 1:1-11), when the two men dressed in white suddenly appeared to the apostles after Jesus was lifted up to heaven, and speak: "why are you standing here looking at the sky?" I think the same is so often the case with us. We keep looking in the wrong places—we keep searching out paranormal locations or past events to find the Risen Lord.

This is often the case with young people who can easily become intoxicated with the addiction toward "spectacular" and "out of the ordinary" experiences. The awesome thing about God is that God is to be found "right here, right now, haven't you heard?" So I wanted to write an anthem, a mission statement of sorts—not just for young people but for all of us—that would announce and celebrate that God's presence is always surrounding us—yes, "God is here!"

I also wanted the song to be experienced with great inclusivity and universality, which is why I asked Tony Alonso, together with Peter Kolar, to create a Spanish translation of the refrain; it is also why that when I recorded the song, I included a children's choir and a group of teens from Benilde-St. Margaret's School in St. Louis Park, Minnesota; and why I wanted a variety of singer-soloist-cantors, to proclaim the verses along with me: Paul Tate, Kate Cuddy, Michael Mahler, Tony Alonso, Lori True, and Tom Franzak. I did a second version together with my friend Jesse Manibusan, who I experienced singing the refrain as a litany to action, and so we included the adaptation "God Is Here: A Litany of Reconciliation" on the original CD, and Jesse brings his passion and convictions to that track with gusto.

Because of the focus on young people, I dedicated the song to the *Music Ministry Alive!* family: team members and participants who gathered together for 19 years to celebrate being church and messengers of hope. Through this community I have discovered, in relentless and faithful ways, that God is most certainly, here. (11.24.17)

CD
MP3
Music

Light and Peace
X-17512
G-3079

GOD IS MY LIGHT

**Music and Text:
David Haas
Inspired by Psalm 27**

God, my light and my life, over and over my life.
God, my light and my life, over and over my life.

God is my light, my living light.
Light that saves me, frees me.

One thing, this I seek:
To live out my life in God's place,
    seeing God's face.

Your beauty I will see in the life free from death.
My hope and my heart will wait for you,
    rest in you.

This was an adaptation of Psalm 27 that I created for the *Light and Peace* collection, a resource of music for morning and evening prayer that initially grew out of my time as composer-in-residence at the St. Paul Seminary School of Divinity, from 1985-1988. It was during this time that I was making intentional efforts to stretch myself not only in my melody writing, but also in exploring some fresh poetic ways to "re-present" some of the psalms.

Psalm 27 has always been a personal favorite. It was not planned, but when I had open heart surgery in 2007—as I was rolled into the operating room, these were the words that came to me, that became my mantra at that moment, during the days of my recovery, and many times since then when I feel most afraid:

Music & Stories GOD IS MY LIGHT

The Lord is my light and my help, whom should I fear;
the Lord is the stronghold of my life, before whom should I shrink?
There is one thing I ask of the Lord, for this I long:
to live in the house of the Lord all the days of my life.
I believe I shall see the goodness of the Lord in the land of the living.
Hope in God, and take heart. Hope in the Lord!

In 1986 when I approached what would become *this* setting of Psalm 27, I wanted to find some fresh ways of expressing this well-known prayer poem, so instead of "The Lord is my light and my salvation," I came up with "God, my light and my life, over and over my life." I tried this approach of finding new metaphors to communicate the meaning of the text on the verses as well...I wanted to have the refrain surround the expression of God's light, which is why it eventually became a sort of canon (as you can hear on the recording).

It was also around this time that the first user-friendly synthesizer came out on the market, the Yamaha DX-7. (Did anyone reading this have this magical instrument back then?) After I bought my own, I would try out different sounds to see what it could do, so when I went to the studio to record "God Is My Light," I decided to use the synthesizer—in fact, I played all of the instrumental sounds on this track—all on the DX-7! I was in overdub heaven!

My dear friend of many years, Bonnie Faber, is the soloist you hear on the recording. I have to say, this is one of the most stalwart vocal performances that I have ever heard Bonnie give—very close to giving birth her son Jonathan, who was born the very next day! Amazing.

While I love so many of the prayers in the psalter, Psalm 27 has been my "light and life," and will always be close to "my hope and my heart." (11.25.17)

CD

MP3
Music

Living Spirit, Holy Fire, Vol. 1;
The Rosary with St. James
X-71633
G-7670

GOD'S CAUSE

God's cause is the only concern of our hearts.
God's cause is our cause.

Music: David Haas
Text:
Inspired from the
writings of Blessed
Theresa Gerhardinger

Over the years I have developed a wonderful relationship with the School of
Sisters of Notre Dame, particularly the Sisters who are centered and grounded at
Our Lady of Good Counsel in Mankato, Minnesota. I have made retreat there
many times and some of these marvelous women— such as Sr. Kathleen Storms,
Sr. Bridget Waldorf, Sr. Dianne Perry, Sr. Lynore Girmscheid, Sr. Catherine
Bertrand, and Sr. Kathleen Bauer—have been true witnesses of God's light to
me and to so many others.

The School Sisters of Notre Dame, established by Blessed Theresa of
Jesus Gerhardinger in 1833, are rooted historically in Germany, and they have
established provinces throughout the world. Blessed Theresa was a woman of
deep wisdom, especially in regards to the spiritual walk and how it is linked to
intentional discipleship. The primacy of prayer is prominent in her writings,
and there are numerous nuggets of wisdom in this regard, my personal favorite
being: "Prayer is the most necessary element for our souls as water is for fish."

But there is another prophetic mantra of hers that has become a real
centering point for my own spiritual life: "God's cause is the only concern of
our hearts." This, for me, embodies the essence of what all spirituality points
toward—the walking with and commitment to bring "God's cause" to life.

Music & Stories GOD'S CAUSE

When my friend Bridget Waldorf was approaching her celebration of final vows on October 26, 2008 (she entered the community in 2001), I wanted to compose something for the liturgy, for her and for her companions who were making this blessed movement and commitment. This was the genesis of this musical setting of what I believe to be Blessed Theresa's mission statement. It most certainly is a reflection of Bridget's mission and passion for ministry, especially with young people.

The original version of this piece is an ostinato, a repeatable mantra, overlaid with verses adapted from other sections of wisdom from Blessed Theresa. The refrain has been adapted for use as a response to various forms of intercessory prayer, as is demonstrated in another project, "The Rosary with St. James." It also has been used frequently for celebrations of Taizé prayer and other contemplative gatherings.

I have been asked, as one who composes music for prayer—am I able to forget that I actually composed a particular piece, let go, and let it enter into my heart and spring forth in prayer for myself? This is one song where I am able to do so, without any difficulty or challenge at all. This has become a prayer for me as much as for others, especially the School Sisters of Notre Dame. I am so thankful for that—having come to know them, and learning of this wonderful insight of Blessed Theresa, my vocation continues to be more and more clarified. To embrace "God's cause" is to ask important things of ourselves—most critically, "am I doing God's work here?" Looking back over the past 40 years I have learned that the music is not in and of itself, the "cause." The cause is found in the homeless person that I drive past when I am in a hurry. God's cause is found when I take the time to be present with the sick, the dying, and those who seem to suffer endlessly. God's cause is found in young people who are fearful and anxious about their future.

God's cause is not to be found in the feeding of my ego, but in the feeding of the hungry. God's cause is not found when we merely talk and sing about the poor; it is for us to discover in the very poor themselves. God's cause must sing *beyond* the song; it must bring beauty beyond the painting itself; it must move and grow beyond the movement of the gift of the skilled dancer; it must bring the poetry to life beyond the metaphors and images of the poem itself. God's cause is advanced when we realize that we have not yet arrived, and that we are truly lost and need to be found. God's cause is the choice to remain *bright*, always shining light on what is life, not death. God's cause is to be *our* cause. (11.16.17)

CD
MP3
Music

God is Here; Do Not Be Afraid, I Am With You;
God Will Delight
X-63102
G-6688

THE GOD OF SECOND CHANCES

Music and Text:
David Haas

Come now, O God of second chances;
    open our lives to heal.
Remove our hate, and melt our rage.
    Save us from ourselves.

Come now, O God, release our demons;
    open our eyes to see
the shame within, our guilt and pain.
    Mend us; make us whole.

Come now, O God, and still our anger;
    open our minds to peace.
Embrace our fear, and hold us close.
    Calm the storm within.

Come now, O God, shake our resentment;
    open our way to choose
the way of love over revenge. Show us a new way.

Come now, O God, and grant compassion;
    open our hearts to love.
May we let go of all our hurt. Help us to move on.

Come now, O God of second chances;
    may we forgive ourselves.
May we become your living sign:
    Children of God's love.

Copyright © 2005 GIA Publications, Inc.

In the fall of 2007, I had open heart surgery. I knew for a few years before this that I would someday have to have a heart valve replacement, but what speeded up the urgency of the surgery was that as a result of a regular visit to the doctor, they saw that my aorta had been swelling up and became so enlarged that we had to do surgery soon. This required two procedures to be taken care of at the same time. So it was a long surgery, about ten and a half hours. For the most part it went well, and so after 8 days, I was allowed to go home.

While I was standing there in my "going home" clothes, saying goodbye and thanking the staff at the nurse's station, I fell faint and dropped to the floor (a good place to be when something like this happens!). After I came to, they decided that I would not be going home after all; they were going to have to re-admit me, as they wanted to keep an eye on me after this happened.

So there I was, back in the hospital bed, and not happy about it all. I wanted to go home. I was agitated and so I was trying to relax and fall asleep. One of the things you learn if you have to be in the hospital for any length of time is just how bad television can really be. I wanted to watch something to take my mind off the fact that I was still there, so in the absence of any TV program worth watching, I asked one of the nurses if they had any videos that I could watch—all I wanted to do was watch something and not have to think, and hopefully, drift off to sleep. It was a short list of options, but I settled on the "Sound of Music." This was perfect—I had seen the movie dozens and dozens of times, which was great. I could watch it, and zone out. So I did.

At some point during the night (while the movie was still playing), I was suddenly startled and saw that there seemed to be about 20 people in the room. A nurse was at my side, sort of patting my leg, telling me that I would be OK. There were machines and people scurrying about—basically, I had gone into cardiac arrest. They came in with the "paddles," and just like in the movies, they placed them on my chest, and I remember feeling myself almost leaping off the bed while they applied them. In addition to all of this and because they were obviously preoccupied with taking care of me, no one bothered to turn off the TV—so the movie was still going, and while all of this was going on, guess what scene from the "Sound of Music" was taking place? It was the scene toward the end, when the Von Trapp Family Singers were singing at the festival, just before they are to escape from the Germans. And yes, they are singing: "So long, farewell." Finally, someone turned off the TV—thank goodness. They finally got me calmed down, and things seemed to improve. However, about two hours later, a second episode occurred. And the next morning, a third.

I WILL BRING YOU HOME

Remember—I was supposed to be going home … thank goodness I did not.

To this day, the doctors are not 100% in consensus as to what caused this to happen. But they were in agreement that as a precautionary measure, I should have a second surgery so they could implant a defibrillator, as a precaution. I had that procedure, and of course, I had to remain in the hospital for a few extra days. As of this writing, ten years later, there has not been any more incidents, and the defibrillator has never "gone off."

In the years that have passed, I am still learning much from this experience. The first thing I have learned is that I never want to see "The Sound of Music" ever again. Secondly, and far more importantly, I have come to realize that in some strange way, this was a "dress-rehearsal," so to speak, for my own death and resurrection. In the years since this event, I have come to know in much less dramatic ways the workings of the one I call the "God of second chances." For some reason, I was not supposed to go home that day. Something was about to happen, and God placed me in an environment where a resurrection, a "second chance," could take place.

I have also learned that while I still fall into the quicksand of my human frailties, the impulse for revenge and to withhold forgiveness only eats away at our well-being. I have learned, and continue to learn, that there is a "new way" that comes to us when we examine the things we do that cause harm and division. I am still learning—and it is a difficult lesson—that shame is a poison and wasted energy in our lives, both in how we knowingly and unknowingly inflict it on others, but also how we often become consumed by it ourselves. Shame is not a reflex or response to the empty tomb; it needs to be exorcised from us, so that the stone can be rolled away, and remain rolled away. I am learning that it is the world and the people in it that create the storms that flood our hearts, the storms we cling to within—and that these can only be calmed if I surrender myself to the God of love and mercy.

I am also learning that this "God of second chances" is walking with me in the midst of all my anxiety and often crippling depression; this "God of second chances" embraces the rat inside of me that I know has been the source of pain to others—and keeps on offering healing, that this "God of second chances" keeps on forgiving me over and over and over again. Non-stop. Relentless. Yes, the doctors, nurses, and the paddles brought me back—a living and concrete sign of the "bringing back" to life that God places before me at all times, places and situations. But it is God alone who offers more than just resuscitation— God offers a new freedom from our anxiety, anger, negativity, self-loathing—

rescuing us time and time again from the quicksand that seems to be so often rising up to our necks. I am learning these lessons and so many more, every day.

God is not only the "God of second chances," but of third, fourth and an infinite number of chances, where an intervention takes place with a new awareness of new life reimagined and experienced. Have you ever had someone come up to you and ask, "have you been *born again?*" I certainly have been asked this many times, and almost always, the statement makes me annoyed and uncomfortable. First of all, as a Catholic, this type of phrase is not common in our lexicon. I *have* come to know, more and more, that we are not just "born again," but we are "born again, and again, and again, and again ..." What happened to me in the fall of 2007 was a prompting of the Spirit, I believe, to awaken me to the reality of the presence of God in my life. I give thanks and praise to God for the gift of life that was restored to me. And I am finding out that this restoration keeps taking place on a regular basis.

As this song, interestingly enough composed prior to these events, tries to express— this God of ours *never gives up on us.* It is not in God's nature to do so. God cannot help but be the ongoing, merciful, and always-forgiving God that we celebrate. It is so difficult to wrap our brains around this—that there is absolutely nothing too awful, too heinous, too horrific, too sinful that we can participate in that will separate us from the love of God. We are always forgiven. We are forgiven before we have what Paul refers to as our "momentary afflictions." We are forgiven in the very midst of our bad choices, and we are forgiven when we carry out those bad decisions. This kind of forgiveness is so very difficult for us to offer to another, and at times even more challenging to offer to ourselves. But nonetheless, we are the children of God, who is the "God of second chances" and ongoing mercy.

It is interesting that while liturgical composers are not called to compose for their own self-interest, there are times when we as crafters of sung prayer need to be honest in admitting that the music we create often speaks to us in a personal way. When I composed "The God of Second Chances" I had no idea at the time how it would speak to me and teach me afterwards. I believe the song to have been prophetic for me—I did not know at the time how it would teach me about the precious gift of life. And it is prophetic in that it has held some power and wisdom, not only for me in the aftermath of my near-death experience, but also speaking and ministering to so many others. That is what prophecy is. It certainly is mystery as well. A mystery that I give thanks for.

Pope Francis has taught us that mercy is the way of God. And that mercy, the offering of "second chances" and so many more chances and opportunities for restoration, are held as promises to and for us. God provides this assurance. May we do everything possible in our lives, to take up this same mission, to become as the song concludes, "children of God's love." (11.20.17)

CD	
MP3	Echo of Faith; I Will Live On
Music	X-50702
	G-5658

THE GUARDIAN'S FAREWELL

Music: David Haas
Text:
John Henry
Newman
(1801-1890)

Softly and gently, dearly ransomed soul,
in my most loving arms I now enfold thee.
And o'er the purging waters as they roll,
I poise thee and I lower thee and hold thee.

And with great care I dip thee in the lake;
and thou without a sob or a resistance
dost through the flood thy rapid passage take,
sinking deep, deeper into the dim distance.

Angels to whom the willing task is giv'n
shall tend and nurse and lull thee as thou liest,
and masses on the earth and prayers in heav'n
shall aid thee at the throne of the most highest.

Farewell but not forever, sister/brother dear,
be brave and patient on thy bed of sorrow,
swiftly shall pass the night of trial here,
and I will come and wake thee on the morrow.

Composers in every genre of music tend to be stereotyped and labeled—put into a box and category in order for people to define the type of music they write. This is certainly true for liturgical composers, and it certainly has been the case for me. I get it. The mass majority of music that I have composed for the liturgy over the years would fall into the category of pop/folk/contemporary, or whatever.

Not everyone knows that I have a strong classical music background. Both

I WILL BRING YOU HOME

of my parents were classically trained, degreed, musicians. My Dad was a pianist, an organist, and a piano and music theory teacher. My mother taught public school music for most of her life at both the elementary and secondary level. My growing-up years were immersed in classical music. I started piano when I was four. We had two grand pianos in our "music room," and recitals held at our home were more common than going out to a restaurant. My brother and I did not have breakfast until we practiced piano—simultaneously—for one hour in the wee hours of the morning, followed by an hour when we got home from school, and another half hour usually before we went to bed. Our growing up was attending concerts and actually meeting well known classical artists. My Dad was vice-chairman of the Saginaw Community Concerts Association for many years, and his job was to pick up the artists at the airport, take them to their hotel, get them to the concert hall, and so forth. I would often get excused from school and accompany him, and often these people came to our house to relax and practice—people like Van Cliburn, Ferrante and Teicher, the cellist Leonard Rose, Lili Kraus, Christina Ortiz, Robert Merrill, and even Arthur Fiedler. It was quite an upbringing. When I first went to college I was a vocal performance major and sang in several opera workshop productions and musicals, with the intention of singing in opera and musical theatre as a career. This is what my life looked like long before I got involved with composing liturgical music.

So from time to time, I have composed something more classical, more traditionally "choral" in nature. This funeral anthem, "The Guardian's Farewell" comes from that side of me, an honoring of my musical training and background.

While she never got to hear it, it is dedicated to the memory of my mentor, friend and heroine, Sue Seid-Martin, who through her ministry and teaching at the University of Notre Dame, St. Catherine University, and the St. Paul Seminary School of Divinity touched so many students and liturgical music leaders over the years. "Farwell, but not forever, sister dear ..." (11.10.17)

CD
MP3
Music

We Are Not Alone
X-89606
G-8331

HAIL, HOLY MARY, QUEEN OF PEACE

Music:
SALVE REGINA
COELITUM
(German, 19th c.)
Text:
David Haas

Hail, Holy Mary, Queen of peace, O Maria!
O fragrance of God's love increase, O Maria!
Mother, servant of God's grace,
womb for Christ, holy birthing place,
first disciple, we embrace:
Salve, Salve, Salve Regina!

Hail, Holy Mary, hope for all, O Maria!
Your song of justice is our call, O Maria!
Poor and broken are held high,
mercy will intensify,
God's reign you personify:
Salve, Salve, Salve Regina!

Hail, Holy Mary, you inspire, O Maria!
With you, God's presence we desire, O Maria!
Vision, wisdom, you instill,
you, the "yes," God's holy will,
faith and courage, you fulfill:
Salve, Salve, Salve Regina!

Hail, Holy Mary, strength and trust, O Maria!
O woman, singer for the just, O Maria!
Mother, model, faith supreme,
pregnant bearer of God's dream,
peace and justice is your theme:
Salve, Salve, Salve Regina!

I WILL BRING YOU HOME

I served only five months in my first full time parish position back in 1981; nonetheless, the people of Our Lady's Immaculate Heart parish in Ankeny, Iowa, invited me back about 30 years later to help them celebrate their anniversary as a parish and to compose a new piece for the occasion. These were the ground rules that were placed upon me: the piece could *not* be heard prior to the festival liturgy, and we would not be able to rehearse it with the assembly—an assembly that included not only parishioners, but also many guests—prior to the liturgy. So it had to be a piece that could be sung by the assembly right on the spot, instantly.

Since the patron of the parish is the Blessed Mother, I right away thought that the piece should have a Marian focus. At the time this brought to mind some of the "Marian" pieces that we would do back when we did not have much repertoire to choose from, or when we were using lots of pop music from the culture in our liturgical celebrations. I remember one time in high school, singing "Let it Be" for the Holy Day of the Immaculate Conception—you know the line, "Mother Mary comes to me speaking words of wisdom …"?...and I have a colleague who told me that many years ago at his parish, when the Feast of Assumption came around, they chose to sing "Proud Mary."

I figured I could at least improve on those choices! So I asked myself: should I try to compose a new setting of the Magnificat? The Hail Mary? Another Marian text? I was not sure what to do. I spent some time perusing and studying several popular and well-known Marian hymns, and I came upon the classic, "Hail, Holy Queen Enthroned Above." I gave myself the challenge to use this tune and create a new text that would be a bit more reflective of the spirit of the Magnificat, Mary's great canticle proclaiming liberty to captives and lifting up the lowly. I knew I was playing with some potential fire: first, because the hymn and its original text is so well known and beloved by many, and second, because the movie *Sister Act* had taken this hymn and popularized it alongside humor and playfulness, and I did not want to do anything that would trigger people's remembrance of the movie. (For many people, believe it or not—especially younger people—the first time they ever heard this hymn was in the movie, and not in church!)

Still, I was determined. As I was beginning to craft the text, I was reminded that the third, fourth, and yes, fifth phrase of each stanza had to rhyme. I am perfectly able to come up with rhymes that do not sound too forced or trite—but three in a row? For several stanzas? Still, I remained determined. While working on the text, I sent drafts of verses to Michael Joncas for his reactions and comments, and he was so helpful not only in his critique of my poetry, but also in helping me remain on good ground theologically.

Thankfully, the hymn was very well received by the people on the day of anniversary liturgy. However, after it became published in 2013, the reactions from some people was not so universally complimentary; some reactions were downright hostile. I knew that I would hear comments from people who preferred the original, traditional lyrics—but I also heard from people who thought I was doing damage to a beloved hymn. Others believed I was guilty of heresy, although they never pointed out what parts of the text were dangerous. A few people were really put off that I included the word "pregnant" on the final stanza. Perhaps they thought it was vulgar? I certainly do not think so, and many others, especially women, have assured me that it is not. And there were still others who told me that the song should be about Mary, not about "peace and justice." I guess those folks never spent any time meditating on the Magnificat. At this point in my public life as a liturgical composer, I had become more used to attacks and smears regarding not only my music, but me personally. This was most profoundly manifested in a website (no longer operational, but still active as a Facebook page) named "The Society for the Moratorium for the Music of Marty Haugen and David Haas." To be honest, such attacks have been painful and difficult to navigate—as I am a very sensitive person with a sometimes very thin skin—but I have to accept (as all composers and performing artists have to do) that once you put your creative work out there for the public to see, you cannot anesthetize yourself completely from these kinds of reactions. It comes with the territory.

So, this adaptation certainly did spark some reactions, which in the end, is a good thing I think. Michael Joncas and others have kindly affirmed me for the attempt—Michael has often reminded me and other composer colleagues that often, our actual *attempts* to try something new and explore different approaches are far more important than whether those attempts are completely successful or widely accepted. At the end of the story (maybe not the end), some will like this adaptation, and others will not like or appreciate it at all. Either way, I am beginning more and more to like it when the conversations and debates get lively! (11.25.17)

CD
MP3
Music

To Be Your Bread; Table Songs, Vol. 1;
Without Seeing You: The Best of David Haas, Vol. 3
X-7164a
G-7164

THE HARVEST OF JUSTICE

Music and Text: David Haas; inspired by Philippians 1:11; Leviticus 19:9, 23-22, Deuteronomy 24:19

May we find richness in the harvest of justice
which Christ Jesus has ripened for us.
Bread for the journey, bread for the hungry,
all for the glory and praise of God.

Gather with patience
    for those who have nothing.
Leave them your riches, and you will receive.
Make room for the poor ones,
    make way for the stranger;
for I am the Lord, the Lord your God.

For to have mercy on those forgotten,
this is my true law, this is my command:
Clothe the naked, be home for the orphan,
be hope for the widow, and welcome the lost.

For to have little is to be in abundance.
To give what remains, to give all we have,
is to walk with the poor ones,
    and become the strangers,
one with the Lord the Lord our God.

While most of the time people compose liturgical music with a particular purpose or event in mind, songs for ritual prayer often come out of faith-sharing types of conversations and, of course, in the midst of breaking open the Word. This certainly was the case with "The Harvest of Justice," composed when I was Director of Music and Liturgy at St. Thomas Aquinas in St. Paul Park, Minnesota (1982-1985).

My time at St. Thomas was truly the period when the energy around composing liturgical music was exploding for me. Primarily, I believe this was the case because I had an actual parish community to write for in the midst of the human journeys that they experience together: births, baptisms, weddings (and divorce), sickness, suffering, crisis, and death. This is the primary "source" material for liturgical composers alongside the scriptures and the liturgy, meaning: real life.

It was also a time when, if I could not find a song to use at Mass that would accomplish what I believed the liturgy was calling for, I would go to "task" and write something myself. It also helped that my pastor, Fr. John Fitzpatrick, and other members of the parish staff—especially Michael Grimes (may he rest in peace), Jan Viktora, Fr. Tom Krenik, and Rhea Serrazin—were so supportive and often fed me ideas for compositions. I also made close friends with those who were part of the parish music ministry, in particular Jim Waldo, Kathy Rustin, Michael LaMotte, Mary Tinucci, Barbie Fritz, Sue Dragert, Mindy Okeson, Lisa Wolf Cressy (I happened to be Lisa's Confirmation sponsor) and Barbara Colliander—who all brought their enthusiasm and talents to many of my earliest published pieces. It was during my three short years at the parish that I composed "We Are God's People," "Lord, You Have the Words," "The Lord Is My Light," "Blest Are They," "All the Ends of the Earth" (this one with Marty Haugen), "We Will Rise Again," "We Are Called," "Song of the Stable," "Jesus, Wine of Peace," the Glory to God that later became part of the "Mass of Light," "Jesus, Heal Us," "You are God's Work of Art," "Alleluia, Sing!," "My Soul is Still," "People of the Night," "Now We Remain," "If Today You Hear God's Voice," "At Evening," "Where There Is Love," "Advent Gospel Acclamation," and a full adaptation of the *Exsultet* (which I have never recorded or published).

I get tired just thinking about it now—but I had so much energy back then, and this was such an exciting time for not just composing the music, but because of the interaction with such gifted servants in ministry; the opportunity to work with three wonderful liturgical ensembles, and a true singing assembly to top it all off! I was luckier than most of my colleagues in pastoral music at the time.

Another piece that came to life during this time was "The Harvest of Justice," born out of some wonderful sharing that I was involved with one afternoon with fellow staff members Michael Grimes and Jan Viktora. I do not remember how we came to share the text from Philippians (1:11), but it was Michael who zeroed in on this image of us holding within our hearts the unique image of the "harvest of justice" that springs forth in us in response to our faith in Christ. It then pulled us toward the sections of Leviticus and Deuteronomy that spoke of gathering the wheat with "patience," with the intention of the bounty going to the poor; in the midst of the leaving of one's richness with the poor ones, they would know the reward from God. This discipline of giving to the poor, the orphan, and the widow, from our riches and blessings was at the heart of the law for the Hebrew people. Immediately the Hebrew Scriptures and Paul came together—that this was the ancient manifestation of sharing the "harvest of justice," and that in Christ, that sharing expands to us as followers.

It seems as though, back then, things were not so rushed—we just suspended the other tasks that were upon us that day, and became very connected in our sharing faith together, which happened many times during my tenure there. Right after our conversation concluded that afternoon, I went down to my "rehearsal room" in the basement of the parish center, and out came this song in just a few minutes utilizing the very scriptures that we had been steeped in just a bit earlier, with a sprinkle of my own love of the teachings of St. Francis of Assisi (the third verse).

While writing it, I was thinking of the flow and choral textures of Bob Hurd's wonderful song, "In the Breaking of the Bread." I am sure that people can hear the influence there. Upon finishing, with my musical fragments in hand, I ran up the stairs (since there were no cell phones back then), and asked Michael and Jan to come down to the piano so I could sing it through for them. They loved it, and they both chose to use it in some of their catechetical programs soon after—and yes, we sang it mass from time to time as well. On both recorded versions of the piece (on *To Be Your Bread* and *Table Songs, Vol. 1*), you can hear Kathy Rustin (a cantor from the parish) singing the verses with me. The song became dedicated to Michael Grimes, and when he died years later after a long battle with AIDS, we sang and prayed "The Harvest of Justice" at his funeral liturgy.

This song, as well as so many that came forth during this time, are such precious gifts and memories to me. I am so grateful and humbled that so many of them have been able to have a life for many faith communities beyond the time I was at St. Thomas Aquinas; and to the people of that community who were the major force that brought these song-prayers to life, God bless you. (11.24.17)

CD
MP3 Music

Who Calls You by Name, Vol. 1;
Alive in Christ Jesus;
Glory Day: David Haas and Friends in Concert
X-80323
G-4749

HE HEALED THE DARKNESS OF MY MIND

Music: David Haas
Text:
Fred Pratt Green

He healed the darkness of my mind
the day he gave my sight to me:
It was not sin that made me blind;
It was no sinner made me see.

Let others call my faith a lie,
or try to stir up doubt in me:
Look at me now! None can deny
I once was blind, and now I see.

Ask me not how! But I know who
has opened up new worlds to me:
This Jesus does what none can do:
I once was blind, and now I see.

This is another wonderful text by Fred Pratt Green, and I knew when I first came across it that I had to find a way of bringing music to its profound poetry. It was created during the time that I was working on the first volume of *Who Calls You by Name*, when I was spending a lot of my travel time as a team member for many of the "Beginnings and Beyond" institutes taking place around the country and beyond, sponsored by the North American Forum on the Catechumenate.

I wanted to find a "song/hymn of the day" to mark each of the three scrutiny celebrations on the third, fourth, and fifth Sundays of Lent, in Year A (the preferred cycle of the lectionary readings to be used when there are the "elect" and other candidates for Initiation at Easter). I wrote "Christ Will Be Your Light" (addressed here also in this book) for the third Sunday, and an ostinato song, "I Am the Resurrection," for the fifth Sunday. But I kept coming up dry for the second scrutiny on the fourth Sunday, which highlights the story of the man born blind. It seemed that I could not come up with anything that would crawl within miles of the standard, "Amazing Grace" ("was blind, but now I see").

Then, rather surprisingly, I came upon this wonderful text and right then and there I knew I had found the treasure that I was seeking. While every word is perfect in this text, the line that still grabs me by the throat is, "Ask me not how! But I know who has opened up new world to me ..."

I found a melody that seemed to lock in well, and I named the hymn tune ARLINGTON, which was the home (Arlington, Virginia) at the time for my good friend and colleague Thomas Morris, to whom the hymn is dedicated. We collaborated on several projects and presented many workshops together years back on Christian Initiation, and he later became the Executive Director of Forum. I recorded it as a solo piece but it truly is intended as a hymn for the assembly to sing, ideally as a response to the homily for this Sunday.

Often, when I experience sadness or anxiety, I think of this hymn, and ask God to come and truly heal "the darkness of my mind." I hope that it has, and will continue to, become a voicing of the same longing for restoration that so many ache for. (11.24.17)

CD
MP3
Music

Winter Grace;
Glory to God: The Best of David Haas, Vol. 4
X-80607
G-3334

HOLY IS YOUR NAME

Music:
WILD MOUNTAIN
THYME
(Scottish Traditional);
adapted by
David Haas
Text:
Luke 1:46-55
Arranged and
adapted by
David Haas

My soul is filled with joy as I sing to God my savior:
you have looked upon your servant,
    you have visited your people.

And holy is your name, through all generations!
Everlasting is your mercy
    to the people you have chosen,
and holy is your name.

I am lowly as a child,
    but I know from this day forward
that my name will be remembered,
    for all will call me blessed.

I proclaim the pow'r of God,
    you do marvels for your servants;
though you scatter the proud-hearted,
    and destroy the might of princes.

To the hungry you give food,
    send the rich away empty.
In your mercy you are mindful
    of the people you have chosen.

In your love you now fulfill
    what you promised to your people.
I will praise you Lord, my savior,
    everlasting is your mercy.

I WILL BRING YOU HOME

I love it when people come up to me and say, "I just love your music, David. My favorite song of yours is 'Holy Is Your Name.'" I always have to laughingly tell them that they are mistaken; I did *not* compose this piece; I just did an arrangement/adaptation of the song. Then they look at me and say: "Oh."

I first came across this piece many years ago while subbing for an accompanist at St. John Neumann Church in Eagan, Minnesota, where my good friend Kathy Eittreim was music director at the time. She had a hand-written manuscript of this piece, and I fell in love with it right away. I later came across it in a liturgical music resource from England. All I did with this piece was try to make it a bit more authentically "folk" in style; I changed all of the male pronouns to second-person, and I also did the vocal arrangement. That is it. Most of all, I guess my association with this piece and giving it a fresh arrangement helped to introduce it to a much wider audience, and for that I am very grateful and give thanks to God.

There are several composers who have taken Celtic melodies and adapted them for use, both in terms of melody and text. Examples that come to mind are "I Sing a Maid" (M.D. Ridge and Michael Joncas) and the incredible "Canticle of the Turning" (Rory Cooney). I have also written new texts to other Celtic and ethnic/folk melodies, such as "Onward to the Kingdom," "Song for the Journey," "Singing Praise to God," "Song of the Body of Christ," "Bound for Life and Freedom," "Know that the Lord Is Near," "You Alone Know Our Hunger," and others. There is something about many of these traditional folk melodies that just transfers so well for assembly participation, and since the majority of these tunes are in the public domain, they are accessible and easy for composers to adapt for liturgical use. In the case of "Holy Is Your Name," we get to sing this gorgeous tune, "Wild Mountain Thyme," and it fits beautifully as a setting of the Magnificat text. It just sings itself. And it prays well, too. (11.10.17)
How shall I sing to God

CD

MP3
Music

I Shall See God;
You Are Mine: The Best of David Haas, Vol. 2;
Do Not Be Afraid, I Am With You
X22607
G-3453

HOW SHALL I SING TO GOD?

Music:
David Haas
Text:
Brian Wren

When life is filled with gladness,
loving and birth,
wonder and worth?
I'll sing from the heart,
thankfully receiving,
joyful in believing.
This is my song, I'll sing it with love.

How shall I sing to God
when life is filled with bleakness,
empty and chill,
breaking my will?
I'll sing through my pain,
angrily or aching,
crying or complaining.
This is my song, I'll sing it with love.

How shall I sing to God
and tell my Savior's story:
Passover bread,
life from the dead?
I'll sing with my life,
witnessing and giving,
risking and forgiving.
This is my song, I'll sing it with love.

I WILL BRING YOU HOME

Brian Wren is an amazing hymn text writer, and I have utilized many of his texts over the years. He has a fresh and direct way with words that are evocative yet accessible to the ear, mind and heart. This is one of my earliest attempts to put music to some of his words.

This hymn has great potential for liturgical use, and many layers of meaning. Above all of them, though, the text articulates beautifully the understanding of why we sing at the liturgy, or better put, why we *sing the liturgy*. At the many workshops that I have presented over the years, the overwhelming question I get is: "how do we get the people to sing?" In other words, what are the strategies, tricks, ideas or recipes to help the people participate more fully in the liturgy?

I get it. The call to foster "full, conscious, and active participation" at the liturgy certainly underscores the question coming from most pastoral musicians. We are looking for greater involvement from the gathered assembly, and are frustrated when they do not participate, fully aware that the major way they are able to do so in worship is by singing.

Over the years I have travelled to all 50 states and several countries, presenting workshops for pastoral musicians, and I have attended and taken part in too many liturgical celebrations to keep track of. I have been to parishes that have the blessing of great acoustics; communities blest with great musical talent and resources in terms of vibrant choirs, ensembles, cantors and instrumentalists. I have experienced parish liturgies where the leadership is excellent and the repertoire is very fine and sound, where they have not only a quality organ but someone who can play it very well, at places where the people are intentionally invited to participate … and yet, in far too many of these communities, the people simply do not sing. They are tight lipped. They look bored, and their energy is minimal.

Likewise, I have been to other parish communities—many of them small and economically poor, where the floor is covered in thick, shag carpeting (thus with horrible acoustics with no reverberation at all), where they have an instrument that more closely resembles a microwave oven than an organ, where there exist poorly chosen repertoire and mediocre leadership from fledgling choirs and not so good cantors, where the instrumentalists have never thought to tune their instruments … and yet, the people not only participate, they often raise the roof!

So what is happening here? The answer, I believe, lies in this: while asking for tips on how to facilitate better singing is certainly a good question with great and sincere intentionality, I believe that there is more important and critical question to ask. Instead of all the time asking, "how do we get them to sing?" we should be asking, "what do they have to sing about?" This is the key here. The parish community, the leadership, the programs, the offerings and the worship experiences—are these helping the people of God express all that is going on in their lives? Is there a connection between what happens on Sunday and what happens in our families, the workplace, our communities, and in our broken relationships and struggles?

"How Shall I Sing to God?" lays this out for us: we sing when we feel grateful, when "life is filled with gladness." We sing when our hearts are stirred and touched by healing, love, understanding, forgiveness. We sing when justice reigns, when peace flourishes, when wholeness is experienced, when a new child is born—when the blessings flow.

We also sing—though we do not acknowledge or empower this to happen as much as we should—when we *need* to sing, in the times of "bleakness," when all that is good seems lost, when we are suffering, and when hope seems absent. We sing because our lives depend on it at times; it sometimes is all we have when the darkness comes. We sing *through* pain, when we are grieving, sometimes while choking through our tears. And yes, we sing when we are angry and want to shake our fists at the world, and sometimes, at God.

As the third and final stanza proclaims, we sing because we have a story to share, to hold up to one another: a story filled with resurrection and hope. We sing because, when we sing, it speaks on a deeper level to what is happening in our lives much more honestly than when we merely speak. We sing with the entirety of our lives. This hymn, I believe, is an anthem and call to service for all of us engaged in the ministry of pastoral music. Some of the most passionate singing and participation that I have experienced has been when the tension and relationship of joy and praise, as well as sorrow and lament—come together. This is the paschal mystery. If our parishes honor the reality of both the blessings and the demons that rise and enter into the lives of their parishioners, then the people will sing. When our church acknowledges the presence of God, but also recognizes that many believe God is also absent and far from them at times, then the people will sing because they will know and experience a community that is walking with them through the terror of life. Yes, we sing with the entirety of our lives. This is how we sing to God. (11.10.17)

CD
MP3
Music

I Am Yours Today (Out of print);
I Will Bring You Home
X-1041b
G-9659

I AM YOURS TODAY

**Music and Text:
David Haas**

O yes, Lord, I am yours today.
O yes, Lord, make this day your day.
You can always find me, you're right here beside me,
and I know that you are always near.
Yes, I know that you are always here.

O yes, Lord, show me how to live.
O yes, Lord, show me how to give.
You are here to help me, you are here to guide me,
you are here to help me through it all.
You are here to help me through it all.

O yes, Lord, I am yours today.
O yes, Lord, make my day your day,
You will be my song now, I will be your voice now,
God, I know that you are with me now.
God, I know that you are with me now.

If they are honest with themselves, every performing musician/composer dreams about someday being able to "make a recording," or to "get published"—to have other people experience what we do, as a composer or as a performer, and hopefully, like it! When I was very young, and later when I began to seriously compose, I certainly had such aspirations, although I was not always confident that it would happen. And this certainly was not on my screen after two and a half years as a vocal performance major at Central Michigan University. I was intending to be a professional classical singer, and I was once offered the opportunity to play and sing the role of Tony in a national Broadway production of "West Side Story" (I was skinny then, had lots of hair, and much more breath control than I do now). After saying no that opportunity (some people think I was crazy) I then took off for Minnesota in the fall of 1978 to attend St. John Vianney Seminary in St. Paul as a seminarian for the Diocese of Saginaw, Michigan. My thoughts then were fixed on whether or not I was being called to be a priest someday.

My musical life did not disappear. I continued my music studies right alongside my study of the theology (my major was both music and theology) and performed in recitals. I continued to study voice, and after a few feeble attempts the year leading up to my Minnesota adventure, I began to compose liturgical music more and more, especially for the liturgical celebrations at the seminary and for the greater campus community at St. Thomas. After composing a few songs (and trying to keep improving the songs that I had already in draft form), I explored what it would take to make a recording.

I had no idea what I was in for, but I dove into the deep end of the pool. First, I had to price out how much money it would cost to do this—in other words, book about 4-6 hours of studio time, manufacture 1000 copies of the LP (cassettes were not as much in the mainstream, and CD's did not even exist at this point), and have someone design a front and back cover. I called a local production company that a friend of mine who played in Minnesota polka bands told me about; and he quoted to me a price of around $1200.00. So, I began to ask friends, mostly back home in Michigan, to help me raise money for this adventure. Thanks to wonderful individual friends like Bill and Dee Rustic, Fr. Ray Oswald and Fr. Joe Schabel, Omar Odette; and the very generous people from several parishes including my home parish of St. Christopher's in Bridgeport, St. Roch's in Caseville, Sacred Heart in Bad Axe, and St. Felix in Pinnebog—I came up with the money, and locked in a date to record. Now remember, I had no publisher at all, and so I was flying blind. I had never been in a recording studio before and was not sure how to proceed, but I did. The choir and instrumentalists were almost entirely made up of fellow seminarians and fellow music students at the college. The rector of the seminary, Fr. Ken Pierre, was very supportive, and my fellow seminarian friend Bruce Kaatz, who had a good ear and knowledge of sound, EQ, and stuff like that (I knew nothing, other than what I liked and what I did not like), agreed to be the producer, my right-hand man for the project.

Due to being extremely nervous, and unable to sleep in the days leading up to the session, I became sick; the night before the session I was worried that I would have no voice to sing with. But friends came by, pumped me up with orange juice, and kept my confidence going. So on January 29, 1979, we went into Cookhouse Recording Studios in Minneapolis to make a record.

We got through the session pretty well. We recorded everything live: instruments, choir, soloists, all at the same time. There were only two pieces where we did more than one take—we simply did not have the time or budget to do go back and do multiple passes. If you listen to the opening track on the album (a song called "He Is the Lord"), you can hear the tempo getting faster and faster, as my adrenaline (and that of everyone else in the room) kept rising. And while my voice got raspier and raspier throughout the night, we still achieved a great energy and spirit as we recorded the tracks. (I had actually never heard the word "track" before that night—I was so uneducated!) We were able to track all thirteen songs in four hours! It was quite an experience that I will never forget. We came back to mix the record in about three more hours a few days later—a process that back then did not include computerized automation. This meant that when we were doing the final mixing from the original two-inch tape to the quarter inch master, five of us—myself, Bruce, two other friends and the engineer (Clyde Green, bless your heart)—were literally crowding around the console, making the moves on the faders and other effects as it was going to tape. Stressful, but exhilarating.

My sister Colleen, who is a very talented visual artist as well as a professor in Ethno-musicology, created the cover image of me from a winter photo of me (wearing a ski jacket!). My friend from home, David Gilmour, took the photo that is on the original back cover, and the overall art direction and layout was designed by one of my brother seminarians, Peter Christensen, who now happens to be the Bishop of the Diocese of Boise, Idaho. The original "store" that housed the inventory of all of the LP's, was the home of my friends Mary and Terri Wollan in St. Paul, and as I began to present more and more concerts, I would take one or two boxes of twenty-five records with me, and sell them myself at the various sites. A second printing was done later, and now the original album is still in the possession of some of the saints who bought the original edition. It came out in a second revised edition a couple of years later, and then some years after that OCP produced an anniversary version—but by now it has been out of print for some time, even though three of the songs ("Jesus, Come to Us," "He is the Lord," and "Fill us with your Word") still appear in OCP's worship resources and as octavos.

This "record" was the beginning for so many things in my ministerial life—somehow, soon after it was released, Michael Joncas got hold of it and called me on the phone. It was the first time we had ever talked to each other. When he identified himself, I almost fainted, because while it had not been officially published yet, I had heard "On Eagle's Wings" and as a result, I thought of Michael as a minor deity. We got together soon after that and that's where the story begins to get more interesting. Around the same time, I also met Marty Haugen. The three of us began to get together on a regular basis to share songs and offer critiques to one another, and a very wonderful collaboration and association was born.

The song featured here is the title song, "I Am Yours Today," and obviously it is representative of those earliest attempts to compose liturgical and religious music; and I know, I know – it sounds so much like John Denver! The recorded version that appears on the accompanying CD with this book is not the original one recorded back in 1979, because on *that* version, my voice suffers from sincere hoarseness. This version, recorded years later—is much better in that regard (I still sound so darn young, though).

While very simplistic perhaps in its message, this song reflects those beginning days of my accepting and saying yes to a call that I soon discovered was not to be an ordained priest, but to nurture a vocation to be a pastoral musician, and a liturgical composer. I believe I made the right choice. (11.14.17)

CD
MP3
Music

I Shall See God; Glory Day:
David Haas and Friends in Concert;
Glory to God: The Best of David Haas, Vol. 4
X-39006
G-3458

I KNOW THAT MY REDEEMER LIVES

Music: David Haas
Text: Job 1:25-27
(alt. DH)

I know that my Redeemer lives!
On the last day I shall rise again,
and in my flesh I shall see God.
On the last day I shall rise again!

I shall see my Savior's face;
    and my own eyes shall behold my God.
On the last day I shall rise again!

Within my heart this hope I hold;
that in my flesh I shall see my God.
On the last day I shall rise again!

This is a song originally composed in remembrance of the great liturgist, seminary teacher and reformer who emerged on the heels of the Second Vatican Council, Fr. Eugene Walsh, SS. I had known about this text for a long time, not aware that it was based in the Hebrew Scriptures (Job 1: 25-27). My longtime memory of these words up until this time had been the beautiful section from Handel's *Messiah*, "I Know that My Redeemer Liveth."

I was thinking about the boldness, courageous honesty, and passionate convictions that "Geno" had throughout his life and ministry, and so I wanted to write something that had a certain intensity to it, and because he loved Gospel-style music, I thought I would look to that as a genre to consider. Around the same time, and I cannot remember the source, I read a biblical commentary on these verses from Job, and the scholar wrote that a more accurate translation of the Hebrew word from which we get "redeemer," would be "avenger," especially when seen in the context of Job's journey. Wow. This changed my attitude toward this text forever, and so while I did not decide to replace "redeemer" with "avenger" (in looking back, perhaps I should have), I did bring together this newly discovered intensity of these verses together with a driving gospel tune. So there you have it. While I will always love Handel's wonderful composition, I believe that with this piece, I tried to focus a different lens on the faith contained in these words.

There are two different recorded versions of this song, my favorite being Kate Cuddy singing it as part of the *Glory Day* concert event. Kate just loves gospel style music. When she gets to sing in this style, she is in heaven. And she just nails it—not only musically, but also the spirit and promise that I had hoped to be communicated with this song. "I Know My Redeemer Lives" was the opening song for the funeral liturgy for my father-in-law William Phang as well. Geno and William, may you both continue to rest in peace. (11.24.17)

CD
MP3
Music

No Longer Strangers
X-29803
G-3949

I PUT MY LIFE IN YOUR HANDS

Music:
David Haas
Text:
Psalm 31:2, 6, 12-13,
15-179
(alt. DH)

Abba, Abba, I put my life in your hands.

In you, O Lord, I take refuge;
     let me never be put to shame.
In your justice rescue me,
     in your hands I commend my spirit.

For all my foes reproach me;
     all my friends are now put to flight.
I am forgotten, like the dead,
     like a dish that now is broken.

I place my trust in you;
     in your hands is my destiny.
Let your face shine upon your servant.
     In your hands I will place my life.

For many years, I wanted to compose a setting of this psalm that is appointed for Good Friday, but I was becoming more sensitized by many of my female friends and colleagues as to the predicament of so many of our texts being exclusive, especially in an overabundance of God images being named in the masculine. I was stuck for a long time with this one because I believed that the crying out in the traditional translation, "Father ..." was important. But I wanted to somehow find a way to make it less "male" and more about the nature of the relationship between God and Jesus, especially Jesus prayed it while suffering on the cross.

I looked at the New Testament address to God offered by Jesus, "Abba." Now, yes, most people will tell us that the closest translation that can be given in English, would be "Daddy." But I learned as I dug deeper, that this "Daddy" reference is less about the relationship between Father and Son, but rather, the relationship between *parent and child.*

While I know I took some strong biblical license in using this title (and I have been chastised by people off and on over the years for doing so), it has seemed to be able to, as I like to say, *pray* well. So, at least at the time, I thought I had come to reasonable solution to my dilemma in terms of the refrain.

The verses are unbelievably vulnerable, and I wanted to be sure that what I did melodically would not overwhelm the intensity and pointed nature of the words. So I channeled one of my favorite composers and choral arrangers, David Clark Isele, the composer of the well-known "Lamb of God" from the *Holy Cross Mass* (also published by GIA). In some of his very unique psalm settings (check out *his Psalms for the Church Year,* GIA: G-2262), he uses a device of implanting a unison tone, with the choral parts expanding and detracting around a single note. I thought this would be a good approach with these verses—verses that also did not necessarily match syllabically.

The first two verses are sung as a very simple, plaintive unison chant, with the third verse expanding chorally and clustering together on the final "let your face shine upon your servant, in your hands I will place my life."

I also thought that this would work well bilingually, so my good friend Jeffrey Judge translated it for me, and then Donna Peña came and sang it in both English and Spanish on the recording. I chose Donna because I knew she would bring a beautiful, lament-like quality to the words. And she did.

Some liturgists and scripture teachers—as well as many who think the inclusive language issue is a canard—criticize my setting because of the use of the word "Abba" in place of "Father." Well, first of all, the issue is not a canard in my humble opinion, and I am saddened that in recent years the issues of inclusive and more expansive language seem to have fallen off in our awareness. Perhaps I was too "willy-nilly" in my making the change. All I can say is that I was trying to grapple pastorally with the image of "Father" in the refrain, and attempted to find a creative and hopefully helpful solution. Regardless of where one stands on this issue, this setting seems to have been successful, and I have learned that many pastoral musicians use it every Good Friday. So, what does one do? Relax. Move on. We do not always have to agree. (11.24.17)

CD
MP3
Music

Before I Was Born;
Without Seeing You: The Best of David Haas, Vol. 3
X-39209
G-4688

I THIRST FOR YOU

Music:
Gaelic Trad.,
adapted by
David Haas
Text:
Psalm 42:2-3;
43:3-5, ICEL

As a deer craves running water,
I thirst for you, my God;
I thirst for God, the living God.
When will I see your face?

Send your light and truth.
They will escort me to the holy mountain
where you make your home.

I will approach the altar of God,
God, my highest joy,
    and praise you with the harp,
God, my God.

Why are you sad, my heart? Why do you grieve?
Wait, wait for the Lord.
I will yet praise God my savior.

As I have already shared, I love Celtic tunes. I do have a tiny bit of Irish in my blood, from my mother's side. Lori True—who is *very* Irish—accompanied me during a workshop experience in Ireland a number of years ago, and during the trip our common love of some of these marvelous folk melodies deepened even more. After that trip, for one of my birthdays, my sister Colleen gave me as a gift a copy of a CD by the well-known Canadian group, the Rankin Family, titled "North Country." One of the tracks on this album is their treatment of a traditional Irish song, "Ho Ro Mo Nighean Down Bholdheach" (No Ro My

Nut Brown Maiden). Lori and I fell in love with this song immediately, and we both kept this tune in our memories for some time.

It was around this time that I also began to delve into the very creative and in my opinion prophetic translation of the Psalter, completed by the hard work of the International Committee on English in the Liturgy (ICEL), simply called *Liturgical Psalter*. The version of Psalm 42/43 really struck me, especially its use of the word "craves" in place of the usual choice of "longs" or "yearns." As I began to recite it out loud, I found an internal rhythm, and remembered the Irish melody, and I found a nice wedding in these two forces. Lori helped and made some very good suggestions, and I was able to complete the piece.

Right away, I thought of Lori singing and praying this, not just because of her beautiful voice, but also her Irish ability to stylize "just right" the feel of this tune. As I said, she helped tweak a couple of the lines in terms of word stress, and then helped me to re-create, with a few changes, the close-knit harmonies for the refrain and the canon that takes place at the end. When we went in to the studio to record this I wanted to be sure that the harmonies would blend as perfectly as possible, so we used the trick of overdubbing her voice—meaning, she sang all three parts that you hear on the recording. In my opinion, it certainly makes for a beautiful listening experience. I have heard it done in many settings with regular choirs, and where the assembly sings the refrain quite easily and quickly. Lori's singing on this is nothing less than gorgeous.

While liturgical music belongs to the entire praying Church, I like to think of this as "Lori's song." She just sings it so beautifully; so prayerfully. So Irish. (11.24.17)

CD
MP3
Music

Creating God;
Glory Day: David Haas and Friends in Concert;
Glory to God: The Best of David Haas, Vol. 4
X-39011
G-3561

I WANT TO CALL YOU

Music and Text:
David Haas

I want to call you by your name while I live.
I will call you: "My God."
I will thank you, I will sing my praise to you.

God calls to me: "Come forth from your grave."
Like an eagle, like an eagle I find strength.

God will forgive, God is tenderness and love.
Love is greater, love is greater than death.

God knows us well, to our God we belong.
God is mercy, God is mercy for our sins.

Over the years as a singer I have been blessed by many teachers and mentors who have helped me truly "find my voice." My first voice teacher, was of course, my mother (who studied voice in college, and was a public school voice teacher for many years, from elementary through high school), who had very strong beliefs (which I share to this day) about how far to push the young voice. I myself have sadly witnessed young singers who have gone through serious vocal damage and at times downright abuse from teachers who pushed these young and vulnerable voices to attempt repertoire and vocal skills that they, as young singers, should have *never* been put through. Too many high-school-aged singers are singing advanced operatic arias, and far too often, they push their voices; Some lovers of musical theater do the same by over-singing and trying to emulate Broadway style singing, which relies heavily on using the chest voice. And of course, a similar type of vocal harm takes place when young singers take on singing pop/ rock styles. Teaching voice, and promoting care of the voice, is a very precious and delicate art.

With me, and with all of my mother's young students over the years, she was careful to not allow me to sing any repertoire that would ask too much of my vocal abilities for my age. Mostly, her belief was that the primary pedagogy for young voices should be to avoid letting them develop bad habits; to always emphasize what we call "head voice" and work hard on developing good breath control. When I went to college to pursue vocal studies as a vocal performance major at Central Michigan University (in Mt. Pleasant, Michigan) and later at the University of St. Thomas (St Paul), my teachers always praised my mother's approach. Sadly, there are many voice teachers who have ruined voices by not paying heed to her wisdom. Jeff Foote—the best voice teacher I ever had—often would say that more singing careers were "sung out of" than "sung into."

Along with my mother and Jeff Foote, I was fortunate to study voice with other good and wise vocal pedagogues like Tim Caldwell and Maurice Jones. Bonnie Faber, Lori True Tim Westerhaus, Bill Gokelman, and I have had serious conversations about this issue many times, and during the years of *Music Ministry Alive!* we took great care to emphasize our concern about vocal health to the young students who attended, and to their teachers who accompanied them.

But I have to say that the first person who truly "taught" and modeled for me what it means to "pray" when you sing was my friend of many, many years, Jo Infante, from my home parish of St. Christopher's in Bridgeport, Michigan. Jo is an amazing woman, who married a wonderful man who was a doctor and a painter, and together they had three children (now all grown up). When the children were very young (this was before I knew the family), Jo's husband Nello was killed tragically in a car accident, hit by a speeding car driven by a mentally unstable man. It was a horrific event for the family, as one could imagine, and yet in the midst of such horror it gave birth to so many amazing graces and testimonies to God's presence. Not long after the accident, Jo stepped forward courageously to offer her talent, but even more importantly her faith, by volunteering to sing at St. Christopher's. It was soon after this that I came to know her, as a young boy in junior high and during my high school years.

We began to sing together in the parish folk group. Jo was never formally trained, but when she sang something special always happened. It was not only that she had a lovely voice, but more importantly, her faith and her knowledge of God's love just oozed out of her. She was also a natural at adding harmonies to whatever the melody was—she could just figure out the right notes to sing and when to sing them. I became close to the family, and would hang out at their house a lot, and together with her kids Lisa, Tony, and Maria (Mimi), I came to know a beautiful family.

I WILL BRING YOU HOME

When I started to compose liturgical music and do a bit of travelling throughout Michigan and some other areas, Jo quickly became my first real "singing partner" during the time around 1977-1980. I have many memories of us being in her car driving off to who knows where, a box of my first LP in the back seat, to sing for various parishes and events. After I left for Minnesota to study, we remained dear friends, and we continued to sing together whenever I came home in those early years. She always seems to get to the heart of a song, and to pull out of it not only its message, but its mission. To this day, she and her family remain a treasure to me.

"I Want to Call You," for me, is a reminder of what I learned from Jo over the years about the relationship of singing, praying, and living the life of faith that we are all called to. She has always been dedicated to the blending together of singing her faith and living her faith. This song was, and continues to be, dedicated to her. This same spirit is seen, felt and heard in the other two women that I have shared about here, who model this same blending of vocal beauty and prayer-filled integrity, Bonnie Faber and Lori True. Bonnie sings this piece on the *Creating God* recording, and Lori on the *Glory Day* concert version. While I have sung it myself from time to time, this really has been for me, and for so many others, a song that celebrates how "blessed we are among women." Thanks to you Jo, for being the source for this song and its sentiment; and thanks to you, Bonnie and Lori, for making it real. (11.16.17)

CD
MP3
Music

I Will Live On; With Gratitude
X-97014
G-8875

I WILL LIVE ON

**Music and text:
David Haas
Inspired by Psalm
118:17**

I will not die. I will live on.
With a song in my heart,
I will witness to God's love.
I will live on. I will live on.

You are my strength and my song, my rescue.
You are the strength in my arms,
    the song in my heart,
the very air that I breathe.

You open the doors of my heart.
You reach and let me in.
You are the song I ache to sing,
the source of all my praise.

You are my rising day, my wings of hope.
My living you have made;
rejoicing fills my life.
Gladness is the sound of my soul!

My mother, Joan Elizabeth (Pierce) Haas, would often say to my brother, sister, and me: "I am going to live forever." She especially would say this during the last year of her life. I was always puzzled by this, even though deep down I of course always believed in the understanding of eternal life. I believe now that it was no mere coincidence that during this same year my interest and passion for the writings of Henri Nouwen was developing in a more focused way. He had an incredible ability to distill, in the simplest of terms, our true vocation, and discover how to answer the call to discipleship with integrity. For Henri, our vocation is simple. We are called to be a "witness of God's love." I had no idea that Mom's declaration of eternal life and Henri's call to witness to God's love would become partners in a song that was about to be pulled out of me.

Among the many amazing charisms that my Mom held and nurtured, one that always remained constant, regardless of the life circumstances that would accompany her, was her absolute confidence that God was real and always working in her life. This was of course instilled in her by the witness of her parents in her growing up in Traverse City, Michigan, and it seemed to permeate everything in her life. Mom attended St. Francis Church and graduated as the valedictorian of her graduating class at the parish high school (there were 20 in her graduating class!).

She often sang for weddings and funerals. When she would come home in the summer months while attending college as a Music and Commerce Major (at Central Michigan Teacher's College—which later became Central Michigan University, where she met my Dad, where my brother also went to school, and where I went for my first two and half years of college), she had the rare and precious experience of being invited to teach singing to the Carmelite sisters in Traverse City, where she was allowed to go into the private cloister where the sisters lived. From that point forward until the day she died, she held a very close relationship with the Carmelites, and always relied on their intercession during difficult times.

Mom then taught music for many years at various schools, and then left teaching when we kids were born and as we grew. Then after we were old enough, she returned to teaching and co-directing high school musicals until the time of her retirement. In the midst of all of this was her dedication, along with my Dad, to church music. She was for a time the director of music and choir director at Mount Carmel Church in Saginaw, at my home parish at St. Christopher's in Bridgeport, and at St. Roch's in Caseville, all in Michigan. Even when she was older and after her retirement, she remained active in the church choir at St. Boniface in Bay City. After my parents moved to Minnesota to be closer to their children, she sang in the choir at St. Joseph's in Red Wing, and she and my Dad were the official "grandparents" for the *Music Ministry Alive!* program that I directed in St. Paul. She was very devoted to praying the Rosary, and at the same time she remained one of the most progressive and "liberal" Catholics I ever knew. She read the *National Catholic Reporter* with great interest every week, and was always very committed to the principles of Catholic Social Teaching. She was, in more ways than I could ever count, a true witness of God's progressive and radical love.

When she died in 2014, the day after Mother's Day, I felt like the bottom fell out. It surprised me that the impact was so huge, because we prepared and knew that it was coming closer and closer in the last year or so of her life. While I knew it would be hard, I also thought that because Dad died a couple of years earlier, that this would be easier. It was not. Not at all. I think that what got me through those initial days was that I threw myself into planning details for the funeral celebration (which she had planned almost to every detail). Actually, Mom had *two* funerals. The first was the mass held at St. Joseph's in Red Wing, Minnesota; but then a couple of months later at St. Christopher's Church in Michigan (which is now named St. Francis De Sales, due to a clustering of parishes in the area), we celebrated the Eucharist again, followed by the burying of her remains at the cemetery there in Bridgeport. It was for this second mass, that I composed "I Will Live On," the refrain inspired and adapted/paraphrased from Psalm 118:17, "I shall not die, but live, and declare the works of the Lord," the psalmist's precursor to my Mom's ongoing reminder to us that she would "live forever." She kept the same song in her heart that was grounded in Henri's challenge, and so I felt compelled to yoke the psalm verse with: "With a song in my heart I will witness to God's love."

One of the joyful memories of this celebration was that the choir was made up of about 30 people who had my Mom as a teacher during the years she taught in high school. The night before, at the music rehearsal, we almost did not get to the music, because of the wonderful stories that were shared by everyone about their memories of my Mom (and my Dad) as one who shaped their lives. It was a beautiful moment during the liturgy to have all of these people whose lives were touched by my Mom, sing and pray this piece.

When I decided to have it published and recorded, I asked my friend Anna Betancourt to translate it into Spanish. Whenever I sing it, however, I do not sing the Spanish—because when I try to sing or speak in Spanish, I sound like a drunk Italian. But when I do sing and pray it—in English—my Mom's presence becomes just as real as it did the day we first sang it at St. Christopher's, proclaiming her vision of living "forever" and being an ambassador of Henri's call to always witness to God's love. She was, and continues to be, a celebration of both.

Yes, Mom, even though I miss you so much, I know that you are still living—forever. You will not die. You—and all of us—will live on. (11.16.17)

CD
MP3
Music

I Will Bring You Home
X-104a
G-9618

I WILL WALK WITH YOU

Music and Text:
David Haas;
Inspired by
Isaiah 58:11

I am here with you, all who live in anguish;
the fearful, the lonely; all who are afraid.
I'll make new your spirit, tend your deepest hurt,
with water flowing endlessly in love.

I know all your ways, and I will come to heal you;
and lead you in comfort, all of you who mourn.
All you near and far, I will grace you with my peace,
with healing that will calm all your fears.

I will always guide you, I will walk with you.
I will hold you in your deepest fear.
I will give you life in all your empty places;
with loving that treasures who you are:
my prize, my beloved, my child.

I will come to you and refresh your shattered dreams,
and free you from the poison
of wasted guilt and shame.
I will hold your story and honor your journey,
with hope that will transform your grief and pain.

I am here beside you amidst the storm and terror;
I will strengthen you with courage
and mend your tattered heart.
I will give you songs to sing
when all seems bleak and hopeless,
with music of forgiveness and joy.

Music & Stories I WILL WALK WITH YOU

At the time of this writing, this is my most recent composition, composed in early September 2017; it is dedicated to my good friend, brother, and fellow composer, Gary Daigle. Since the passing of my parents and other key people in my life in recent years, after turning 60 and confronting challenges of vocation and discernment, it has been a most challenging time for me in coping with loss, endings, sadness, and the anxiety that comes with new beginnings. This has brought about periods of tremendous self-doubt, fear, sadness and, at times, a deep sense of emptiness.

I am not sure nor do I remember how I stumbled upon it, but this verse from Isaiah was placed before me: "I will give you life in all your empty places" (Isaiah 58:11). From this, rather quickly, the first draft of the song began to take shape and form. During periods of vulnerability and loss (the circumstances that led to this song's creation), I continue to learn and experience the important reality that the ministry of compassion is not "providing services" for others, but rather, walking with one another in the midst of their pain and suffering.

This is at the heart of understanding the comfort and healing that God gives, and what we are called to do in response to that lavish outpouring of grace. Simply put, God walks with us and is present to us. Good friends are people who take on that same stance and attitude with us in the path of our brokenness, and they, by that attentiveness, teach us how to serve others. I have been, and continue to be, so very blest by the presence of such friends in my life. Gary is one among many, and we have talked about this with each other from time to time when we both have known dark times. In this walking with each other, I know Gary to be my brother. What a most holy gift this is!

Whenever I finish a new piece, I am of course always grateful that I had at that moment, "one more in me." I hope that if no more songs are able to come to life, I can be grateful for this particular one being the last. I pray that I may have the grace to remember and hold on to the wisdom that the Spirit blessed me with in the final verse of this song: "I will give you songs to sing when all seems bleak and hopeless, with music of forgiveness and joy." Perhaps there are not many—if at all—more songs to compose. But God does and will provide a new kind of music that will sustain us beyond any final notes and words that are put to paper, "the music of forgiveness and joy." That should be more than enough. (11.16.17)

CD

MP3
Music

**God Has Done Marvelous Things;
Glory to God: The Best of David Haas, Vol. 4;
Glory Day: David Haas and Friends in Concert**
X-80608
G-4736

INCREASE OUR FAITH

Music:
David Haas
Text:
Luke 11:1-13; 17:5
(alt. DH)

Lord, increase our faith.
With all our heart, may we always follow you.
Teach us to pray always.

So I say to you: "ask you will receive;
seek and you will find.
Knock, it shall be opened to you."

Whoever asks, they shall receive;
whoever seeks shall find.
Whoever knocks, the door will be opened.

If you, with all your sins, know how to give,
how much more will God
give to all those who cry from their hearts!

The words of this refrain and the words of the verses come from totally completely different chapters in Luke's Gospel; still, when I wrote this piece, I felt that they were very much in tune with each other. The text of these verses occur right before and right after Jesus teaches the "Lord's Prayer" to the disciples. It is as though these verses (and the verses that precede and follow) are a mystagogical reflection upon the prayer itself, putting Jesus' teaching in context of how they are to live; as to what living the "Lord's Prayer" actually looks like.

"Increase Our Faith" was composed in total darkness. Let me explain. I was speaking at one of the annual conferences of the National Association of Lay Ministry (I do not remember where), and one night, I was restless and I simply could not fall asleep. So at about 2 a.m. I got up, got dressed, and left my hotel room and took the elevator to the ballroom level, and into the actual ballroom where all of the major plenum events were taking place. I remember that there was a piano on the stage. But I looked and looked and looked, and I could not find any light switch. I stumbled and knocked over a bunch of chairs, banged my knee on a couple of them, and found my way up to the stage, and like a blind man (and I felt as though I was), I sat at the piano and starting doodling around. And it was right there and then that my fingers found a chord progression, and I wrote, "Increase Our Faith."

After I finished it, I again stumbled in the dark and got back up to my room as fast as I could, because I did not want to forget what I wrote. I sat down at the desk in my room, took a sheet of paper, and wrote out five lines to resemble staff paper, and wrote down the notes and the words. Later it came to be a part of the *God Has Done Marvelous Things* project, and we also sang it for the *Glory Day* concert. I remember the blessed Derek Campbell singing one of the verses. You can see and hear him sing it on the video. Talk about increasing faith. Derek died a number of years ago. I miss him.

This was a first for me: that is, composing in total, literal, darkness. I cannot remember now if, after I got the music and words written down, I was able to fall back to sleep. As I get older (as is the case for many), I do not sleep as soundly or as much as I would like or need. Lord, please, as I continue to age, not only increase my faith, but also, please, increase my sleep. (11.24.17)

CD
MP3
Music

Psalms for the Church Year, Vol. 3
X-21205
G-3264

IN GOD ALONE

Music: David Haas
Text: Psalm 62
(alt. DH)

In God alone is my soul at rest,
    the God who is my help.
The Lord is my rock, my strength and my hope;
my fortress, my God.

Only in God is my soul at rest,
    from my God comes my salvation.
God is my rock, the salvation of my life.
I shall not be shaken, for the Lord is my strength.

Only in God is my soul at rest,
    from my God comes my hope.
God is my rock, my salvation and my hope.
I will rest in the Lord, I will not be afraid.

Glory and safety, God is my joy.
    God is my rock and my strength.
God is my refuge, I trust with all my heart.
Pour out your hearts before the Lord.

This setting of Psalm 62 was in response to a commission I received to compose the responsorial psalm for the 10th Annual National Convention of the National Association of Pastoral Musicians, held in Minneapolis.

I have come to find out over the years that this setting has been a favorite for many. This refrain holds a rich choral texture—arranged by my dear friend Rob Glover—and it also truly celebrates the role of the cantor. The verses underscore, by the sweep of the melody (hopefully wedded well to the words), how critical this ministry is for every parish and faith community. Not merely a "song-leader" who directs the people when to come in, I would assert that the cantor—in particular, when taking on the role of the psalmist— is a more critical ministry than the organist, the other instrumentalists, and yes— even the choir. So often people will refer to a particular liturgical celebration having "only" a cantor. This saddens me, and I believe that the development of quality cantor ministry should be a top priority for pastoral musicians and parish music directors.

The cantor is many things: yes, a song leader, and yes, an animator of the people's song. But it is in this image of the "psalmist"—the psalm singer for the community—that we find our deepest understanding of this profound ministry. In ancient Judaism, the most desired qualities hoped for in the cantor were not necessarily about having the most beautiful voice. What was most important was that this person was truly and intimately connected and tethered to the community, so that they could, with integrity, sing the psalms (which are cries of praise and lament) on behalf of the people. We sometimes forget that the responsorial psalm is a reading from scripture—God's word, proclaimed in song. This is why it is prayed and proclaimed from the ambo. It is the word of God. With that understanding, a sense of humility, awe, and gratitude should accompany the musical skill called for. This humility and focus is modeled so beautifully by Lori True who, whenever she approaches the ambo to lead the psalm, silently with each step calls out to God, "Not me, but you. Not me, but you."

As I reflect on this setting of Psalm 62, I think of my friend Robin Medrud who sings the verses so beautifully on the original recording. My friend David Dreher from Pittsburgh also comes to mind, as he was the cantor who so powerfully proclaimed the "premiere" of this psalm at that very NPM convention in 1987.

I think of so many wonderful cantors who have truly served in this ministry as Spirit-filled servants of sung prayer. We all know those people who help bring the psalms to life through their surrendering to the text and prayer appointed. We did not use the word "cantor" back when I was really young, but I think about my friend Jo Infante from my home parish of St. Christopher in Bridgeport, Michigan, who (as I have shared elsewhere in these pages) was the first who modeled for me what it means to pray when you sing. Again, I cannot help but give thanks to God for my friend and partner in ministry, Lori True, who truly embodies all of the qualities—musical, liturgical, and pastoral—that are called for in this most important ministry. I also think of people like Bonnie Faber, of Derek Campbell and Mike Hay (may they both rest in peace), David, Robin,

I WILL BRING YOU HOME

Mary Werner, Lisa Cressy, Anna Betancourt, Michael Connolly, Kate Cuddy, Stephen Pishner, Andrea Goodrich, Kevin Walsh, Kathy Rustin, Christopher Walker, Jo Mabini Greene, Jim Waldo, George Miller, Lisa Habeck, Barbara Bridge, Tony Alonso, Zack Stachowski, Becky Gaunt, Paulette Ching, Carol Porter, Chrissy Fritzen, Barbara Conley Waldmiller, Thomascena Nelson, Steve Herring, Fiona Dybal, Larry Hylton, Juliette Countiss, Matt Maus, Erin Schwanger, Freda Mhrywold, Nova Nelson, and Michael LaMotte, all of whom, among hundreds of others, have served so lavishly as cantors over the years. I think of some of the younger cantors who make me cry when they lead with such incredible joy and passion, like Katherine True, Ryan Slattery, Ellen Larson, Julia and Clare Reimann, Doug Starkebaum, Tyler Jensen, Harrison and Phoebe Crenshaw, Angie Flake, Abbey Scherrer, Elena and Lily Cressy, Cameron Cabot, Rachel Armstrong, Greg Papesh, Jack Johnston, Danielle and Madeline Peterson, Kelly Mueller, Christine Frenzel, Lucy Sedor Franzak, Nina Hayes McGuane, Daniel Franzak, Doug Starkebaum, Stella Garcia, Brenna Kelley Starkebaum, Abbie Rivard, Jes Garceau, and so many other talented young saints who totally "get it."

"In God Alone" is one among hundreds of psalm settings that I have composed over the years. The psalms, these wonderful pieces of Scripture, are critical for both my spiritual life *and* for all liturgical celebrations. The psalms are the center for those called to be liturgical composers. When I think of how the psalms have shaped my life and how central they are to the life of prayer for all, I cannot help but think of this marvelous quote from St. Ambrose:

> *What is more pleasing than a psalm?*
> *David himself puts in nicely:*
> *"Praise the Lord," he says, "for a psalm is good" (Psalm 146: 1)*
> *And indeed!*
> *A psalm is the blessing of the people,*
> *the praise of God,*
> *the commendation of the multitude,*
> *the applause of all,*
> *the speech of every person,*
> *the voice of the church,*
> *the sonorous profession of faith,*
> *devotion full of authority,*
> *the joy of liberty,*
> *the noise of good cheer,*

and the echo of gladness.
It softens anger,
it gives release from anxiety,
it alleviates sorrow;
it is protection at night,
instruction by day,
a shield in time of fear,
a feast of holiness,
the image of tranquility,
a pledge of peace and harmony,
which produces one song
from various and sundry voices in the manner of a cithara.
The day's dawning resounds with a psalm,
with a psalm its passing echoes.

When reflecting on all of this, I feel the Spirit moving through Psalm 62—for in the singing and praying of any psalm, ultimately, we are confessing with the entirety of our heart, that it is "in God alone" where we place our trust, our faith, and yes—find our rest. (11.11.17)

CD
MP3
Music

Reach Toward Heaven
X-56608
G-6159

IN THE POWER OF CHRIST

Music: David Haas
Text: 2 Corinthians
12:9-10; Galatians
6:14-18 (alt. DH)

The grace of God is all we need;
our strength is made perfect in our weakness.
May we boast in the pow'r of Christ
    who dwells in us.

I am content with weakness and insult,
and hardship, and distress for the sake of Christ.
When I am weak, then I am strong.

There is no other boast than in the cross of Jesus,
through whom the world has been crucified,
    for the glory of God.
When I am weak, then I am strong.

Peace and mercy be to all who follow
    to Israel of God.
    May the grace of God be with you.
    When we are weak, then we are strong.

One of the most profound yet maddening mysteries of our faith is the realization that power never achieves for us what we so desperately want or need. But our pursuit of power, control over our lives, of climbing and ascending—both professionally and personally—always pulls us in. And it always, in the end, fails us. It is only when we embrace our weakness and brokenness, when we do not run away but lean into "insult, and hardship, and distress," that will we be able to see clearly, live and love more rightly, and become more whole. This is central to understanding the mysterious life and spirituality of Paul (who is the author of these passages from 2 Corinthians and Galatians), inviting all of us to direct our allegiance to Christ.

This piece, for me (and this may sound contradictory and strange) is arguably the best "hard" song that I have ever composed, because what it is asking of me, and all of us, is so difficult, most challenging and painful to accept.

But difficult or not, these passages express the *entré* into what it means to follow Jesus; one could say it communicates the "non-dysfunctional" truth about discipleship, which requires taking up the cross and holding that cross, and the suffering that it promises, close to our hearts. This is why this piece is appropriate for various celebrations of the catechumenate, and in particular, the Rite of Acceptance/Welcome. During this ritual the catechumens are signed from top to bottom with this cross. And remember, this signing also is found at the very beginning of the ritual for Infant Baptism. Recall how this begins. The priest invites the parents and God-parents to join him to "trace the sign of the cross" on the child's forehead. We need to stop and think about this for a moment. At the very beginning of this joyful celebration of Baptism, the first ritual gesture that takes place is the signing the baby with a symbol of an instrument of death. The same is true for those of us who still, when entering a church space, dip our hands into the holy water and sign ourselves with that same cross. The same is true whenever we genuflect and sign ourselves; the same is true when we pray the prayer of grace before a meal—we wrap ourselves in the cross. This, even though most of the time we are not conscious or attentive to it, is the act of surrendering ourselves to the "power of Christ" that we sing about in this song-prayer.

When we sit in the reality of our weakness we should cultivate some compassion for ourselves, because in such struggles, we need to remember that we are not alone. Our weakness and brokenness need not scare us. We believe in a God who may sit very high, but who also looks low, bending down and choosing to walk with us as *human*, in our most vulnerable places. Brokenness. Weakness. "When I am weak, then I am strong."

The great spiritual writer, Fr. Richard Rohr, has often said that the work of spirituality comes down to what we do with our pain. This is the "whole" and "holy" life. When we are able to honestly and courageously face our pain and weakness, our beautiful selves will be more revealed to us and to the world.

I need to keep this wisdom ever before me, not only in my efforts as a minister, but in how I move forward, cope, and yes, celebrate what it means to be Christian, to be a follower of Christ. It means that I am not to move forward with boasting in myself, my achievements, my status, or my opinions. No, I am to boast "in the cross of Jesus, through whom the world has been crucified." Then God's glory can shine through. Yes, "when we are weak, we are strong." As bizarre and self-defeating as it may sound, may we all pray for such weakness. (11.16.17)

Echo of Faith
X-50701
G-5657

IN THE TIME OF GOD

Music:
David Haas
Text:
Psalm 72
(alt. DH)

Justice shall flourish in the time of God,
with the promise of peace, with the promise of peace.
Justice shall flourish in the time of God,
with the promise of peace forever.

Give to the one who rules
    the judgement of your name,
justice and righteousness
    to all who come to pow'r;
and truly lead with integrity and right,
and the poor will receive their due.

Justice will flower in the days of those who lead,
and peace will abound till the moon be no more!
May the one with power rule from sea to sea,
from the river to the ends of the earth!

The one whom you call will hear the poor's cry,
the lowly and the powerless who have no voice.
Pity and compassion for all who have been lost,
and the lives of the needy will be saved.

May this name live on forevermore,
as long as the sun, the name shall remain.
May all find the blessings of God,
All nations will sing for joy!

I WILL BRING YOU HOME

Psalm 72, with the refrain, "Justice shall flourish in his time, and fullness of peace forever" is situated as the responsorial psalm for the Second Sunday of Advent in Year A. This is a tough one to understand, being one of the "kingship" or "messianic" psalms, but at the core of its message is the description of a utopian or perfect society, where justice, peace, and economic security can "flourish." The enthronement of the king involves his responsibility as mediator, or ambassador, for God's restorative justice and blessing upon the people.

This psalm's connection with Advent and the birth of Jesus is clear, as it speaks to the earthly king to come, the long-awaited Messiah. But it is a two-fold coming or "Advent" that we hold on to during this season. We celebrate the historical birth of Jesus, but we also wait and ache for the coming of the messianic presence at the end of time. We believe the incarnation to be true indeed, but at the same time, we are still waiting. We wait for this justice and peace to be real and flourishing, and we believe that it will happen, as I paraphrase in this setting, "in the time of God." On the recorded track of this song (which appears on the CD collection, *Echo of Faith*), the tempo unintentionally speeds up and rushes a bit. Most of that I would probably attribute to my adrenalin pumping up while playing the piano, but I would also suggest that this push of energy was intentional…that it signifies the excitement and anticipation of the season …?

Well, I gave it a shot. Nice try, David.

Advent has always been a favorite time of year for me. I guess I am always in a state of waiting—so this is most certainly my season! I also love this season because of the fact that it seems so impossible to celebrate Advent in a culture where Christmas begins around Halloween! That may seem contradictory, but I am attracted to Advent because it is so *subversive*; it challenges us, if we quiet down our lives enough to hear the message. As Paul Simon would say, "slow down, you move too fast." (I should have thought about that and had a metronome next to me when I recorded the song.)

Advent is *not* a "mini or quasi" Lent of some kind, and is not intended to be penitential in nature. It is a joyful season that David Livingston, to whom this setting is dedicated, brings about so wonderfully in the recorder parts he plays on the recording; a joyful season where we *take our time* to invest in what seems impossible so much of the time, a season when "justice shall flourish" and the "promise of peace" can seem to be, just a little bit closer for us. The readings appointed for this Second Sunday of Advent serve as bookends for this psalm: first, the Isaiah announcement (Isaiah 11: 1-10) that the "wolf shall be a guest of the lamb, and the leopard shall lie down with the kid; the calf and the young lion shall browse together," where "there shall be no harm or ruin."

In the second reading (Romans 15: 4-9), Paul calls down a blessing upon us all from the "God of endurance and encouragement." And then the gospel booms loudly (Matthew 3: 1-12) with John the Baptist calling us to repentance, "for the kingdom of heaven is at hand!"

Regardless of the tempo—whether it be a rushed and hurried time during the days of Advent, or a calmer, more reflective time of pondering the final reign of God coming into our midst, let us be sure of one thing that is central to our faith: that God's "justice *shall* flourish" and the "promise of peace" *will* be forever. That is, if we choose to respond and live accordingly, and surrender the outcome to "the time of God." (11.24.17)

CD
MP3 Music

God Has Done Marvelous Things;
Table Songs, Vol. 2;
Without Seeing You: The Best of David Haas, Vol. 3
X-80343
G-4732

JESUS, BE WITH US NOW

Music and Text:
David Haas

We come before you with all we have,
the work of our hands.
Broken and poured out, sign for the world.
Jesus, be with us now. Now.

Broken, your people, we who are your own.
Mend us in the shape of your love,
    formed in you!

Scattered and fractured, frozen in our fear.
Bind us, unite us as one, strangers no more!

With singing and in silence,
    we come with open hands.
In blessing, in breaking the bread,
    we become you!

I have friends who have teased me over the years about my compulsion to use the word "now" in so many of my liturgical songs: "Now We Remain," "Now it is evening," "Jesus, heal us now," "To be your bread now," and a host of others. One friend once said, "David, you seem to be very impatient—you always want things to happen *now*." Those who know me well would most likely agree. I have never been good at waiting for things. I hate it whenever I have to stand in a line for something. I am not good at process. I frustrate others in conversations and at meetings, whenever we are discerning a decision to be made—as I want to have it decided quickly, not with any need to "process it for a while." I want to decide, *now*. In recent years, I have been trying to balance this. (It's not going so well.)

Music & Stories JESUS, BE WITH US NOW

So, in addition to the other songs already mentioned, here is another "now" song.

"Now" obviously names an urgency, and in the struggles of life, in the midst of a broken world, in times of conflict and hurt, we want God to intervene—not on some future timeline, but *now*. Right here, right now. *Now*. This I believe, is the hope that we yearn and ache for when we come to the table, humbly recognizing that we are who we are—flaws and all—and waiting for the Christ to be more than present in the elements of bread and wine, but to be here, *now*, in our presence, in the presence of our lives, in the presence of a world desperately needing to be healed and transformed into the "sign for the world." We long for a way to pull the presence of Jesus out of the tabernacle, so it can seep into the lives and the cries of God's people. This is what Eucharist is. To celebrate the Eucharist is to "give God thanks and praise." We give our thanks and praise in the midst of our brokenness, our questions, recognizing that we are "scattered and fractured," facing the truth that we often are "frozen" in fear, and reaching out for a sign, so that we can become the living sign, *now*.

I love writing descants, and the descant on this refrain is a doozy. On the two different recordings of this song that I have done, my friends and power-tenors David Fischer and Michael Mahler bring the descant to life with the drama it needs. I don't think this song gets used very often, but it is a favorite of mine. Alec Harris, president of GIA Publications, has told me it is his favorite "Haas" song. Maybe it is because he knows me well; he "gets" me, and has been a most patient friend at GIA, especially when I am impatient, restless, and want things to happen, *now*. (11.12.17)

CD
MP3
Music

A Changed Heart
X-82208
G-7728

JESUS CHRIST IS LORD

Music:
David Haas
Text:
Philippians 2:6-11
(alt. DH)

Emptied and humbled, obedient to death,
Christ embraced the cross.
Jesus Christ is Lord!

Although he was in the form of God,
he did not claim equality
    with God as something to be grasped.
But Jesus chose to empty himself,
and take the form of a slave,
    human and broken like one of us.

Being found in human form,
flesh and blood like each of us,
    Jesus humbled himself.
He embraced his death, death on a cross,
and yet our God did lift him high,
    with a name above all names.

So at the name of Jesus,
all knees on earth will humbly bend,
    in heaven, earth, and all below,
and with one tongue proclaim and sing
all glory to our creator God:
    "Jesus Christ is Lord!"

In the same biblical tradition as the Suffering Servant Songs found in Isaiah, this powerful canticle from Philippians, heard on Palm Sunday at the beginning of Holy Week, is known by many as the "Kenosis Hymn." *Kenosis* is basically, the act of "self-emptying" at the heart of the understanding of Jesus' passion. In this New Testament canticle we have an important and prophetic summary of Paul's theology of power and how Jesus shakes up the usual models of leadership.

Jesus does everything *but* grasp or manipulate power. Rather, he empties himself and surrenders the trappings of status and power that most seek. Jesus' power is transformative, seeking the most unusual path of reducing oneself to slave status and freely choosing to be emptied of all of the seductions associated with domination. Here is the discovery of discipleship, because Jesus rejects these seductions, which you and I confront on a daily basis in our lives: in our places of employment, in our relationships, and yes—even in our ministry in the church. The lure of choices that lead to power is sometimes obvious, sometimes subtle and hidden. Leadership is a tricky thing, and the qualities of humility, self-sacrifice and "other-centeredness" are sometimes not intrinsic to the seminars, books, and other training materials that guide us to become leaders.

Paul's canticle presents a Jesus who utterly fails at achieving power and influence as the world presents it. But Jesus was not interested in that kind of success. Jesus was about something completely different, something that moved radically against the agreed-upon values and belief systems of leadership and power.

The same was true for the early Christian community. Proclaiming "Jesus Christ is Lord" was seen by the political authorities as a major affront to the status quo of the state. It signaled turning allegiance and honor from Caesar and giving them to God. It was considered to be an act of treason. These four words made up the earliest creed, the most fundamental profession of faith for those who risked everything to be followers of the Way—namely, the way of Jesus. For them, following Christ required the surrender of all things the world finds attractive, all things that their culture—and ours—values and rewards with high honors.

The simple truth is this: to follow Jesus, to be a Christian, is hard. It means more than tolerating or accepting being humbled and emptied of self. It's more than giving assent to the struggles and sacrifices that come with discipleship. It means embracing the life of surrender, freely choosing and rejoicing in obedience to the way of Christ. It means seeing the reality and cost of humility and emptiness as a most precious gift.

I WILL BRING YOU HOME

This brings my life and vocation as a pastoral musician, and even more so as a liturgical composer, to its most humble, yet necessary, center. I am called to be emptied, to surrender myself not only to the liturgical rites, actions, and seasons. I am called to empty myself of all of the things that can come so naturally with being a musician, a "performer," and an artist. Ego so often gets in my way. Ego and self-absorption can overwhelm, take over, and sometimes even poison my work; when it ceases to be ministry, it can become an exercise in narcissism. I need to constantly, daily, renounce the things that lead me down this path. As I get older, it does not get any easier, but it becomes clearer and clearer that this is what I am called to do. I am called to empty myself, and name Jesus as the Lord of this ministry of sung prayer. Join me, as all of you reading this reflection are ministers of music in some way—most profoundly and ultimately, as members of a praying assembly—in following this call to kenosis. (12.11.17)

I Am Yours Today (Out of print)
X-1041b
From OCP: 30114186

JESUS, COME TO US

**Music and Text:
David Haas**

Jesus, come to us, lead us to your light.
Jesus, be with us, for we need you.

Lord, we come before you; listen to our prayer.
Fill us all with hope and your love.

Lord, we come to praise you
    for your faithfulness through night.
You will be with us, this we know.

Lord, you give us wonders, your glory to all.
We believe in you; come to us.

"Jesus, Come to Us" is one of my earliest liturgical songs, and was a part of that first self-produced LP that I did back in 1979, *I Am Yours Today*. While I now see the weaknesses in the lyrics ("you will be with me, this I know"—geez!), I still find it to be a song that seems to "pray" well for people.

I composed it originally, if memory serves, as a song for children's choirs and for liturgies with children, but it eventually became a communion song at St. John Vianney Seminary (St Paul) when I was a student there. While most of the songs from that first LP of mine have drifted away, this song still remains in the repertoire of many liturgical ensembles, and still appears in several of the hymnals and print resources of OCP Publications.

While by no means intentional at the time when it was written, folks have told me that it has been their choice for parish celebrations of First Eucharist. Makes sense, when looking at the words. I love it when other people can see something in a song that you yourself as the composer were not able to see yourself. Very cool. (11.16.17)

CD
MP3
Music

Who Calls You by Name, Vol. 1;
Alive in Christ Jesus; With You By My Side: Vol. 1:
The Journey of Life; Give Me Jesus
X-41605
G-3248

JESUS, HEAL US

Music and Text:
David Haas

Jesus, heal us, Jesus.
Jesus, hear us now.

All who fear the Lord: Wait for his mercy.
All who love the Lord, come, he will fill you.

All who fear the Lord: Follow his ways.
All who love the Lord, hope in his goodness.

All who fear the Lord:
   Keep your hearts prepared.
All who love the Lord,
   be humbled in his presence.

All who fear the Lord: He will uphold you.
Let us cling to him,
   let us fall in the arms of the Lord.

This song was written during my time at St. Thomas Aquinas in St. Paul Park, Minnesota (1982-1985), for one of our communal services of the Anointing of the Sick. The intention was to write something very practical—I wanted to write a very, very simple refrain that could easily memorized and sung during the laying on of hands.

In the early days of its use, I never thought that it was a great song. But it seemed to work for that anointing liturgy, so I hung on to it. About a year or so later, someone asked me if knew of any piece of ritual music that could be utilized during the laying on of hands at a similar liturgy. I said that I had a piece that I had written quickly a while back, and so I shared it with him. After a while, word got out among my pastoral musician colleagues in the twin city area that I had a song for the Anointing of the Sick, and it began to be used more and more. I realized that it was publishable, but I was not sure during this time what collection I should include it on; I settled on having it be a part of the first volume of *Who Calls You by Name*. I felt it could also be a common song to use during the season of Lent, for communal celebrations of reconciliation.

It has appeared over the years in various hymnals, so I guess I learned something from the experience of this song. When you compose something authentically, without guile, for a specific ritual moment or occasion, chances are it will work well at another parish. Ever since then, I have continually tried to remember this. Think about the ritual moment. Think simply. Think about how the song fits the liturgical action and how quickly it can be picked up by the assembly. Think about it possibly being done by memory. Songs that follow these types of guidelines may not always be the most gorgeous of compositions, but they do present an opportunity of helping the community have an investment in the liturgy. (11.24.17)

CD
MP3
Music

To Be Your Bread; Table Songs, Vol. 1;
Glory to God: The Best of David Haas, Vol. 4
X-26507
G-3027

JESUS, WINE OF PEACE

**Music and Text:
David Haas**

Jesus, wine of peace, wine of love;
may we drink of you;
may we taste your presence;
your promise; our future.

You will never be alone; I am with you.
Drink well, drink and live.

You will never thirst again; I will fill you.
Drink well, drink and live.

No more weeping, no more pain in my kingdom.
Drink well, drink and live.

This is another song that was pulled out of me by my friend and mentor back in the eighties, Sue Seid-Martin. There was a circle of us back then who were part of the St. Paul Seminary School of Divinity community (students, faculty and staff), and we would often gather together spontaneously and talk about liturgy, music, ministry, and a host of other topics. These people included people like Sue, Bonnie Faber, Steve Brodersen, Dave Belt, Michael Byron, Barb Conley-Waldmiller, Larry Snyder, Jim Moudry, Carole Kastigar and John Estrem, and boy—these conversations were often like small intimate seminars where we all learned so much, and grew together in our understandings, particularly about ritual and ritual music.

I remember one of these informal "town halls," focused on the Eucharist and the need for communities to receive a more in-depth catechesis regarding the ritual action and the spirituality that revolves around these actions. We all agreed that the most likely and obvious "pedagogy" would be effectively enshrined in the texts that we sing and pray with during the ritual sharing of communion. As an aside, I remember Sue leaning over and saying to me, "David, we have so many communion songs that focus on the 'bread.' Someday you should compose a song that centers in on the symbol of the cup, and the sharing of that common cup." I always knew that when Sue shared an "instruction" like that, you need to respond quickly. That was all that I needed, and later that very day, I sat down and composed "Jesus, Wine of Peace." She was so surprised when the very next day, I sat down and played through it for her. I remember that her first reaction was, "we are going to use this song this Sunday."

Wine is often referred to as the "elixir of love," and I could not help think about that while composing this piece. I remembered when I was a vocal performance major in college, learning and singing the aria "Una furtiva lagrima" from Donizetti's well known opera, "L'elisir d'amore," when translated is, "The Elixir of Love." This aria is a gorgeous and moving romantic song of aching love and desire, and at one point, the tenor singing recognizes: "What more need I look for? She loves me! Yes, she loves me, I see it. I see it" (this is a rough English translation from the Italian). Now, what does this have in common with the Eucharist and our sharing in this most holy meal? In a way, everything! The word "Eucharist" basically means "thanksgiving." Our sharing in communion is a communal recognition of God's love for us, made real in the broken and poured out life of Jesus. In other words, to paraphrase and adapt the words from the aria: "what more do we need, other than this saving meal? God loves us! Yes, God loves us! We can see it. We can taste it." This is why each verse of "Jesus, Wine of Peace" concludes with the invitation to "drink well and live," leading me to fuse together in the text the sharing of the consecrated wine as a meal and feast of love, one that we want to continue to take part in, so that we may "taste" the promise of what the "real presence" offers us:

Jesus, wine of peace, wine of love;
may we drink of you;
may we taste your presence;
your promise; our future.

I am grateful that Sue planted the seed in me to create this song. While it is an over-simplification to reduce it this way, for me, the song helps me to remember and hold close the precious gift that the Eucharist is for us. In the bread we are sustained in Jesus' body. In the wine we are calling to mind how we are soaked in the love of the blood of Christ. Put it all together, and we have a sacred and holy meal and sacrifice, where in our common sharing, we can see and celebrate the presence of the Lord in our midst in this very moment, but also pointing toward the future banquet in heaven. (11.12.17)

CD
MP3
Music

No Longer Strangers;
Without Seeing You: The Best of David Haas, Vol. 3
X-80519
G-3956

LIKE A LITTLE CHILD

Music:
David Haas
Text:
Psalm 131;
Psalm 42:2-3, 12
(alt. DH)

Like a little child in its mother's arms,
my soul will rest in you, my soul will rest in you.

My heart is not proud,
my eyes do not seek the ways from above;
the things that are great.
The marvels beyond are not what I need,
for you are my peace.

Quiet and still,
my soul is calm in your sweet embrace,
like mother and child.
My hope is in you; my heart is full,
for you are my peace.

As the deer
that longs for the stream, my soul longs for you,
to see your face.
To you I will sing and offer my thanks,
for you are my peace.

Edward's Syndrome, otherwise known as Trisomy 18 Syndrome, is a chromosomal condition that usually results in a devastating prognosis. It is often called Trisomy 18 because in such cases, infants are born with three copies of chromosome 18. For many parents who have children with this condition, the baby often miscarries or is still born. Most survive no more than a few days or one week at best.

I WILL BRING YOU HOME

This was the prognosis for Steve and Judy Petrunak when their first child, Daniel, was born. As anyone could imagine, this was a very painful experience for Steve and Judy and for the members of their extended family, and many of us who are close to the family. While Daniel defied all odds and lived ten and a half months, he still was taken from us far too soon. Yet, Daniel's life was, and continues to be, a source of strength, inspiration and courage for the family and for so many of us.

This setting of sections of Psalm 131 and Psalm 42, was composed when I heard the news of his passing. We sang and prayed it at little Daniel's funeral.

Nothing more to say. (11.24.17)

CD
MP3
Music

Living Spirit, Holy Fire, Vol. 2; Give Me Jesus;
God Will Delight
X-80301
G-7166

LOOK TO CHRIST

**Music and Text:
David Haas**

Look to Christ to be your light; follow.
Leave behind your former self and live.
Don't look back, don't be afraid: follow.
Come to Christ,
walk with Christ, and live.

Who is the one who sees
    everything we say and do?
Who is the one who knows us and still forgives?
Who is the source and fountain of grace
    that quenches our thirst?
Jesus the Christ: the Son of the Living God!

Who is the one who gives new sight
    to those who are blind?
Who is the one who washes and makes us new?
Who is the one who opens our eyes
    that we may believe?
Jesus the Christ: the Living Light of God!

Who is the one who weeps for us?
    Who can this be?
Who is the one who rolls the stone away?
Who is the one who cries to us all
    to come out and live?
Jesus the Christ: Resurrection and Life for all!

I WILL BRING YOU HOME

As one among many who have been in and out of therapy over the years, you would think that we would find not only one, but several paths to uncover and discover wholeness, serenity and courage. But as Christians, our stance is that all human efforts to bring us sanity must, at the core, be rooted in our ongoing conversion and choice toward the Risen Christ.

This song celebrates that conversion, the process of daily being born again and again and again and again. As I grow older I find that my desperate need to put Christ at the center of all things increases with intensity. I am discovering that my ache for wisdom is greater, not less, than it has been in the past. As I hopefully mature, I am seeing that such maturity comes only in a daily surrender: both in my individual walk, and also among the community of believers that I walk with. And as I move toward retirement, I am seeing a new conversion in need of taking place in the necessary journey of simplifying, leaving behind the baggage, burdens and old possessions, and facing the future not with dread, but with a joyful acceptance and even anticipation.

With the restoration of the catechumenate that became embodied in the *Rite of Christian Initiation of Adults,* we have come closer to seeing how our liturgical rites and communal prayer ritually proclaim the word of God on the pathway to conversion. Every step of the RCIA process enters into this journey. Digging deeply into the "purification and enlightenment" of the Lenten season, we come to experience this journey with life and vibrancy in the three conversion stories found in the Gospel of John that we hear on the Sundays when we celebrate what we call the "scrutinies." These occur in the Year A readings on the third, fourth, and fifth Sundays of Lent. Here we see our call to "look to Christ" most fervently presented to us.

The first of these is found in the story of the Samaritan Woman (John 4: 5-42), where we see a woman going to the well to get water, and she ends up getting something else altogether. She faces Jesus and at the same time comes face to face with herself, through a prophet-presence that chooses to burst open one of the taboos of that day and culture (a man talking to a woman alone, and a Samaritan woman at that). He breaks this taboo for the sake of her life, encouraging her to "look" to what is possible and promised for her. Jesus does more than confront her with the humanity embodied in her choices—he sets her free to live life to the full. After he most assuredly exposes her secrets and shame—unvarnished and not glossed over—he transforms them, leading her to a response full of unabashed joy and celebration.

The woman experiences what we sometimes, without astonishment, refer to as "unconditional love." After exposing her humanity and brokenness, Jesus not only continues to love her, but she comes to know that love now even more than ever. She first recognizes who this presence is ("I can see that you are a prophet"), and then, unable to contain herself, she gives witness to what has happened to her, taking her exposed life and holding it as a source of joy in who Jesus is and who she is not ("come and see a man who told me everything I have done."), finding great freedom in that distinction. Conversion. She looked to Christ. So must we.

Who is the one who sees everything we say and do?
Who is the one who knows us and still forgives?
Who is the source and fountain of grace that quenches our thirst?
Jesus the Christ: the Son of the Living God!

In the equally marvelous story of the Man Born Blind (John 9: 1- 41), we come to face to face with the fact that usually when we condemn another, we are doing so because we cannot face our own shame. This story of conversion is far less about the blind man—or anyone else we see as afflicted, whether that affliction be physical, psychological, or spiritual—than it is about *us*. The afflictions of others often expose our own flaws and shortcomings, and the parts of ourselves that are crying out for healing, for restoration. In other words, to be able to see, for whatever reason, we seem to have to rationalize our own short-sightedness, our own blindness, so we take our self-loathing and cast it upon someone else. Like the blind man, we cannot "see" what those who are afflicted in more obvious ways are able to see so very clearly: how desperately they are in need of God. In their vulnerability, the mud that they have accumulated has become a healing balm, and has opened their eyes to this deep need and brought them close to God. They often know the Lord in ways that we cannot see—we are too blinded by our arrogance, our pride, and our common addiction to being "right."

In this story the man is seen as a beggar, and I believe this is key to understanding why we are in such need of ongoing conversion. We have forgotten how to beg. We have forgotten how to lay ourselves at the feet and mercy of Jesus; in fact, we have a difficult time even seeing that we are in such critical need of this mercy. Jesus exposes the arrogance that we hold on to at the end of the story: "If you were blind, you would have no sin; but now you are saying, 'We see,' so your sin remains." The blind man is the one who could see. The afflicted ones in our midst, the "least of these," have often seen what we have not yet seen. Conversion. The blind man looked to Christ. So must we.

I WILL BRING YOU HOME

Who is the one who gives new sight to those who are blind?
Who is the one who washes and makes us new?
Who is the one who opens our eyes that we may believe?
Jesus the Christ: the Living Light of God!

In the final story of the three, the story of the raising of Lazarus (John 11: 1-45) confronts us with the greatest affliction of all, the one that moves beyond our own personal challenges (The Samaritan Woman) or the arrogance of a "mob mentality" (The blind man). Here we are faced with the ultimate conversion, the choice to move from death to life.

As I have shared previously, when we read the gospel stories we need to be attentive to not only what is there in the narrative, but also, to what is *not* there. Nowhere in this story does it state that Lazarus wanted to "come out." That is certainly the case with me when I am in the midst of my darkest days. It is much easier, it seems at the time, to isolate and remain in the false comfort of my tomb. We all do this to some degree. Jesus did so as well, as see in the story. Right after he receives the news of Lazarus being ill, "he remained for two days in the place where he was." He too, was stuck. But eventually, Jesus gets up and makes a move. I am not a scripture scholar, but I remember hearing someone tell me that one translation of the name Lazarus is "God to the rescue." This is what is happening here—God is coming to the rescue. And Lazarus, like all of us, is most certainly in need of rescuing.

In this story, one of the few times we see Jesus weep, we also see clearly how God feels about us. This weeping, this grieving, needs to take place for true conversion to take hold. Those who love us the most are often the ones who cry for us the most. We can only move forward into life if we grieve and cast out all that is dying in our lives. We need to grieve when we realize that some things *need* to die. In the story, this grieving precedes the rescue that is about to take place; the same grief is also before us in our own need for rescue and liberation. Then, the command can be heard—and it is most certainly a command, not a mild request: "Lazarus, come out!" And he did. And so must we. Conversion. Mary, Martha, and yes, Lazarus—looked to Christ. So must we.

Who is the one who weeps for us? Who can this be?
Who is the one who rolls the stone away?
Who is the one who cries to us all to come out and live?
Jesus the Christ: Resurrection and Life for all!

At the heart of all of these conversion stories is the exploration of this fundamental question: What is the Resurrection, really? What is the promise that is held for us? We know that these stories do not end with the final sentence.

All stories are true, even if only some of them took place factually in time and space. In the case of these rich scriptural stories, regardless of whether they actually *literally* happened, there is something so very true about them all. The Samaritan woman (and as is the case with all of us) after this experience most certainly had more and more struggles in her life that exposed her humanity and weakness. While the blind man's sight was restored, he probably suffered a continual rejection from society, if for nothing more than the fact that he lived in such perverse poverty. And Lazarus—obviously, in the literal sense, did not literally, "live forever." He would certainly die a physical death someday. He was not "saved" from that eventuality.

The promise of the resurrection is *not* that all suffering, blindness, shame and death will be banished from our lives. The promise is *not* the naïve belief that we will never suffer and experience evil, or oppression, or sadness, or sickness—or death. The promise of the resurrection is this: that such evil, oppression, sadness, sickness and death—*will not win*. It will not be the last word. It will not be the ultimate destiny of our existence. This is what is promised to us.

So how do we keep our faith in this promise alive? We look to Christ. (11.14.17)

Before I Was Born
X-44812
G-4800

LORD, IT IS GOOD

Music: David Haas
Text:
Psalm 92:1-13
(Refrain, alt. DH)

Lord, it is good to give thanks to you.
Lord, it is good to give thanks to you,
to praise your name, to praise your name.

How good to thank you, Lord,
    to praise your name, Most High,
to sing your love at dawn,
    your faithfulness at dusk
with sound of lyre and harp,
    with music of the lute.
For your work brings delight,
    your deeds invite song.

I marvel at what you do, Lord,
    how deep your thought!
Fools do not grasp this,
    nor the senseless understand.
Scoundrels spring up like the grass,
    flourish and quickly wither.
You, Lord, stand firm forever.

See how your enemies perish,
    scattered to the winds,
while you give me brute strength,
    pouring rich oil upon me.
I have faced my enemies,
    heard them plot against me.
The just shall grow like palm trees,
    majestic like cedars.

Music & Stories LORD, IT IS GOOD

In 1997 I was a member of the liturgy planning team for the bi-annual National Catholic Youth Convention (NCYC) held in Kansas City. The team was led by Jean Bross-Judge, and the other members of this group included my good friends and colleagues, Kate Cuddy, Bob Piercy (may he rest in peace), Fr. Ray East, and Art Zannoni. This particular year over 17,000 teenagers from all across the United States were to be in attendance (the conferences since then have exceeded this number several times). Our task was to plan and coordinate several prayer services and the closing Eucharistic celebration, and to help empower many talented young people who were part of the various liturgical ministries, including music.

I was asked to compose the responsorial psalm for the closing liturgy, and the appointed psalm for the liturgy was Psalm 92. I was happy that this was the text because it is a psalm of thanksgiving, and that lent itself to the occasion. While I believe young people love *all* styles and genres of music, in this case, I specifically chose to compose something in a pop-style. At the time, I was—yes, I admit it—a fan of a Minneapolis based family band, "The Jets," who achieved great popularity for a while. They used to record at the same studio in Minneapolis where I worked, and there were a few times when they were in one of the other studios in the building—but I never had the courage to introduce myself. Anyway, I really loved their song "You Got It All" and so this setting of Psalm 92, "Lord, It Is Good" is highly influenced by that song and their style. You can tell, I think, if you know their music, how that comes across on the recording (*Before I Was Born*), beautifully sung by Lori True and David Fischer.

While I never met "The Jets," I did one evening meet up with Donny Osmond, who was recording in the room right next to where I was working. We had a great conversation about his music *and* mine. It was great. Despite his fame, he presents himself and acts like a regular guy, and he has a great sense of humor. The only bad thing about this meeting was that I remembered that we were the exact same age—despite the fact that I looked old enough to be his uncle, while he looked like he was just recently confirmed. (11.25.17)

CD
MP3
Music

Echo of Faith
X-50705
G-5661

LOVE NEVER FAILS

Music:
David Haas
Text:
1 Corinthians 12:31;
13:13 (alt. DH)

If I speak with the tongues of the earth,
if the angels fill my mouth,
yet do not have love, I am but a sound.
If I prophesy and understand all things,
if mountains shake by my faith,
without love I am nothing at all.

Love is patient, love is kind,
love rejoices in the truth.
It bears all things, believes all things,
it hopes all things, endures all things.
Love never fails.

If I give away everything I own;
give my body to be burned,
yet do not have love, I gain nothing more.
Prophecies will cease, tongues will be silent,
Knowledge will be no more,
the partial will pass away.

When I was a child,
I talked, thought, and lived like a child.
But now that I have grown,
    I have put these things aside.
My knowledge is imperfect now;
    then I'll know as I am known,
that faith, hope and love remain,
and the greatest of these is love.

Copyright © 2001 GIA Publications, Inc.

Music & Stories LOVE NEVER FAILS

These sections from First Corinthians are the most common and usually chosen readings for marriage celebrations, not just for Catholics, but for any Christian couple. It is certainly understandable as to why. The sentiments held in these verses are the "gold standard" for what it means to live in a committed life and covenant of love.

I wanted to see if there was a way, however, that the scripture could shift its emphasis beyond the "love is patient, love is kind" lines only, and go a bit further as to what follows:

Love rejoices in the truth.
It bears all things, believes all things,
it hopes all things, endures all things.
Love never fails.

I worked on this for a while, wanting to build a sense of intensity in what would hopefully be an assembly refrain, regarding these attributes of *bearing*, *believing*, *hoping* and *enduring*. For me, it had to have sort a musical kind of anxiousness so that its message could "hit home" with every person about to make such a commitment.

Of course, this four-fold template of *bearing, believing, hoping* and *enduring* is not a commitment that begins and ends on the wedding day; nor it is limited to marriage itself. Certainly this was not Paul's intent when he first wrote this section of this letter to the church at Corinth. The sacrament and celebration of marriage is most certainly a celebration where we celebrate the nature and challenge of God's love—but it is not limited to the bride and groom alone. This is a problem that we have with sacraments in general, but particularly with marriage, because of all of the cultural and potentially narcissistic dynamics that surround this particular sacrament.

Sacraments are not magical things that happen to an individual. Sacraments always, always, always—happen to a *people*, a *community*. As a church, we have failed miserably in how we teach about sacramentality. There are many who would be shocked to hear that in the case of infant baptism, for example, the ritual is *not about the baby*. It is about *us*, we who gather around this child, this beautiful work of art, with parents and godparents, to recognize God's presence. Yes, we recognize God's presence in the baby, but to expand the power of the moment even further, we also recognize God's presence and action among *us*—*because* of this baby being born and honored on this day. The Eucharist is not limited to our receiving the physical bread and cup, the presence of Christ in

205

food and drink as individuals… it celebrates not only what is happening in the bread and wine, but again, what is happening to *us*, as a result of our sharing in this meal. The sacraments of reconciliation and anointing are not just about individuals being forgiven and praying for healing; they are about proclaiming to us that we are a forgiven people; a people who, in relationship with each other, are healed and made whole. Ordination is not only about what is happening to the new priest—it is about *all of us* who are called to serve and lay down our lives for others.

The same is true with marriage. In other words—sorry to break this news—the wedding is not about the couple in particular, and it is most certainly not the "Bride's day" as popular culture and glossy magazines would lead us to believe. Weddings are not about the couple, or the bride—weddings are about *us*, and more importantly, about *Christ!* They are about us, in that the bride and groom (*not* the priest) are seen as the primary ministers of the sacrament; as a result, by their love, the couple bears witness to how *we* are to grow in our relationships and covenants of love. They are about Christ, because with marriage (and all of the sacraments), it is *Christ* who is to be proclaimed, announced and celebrated through the vessel of the bride and groom, not the other way around.

If we accept this (and this requires a gigantic shift in our thinking), then the message of First Corinthians here has consequences and challenges for us all. We are *all* called to *bear, believe, hope* and *endure* with one another, and for one another. In all of our relationships. In all our circles of commitment. In all situations where we bind ourselves in covenant. And Christ is the central source of our response to this call, because Christ is the embodiment of God's love, a love that never fails. (11.24.17)

CD

MP3
Music

I Shall See God; Blest Are They:
The Best of David Haas, Vol. 1;
Glory Day: David Haas and Friends in Concert;
God Will Delight; With You By My Side, Vol. 1:
The Journey of Life; Give Me Jesus;
The Rosary with St. James
X-89701
G-3447

MAGNIFICAT

Music:
David Haas
Text:
Luke 1:46-55
(alt. DH)

All that I am,
sings of the God who brings new life
    to birth in me.
My spirit soars on the wings of my Lord.

My soul gives glory to the Lord,
    rejoicing in my saving God;
who looks upon me in my state,
    and all the world will call me blest;
for God works marvels in my sight,
    and holy, holy is God's name.

God's mercy is from age to age,
    on those who follow in fear;
whose arm is power and strength,
    and scatters all the proud of heart;
who casts the mighty from their thrones,
    and raises up the lowly ones.

God fills the starving with good things,
    the rich are left with empty hands;
protecting all the faithful ones,
    remembering Israel with mercy;
the promise known to those before,
    and to their children forever.

I WILL BRING YOU HOME

I love the Gospel of Luke for many reasons. First of all, Luke (in both this Gospel and its companion book, the Acts of the Apostles) is the author most consumed with the presence and activity of the Holy Spirit. Secondly, this is the gospel that holds up more than any other the role and dignity of women. This is the gospel where we see Jesus praying the most often. Another reason I love this gospel, which is dear to my heart—and my stomach—is that Jesus eats in the pages of Luke, more than in the other gospels. The meal-ministry of Jesus is most prominent here.

The final reason that I love the Gospel of Luke so much is that it is the most *musical* of all of the gospels. It has a lyrical phraseology that makes one want to sing—here we find actual *canticles* that give a melodic and tuneful message of God working in our lives. In the opening chapters and verses we have the *Benedictus* (Canticle of Zachary) in Luke 1:68-79. We have the *Gloria in excelsis* (Glory to God in the Highest), the song of the angels to the shepherds, in Luke 2:14. We also have the *Nunc Dimittis* (Canticle of Simeon) that appears in Luke 2:29-32.

But my personal favorite of the beautiful Lukan canticles would be the *Magnificat* (Canticle of Mary) that breaks forth in Luke 1: 46-55. This version was my third attempt at composing a setting of this beloved text. My first try was "Tell Out My Soul," which utilizes a strophic translation by Timothy-Dudley Smith and is a part of the evening prayer setting from the *Light and Peace* resource for the Liturgy of the Hours (since this canticle is the central canticle for celebrations of evening prayer), released in 1986. The second opportunity came with my adaptation and arrangement of "Holy Is Your Name," which is wedded to the wonderful and well-known melody "Wild Mountain Thyme." With this setting I wanted to present the canticle and the persona of Mary in a different way than we often experience her, or have come to believe about her.

The Blessed Mother is often presented to us as a demure, submissive and subservient woman, but the *Magnificat* presents us a much different picture. First of all, the author of Luke is actually placing on the lips of Mary a song that is not exactly original to her; it is a re-voicing of what is referred to as the "Canticle of Hannah," which appears in 1 Samuel: 2-10. (I have composed a setting of this canticle, entitled "God Walks With Us," available from GIA: G-9466.) This prayer from the Hebrew Scriptures finds itself on Mary's lips and in her heart, as Mary's response to Elizabeth's witness. We need to remember that Mary was Jewish, and so she is singing out of that religious tradition and spirituality. This canticle also connects together the prophecy of God's presence to the Hebrew nation and this new manifestation of God's presence—the birth of a savior (a deliverer) who will bring justice and righteousness to the world. With that as a backdrop of understanding, in this prayer we find Mary singing in her conviction of who this Jesus is to be, and her role in offering her "yes" to that invitation to be the human vessel of this presence breaking forth.

While I love praying the "Hail Mary, Full of Grace" prayer, we need to be aware that it is not biblical. But the *Magnificat* is, and it presents Mary right away as this harbinger not only of the birth of a child, but the birth of transformation for the nations.

This canticle, while a prophetic and startling song, it is also a most joyful expression of the entirety of Mary's response to the angel's invitation, a response that is to be ours as well. That is why the image of our "soaring" in the refrain is chosen here: "My Spirit soars on the wings of my Lord." Mary loses herself ("all that I am") in the enormity and awesomeness of God's presence and gift to her, she is taken up on the "wings" of God's tremendous gift.

Musically, it probably is obvious that I am influenced by the musical styles that I grew up with, in this case (as it is with other pieces of mine), one can hear the tinges of the Beatles, Elton John, and Billy Joel. In fact, well after the song was published and recorded, I myself recognized the nod to Elton John's "Rocket Man" in the verses. With the refrain actually interrupting and overlapping the end of the verses, I am trying to intentionally embody in a musical manner how, when we come to grips with the litany of God's justice being sung relentlessly, we cannot contain ourselves, and so we burst in with the response. I am not sure praying communities "get" that intention, but that was the thought in designing the piece in this way.

This setting is intended to be a courageous announcement of God breaking into our midst; proclaimed by a most unlikely source: a teenage girl (OK, youth ministers—here is a curriculum for you to implement)—and not just a teenage girl, but one who is a container of the strength of God, and the strength of God's promise. That is why the piece is dedicated to my long-time friend, Andrea Goodrich. Andrea is a living witness of such strength, and her life of ministry as a veteran pastoral musician is most certainly, like Mary, a model for us all.

Whenever I get asked by people if I have a favorite composition that I have written—I have to say, this is one that finds itself very close to the top of the list. (11.11.17)

CD
MP3
Music

Creation God; Mass of Light (Revised)
X-7771CD00
Original Version: G-3341
Revised Order of Mass 2010 Version: G-7771

MASS SETTINGS
MASS OF LIGHT

Music: David Haas

Every liturgical composer, in addition to holding the psalms as central to their vocation, at some point, to my thinking, needs to delve into the waters of composing at least one mass setting. Now for myself, I was very intimidated to do so for quite a while, because when Marty Haugen created the iconic *Mass of Creation,* I felt as though the standard had been achieved, alongside Richard Proulx's *Community Mass*—so for a long time I just did not go down that road. Composing a mass setting is a big challenge. When I was at St. Thomas Aquinas Parish in St. Paul Park, Minnesota (1982-1985) I attempted and made a few sketches of a "Mass in Honor of St. Thomas Aquinas." It was awful. For a while I had put it in a drawer. Later on, it made a permanent home in the waste basket.

In high school I was on the track team, but I was not a long distance runner. I did the sprints. I thought that this was my calling as a composer of music for the liturgy. Short sprints. Songs. Psalms. Acclamations. The only "mass part" that I felt good about was the *Glory to God* that I composed for the 100th Anniversary celebration for St. Thomas Aquinas. Many wanted me to compose a mass. No, not now. I would stick to doing the sprints.

Then, sometime in 1987 I was contacted by Ken Mervine, the director of music at St. Ann's Church in Raritan, New Jersey, who asked me to compose a complete mass setting for the parish, including a sung Eucharistic Prayer (and it had to be what was then Eucharistic Prayer IV). I mustered up my courage and went to work on this setting. Originally I thought would be Lenten in character, sung *a cappella,* but I quickly abandoned that thought when Ken told me that he wanted it to have the same options that Marty had designed for *Mass of Creation*, a setting that would include keyboard, organ, guitar, full choir as well as obbligato instruments and brass. I made a conscious decision to use *Mass of Creation* as the prototype, to go for it. Since I had a Glory to God setting already completed, I decided that E major / E minor would be the harmonic landscape. This resulted in the *Mass of Light*, which, surprisingly, became a staple for many parishes for 22 years, appearing in several GIA hymnals.

This level of success, especially in regards to the Glory to God, is what made things quite challenging when I was strongly encouraged to revise this setting in accordance with the new Order of Mass translations a few years ago, going through the process of "retro-fitting" new texts to an already established setting. As a composer, the issue was this: how was I going to be able to make these new texts sound fresh and vital, without sacrificing certain rhythmic and melodic devices that made the original version appealing? This process goes against the basic principles of liturgical composition: one usually begins with the text, and then the melody and harmonizations follow. With each part of *Mass of Light* I had to make a conscious decision whether to stay as close as possible to the original familiar melodic writing (possibly confusing people who have closely linked the melody and text), or, to start over with new melodic material (which would, in the end, make it no longer really the *Mass of Light*). As was the case with *Mass of Creation, Community Mass,* and other popular mass settings in the GIA catalog, I, together with the editorial staff at GIA chose to keep *Mass of Light* as close to the original as possible, recognizing the changes that had to be made.

I went to work on the revision. The most challenging component was of course, the Glory to God. In this case the text was radically different, and I was told that word "sing!" that was in the original refrain had to be removed altogether—so this would be difficult. In the process of it all, I really believed that the setting would sort of drift away; I wondered if it would cause confusion, and suspected that the compromises that had to be made might make it less appealing to use. But we put it together. I was (and continue to be) not very happy with the changes, but much to my surprise, it has continued to be successful and utilized by many parishes.

I am conflicted, especially about the Glory to God, of which I talk about elsewhere in this book. I have moments when I wished I had not agreed to have it revised, and just let it remain as it was, and if it went off to "Glory to God 'heaven'" and was never sung again, that would be fine. I still do not know how I feel about it all. But the fact that *Mass of Light* is still widely used helps me in being at peace with making all of the changes. Even to this day, with all of the revisions that had to be made or forced—of all the mass settings that I have composed over the years, this still remains the most popular. I do however really miss the absence of a musical rendering of the Eucharistic Prayer. I just have not yet been able to work on this. Again, I am conflicted, for a host of reasons. Maybe someday. (11.22.17)

CD
MP3
Music

Mass for the Life of the World;
Mass for the Life of the World (revised)
X-7845CD02
Original Version: G-3889
Revised Order of Mass 2010 Version: G-7845

MASS SETTINGS

MASS OF LIFE OF THE WORLD

Music: David Haas

Of all of the mass settings that I had composed up until the revision mandate, the only other setting I have reworked was *Mass for the Life of the World / Misa Para Vida Del Mundo*, originally composed and published in 1993.

My influences in creating this setting originally had several sources. During this period I was greatly influenced by gospel-style compositions for liturgy, especially those of Leon Roberts and Clarence Rivers (in this mass, there are several "nods" towards these two heroes of mine). This was also a time when I began to become very involved with the Malia Puka O Kalani parish community in Hilo, Hawaii under the pastoral leadership of Fr. George DeCosta, Joe Camacho and many other very creative people. Lastly, I was also beginning to see the importance of bridging generational gaps, and the rising need and call for more bilingual liturgical music in order to be more inclusive of the rising Hispanic population in the United States. The end result is a multi-cultural "experiment" I guess, reflecting gospel-style melodies and progressions, Pacific rhythms and sounds, and language diversity, arranged for intergenerational choirs and cantors.

There are many people who played a role in bringing this setting to life, especially Jeffrey Judge who did the original Spanish translation, and Fr. Ron Krisman who re-worked it to work with the new translation. I also thank Joe Camacho for allowing his wonderful setting of the Penitential Act to be included, and for allowing me to adapt it—more than once! Rob Glover did many of the choral arrangements, and Brian Streem worked closely with me to problem-solve in making the text adaptations work.

CD	
MP3	We Give You Thanks
Music	X-43600
	G-4990

MASS SETTINGS
JESUS, THE COMPASSION OF GOD

Music: David Haas

Mass: Jesus the Compassion of God was composed and published in 1998 as a commission from my long-time friend Fr. Jim Bessert, for the dedication of the church renovation and his installation as pastor of St. Boniface Church in Bay City, Michigan. Jimmy and I go way back, to the time when I first was discerning entering the seminary, and he was very close to his own ordination. He has been a part of the Haas family for many years and for a short stint was my parent's pastor at St. Boniface. It was during this time that the commission to compose this mass came about.

The driving force behind the framework for this mass was Jimmy's love of my communion song "We Give You Thanks," which he had heard a few months before. He placed the idea in my head that it would be cool if the mass setting could utilize the same melodic motifs and phrases that were part of that song. We also both were intrigued by the then-recent publication of the *Eucharistic Prayers for Various Needs and Occasions*, in particular, the prayer titled, "Jesus, the Compassion of God." I found that implementing the melody of "We Give You Thanks" worked rather easily with the ritual acclamations, which was good news. Unique to this setting is the fact that, in addition to the usual parts of the "ordinary" of the Mass, I composed a call to worship, an acclamation/processional for Children's Liturgy of the Word, an alternative Lenten Gospel Acclamation with an original text, an acclamation song for the dismissal of catechumens and candidates for initiation, a setting of the general intercessions (based on the Zimbabwe song, "If You Believe and I Believe"), an acclamation for sending forth the Eucharistic Ministers to bring communion to the sick and homebound, and a sung final blessing.

In particular, I happen to personally like the "Sing Alleluia" gospel acclamation, and while this setting of the mass has not been revised for the new translation, I still believe that this particular acclamation is successful and it is used quite often. When we recorded this mass, I was thrilled that Jimmy was able to join us in the studio and sing the Eucharistic Prayer and other presidential texts. Every once in a while people will come up to me and share with me their love of this setting and get asked if it will ever be adapted for use utilizing the revised texts. GIA has not asked for this to happen. It probably will not. But one never knows. (11.22.17)

CD
MP3
Music

Do This in Memory of Me
X-55400
G-5433

MASS SETTINGS

DO THIS IN MEMORY OF ME

Music: David Haas

There are many who have no knowledge at all of this setting, mainly because it was originally composed as a Holy Communion setting for Christ Lutheran Church in Charlotte, North Carolina. Christ Lutheran is a marvelous vibrant community, where I have come to know and become friends with their music director of many years, Mark Glaeser. Mark wanted a more contemporary style in the music, in the vein of Marty Haugen's, "Now the Feast and Celebration," to fit in with the musical landscape of the repertoire sung at their contemporary service. I remember remarking during several of my visits to this congregation over the years, that they were most "Catholic repertoire centered" Protestant church I had ever attended.

The common ritual elements for this Holy Communion setting that could be used very easily in Roman Catholic settings are the Kyrie, the Glory to God, two gospel acclamations, the three Eucharistic Acclamations, and the Lamb of God. The setting also includes a gathering hymn (with a beautiful text by Ruth Duck), a musical setting of the Lutheran Order of Confession and Forgiveness, Bidding Prayers, a version of their common text "This is the Feast," a concluding canticle (Canticle of Simeon), and a communion song that bears the title of the entire setting, "Do This in Memory of Me." This setting is still a viable option for Lutheran communities in its present form, but while there was an initial desire to do so, the "mass parts" that are common to Roman Catholic parishes have not been revised to meet the newer requirements. (11.22.17)

| CD |
| MP3 |
| Music |

Mass for a New World
X-7803CD00
G-7803

MASS SETTINGS

MASS FOR A NEW WORLD

Music: David Haas

When the news came down that we had a new revised text for the Order of Mass that was to be implemented, GIA asked me, along with other composers, to create a brand-new setting from scratch. While I was not (and still am not) happy with these new translations, I was pleased that I did not have to retro-fit new texts to already existing melodies; I could actually create something new. This was the impetus for *Mass for a New World*. It was to be included—untested, which made me nervous—in the forthcoming *Gather: Third Edition* hymnal. So I, and the other composers who were invited to create these settings (Marty Haugen, Tony Alonso, Sally Ann Morris, Fr. Ron Krisman, Chris de Silva, Fr. Liam Lawton, Randolph Babin, and Norah Duncan) had to get to work, and fast. I decided that I wanted to try and "vet" this new setting—so I presented it at various workshops and with music director colleagues, and this was very helpful to me as I worked on this project.

In looking back, the rush to "crank out" these settings might not have been altogether wise, but we were under the pressure to respond to this new need, and at the time many of the composers (including myself) and the staff at GIA were not totally confident that the revised versions of already existing settings would be well received. I decided, as many of the other composers did, to create a very simple setting that would be accessible and comfortable for people grappling to sing and pray with these new translations. That is why many of the vocal arrangements are very simple. In addition to the usual ritual texts that were to be set to music, I also added a Lenten gospel acclamation, a sprinkling song (adapted from my "Water of Life"), and a setting of the Lord's Prayer.

While I do receive feedback that the mass has been used in various parish communities, the piece that seems to have "popped" and stood out is the Gospel Acclamation, which includes various sample gospel verses for the various seasons and Ordinary Time. The refrain to this acclamation has also been expanded into an independent song/canticle: "Alleluia: Our God Is Speaking" (G-7727). Its dance-like quality seems to sing itself. My mother liked it so much, she requested it to be the gospel acclamation for her funeral liturgy. (11.22.17)

CD
MP3
Music

God is Everywhere!; Mass of Christ, Our Hope
X-7114CD00
G-7114

MASS SETTINGS
MASS OF CHRIST, OUR HOPE

Music: David Haas

The motivation to create this most recent mass setting came while I was a member of the campus ministry team at Cretin-Derham Hall High School in St. Paul, Minnesota a few years ago; a school that is sponsored by both the Sisters of St. Joseph of Carondelet and the Christian Brothers. Being a part of this community was one of my most fulfilling pastoral experiences, and it was environment where I was free to not only be creative, but also to touch and be touched by the lives of so many wonderful students.

I sensed the need to create a setting that would appeal and speak to the entire school community, which only meets to celebrate the Eucharist together about once a month. The student body, faculty and staff—some who go the church on a regular basis, and many who do not—presented a unique challenge for me to create something that could unify our common prayer together and be simple, accessible, and engaging—something to help foster their participation. While this mass setting was created originally for a high school age audience, I hope that people do not see it as a "youth mass." It rose out of an experience of the young church, but I really hope that people can see it as inter-generational, able to minister to people of all ages.

One of the centerpieces of this Mass is a musical setting of one of the *Eucharistic Prayers for Masses with Children*, which have acclamations to be proclaimed by the assembly throughout the prayer. I also deliberately composed settings of all three memorial acclamations, and created a processional piece for the dismissal of children for parishes that choose to celebrate a unique Liturgy of the Word with children. Also included are a Lenten Gospel Acclamation, a dismissal song for catechumens and candidates for Initiation, and a setting of the Universal Prayer (Prayers of the Faithful).

I WILL BRING YOU HOME

In regards to this setting I particularly am happy with the "Glory to God," as I wanted to compose something that would have the same energy as the setting in *Mass of Light*. I am also fond of the Lamb of God, partly because I wanted to somehow respond to the new directive that additional tropes (such as Bread of Life, Saving Cup, Prince of Peace and other names) were no longer able to be used, which meant that only "Lamb of God" could appear in the litany. Because I believe so strongly that this litany should accompany the entire length of the breaking of the bread and preparing of the cups for communion, I wanted to find a way to extend the litany and yet still follow the new guideline. I chose to use the image of "Lamb of God," but to extend it by singing the invitation to each litany response in a different language. On the recording you can hear examples such as "Agnus Dei" and "Cordero de Dios," along with the English response.

I continue to be so grateful to the Cretin-Derham Hall community that brought *Mass of Christ Our Hope* to life. I now have dear friends as a result of my time there, such as Lou Anne Tighe, Jackie Bohrer, Peter Gleich, Frank Miley, Janet Watson, Mary King and Peter Watkins, as well as many of the students who I had the privilege to walk with during those years. I chose the image of "Christ Our Hope" because it continues to be my experience, from working with young people over the years, that they provide a genuine hope for the Church and for the world. God bless CDH!

I have a strong feeling that I am done composing Mass settings. There are plenty to choose from, and I believe that our younger and emerging composers will be giving us some of the best to come. Good luck and blessings to them. (11.21.17)

CD

MP3
Music

I Am yours Today (Out of print);
I Will Bring You Home
X1041i
G-9659

MIMI'S SONG

**Music and Text:
David Haas**

You wake up each morning, you open your eyes.
You fall out of bed, you see the beautiful sky.
You see the sun a-shin'in, the bluebird, see him fly.
This is from heaven, God's wonderful surprise.

Mimi, look to the sun.
Look to the rain fallin' down.
Look to the sky and all around you too.
God gave life to you;
and I'll never stop thanking God for you.

Look to your family, and look to your friends,
look up to God when all happiness ends.
He is with you today, and tomorrow he will be too.
Now you will know that he really does love you.

Your very happy smile and your beautiful eyes,
the love that you show us reaches up to the sky.
You're very special to me and to all of us here.
You're special to God who is very real and near.

This was the very first actual song that I ever wrote. I mean, when I was very young I would sit at the piano or with the guitar and make up little tunes here and there from time to time, but this was the first time an actual complete song was conceived and finished.

I was a freshman in high school, and around this time I had had already become very close to a family who lived behind our house and across the field from our back yard. Jo Infante, who had lost her husband in a horrific car accident just a few years before, had three children—Lisa, Tony and Maria. After her husband died, Jo began to become more involved at our parish in Bridgeport, and that is how I got to know her; I played guitar in the parish "folk" group, and she was one of the singers. Jo was, and still is, one of the most amazing and courageous women I have ever met, and while she was never formally trained in music, when she sang at church, she radiated a joy that was very difficult for me to understand, knowing the profundity of the loss that she carried in her life. Losing her husband at an early age, raising three children all on her own, and so much more—it was (and still continues to be for me) quite astonishing.

Around this time, I used to hop over the fence in my back yard with my guitar, and I would hang out at the house with her, her kids, and others who would come over, and we would sing and sing. While I was still very young, Jo was a good listener, always very affirming and attentive to me, and this continued throughout my high school years and beyond. I also really enjoyed being with her children, and I guess I was a sort of big brother to them during this time when they were still in many ways grieving the loss of their father and trying to navigate their way through these growing up years.

Maria—whom we all called "Mimi"—was about to make her First Communion. These were the days when people would often, for special occasions, have a "home mass," and that was to be the case for Mimi. There would be family and a few close friends, and Jo and Mimi asked me if I would come, play the guitar and lead the singing for the mass. I said of course, and then almost immediately I asked, "could I write a song for the occasion?" I am not sure where this came from, because I really had never composed a song before. They enthusiastically said, "my goodness, yes!" When I think about it now, I wonder what Jo was really thinking at the time when she gave her assent. I knew she believed I was talented, or she would not have asked me to play or sing for this special day. But I am not sure she had confidence as to whether or not I would follow through on writing the song, or whether or not it would be any good.

Well, by the night before the mass, when I was sitting on my bed with my guitar and nothing at all coming to me, as one could imagine, I was becoming quite anxious. I looked at my wall, which had a poster (I do not remember who gave it to me) that said, "I never stop thanking God for you." While it probably said at the bottom or on the back that this was a quote from Ephesians 1: 16, I did not realize at that time that this was from the Bible. That quote resonated with how I felt about the Infante family and Mimi in particular at that moment, and so that line became the springboard for my finishing the song, although it took into the very early hours of the morning.

The mass for Mimi was very beautiful for her and for all of us, and the song was a very special moment. It did not spark in me any kind of vocational dream that I would someday become a composer; I was just relieved and happy that I finished the song, and got through it!

Mimi married years ago and moved to Rome, where she too has raised children of her own. She and her kids still live there. I miss her. For some reason, she often calls me "Chuck." I miss that. I always seem to miss her when she comes home to Michigan to visit. But I know and believe that she still "looks to the sun." And I hope that she and the entire Infante family know that "I'll never stop thanking God for you." (11.25.17)

CD
MP3
Music

God Has Done Marvelous Things
X-39814
G-4738

THE MUSIC OF CREATION

Music:
David Haas
Text:
Shirley Erena-Murray

For the music of creation,
        for the song your Spirit sings,
for your sound's divine expression,
        burst of joy in living things:
God, our God, the world's composer,
        hear us, echoes of your voice—
music is your art, your glory, l
        et the human heart rejoice!

Psalms and symphonies exalt you,
        drum and trumpet, string and reed,
simple melodies acclaim you;
        tunes that rise from deepest need,
hymns of longing and belonging,
        carols from a cheerful throat,
lilt of lullaby and love song,
        catching heaven in a note.

All the voices of the ages i
        n transcendent chorus meet,
worship lifting up the senses,
        hands that praise, and dancing feet;
over discord and division music
        speaks your joy and peace,
harmony of earth and heaven,
        song of God that cannot cease!

Music & Stories THE MUSIC OF CREATION

Ministers of music come in all shapes and sizes. They hold various and different opinions and tastes about what music is best to serve the liturgy, and they have different levels and abilities and varied gifts. Some are singers and others are players; they are young and old, women and men, adults and children. They sing in many different languages and come from every known culture and race—and yes, they are members of the assembly. This diversity is a blessing, but it also pulls us apart at times. In the early days that followed Vatican II, liturgical music was in a bit of chaos—in fact, before that, we did not even use words like "liturgical" or "pastoral" or "ritual." It was church music, or sacred music.

Almost overnight, the organ was no longer the only instrument that we heard in church—it was like one day people showed up to mass, and my goodness, there were guitars there! And tambourines, and flutes, and then later, the piano arrived. The so-called "traditional" musicians dug their feet in, and the young "hippie folk" musicians were knocking at the door. Lines began to be drawn.

Ever since then, we have had various degrees of battle in the "worship music wars." They have waxed and waned over the years but never really gone away. The judgment and sense of superiority comes from every corner; no one style or genre of music is totally free from those who think in terms of a "mutual absolutism" that seeks to divide and isolate the other.

In my workshop presentations over the years I have encountered musical snobbery from many different vantage points. Some tout that they only approve of doing "traditional" music, and that Gregorian Chant is the only true sacred music…others also say they insist on "traditional" music, but this group considers "traditional" to be almost synonymous with "classical" music—anything that does not sound too modern.

The so-called contemporary pastoral musicians are not off the hook here. Some in *this* group maintain that nothing composed prior to 1977 has any place in the liturgy. Many have no appreciation or even knowledge of any of the more traditional repertoire or music from the sacred treasury. I presented a workshop one time for a group of college students, and while having a discussion of this topic of musical diversity and tolerance, one young man about 19 years old stood up and said, seriously, "Oh, we do a lot of traditional music." When I asked him to name some of this music, he replied very innocently, "well, like your stuff."

There has also been throughout this time an additional fervor as to what the role of the congregation is, in terms of music. Choirs and ensembles in some places want to sing on their own, and not have the assembly join in with them, wanting to perform rather than support. Communities will find themselves divided over the kind of music they "like" and be very opinionated about what styles of music they want to hear, pray and sing with. Mirroring secular culture, people are fearful of diversity and at times show their disdain when the music of different cultures and languages enters into their prayer life. The Body of Christ, in many cases, has forgotten how to behave at all like a body that lives and prays together, or like a family that celebrates and revels in its many expressions.

There are a lot of issues that come to the surface here, but the overall one, I believe, is the need for all of us to come together and look in the mirror, and come to honor and reverence all of the many musical ways in which people offer praise and prayer. Some people argue, "well, I don't like contemporary music," or "I don't want to sing the old traditional hymns," or "we do not have any Hispanic people in our parish—so why are we singing in Spanish?"

To any of you who hold these and similar convictions, I would say this to you: *It is not about you.* It is about recognizing how large God is, how diverse we all are, and how large our prayer and expressions need to be. We need anthems and songs that bring us together. One of my favorites that does this is the text of Sr. Delores Dufner, OSB, "Sing A New Church." There are many others.

This song, "The Music of Creation," with its joy-filled text by Shirley Erena Murray, is an invitation holding a message to help bring us together; to gladden our hearts, and to truly be, for pastoral musicians, *our* song and prayer of Thanksgiving! Sing it, or pray with the words. Give it a try. Who knows? You might end up liking it!

For me, the marvelous lyrics of this song provide great clarity and serve as the great equalizer for finding common ground in our musical diversity in worship. These many "divine expressions" do not even begin to come close to offering an adequate praise to God, but they sure come as close as just about any psalm, hymn or canticle that I have ever come across. The line in the first stanza that cries out to our God who is the "world's composer" reminds me of what is proclaimed in the opening line of the US Bishop's statement on liturgical music, *Sing to the Lord (STL):*

God has bestowed on his people the gift of song.
God dwells within each human person,
in the place where music takes its source.
Indeed, God, giver of song,
is present whenever his people sing his praises. (STL, 1)

In other words, music – *all* music, not just liturgical music – is God's idea! Music is a most precious gift, and God is the "giver" of this gift, as Shirley continues to proclaim: "music is *your* art, *your* glory …" Who has any right whatsoever to determine a particular style or genre is worthy of the praises being sung in our vocation of liturgical music? Who can possibly claim to be the arbiter of what instruments are the most appropriate or not? If and when we accept this statement that claims that God "is present whenever his people sing his praises," then we have made a covenant that honors the galaxy of ways God is to be praised. This is, in a way, for all of us who are pastoral musicians, our experience and expression of the "real presence."

Shirley just begins to touch on the myriad of ways this praise takes place and how this presence is seen, heard, listened to, and *joined with*: "Psalms and symphonies exalt you, drum and trumpet, string and reed …" And this sung prayer comes forth in the "simple melodies" and the "tunes that rise from deepest need, hymns of longing and belonging, carols from a cheerful throat …" My goodness, this pulls together the three-fold judgment referenced in *Sing to the Lord* when it speaks of the liturgical-pastoral-musical judgments. This hymn calls us to shoot for the stars—to not only "catch heaven in a note" (why could I not have come up with that lyric!), but to stay the course in the very mission of our sung prayer, where we are called to foster an integrity-filled "lifting up the senses" that conquers all "discord and division," building the reign of God: "harmony of earth and heaven, song of God that cannot cease!"

This is the heart of our vocation as music ministers. Anything short of this is to close our eyes and hearts to the musical gifts we have been given. This song, these words—that I had a great delight bringing music to—is our "theme song" as pastoral musicians. (12.18.17)

We Have Been Told;
Blest Are They: The Best of David Haas, Vol. 1
X-34006
G-2662

MY GOD AND MY ALL

Music and Text:
David Haas
Adapted from a
prayer of St. Francis
of Assisi

My God and my all, how I long to love you;
and give you my heart, and give you my soul.

Show me the way to love,
    and give of my life to you.
    Then I will live. Then I will rise.

And I will live with you,
    and I will die with you—
    weeping for love, weeping for joy.

I, like so many, have always loved St. Francis. I grew up knowing Franciscans, especially the Capuchins who ran a retreat center not too far from my childhood home. When I was in the seminary, I was even considering entering the Franciscans for a time. I remember seeing for the first time Franco Zeffirelli's film about Francis, *Brother Sun, Sister Moon*. While I know the movie has many historical inaccuracies, I still get caught up in the Franciscan charism that is captured in that movie.

Just about every Christian I know loves the prayer, "The Prayer of St. Francis." What a lot of people do not know is that, though it captures the spirituality and wisdom of Francis, it is absent from his writings, and this prayer that we all know well only traces back to 1912.

The refrain for "My God and My All," however, is grounded in a mantra that Francis himself was known to have prayed quite often as a prayer of meditation that he would engage with for hours at a time.

In line with the utter simplicity of Francis and the Franciscan "rule," this is an intimate song. Simple, direct, and tender. For Francis, following Christ meant to give up everything, to surrender all. This is a song and prayer of surrender, containing a commitment to offer up everything to Christ, and to the Body of Christ. I have to say, I fall short of following the simple direction illuminated so greatly in this song.

I have composed other songs from Francis' writings and prayers, and from Franciscan-inspired sources; this was the first, and it continues to be a profound prayer for me. This song is intended to be sung with guitar accompaniment. Even though piano and trumpet were the instruments I studied formally, I would play the guitar a lot when I was young. It became the first instrument that I would play in church (my Dad was the organist, but I never got the knack for that). Then, as the piano became more and more present in both our worship spaces and in the repertoire (beginning around the early 1980's), I began to write more and more for the piano as the primary accompanying instrument. I still compose guitar-based pieces, but I have to admit, the guitar does sit in its case a lot more as I have gotten older. I miss it. Gotta get it out of the case more often. (11.12.17)

CD
MP3
Music

I Am Yours Today (Out of print);
I Will Bring You Home
X-1041g
G-9659

MY LORD AND MY GOD

**Music and Text:
David Haas**

Lord, here is my prayer to you.
Lord, help me to be close to you.
For you are the one who protects me.
You are the one who sets me free.

Lord, help me to find you.
Lord, help me to see you
as God who is loving and a God who is kind,
and a God who will help me find my mind.

Lord, help me to follow you.
Lord, help me sing this song to you.
A song that will give me a brand new start,
and a song that will keep you in my heart.

My Lord and my God.

Copyright © 1979, 2017 GIA Publications, Inc.

Not counting "Mimi's Song" that I wrote when I was in the ninth grade several years earlier, this was the very first religious song of any kind that I ever composed.

Its story begins in the summer of 1977 (40 years ago), and I was sitting in the office of the vocation director for the Diocese of Saginaw (in Michigan), Fr. Bob DeLand. I was having that first meeting about the possibility of me entering the seminary. After talking a bit and finding out that I was a musician, he got on the phone right then and there and called one of his other seminarians, Jimmy Bessert, and put me on the line with him. After about a five-minute discussion, Jimmy told me that two days later he was going to be driving to Baltimore to attend a national liturgical music workshop, and that I should go with him. So, without ever meeting him before, here we were in his Chevy Vega on our way to Baltimore. On the drive along the way with my guitar in tow, we talked a lot and got to know each other very quickly; there was a connection that we both felt immediately. We talked about music, about the church, and shared with each other our stories as to how we got to this point in our lives; and we *laughed* a lot, harder than I ever I had before! Jimmy has a very quick and clever wit, and this was the beginning of a life-long friendship that remains to this day.

The workshop was amazing, and its impact on me would dramatically change the course of my discernment. The event was held at St. Mary's Seminary and was called "Summersong," co-sponsored by what was at that time the primary publisher of contemporary Catholic liturgical music, North American Liturgy Resources (NALR). Throughout that week, I met and went to workshop sessions by people I had mostly never heard of before. With the exception of Joe Wise, who was there, these were brand new names to me: Ed Gutfruend, Tim Schoenbachler, Tom Conry, Robert Twynham, Bernard Huijbers, and Grayson Warren Brown. During these sessions we sang through brand new music from these composers. I remember Tom passing out photocopies of hand-written scores to two new songs that he had just written, "Ashes" and "Anthem." Ed led us in his arrangement of a Quaker song that I had never heard before, "How Can I Keep from Singing." Bernard Huijbers conducted music for a liturgy that included pieces like "When from Our Exile," "Awake from Your Sleep," and "Even Then."

Bob Twynham presented an organ recital of music by Messiaen and Langlais—I had heard a lot of organ music from my Dad over the years, but these were amazing sounds and astonishing harmonic structures that were brand new to me. Grayson led what could have only at the time be described as a revival meeting with brand new and exciting gospel hymns. Tim, who happened to be a classmate of Jimmy, sang "Lord of the Dance" and his arrangement of "Speak, Lord," and Joe Wise shared songs like "Watch with Me," "This is my Gift," and yes, "Take All the Lost Home." There were other workshops about liturgy planning, the sacraments, techniques for encouraging congregational participation, and instrumental skill-building, and lots and lots and lots of jam sessions where we would get out our instruments and sing for hours. Suffice it to say, I was completely taken in. The 100 or so participants were joyful and filled with an overwhelming zeal for liturgical music and ministry. These are my kind of people, I kept saying to myself, and I began to see how and where God was taking me. I wanted to be a part of, what was for me, this new energy and excitement that, with the risk of sounding hokey, truly inspired me.

I WILL BRING YOU HOME

During one of the evenings after most of the people had been asleep, I walked outside with my guitar and stood in this beautiful grotto area outside the seminary chapel, and prayed for a while. Then I began to play my guitar, and a chord progression that I just learned in one of the sessions led to me coming up with this song, "My Lord and My God." It was a painfully simple song (again, like many of my early liturgical "folk-style" songs, it sounds a lot like John Denver), and it reflected the fact that I did not know much about writing lyrics, but even so, what I wanted to say was so true. I felt God's presence in my prayer. I was seeking guidance for what I wanted to do in this chapter in my life, asking God to "help me find my mind." I was looking not at this point to be a prolific liturgical composer, far from it. But I did know in those moments, and during that week, that I wanted to sing and play and pray to God "a song" that would "give me a brand-new start, and a song that will keep you in my heart." For whatever reason, the final words were my echo of Thomas after he experienced the risen Lord, "my Lord and my God."

I knew at that time that this was not an incredible song by any means. But I knew something new was stirring. And it was humbling, powerful, and very cool.

After that conference and upon returning home, I started to write a few more songs. Jimmy went on to be ordained a priest soon after and I went on to Minnesota, and well, as they say… (11.27.17)

CD

MP3 Music

Who Calls You by Name, Vol. 2;
Alive in Christ Jesus;
Blest Are They: The Best of David Haas, Vol. 1
X-34005
G-3654

MY LORD WILL COME AGAIN

**Music and Text:
David Haas**

My Lord will come again, my Lord,
my Lord will come again,
my Lord will come again,
my Lord will come again!
My Lord will come again, my Lord,
and the kingdom will have no end!
Amen! Amen! My Lord will come again!

I will bless the Lord at all times!
    I will praise God with all my life!
For the Lord our God is risen,
    and death will be no more!
Amen, Amen, my Lord will come again!

I will sing to God a new song;
    make music to my God while I live!
For the Lord our God is with us,
    and death will be no more!
Amen, Amen, my Lord will come again!

God will wipe all tears from our eyes!
    The world of the past will be gone!
And sadness, pain, and mourning:
    these will be no more!
Amen, Amen, my Lord will come again!

I WILL BRING YOU HOME

So, I am thinking *Ascension*. I'm thinking about the notion of Christ coming again. And all that comes to my mind is a wonderful song by Joe Wise that I sang when I was about 10 years old in catechism class, called "My Lord Will Come Again." The words go like this:

My Lord will come again,
my Lord will come again;
He'll come again I know,
I know, I know, I know, I know;
So sing, my soul, and laugh, and dance,
and skip, and run,
and shout for joy, he'll come.

I wanted to write something that had a similar sense of freedom, abandon, and simplicity in the message. So I came up with my own version of "My Lord Will Come Again," that would include a sort of Gospel-Spiritual like feel, with a Jackson Five kind of accompaniment in the refrain—I mean, listen to Bobby Fisher playing the guitar on the recording—it sounds like the opening groove on "Oh Baby, Give Me One More Chance." Seriously.

Anyway... I added an SATB arrangement on the refrain, and I had my Ascension song. I have always admired the wonderful SATB arrangements that my good friend Rob Glover creates; and because we are of a similar age, and he would also have remembered the old Joe Wise songs, I chose to dedicate this song to him. The joy of this song certainly calls to mind the joy of the influence of Joe's music and witness in my life; my love of the Spirituals and Gospel music; and my friendship with Rob. So it all connects with the Ascension. The Lord is coming again—to me, Joe, Rob...and yes, even the Jackson Five. (11.24.17)

CD
MP3
Music

When We Are Weak, We Are Strong;
I Will Bring You Home
X-101114
G9471

MY ONLY DESIRE

Music and Text:
David Haas

In you alone my soul is resting;
in you alone my strength will soar.
You—my wall of endless safety,
my dwelling place, my solace and my home.

In you alone my hope will flower;
in you alone my soul will shine.
You—the presence of sweet mercy,
healing for my broken heart and mind.

You alone,
You, my only hope.
You, my only song.
You alone, my only desire.
You, my only desire.

In you alone I find new glory;
in you alone I am complete.
You—the gift of flowing freedom,
my fountain of all holiness and grace.

In you alone I find direction;
in you alone I know my path.
You—my compass and my vision,
my Alpha and Omega all my days.

I WILL BRING YOU HOME

In the fall of 2016 I was fortunate to have the opportunity to travel to the Pacific Rim and Asia, on what I now refer to as my "Lumen Pacifica Tour." During a three-week period, I presented workshops and concerts in Guam, the Philippines, and Singapore—my first time to all three places—and Hawaii, where I have been blest to be numerous times over the years. It was truly a highlight of my ministerial life, as I encountered so many wonderful people, devout and passionate about their faith, and also—lovers of music! I swear, everyone in Guam, the Philippines and Singapore is in a choir of some kind. I wonder, is it a requirement of citizenship? My goodness, at every place where I visited and presented I was so inspired and moved by choirs who were not only full of musical talent and sensitivity but who witnessed so powerfully their love of God and God's people. I was also able to meet some of the liturgical composers who dwell in this region of the world.

While in the Philippines, I presented an all-day workshop and evening concert at Ateneo University in Manila, a well-known Jesuit institution that has served the people with tremendous resources and music under the umbrella of "Jesuit Communications/Jesuit Music Ministry." At the evening concert, I was the special honored guest performer along with three incredible vocal ensembles and music ministry leaders: The Ateneo Chamber Singers; Bukas Palad (which means, "open palm"), and Hangad (which translates as "desire"). All three of these choirs shared their gifts so generously, and I was thrilled to hear some of their arrangements and renderings of some of my compositions. It would seem that the biggest hits in the Philippines include "You Are Mine," "Without Seeing You," "Now We Remain," and surprisingly, a not-so-well known wedding song of mine, "Love Never Fails." I was so powerfully moved, again, not just by their incredible musicality and gorgeous arrangements, but their absolute joy and dedication to their ministry. They each had a portion during the concert to feature their unique gifts; I did a "set" of music by myself, and then the evening concluded with all three groups combined, joining me for several songs. At the afternoon rehearsal, at the last minute, I passed out the SATB refrain for my piece, "I Will Live On," and with only one run through, they gave me chills as they added beautiful improvised harmonies and descants to my SATB arrangement. When we did it at the evening event for the audience who came (over 1,000 people!), it traveled to a place of exquisite beauty and prayer. I will never forget that evening.

After the concert, all three choirs and their organizers had me join them for a wonderful dinner, and throughout the evening they all sang to me—right there in the restaurant! It was amazing, and my tears almost turned into quite the puddle on the floor. I was sitting at the table with the members of Hangad, and instantly I felt as though I had made several life-long friends. We talked and laughed, and they shared with me more about the name of their group (again, which means "Desire"), and I was so taken with this image and how powerfully it speaks about the journey of faith and conversion. We had such a great time that the very next evening, the members of Hangad and I shared another meal together, and shared in more storytelling, music, and the sharing ensued throughout the evening. Such an incredible evening—and I lamented when we had to say both goodnight and goodbye.

After returning home, the memory of this most loving, gifted, and Christ-centered ensemble/community stayed with me, and I kept thinking and praying more and more about this image of "desire." So one afternoon thinking about them, in one sitting, I composed this song "My Only Desire," as a gift to Hangad. I quickly did a very simple recording of it, of just myself singing, and included it as the concluding song on my recorded collection, *When We Are Weak, We Are Strong*. Soon after that, because I wanted (for selfish reasons I guess) to hear Hangad sing it, I composed an SATB arrangement. I remember when they sent me a video of them rehearsing it, and I broke down and cried, it was so beautiful. I never imagined that they would record it and include it on a new CD that they were putting together celebrating their 26th anniversary. It is that recorded version, sung by Hangad, that you hear on the CD that is partnering this book.

The first verse of the song begins with a nod to the opening lines of Psalm 62 ("In God alone is my soul at rest"), and it was there that I found the recurring theme of the entire song—that it is God alone who is the source of our life, our joy, our survival and our call to ministry, whether it be in music, religious education, evangelization, working with youth, pastoral care, social justice activism, care for the poor and the elderly—everything that is at the center of Gospel living. Only God can sustain us in our life. And this recognition feeds our "desire" to become more tethered to the Spirit of God, to the presence of God, to the activity of God's people. This desire is ongoing, relentless, and infinite. Such is the case also in my love for Hangad, and also for Bukas Palad and the Ateneo Chamber Singers, for all that they provide to announce God's presence in the life of the people in the Philippines and beyond. Keep the *desire* burning. Keep the energy of desire ever present in your ministry of music, so that all of us who are the recipients of your blessed ministry can also join in the "only song" that is God alone. (11.17.17)

CD

MP3 Music

Where the River Flows; Without Seeing You: The Best of David Haas, Vol. 3; Glory Day: David Haas and Friends in Concert
X-80511
G-4336

MY SONG WILL BE FOR YOU FOREVER

Music and Text: David Haas

My song will be for you forever,
    you, the music in my heart,
for your love is all around me,
    and your goodness always here.

You have clothed me in your promise;
    you, my love, my light, my friend.
You, the way and path before me,
    you will lead and guide me home.

    My song will be for you forever;
    You, the music in my heart.

I am here to be your servant;
    you anoint me with your love.
You will hold me in my longing,
    all my hope in your embrace.

With your voice, you sing within me;
    you, the one who knows me well.
You, my joy, my life and blessing,
    when you call, you know my name.

I will pledge my love forever,
    I will call your name out loud.
I will reach my hand out to you,
    and I know you'll reach for me.

Copyright © 1995 GIA Publications, Inc.

Roman Catholics have always had a unique language about how we talk about God and our relationship with the transcendent. While our discourse has evolved, most Catholics still feel uncomfortable when someone comes up to us and asks the question, "do you have a personal relationship with Jesus?" It always makes me uneasy, and I am not sure why. I guess it is just because I did not grow up talking that way. I mean, how does one have an intimate and close relationship with a historical person who lived so long ago? How are we intimate with the divine?

I have come to learn over the years more about the distinctions between the "Jesus of history," and what some theologians name as the "Christ of faith." Some people never move beyond the historical Jesus. Not that it is wrong-headed to reflect on Jesus' life on earth, but the problem is that we cannot verify much about Jesus of Nazareth. Not really. The four gospels give distinct and diverse aspects into his life on earth (and we have additional evidence, albeit not detailed, from Josephus in the first century), often holding different versions of the same stories. Just one among many examples is how these documents address the birth of Jesus. Matthew and Luke provide what we call the "infancy narratives," but Mark, and certainly John, hold absolutely no concern about the origins of Jesus' birth nor about his childhood and growing up years. Mark begins with Jesus as an adult; and John presents a more mystical and deeply theological rendering. In our present time, when people are anxious to have facts and history verifiable and researched for accuracy, doing so with the New Testament and the life of Jesus is difficult if not impossible. We need to see the Bible not as history, but as *faith literature*. So how exactly do I develop a personal relationship with Jesus, at least in terms of how I understand having relationships with the people in my life?

What this gets to, and what "My Song Will Be For You Forever" attempts to express, is that while we certainly believe that Jesus is present in the consecrated and shared bread and wine, and fully present in the bread reserved in the tabernacle; while we have come to know more and more how Christ is present in the proclaimed and preached word of God; while many experience God being real for them in the beauties of creation—what we need to celebrate and honor more and more, is that the primary revelation and incarnation of Jesus is to be found, discovered and nurtured—in *each other*, in human beings! To put it plainly, yes, I *do* have a personal relationship with Jesus the Christ when I am invested in the *Body of Christ*, and that is you and I—the baptized, the holy people of God who have been called by name. As I heard someone once say, if we cannot find the presence of Christ in each other, we will never understand the power of that presence in the bread.

We most certainly *do* have a personal relationship with Jesus, grown out of his invitation to us to love and connect with our brothers and sisters around us. When we are tethered to one another, and most especially when we *serve* one another—when we see Jesus in one another, in a spouse, a partner, a parent, or a child, in a relationship that is deeply personal, intimate, vulnerable, and loving—we are then even more tethered to Christ in a most intimate way:

When the Son of Man comes in his glory,
and all the angels with him,
then he will sit on the throne of his glory.
All the nations will be gathered before him,
and he will separate people one from another
as a shepherd separates the sheep from the goats,
and he will put the sheep at his right hand and the goats at the left.
Then the king will say to those at his right hand,
"Come, you that are blessed by my Father,
inherit the kingdom prepared for you from the foundation of the world;
for I was hungry and you gave me food,
I was thirsty and you gave me something to drink,
I was a stranger and you welcomed me,
I was naked and you gave me clothing,
I was sick and you took care of me,
I was in prison and you visited me."
Then the righteous will answer him,
"Lord, when was it that we saw you hungry and gave you food,
or thirsty and gave you something to drink?
And when was it that we saw you a stranger and welcomed you,
or naked and gave you clothing?
And when was it that we saw you sick or in prison and visited you?"
And the king will answer them,
"Truly I tell you, just as you did it to one of the least of these
who are members of my family, you did it to me."
(Matthew 25: 31-40)

So there it is. This is what this song is—it is a love song to God, expressed by how that love is experienced through, with and in the walking beside our sisters and brothers. (11.12.17)

CD
MP3
Music

As Water to the Thirsty; Psalms for the Church Year,
Vol. 3; I Will Bring You Home
X-26514
G-3498

THE NAME OF GOD

Music:
David Haas
Text:
Psalm 116
(alt. DH)

I will take the cup of life,
I will call God's name all my days.

How can I make a return
    for the goodness of God?
This saving cup I will bless and sing,
    and call the name of God!

The dying of those who keep faith
    is precious to our God.
I am your servant called from your hands,
    you have set me free!

To you I will offer my thanks
    and call upon your name.
You are my promise for all to see.
    I love your name, O God!

Copyright © 1987 GIA Publications, Inc.

"The Name of God" is an adaptation of Psalm 116, based on the commonly found refrain text, "The cup of blessing I will take up, and call upon the name of the Lord." I have enjoyed lingering with the psalms, and in particular, discovering creative and more contemporary ways of stating the same message. This setting was composed originally for the first Mass of Thanksgiving for a good friend of mine following his ordination to the priesthood. I created additional refrain texts as well, to make this more versatile for other liturgical celebrations—especially for the Evening Mass of the Lord's Supper on Holy Thursday, where Psalm 116 is the appointed psalm.

I WILL BRING YOU HOME

I remember this being composed rather quickly, and while that is always a blessing, it sometimes makes me nervous. But "The Name of God" seems to be a favorite for many, and when I am pressed to name a favorite composition of mine, this often pops into my head right away. While it is not one of the appointed psalms for celebrations of the Order of Christian Funerals, it has been chosen many times as the responsorial psalm for the Funeral Mass. This was the case for the funeral masses for both of my parents, especially considering the sentiment of the second verse: "The dying of those who keep faith is precious to our God."

Alive in its Eucharistic imagery, this is a psalm of thanksgiving and gratitude. When we are grateful and thankful, the best part of ourselves is revealed to others, and we see how only good things will come to us from living our lives in this spirit. When I am grateful, I am choosing right then and there to abandon resentment and the need for revenge; my feelings of jealousy of others begins to melt away. I am less consumed with myself and my own selfish needs, and my creative muse flourishes.

I am my best self when I am thankful. The richest creations spring forth when my gratitude does the same. I feel as though when I am grateful, my responses are more creative, more beautiful, and more authentically grounded in ministry and service. When I am grateful, my giving becomes more lavish and more honest, because it comes from a place of complete freedom. The third verse of this setting proclaims this truth: "To you I will offer my thanks and call upon your name. You are my promise for all to see. I love your name, O God."

God, help me to always be thankful and filled with gratitude. I lift to you the cup of life that you promise for us, and I call out your name. May I do so forever, all my days. (11.12.17)

CD

MP3
Music

No Longer Strangers; Glory Day: David Haas and
Friends in Concert; Without Seeing You:
The Best of David Haas, Vol. 3
X-29813
G-3957

NO LONGER STRANGERS

Music:
David Haas
Text:
Ephesians 2:4-8,
11-14, 18-22
(alt. DH); David Haas

We once were lost; without hope, without God;
but now in Christ Jesus, we have been found!
Saved by the promise of God!

No longer strangers, no longer lost and alone!
No longer strangers, now we are saints!
We are one in the house of God!

We once were cut off; but now we are brought near,
for Christ is our peace, we were broken—now whole!
One spirit, one Body of Christ!

We who once were dead, now we live in the light,
we follow Christ Jesus, abundant in grace!
Who saved us, who raised us to life!

In my earliest days of writing liturgical music I remember listening over and over
again to the recordings of John Michael Talbot, especially his recording of "The
Lord's Supper" that he created soon after his conversion to Catholicism. I was
amazed and inspired by his passion and energy—not to mention his incredible
guitar playing—and always waited with excitement for the next album to come
out. Among several of his subsequent album releases was a collection he did
with his brother Terry, called *No Longer Strangers*. The message, and *especially* the
arrangement (with its tight vocal harmonies), grabbed me from the start. After
that, this passage from Ephesians became new for me.

But what finally brought *my* setting to life—many years later—was my
ongoing involvement with my home Diocese of Saginaw, Michigan, and in

particular with the Lay Ministry Formation program that was directed by my mentor and friend, Sr. Roberta Kolasa, SJ, and Sr. Jo Gaugier, OP. They were always looking for music from me to create and lead during their various retreats events. For one retreat, this passage from Ephesians came to mind as well as the Talbot song. I was so hooked on gospel music at the time (after writing songs like "We Are Called," "We Will Drink the Cup," and others), that I wanted to bring that style to this piece. So this is what brought my version of "No Longer Strangers" to birth.

When the time came to record, I wanted it to be very authentic and taken up a few notches in terms of vocal prowess, so I reached out to my friend Kate Cuddy, and right away she recommends a musician-singer friend of hers, Gwen Matthews, and so we invited her to the studio to give this song a spin. Well, my goodness … I ran through it once for her, and she had it down, and more! Then you add the piano and organ prowess of Minneapolis music giant Ricky Peterson alongside the guitar virtuosity of Bobby Fisher, and wow—it was unlike anything I had put on a recording before up until this time. The choir sounds awesome on the track as well.

It is quite astonishing that our God is so in love with us, that we are brought so very close, always finding there, a deep, vulnerable and covenant relationship where we are not only "no longer strangers"—but also named as "saints." It is hard to accept. But it is the truth. I keep forgetting this. I need the Church, the community: *you all*, the Body of Christ, to keep reminding me and each other—that we are one in house of God, together. Always. (11.24.17)

CD   We Have Been Told;
Blest Are They: The Best of David Haas, Vol. 1;
Give Me Jesus

MP3   X-265151
Music   G-2709

NOW WE REMAIN

**Music and Text:
David Haas
inspired by
2 Corinthians 4:10**

We hold the death of the Lord deep in our hearts.
Living; now we remain with Jesus the Christ.

Once we were people afraid, lost in the night.
Then by your cross we were saved;
dead became living, life from your giving.

Something which we have known,
    something we've touched,
what we have seen with our eyes:
This we have heard; life giving Word.

He chose to give of himself, became our bread.
Broken, that we might live.
Love beyond love, pain for our pain.

We are the presence of God; this is our call:
Now to become bread and wine;
food for the hungry, life for the weary,
for to live with the Lord,
    we must die with the Lord.

This is one of my earlier songs, composed during the time that I served as Director of Music and Liturgy at St. Thomas Aquinas Church in St. Paul Park, Minnesota (1982-1985), and it was composed specifically for one of the choirs that I led there, named as the "Emmaus Music Ministry." They were named after the Emmaus story in Luke, because one of the very first pieces that I introduced to them was a hand-written score of a new unpublished song by Bob Hurd, "In the Breaking of the Bread." This wonderful song (it has become very popular over the years) almost instantaneously centered us in what our mission was to be—people who are walking on the road, and encountering the Risen Christ in the sharing of the stories, and recognizing him in "the breaking of the bread"— and choosing to lead sung prayer in that same spirit.

The Emmaus ensemble served as the music ministry for the Saturday evening 5:30 p.m. Mass throughout my tenure there at St. Thomas Aquinas and, while not intentionally at the outset, became a "laboratory," so to speak, for some of my earliest compositions, such as almost all of the psalm settings found in *Psalms for the Church Year* (my first GIA project, a collaboration with Marty Haugen), as well as "Blest Are They," "We Will Rise Again," "Jesus, Heal Us," "The Harvest of Justice," "People of the Night," "You Are the Voice," and many more.

The first among these was "Now We Remain." I was calling to mind 2 Corinthians 4:10, where Paul teaches, "we carry in our body the death of the Lord, so ours may be the gift of his life." This amazing mystery—that we hold within ourselves the core of Jesus' suffering, and that we too, share in that journey that leads to an ongoing and relentless rising—for me, cried out for song. It did not take long for words and melody of the refrain to fall out of me. Then other favorite passages from the New Testament filled out the verses, along with the increasing acknowledgement of the paschal mystery that concludes the third verse: "Love beyond love. Pain for our pain."

The song has become popular over the years during the paschal times of Lent, Triduum, and Easter, and is has been included in many hymnals and other resources. It seems to be a favorite among my liturgical music friends in the Philippines and Singapore as well, where it was at the top of the list of requests when I was sharing my songs there. I remember watching the popular movie, "Close Encounters of the Third Kind" not long after this song was published, and hearing a bit of melodic similarity to the five-note motif in the movie where the scientists were able to communicate in friendship with the alien life forms. I only hope that this song has communicated well for sung prayer.

So, to those of you who made up that original ensemble of singers, players and instruments of God's song, the Emmaus Music Ministry: Kathy, Mindy, Rose Ann (Red), Jeanne, Jim, Michael, John, Mary, Barbara, Sue, Barbie, and all who followed—this one was, and still is, for you. Thanks for some wonderful times sharing our faith in music, and for inspiring a song that will hopefully continue to open a wider circle for singing the Paschal Mystery. (11.19.17)

CD
MP3
Music

God Is Everyhwere!
X-95902
G-8851

ONE HEART, ONE MIND

Music and Text: David Haas; Inspired by Acts 4:32-35

May we be of one heart, one mind,
giving our lives for each other.
All that we are,
we hold in common by the grace of the Lord.
May there be no one among us
who is in need or alone.
May we be of one heart, one mind.

Grounded in hope, strong by faith,
filled with joy, led in peace:
Blest by God, one in the Body of Christ!

Courage lived, wisdom shared,
mercy shown, truth be told:
Blest by God, one in the Body of Christ!

Wonders and signs day by day,
one in love, offering praise:
Blest by God, one in the Body of Christ!

Unity, generous hearts,
table spread, breaking bread:
Blest by God, one in the Body of Christ!

Spirit poured, prophecy sung,
visions and dream by old and young:
Blest by God, one in the Body of Christ!

I WILL BRING YOU HOME

From the fall of 2012 through the spring of 2016, I had the wonderful privilege to serve part-time on the campus ministry team for Cretin-Derham High School in St. Paul, Minnesota, a wonderful school infused with the charisms of the Sisters of St. Joseph of Carondelet and the Christian Brothers. Since leaving that position, I continue to be the animator for a monthly Taizé prayer community there at their beautiful "Pax Christi" Chapel. I wish that when I was in high school I could have attended a school such as this, a school that beyond lip-service, is centered in Christ and sees that presence as intrinsic to every aspect of its life and mission.

"One Heart, One Mind" was composed for the liturgical celebrations of the CDH community, to reflect the mission embodied in their CASA program: an outreach effort, consisting of students, faculty and staff, that takes place in small group communities in the school. When this program was initiated, I was inspired by the school's efforts to be more connected with the students, and immediately, that wonderful line from Acts 4:32 came to my brain, speaking about the early Christian community that sought to be "of one heart and one mind." That image served as the impetus for this song, one I hoped could be not just a prayer for them during the sharing of Eucharistic communion at their school liturgies, but also a rallying cry for their mission to be their own unique Christian community, to and for each other.

While the refrain was to be seen as the umbrella message of who CDH was as a community, the first two verses were intended to illuminate the eight names or "titles" of the specific intentional communities that make up CASA at CDH: *Hope* ("grounded in hope"), *Faith* ("strong by faith"), *Joy* ("filled with joy"), *Peace* ("led in peace"), *Courage* ("courage lived"), *Wisdom* ("wisdom shared"), *Mercy* ("mercy shown"), and *Truth* ("truth be told"). These images are at the heart of what the earliest Christian communities ached for, and what we are called to lean into as the Church today. The remaining verses continue along the same lines, and this song quickly became one of their standard communion songs. It is one of the songs on my recorded collection, *God Is Everywhere!* along with a mass setting also composed originally for CDH (*Mass of Christ, Our Hope*), and other pieces that were part of their prayer life while I served there. Many of the talented young students who were part of the school liturgical choir during my time there are featured on the recording, and you can hear these young saints' wonderful faith in their singing.

The verse from the Acts of the Apostles that grounds the refrain is heard in the first reading for the Second Sunday of Easter (Year B); several of these sections from Acts make up an important part of the Liturgy of the Word for the entire Easter season each year. Years back I led a parish mission at a parish that began on this Sunday and was invited to preach the homily at the weekend masses. I chose to focus on this passage, which in its entirety, proclaims:

The community of believers was of one heart and mind,
and no one claimed that any of his possessions was his own,
but they had everything in common.

With great power the apostles bore witness
to the resurrection of the Lord Jesus,
and great favor was accorded them all.

There was no needy person among them,
for those who owned property or houses would sell them,
bring the proceeds of the sale,
and put them at the feet of the apostles,
and that were distributed to each according to need. (Acts 4:32-35)

I took time to reflect on these actions of the "community of believers." Consider their intention to renounce all their possessions and hold everything "in common," and their intentional sharing of riches and gift with each other "according to need." As a result, there would be "no needy person among them." I attempted to contrast this with how in far we are in our present day and age from embracing such values in our actions, our policies, and our politics; and how Easter is an invitation and a mandate to make real what rising from the dead concretely looks like if we are to call ourselves disciples.

After the mass was over, a very angry woman came up to me and said, "that's communism." My only response that I could come up with at the time was: "No, it's the word of the Lord." Now, I would add: "it is Easter." (11.19.17)

CD
MP3
Music

With You By My Side, Vol. 1: The Journey of Life
X-51710
G-5815

ONE MORE SONG

Music and Text:
David Haas

Time goes on far too fast;
and we wish these days would always last.
There comes a time, and here we are.
It is time to go and chase that star.
But together or apart, you are always in my heart,
    when I sing!

One more song,
    one more day to remember the times we've had,
    to celebrate the love that we've shared.
    One more time, one great prayer,
    and in hope we'll live a future
    where we will have a new song to sing!

As we go from this place,
I will always remember your face;
and how we must say "goodbye."
When I speak the words it's hard not to cry.
But together or apart, you are always in my heart,
    when I sing!

Stand with me, and we'll shine;
come and take my hand just one more time.
We will dance just once more;
let us sing our song like never before.
But together or apart, you are always in my heart,
    when I sing!

God our song!
God our light!
We will build a bright tomorrow
and live the dreams we hold now in our hearts!
Give us faith on the way,
to climb the highest mountain
and we'll become your new song to sing!

Copyright © 2002 GIA Publications, Inc.

Before I served as a part of the campus ministry team at Cretin-Derham Hall in St. Paul, I was a part time member of the staff at Benilde-St. Margaret's School in St. Louis Park, Minnesota for 13 years (1998–2011). I was so totally inspired by my wonderful friend Kate Cuddy, who was the choral music teacher there during this time, and by the marvelous ministry she offered as a teacher and advocate for her students. Kate's musical abilities had been obvious to me for some time at this point (pianist, vocalist, and arranger), but after attending a couple of the BSM choral concerts, I realized that she not only was a marvelous teacher who was able to pull out of her students the very best that they had in themselves, but she truly *loved* them in the deepest understanding of the word. She served as a true mentor and guide for her students, regardless of the level of their musical talent and regardless of how they were seen by their peers and other teachers at the school. It was this combination of gifts that she also brought while she was an integral team member for the *Music Ministry Alive!* program for most of its years.

After one of the concerts I attended, I remember going up to her and the BSM school president at time, James Hamburge, and said I would love to do whatever I could to help support the wonderful cause of the music program there. That resulted in me performing a benefit concert for the music program, and a year later I accepted a part time position as Campus Minister/Artist-In-Residence. It was a wonderful chapter of my life. Being able to work side by side with Kate and to be able to be a small part of the lives of so many wonderful students was very formative for me. I still keep in touch with some of those students, among them Michael Mahler, who is himself now a published composer with GIA Publications as well as a very successful actor, director, and composer of musical theatre.

"One More Song" was composed for the BSM graduating class of 2000

I WILL BRING YOU HOME

(which included Michael), as they completed their four years. Honestly, it is not a "liturgical" song. While participatory, is more of a musical celebration of young people and their connection and friendship with each other, offering their gratitude to God for leading them in their lives at this point of their journey. The recording of the song includes Michael and other BSM alums as soloists, and makes me smile every time I listen to it. I hope that it can continue to be an anthem for young people who are striking out beyond the cocoon of their school experience, grateful for what they have been given. (11.19.17)

Reach Toward Heaven;
Do Not Be Afraid, I Am With You
X-56611
G-6162

ONLY YOU

Music and text
for refrain:
David Haas
Text for verses:
Psalm 16 (alt. DH)

You, you, you, only you.

Protect me from fear, my trust is in you;
for you are my guardian, my happiness.
I find my delight in all that is yours,
in all that is yours on the earth.

My share and my cup, you draw out my lot,
and it pours out, without hesitation;
lovely indeed is my estate.
My home and my heart is joy beyond joy.

I bless you who brought me through to this day,
even at night, in tender times;
my trembling soul is tethered to you,
your presence is here, always here.

You will not abandon my soul to the dark,
the terror before me will not overwhelm me;
you will show me the path for my life,
your presence is joy, your hand my delight.

By now, it should be obvious in reading many of these stories and reflections that I love the Psalms. These ancient prayer-poems wed together my spiritual life with my vocation as a liturgical composer.

The psalms have an amazing universality, and they carry an equally amazing spiritual and psychological insight within them that touches upon every possible human emotion and life condition. They embody not only the more welcome attitudes of peace, wisdom, gratitude and comfort, but also the human dynamics of angst and anxiety of sadness, hopelessness, doubt, anger —and the demons of rage, revenge, violence and destruction. Some of the emotions and desires in these poems are not necessarily the actions of God, but how we sometimes *wish* God would act. This makes them so very real and human. Nothing escapes expression in the Psalms—it is all here, in these poems that speak not only to the Judaeo-Christian culture but also to many other religious traditions.

The psalms stretch across the entire history of the spiritual practices of Christianity, bringing us closer to the person of the historical Jesus than the writings found in the New Testament. We often forget that the writings of Paul, and even the gospels, were written well after the earthly life of Jesus. The earliest gospel to be written, Mark, was likely written not by an actual apostle or disciple of the earthly Jesus (the same is true for the other gospels and all of the other books in the New Testament), and it does not appear to have been written until around the years 70-75. So when we try to capture the actual literal spoken words of Jesus with only gospels as our source, any attempt at "absolute accuracy" is doomed to be anything but accurate at all.

The psalms give us a strong set of insights into the life of Jesus. Because Jesus was a Jew, many of these prayers would have been on his lips and in his heart—so here, we have words and sentiments that would have been central to his life. So while these are Jewish prayers, in the liturgy they help to inform and center our Christian faith. This understanding has changed forever not only how I have approached the psalms in my own spiritual life, but also how I understand them to function in the Liturgy of the Word at every celebration of the Eucharist. The responsorial psalm has not been tapped much in our liturgical planning or in our preaching, but yet, in these words we are given not only clues, but often a deep clarification about the central message of the gospel appointed for a particular celebration.

We are then able to see how the psalms are at the center of the official prayer of the Church, the *Liturgy of the Hours*. Living most of my life in the twin city area of Minnesota, I have been surrounded by this experience, primarily through the religious practices of the Benedictine monks at St. John's University in Collegeville, just an hour or so north of where I live. The daily pattern of prayer in monastic communities is centered in the psalms. The psalms are an amazing resource for meditation and contemplation, and the Judeo-Christian practice of chanting the psalms leads very naturally to the meditative practices of some non-Christian patterns of prayer—so much so that having spoken with more than one non-Christian, and after reading about and speaking with practitioners of Zen Buddhism, I have learned that many of them also see the psalms as a path to enlightenment.

It was out of my thinking about this, and my beginning experiences in meditation myself, that this setting of Psalm 16, "Only You" came to be. I have always been in love with this particular psalm, with its common cry of reaching to the "path of life," and I had already by this time composed versions of Psalm 16 twice before ("The Path of Life" from *Who Calls You by Name*, and "Show Me the Path," in the original collection of *Mass for the Life of the World*). Since I wanted to compose a psalm setting in a meditative-mantra style, the phrase, "you will show me the path of life" kept ringing in my heart. While I knew that the "path" was God, I wanted to find a way to address God directly, and with the intention of becoming immersed in this recognition, as a path to meditation. That is where I came up with the simple and direct address as "You," and the decision to have this be a repetitive thought.

Again, like the other two versions of Psalm 16 that I created, "Only You" is not chosen very often for liturgical use, from what I can tell. Maybe Psalm 16 and I just are not finding each other. I get teased by some about the refrain. Some find it boring; others I think, find it to be overly simplistic and a bit silly. But I still love Psalm 16, and this version remains my favorite of the three settings I have attempted. When I have led it at concerts or at Taizé services, it seems to achieve my desired effect, and *affect*. "Only You" is among the pieces of mine that, when I sing it, I am able to let go of the fact that I am the composer, and a result, I am able to pray. I hope others can as well. That would be enough for me. (11.21.16)

CD	No Longer Strangers; Without Seeing You: The Best of David Haas, Vol. 3; Glory Day: David Haas and Friends in Concert
MP3 Music	X-39008
	G-3954

ONWARD TO THE KINGDOM

Music:
MAIRI'S WEDDING
(Celtic Traditional)
Text:
David Haas

Sing we now, and on we go;
    God above, and God below;
Arm in arm, in love we go onward to the kingdom.

Star above to show the way,
    through the night and into day,
with the light we won't delay
    onward to the kingdom.

Come now sisters, brothers all,
    time to heed the Lord's call,
we will travel standing tall
    onward to the kingdom.

In the promised land we'll be one with God,
    where all are free,
the deaf will hear, the blind will see
    when we reach the kingdom.

"Onward to the Kingdom" is an original text of mine wedded to another wonderful Celtic melody. I heard somewhere that this tune originally was a drinking song. My friend and one among many mentors, Fr. Jim Dunning, used to say that Protestants cry in their beer; Catholics drink it. More accurately and verifiable, this tune is known by many as "Mairi's Wedding." There is some debate whether it is of Scottish or Irish origin; regardless, the words are familiar to many:

Chorus:
Step we gaily, on we go,
heel for heel and toe for toe.
Arm in arm and row on row,
all for Mairi's wedding.

Verses:
Over hillways, up and down,
myrtle green and bracken brown.
Past the shielings, through the town,
all for sake o' Mairi.

Red her cheeks as rowans are,
bright her eye as any star.
Fairest o' them all by far
is our darling Mairi.

Plenty herring, plenty meal,
plenty peat to fill her creel.
Plenty bonny bairns as well,
that's the toast for Mairi.

I first learned this song from John Gilmour, my guitar teacher from high school and my early college days, who is also the older brother of my best friend from back then, David Gilmour. The Gilmour family has been a well-known family for many years in my home town, Bridgeport, Michigan; John and David's parents grew up with my Dad when he was a youngster. John, brother Greg, and another friend of theirs, Mike Jahncke, had a group years ago called the "Gilmour Brothers," and they were local celebrities with their recordings and performances around the Michigan area and other parts of the Midwest (they still do annual reunion concerts together back in Bridgeport from time to time). They used to sing "Mairi's Wedding" all the time, and I always loved it, and years later I thought it would be a great tune for a liturgical song, because of the catchy melody that practically sings itself. There are many "covers" of the song and it has been interpreted in varied ways as well—sometimes as a very gentle song, and other times, it is presented in a very aggressive and upbeat manner. My version is somewhere in the middle, feel-wise, inspired by the approach the Gilmour Brothers presented. Whenever I sing "Onward to the Kingdom"

I WILL BRING YOU HOME

I remember the Gilmour Brothers, and am reminded of the Irish and Scottish blood that comes from my mother's side of the family.

I wanted this new text, "Onward to the Kingdom" to retain some of the images found in the original refrain, so I kept in some of the lines, "on we go" and "arm in arm"—that keep the united family theme moving, but instead of going "off to Mairi's wedding," we are going "onward to the kingdom," which is, actually, the great and final wedding feast of the reign of God. Because of the reference of the second verse regarding the "star above to show the way, through the night and into day, with the light we won't delay," many have chosen to use this song for the Feast of the Epiphany. I was not conscious of this when I wrote the words originally, but I can see how folks have made the connection. It then follows, in light of that epiphany—that manifestation—that the final verse of the "promised land," where we will all be "one with God, where all free, the deaf will hear, the blind will see when we reach the kingdom" provides a good conclusion to the message of the song.

I always enjoy singing and leading this song, and I can tell, not only by their singing, but through the joy on their faces, that the people seem to enjoy it as well. I just wish that more of it could come true, where all of us could truly move forward "arm in arm, in love" along the path that God provides us. We are told that the kingdom of God is within us. I know I need to do more to recognize that, and lock arms in love with the people of God to make the kingdom come. May it one day, be so. (11.12.17)

CD
MP3
Music

Reach Toward Heaven;
With You By My Side, Vol. 1: The Journey of Life;
Do Not Be Afraid, I Am With You
X-56613
G-5817

THE PEACE OF GOD

Music:
David Haas
Text:
Philippians 4:5-9
(alt. DH)

Let your gentleness be known,
so all may know the Lord is near.
Do not worry, do not worry;
reach out to God in prayer.
Stay with all that you have learned,
and all that you have heard and seen,
and the peace of God,
the peace of God will be with you.

Whatever is true,
whatever is just, all that is pure and pleasing
and all that is worthy of praise:
think on these things.

And the peace of God,
the peace of God beyond all understanding
will guard your hearts,
and guide your minds in Christ Jesus.

The morning of September 11, Helen and I were at home eating breakfast with our three house guests, Stephen Petrunak, Bobby Fisher, and Tom Franzak. They were in town along with Eileen Bird (who was staying with Lori True) to be part of a recording session that day for a new project. Just by accident, I turned on the TV, and our eyes became fixed on what was happening that morning. Unable to find adequate words or rational sense as to what was going on, some force was able to get us into the car and we drove to the studio, pretty much in silence. When we arrived, the others: Lori, Eileen, and three of my other musician friends, Dik Hedlund, Marc Anderson and Gordy Knudtson were already there with our engineer, Steve Wiese, watching the events as they continued to unfold on TV. We were paralyzed as to what to do. Should we continue on with the session or not? I remember it was Marc who finally said, "well, let's be about love today," and so we went and did the session, and all of the emotions we were feeling came through in our playing. The list of songs to record included a new version of "We Are Called," and I clearly remember Bobby Fisher playing the guitar solo filled with all of the angst we were feeling that day. It was through sheer determination of will that we got through that session. Tom, Bobby, Stephen and Eileen, soon after we finished, rented one of the few cars they could find (since all flights were cancelled) and left Minneapolis—they wanted and needed to be with their family, as so many did during those days.

"The Peace of God" was one of the songs for this project, and I believe we recorded it the very next day. I had already decided that I wanted the song to be intimate and not heavily arranged. I recorded the piano track, and sitting there with Lori we decided to do all of the vocals ourselves, just the two of us. So that is what you hear on the recording. It was our prayer amid the terror and pain that was going on during those days and long after. It has continued to be a prayer for me, as these words of comfort are words that I—that all of us—need to embrace in the most anxious of times. (11.25.17)

Glory Day: David Haas and Friends in Concert
X-39001
G-4745

PERFECT CHARITY

(Song Before the Cross)

Music:
David Haas
Text:
Inspired from the
"Prayer to the
Crucifix"
by St. Francis
of Assisi
(alt. DH)

Most High, Glorious God,
enlighten the darkness of my heart;
give me right faith, sure hope, and perfect charity.
Fill me with understanding and knowledge,
that I may fulfill your command.

Grant us your humility,
    and the fragrance of your most holy Word.
May we in your presence alone find our joy,
    which leads us all to you.

You alone take our burdens
    and clothe them in the blanket of your love.
May we share the treasure,
    and know the measure of the glory of your cross.

Save us from our pride,
    may we not exalt ourselves over one another.
Help us to seek simplicity,
    then we'll know the beauty
    of the promise that is you.

I have already shared elsewhere in this book that I hold a special place in my heart for St. Francis, and so this song gets to the heart of the Franciscan spirituality that I have come into contact with over the years (which include every flavor of Franciscan orders, including the Capuchins, the Conventual Franciscans, the Franciscan Sisters, the Poor Clares, the TOR's, and many Secular Franciscans— all of them).

I WILL BRING YOU HOME

It was 1996 and I was in the midst of intense planning for an upcoming made-for-TV production that was being produced by what was then St. Anthony Messenger Press (they are now "Franciscan Media") in Cincinnati, Ohio. An original idea of my editor there, Lisa Biedenbach, it was to be a concert held at Mount St. Joseph College that would feature my music, and it would be released as a video and a CD, produced and directed by Ron Riegler and Fr. Greg Friedman, OFM (it became *Glory Day: David Haas and Friends in Concert*). I was fortunate to have been given a budget that could include some of my favorite singer and instrumental friends: Lori True, Kate Cuddy, David Fischer, Derek Campbell, Tom Franzak, Gordy Knudtson, Marc Anderson, Kenni Holmen, Stephen Petrunak and Bobby Fisher, not to mention a great group of dancers led by the inexhaustible Bob Piercy, which included Joe Camacho, Jean Bross-Judge, and Donna Anderle, as well as my young friend, Sarah Hudetz. The technical aspects of the event included a six-person camera crew, sound people, make-up artists—everything, as they say, but the kitchen sink.

While making the musical choices for this event, I realized that what was missing in the lineup was a song inspired by St. Francis. Since it was an event bearing the Franciscan banner, I wanted to write something to honor their patron, something that would serve as a musical "opening prayer" for the concert. So I composed "Perfect Charity," based on Francis' well-known "Prayer Before the Crucifix." The words of the refrain, word for word, make up this prayer that Francis used to recite during 1205-1206 while he was discerning his vocation. He would do so in a small abandoned church of San Damiano, outside the borders of Assisi. The Byzantine crucifix he prayed before is now venerated in the Basilica of Santa Chiara in Assisi; it has been replicated as an important icon and symbol for Franciscans around the world. It was before this cross that Francis would offer this prayer, and Franciscan scholars believe these are the earliest words that we have from him. These words truly set the tone and charism of Francis' entire life—a life dedicated to simplicity, prayer, poverty, and wisdom—all expressing the eagerness to serve the will of God. It is a prayer of surrender that profoundly accepts who God is, and who we are.

Many people do not know of this song, since it only appears as the beginning of the *Glory Day* concert CD and video. I have thought from time to time that I should do a recording and music project dedicated to St. Francis. Maybe someday. I also have never been able to visit Assisi. I really hope I can get there someday. While the song is dedicated to Lisa Biedenbach and the people who were then part of the St. Anthony Messenger Press family, I also offer it also as a prayer of thanksgiving for all of my Franciscan friends—especially Fr. Peter

Damian Massengill, OFM Conv; Fr. Bob Hutmacher, OFM; Sr. Delores Rocker, OSF; Fr. Richard Rohr, OFM; Fr. Dan Horan, OFM; Fr. Ed Foley, OFM Cap.; Bro. Rufino Zaragoza, OFM; Fr. Chuck Faso, OFM; Fr Greg Friedman, OFM; Fr. Jeremey Harrington, OFM, and the memory of the well- known author, Fr. Michael Crosby, OFM Cap. God bless the Franciscans! (11.25.17)

CD

MP3
Music

As Water to the Thirsty; Walking by Faith;
Glory Day: David Haas and Friends in Concert;
Blest Are They: The Best of David Haas, Vol. 1
X-17712
G-3505

PRAYER FOR PEACE

**Music and Text:
David Haas;
Inspired from a
Navajo Blessing**

Peace before us, peace behind us,
    peace under our feet.
Peace within us, peace over us,
    let all around us be peace.

Love before us, love behind us, love under our feet.
Love within us, love over us, let all around us be love.

Light before us, light behind us,
    light under our feet.
Light within us, light over us,
    let all around us be light.

Christ before us, Christ behind us,
    Christ under our feet.
Christ within us, Christ over us,
    let all around us be Christ.

Alleluia!

Peace before us, peace behind us,
    peace under our feet.
Peace within us, peace over us,
    let all around us be peace.

"Prayer for Peace," was inspired by a greeting card that I came across while I was a guest of Marty and Linda Haugen in the midst of their sabbatical year at

Music & Stories PRAYER FOR PEACE

Holden Village (1985-1986), near Lake Chelan in Washington State. Holden Village is an intentional community of the Evangelical Lutheran Church in America (ELCA) and during this time, Marty served as their "Village Musician." The village is located high in the Cascade Mountain region and is quite isolated; there was no phone service, TV or other modern communication technology. It was the first and last time I ever went cross country skiing. Also, in one of their buildings, the village community had a gorgeous nine-foot grand piano, and I spent many hours during my visit playing and composing at this beautiful instrument in the private and quiet time I was able to enjoy. I found out that the prayer on the card was a Navajo prayer, and it was translated as:

Peace before me
Peace behind me
Peace under my feet
Peace within me
Peace over me
May I be surrounded in peace

This immediately became the message of a song, which I then adapted, moving the "me" to "us," and then I added additional verses with the message of love, light, and Christ. It was created to be very, very simple; almost mantra-like, and over the years it became a closing song for many of my concerts.

After the song was recorded and published in 1987, it was brought to my attention that the original prayer actually does not say "peace," but rather, "beauty." Here is a rendering of the original blessing that I was able to come across:

In beauty I walk
With beauty before me I walk
With beauty behind me I walk
With beauty above me I walk
With beauty around me I walk
It has become beauty again

Hózhóogo naasháa doo
Shitsijí' hózhóogo naasháa doo
Shikéédéé hózhóogo naasháa doo
Shideigi hózhóogo naasháa doo

I WILL BRING YOU HOME

T'áá altso shinaagóó hózhóogo naasháa doo
Hózhó nastily' Hózhó náhásdlíí'
Hózhó náhásdlíí' Hózhó náhásdlíí'

Today I will walk out, today everything negative will leave me
I will be as I was before, I will have a cool breeze over my body.
I will have a light body, I will be happy forever, nothing will hinder me.
I walk with beauty before me. I walk with beauty behind me.
I walk with beauty below me. I walk with beauty above me.
I walk with beauty around me. My words will be beautiful.

In beauty all day long may I walk.
Through the returning seasons, may I walk.
On the trail marked with pollen may I walk.
With dew about my feet, may I walk.
With beauty before me may I walk.
With beauty behind me may I walk.
With beauty below me may I walk.
With beauty above me may I walk.
With beauty all around me may I walk.

In old age wandering on a trail of beauty, lively, may I walk.
In old age wandering on a trail of beauty, living again, may I walk.
My words will be beautiful...

In digging even deeper, I came to learn that this blessing is a celebration of balance in one's life alongside the presence of beauty that is embodied in the nature of the universe, the world, all of humanity, and the nature of time, space, creation, growth, motion, order, and control. This is all part of the cycle of life. And while my piece was composed, recorded and published before I knew all of this—I have come to see that the images of peace and beauty are most certainly consonant with each other. To be people who embrace peace, love, light and the risen Christ—is to be people caught up in the "beauty" of God.

Among the many joys that have come with this song is that it has become a favorite for children's choirs, and it also has been interpreted beautifully in ASL (American Sign Language). Every time I have sung it with others proclaiming the same words in this beautiful language, it brings me to tears. I am amazed how various cultural groups have adapted some of my songs over the years, and this song has been among them. My favorite cultural adaption of "Prayer for Peace" has been witnessing the beautiful dance that my friend from Hawaii, Joe Camacho, created for this song through his cultural language of ancient hula. You can see Joe's wonderful gift with this in the version of "Prayer for Peace" that features him on the video of *Glory Day: David Haas and Friends in Concert*— produced as a DVD from Franciscan Media.

I still hold a very strong memory of when we recorded the song in 1987, and included it on the *As Water to the Thirsty* collection, at Metro Studios in Minneapolis. I decided to dedicate an entire evening to record the song, including some of my favorite people from many different walks of my life— some of them musicians, some of them not. We shared a catered meal, followed by what I would call a musical "prayer meeting" with these 70 plus people who stood on risers before me. We prayed for peace that evening. It is captured on the recording when you hear the throngs of people singing throughout. Featured soloist friends included John Foley, Jo Infante, Bob Hurd, Jeanne Cotter and local Minneapolis jazz vocalist, Susan Oatts Tucker. The tenor and bass vocal "mantra" that you hear on the "Alleluia" verse was my friend Bob Harvey and I, singing both parts about 20 times over and over as overdubs. It took a long time, but it was fun. I also added some vocal overdubs as free flowing descants on the "outro" of the song, and a Native American drum to give reverence to the roots of the song. I remember that evening with such gratitude, and every time I hear the track, I get taken back to those sessions.

Peace still seems so elusive in our lives. In fact, it seems that its ability to reign above the darker forces of war, racism, hatred, discrimination and intolerance of every kind, becomes drowned out. We need more than just 70-some voices. We need the voices of all of creation to sing, pray, and dance the message and hope that only peace can provide, a peace that comes with embracing the Spirit of God. (11.19.17)

CD
MP3
Music

Living Spirit, Holy Fire, Vol. 1
X-71621
G-7668

PRAY THROUGH US, HOLY SPIRIT

Music:
David Haas
Text:
Mary Louise Bringle

Pray through us, Holy Spirit,
   with deep and wordless sighs,
from fainted whispers of daybreak
   to the hush of evening skies.

Pray through us, Holy Spirit,
   in shimmers of delight
that spark our joy in creation
   —gifts of touch and sound and light.

Pray through us, Holy Spirit,
   when anxious and distressed,
until we lay down our burdens
   in your arms of quiet rest.

Pray through us, Holy Spirit,
   for frail and troubled lands,
so we may aid in their healing
   and enact what Love commands.

Pray through us, Holy Spirit,
   that till our labors cease
we may draw strength from your goodness
   and unfurl your wings of peace.

The text for this hymn was created by Mary Louise (Mel) Bringle, a highly revered text writer, theologian and professor from North Carolina. Mel's texts appear in many hymnals in the English-speaking world, and composers of various denominations—such as Marty Haugen, Lori True, Tony Alonso and many others—have created musical settings of her words. I have set several as well, and I have to say this is one of my favorites.

What grabbed me about this text was the use of the word *through*. In our prayer piety many of us speak about praying *to* the Spirit, and *in* the Spirit ... but in the tradition of intercessory prayer, here we call upon the Spirit to pray "through" us. I believe this is also a very healthy and fresh way to think about our devotion to the saints.

Also, when we think of the Holy Spirit, we of course honor it as part of our devotion to and doctrine of the Trinity. We also employ this third person of the Trinity when we think of people who inspire us. We speak of someone being "Spirit-filled," or "Spirit-led," or "Spirit-driven." These are wonderful ways to honor how the divine works in people. Prayer centered people are people who allow the Spirit to dwell in their hearts and minds, and through that indwelling, their prayer is already heard, already part of the holy conversation, already being received. This opening and indwelling becomes a part of who we are, opening the eyes of our mind to listen to God's answer. When we cannot find the words to adequately express our thoughts, our desires, and our hopes—the Spirit takes over, and prays through us, as Paul affirms:

"... the Spirit helps us in our weakness;
for we do not know how to pray as we ought,
but that very Spirit intercedes with sighs too deep for words.
And God, who searches the heart,
knows what is the mind of the Spirit,
because the Spirit
intercedes for the saints according to the will of God" (Romans 8: 26-27)

Mel's insight here is that we do not so much offer our own prayers, but rather, recognize that these prayers of the Holy Spirit already dwell in our hearts, made manifest in and through us.

This raises for me issues and questions about the Sacrament of Confirmation, which some have said is a sacrament still in search of a theology, at least as it is practiced in much of the Roman Catholic sacramental system. The way in which Confirmation programs and rituals are experienced often reveals an incomplete understanding of the Spirit and a lack of clarity around what exactly is "happening" in the sacrament, especially for young people. When the Bishop lays hands on the confirmandi, the words spoken are, "receive the Holy Spirit." Art Zannoni, a theologian and scripture scholar, (and my Hebrew Scriptures professor when I studied theology) shared that what is happening in this ritual act of laying of hands, is that rather than magically infusing the Holy Spirit into the person of the "confirmand," the Bishop, in the name of the gathered assembly (that would mean, the Church, the Body of Christ), is calling for the Spirit to be "released" rather than "received." In other words, the Spirit of God is already *there and present* in this baptized person. Sadly, we reduce Confirmation to being the event where people "get the Spirit." What all of the Sacraments of Initiation (Baptism, Confirmation, Eucharist) proclaim, is that the Spirit of God is *already present,* moving; stirring in our lives. Confirmation is when we, in an intentional and focused way, call upon, the Spirit to be "released," so that they—and we—can all live, pray, and act "through the power of the Holy Spirit."

From time to time, I pause to reflect and meditate on these powerful words from Mel Bringle. I invite all of you to do so as well. Take some time and linger on this text and allow the Spirit, which most certainly worked "through" Mel in crafting this text, come and work and pray "through" us. (11.19.17)

	Psalms for the Church Year	
CD	Vol. 1	X-80323
MP3		G-4749
Music		
MP3	Vol. 3	X-21200
Music		G-3325
MP3	Vol. 8	X-38700
Music		G-4579
MP3	Vol. 9	X-43000
Music		G-5041

PSALMS FOR THE CHURCH YEAR

Volume One:
Marty Haugen
and David Haas

Volume Three:
David Haas
and Jeanne Cotter

Volume Eight:
David Haas

Volume Nine:
David Haas

Psalms for the Church Year came to birth in the early 1980s, during the time that I was Director of Music and Liturgy at St. Thomas Aquinas in St. Paul Park, Minnesota, and while Marty Haugen was Director of Music at St. Bonaventure Parish not far away in Bloomington. Marty and I had been friends now for about two years, and this was the beginning of the days when he and I, along with Michael Joncas, would gather together on a somewhat regular basis to share music and offer critique and support. Out of our own yearning to locate good responsorial psalm settings that were composed in a more contemporary style, Marty and I were busy composing psalms for our parish liturgies, and we began to talk about pulling them together to begin a new resource of our own, focusing on the common/seasonal responsorial psalms that are presented in the Lectionary, created with accompaniments that would work equally well on the piano (which was still a relatively new instrument to be utilized in the liturgy at the time) or the guitar—or the two in combination with each other.

We both were admirers of "Psalms for Feasts and Seasons" by the Australian composer, Christopher Willcock, SJ, containing the seasonal psalms in a more "classical" style. We used this as our template. Between the two of us we already had most of these appointed psalms set to music. They were already tested and utilized in our parishes. We decided we would fill out the resource by composing the remaining psalms needed, and also include settings for Holy Thursday and Good Friday. It was from this design that *Psalms for the Church Year* came to be. Marty already had two recorded and published collections with GIA ("With

I WILL BRING YOU HOME

Open Hands" and "Gather Us In"), but for me, this would be my maiden voyage in having my music published by GIA.

It was the very first publication to be released under the banner of the "Celebration Series" that continues to this day from GIA. Some people still refer to this first volume as the "Celebration Psalms." After it was released it took off like wild-fire, and it continues to be a staple resource for many pastoral musicians. Due to its popularity, Marty developed a second volume in 1988; Jeanne Cotter and I followed up with a third collection the following year. Over the years other composers added to the series, such as Rory Cooney, Gary Daigle, Roy James Stewart, Malcom Kogut, John Foley and the Dameans. I came back to the series in 1997 and 1999 with Volumes 8 and 9.

From the very first volume—still the biggest "seller" among all of the volumes— some of Marty's most beloved psalms that stand out are his two Advent psalms: "To You, O Lord" (Psalm 25) and "Let Us See Your Kindness" (Psalm 85); "Be Merciful, O Lord" (Psalm 51 for Lent); his two wonderful Easter Psalms, "Let All the Earth" (Psalm 66) and "Let Us Rejoice!" (Psalm 118); and "Taste and See" (Psalm 34) and "Your Love is Finer than Life" (Psalm 63). These have all become classics.

Of my included psalm settings, the Ordinary Time psalms seem to pop out. "Lord, You Have the Words" (Psalm 19) was intended to be a very simple rendering, composed after the father of Kathy Rustin (one of the parish cantors at St. Thomas Aquinas) had passed away. While Psalm 19 with this refrain is not one of the appointed psalms for funerals, I kept thinking that the "words of everlasting life" provides a central source of comfort for those who are grieving.

Out of all my contributions to this volume, "The Lord is My Light" (Psalm 27) is the best-known, in use by not only Catholics but Protestants as well. Psalm 27 has always been a favorite among the psalms in my own prayer life. If memory serves, this was my first attempt at doing anything other than "stacking" the same melody for each of the verses, shaping the text to fit the existing tune. The final verse ("I believe I shall see the goodness of the Lord in the land of the living …") seemed to cry out for something a bit bolder and proclamatory; it really seems to me to be a profession of faith. I remember this being the psalm that I sang to myself as I was being wheeled into the operating room when I had heart surgery years ago … and it continued to be the psalm that I sang to myself when I had to start working on the treadmill during the recovery time that followed (as I write this, I am feeling the pangs of challenge—that I need to get back to that treadmill). "I Will Praise Your Name" (Psalm 145) has been included in several hymnals as well over the years, and famous for that surprise

2/4 measure that takes place in the middle of the verse. Some like it, for some it drives them crazy. I like it.

My setting of Psalm 95, "If Today You Hear God's Voice," has also proved to be popular, and this is a special piece for me, because it is dedicated to my sister, Colleen. Many have noticed at the top of the page that it is dedicated to "Toosie" Haas. "Toosie" and Colleen are the same person, the former being a nickname she was given by my father when she was a little girl; it stuck for a while. The story is too long to tell. Suffice it to say, she does not go by that name anymore. She is most definitely, and eternally will be—Colleen. So if you ever meet her, remember that.

"We Are God's People" (Psalm 100) was my very first attempt to compose a "Taizé-like" piece, featuring an ostinato refrain with verses accompanying it simultaneously. The verses demand a bit of vocal prowess, but they are fun to sing for cantors once they get the hang of it. I have found that many have been a bit squeamish to actually sing "We Are God's People" in the way that I intended it, and so they do it in the traditional manner, of the refrain and the verses being sung alone, without the yoking together. Both Psalm 95 and 100 are appointed and classic psalms to be sung for celebrations of morning prayer, and I have experienced both of these settings in that prayer environment.

One of the most popular and commonly used settings from Volume One is the Christmas psalm, "All the Ends of the Earth" (Psalm 98) that is listed as a collaboration of both Marty and me. People ask from time to time how this collaboration took place. It is an interesting story. When Marty and I were working on this project we discovered that each of us had our own version of Psalm 98. The coincidence that we discovered was that both settings were composed in 6/8 time. As we looked at both, we thought my refrain had a shine to it, and Marty's verses of his setting had a very engaging movement both melodically and rhythmically, and so, yes—you guessed it—we just pasted the two together! So that is how the "collaboration" happened. Not the usual, typical or recommended way to collaborate … but it worked.

Marty's Volume 2 includes some wonderful settings that have also become a part of the repertoire for many parishes, especially "You Will Show Me the Path of Life" (Psalm 16), and of course, his iconic "Shepherd Me, O God" (Psalm 23). Both Michael and I have stated many times how we wished we could have written this! Truly a gift of prayer to the Church. Other stand-outs from Volume 2 include "Let Your Mercy Be on Us" (Psalm 33), "Lord, Make us Turn to You" (Psalm 80), "God Has Done Great Things for Us" (Psalm 126), "Blest are Those who Love You" (Psalm 128), "Bless the Lord, My Soul" (Psalm

147), and his setting of the Isaiah 12 canticle, "With Joy You Shall Water," that seems to visit most Easter Vigil celebrations.

The third volume that Jeanne and I put together includes her gorgeous setting of the lament "Let My Tongue Be Silenced" (Psalm 137). It is not widely known, and if you are not aware of it, get thee to it right away. It is one of her best liturgical compositions ever, in my opinion. Of my offerings in this volume, some that have gotten attention are four psalms that I share stories about elsewhere in this book, "The Name of God" (Psalm 116), "They Who Do Justice" (Psalm 15), "The Fragrance of Christ" (Psalm 138), "In God Alone" (Psalm 62), and my setting of Psalm 51, "Create in Me," where I utilize some fun chromaticism.

Years later I put together Volumes 8 and 9, which contain several psalms that are appointed for particular celebrations. "The Lord Will Bless All People" (Psalm 29), composed in a "Taizé" fashion, is composed specifically for the Baptism of the Lord or to be used as a piece during the sprinkling rite. The version of Psalm 25, "To You, O Lord," utilizes the chant melody of "O Come, O Come Emmanuel" for when this psalm appears during the Advent Season. "Everlasting Grace Is Yours" (Psalm 136) tries to honor the internal litany-like nature of the verses, with a call and response format, and I heard it as a bit more "folky" in this version. Again, for the Easter Vigil.

There are two different versions of Psalm 117 (this psalm happens to be the shortest in length of all of the psalms in the Psalter) in these two volumes: "Go Out to All the World," followed by "You Will Be My Witnesses," which I originally composed for celebrations of Confirmation. A personal favorite of mine is "Our Eyes Rest on You," a setting of Psalm 123 utilizing one of the beautiful translations from the ICEL *Liturgical Psalter*. The usual refrain we hear for this is "Our eyes are fixed ..." and I just love the image of our eyes being able to "rest" on God. Just love it. "God Is Ever Wakeful" (Psalm 121), "As Long As I Live" (Psalm 146), and "I Call to You, God" (Psalm 17) also utilize the ICEL translation, which sadly, is no longer available as a published resource.

"Throughout All Time" (Psalm 89) is a personal favorite of mine, and is also featured separately in this book. Another favorite is my setting of Psalm 119, "How I Love Your Commands," that holds some big vocal leaps in the verses. Cantors have cursed me from time to time when they have had to sing this, but at the same time they tell me how much they love the melody. Temperamental cantors—go figure (usually sopranos—I'm just sayin'). For those looking for an upbeat psalm of praise, check out my version of Psalm 148, "Praise in the Heights."

"Psalms for the Church Year," in particular the very first volume, served as the beginning of a lifetime of discovering and exploring musical ways to express the power, diversity and beauty of these ancient prayer-poems. To this day, Marty and I continue to compose new settings of the psalms, and we have furthered this passion in two resources that have been released in recent years, especially with the advent of the newer revised "Grail" translation that is now approved for use with the Lectionary. Marty has collaborated with Tony Alonso on a four-volume series entitled "Lyric Psalms," and I, together with Lori True, Paul Tate, Stephen Pishner, and Sr. Kathleen Harmon, more recently produced a four-volume series of settings of responsorial psalms (along with musical versions of gospel acclamations and the universal prayers, entitled *Cry Out with Joy*, that is also addressed in this book). Both resources are available from GIA.

I am grateful to Marty and GIA for the process in creating and for the ongoing popularity of the *Psalms for the Church Year* endeavor. Some of have said that the first volume has set the standard for contemporary composers in their approaching creating settings of the psalms. I am not sure if is the standard, but I am proud of our taking on this wonderful project, and happy that it has served people's prayer so well. (12.18.17)

CD

MP3
Music

To Be Your Bread; Come and Journey;
Blest Are They: The Best of David Haas, Vol. 1;
With Gratitude
X-100613
G-3340

SEND US YOUR SPIRIT

**Music and Text:
David Haas**

Come Lord Jesus,
send us your Spirit, renew the face of the earth.
Come Lord Jesus,
send us your Spirit, renew the face of the earth.

Come to us, Spirit of God,
breathe in us now, we sing together;
Spirit of hope and of Light, fill our lives,
come to us, Spirit of God!

Fill us with the fire of your love,
burn in us now, bring us together;
Come to us, dwell in us,
    change our lives, O Lord,
come to us, Spirit of God!

Send us the wings of new birth,
fill all the earth with the love
    you have taught us;
Let all creation now be shaken with love,
come to us, Spirit of God!

This is an "oldie," written while I was still in the seminary, and during a time when I was playing the guitar more often than I do now. During my high school and early college days I played a lot of John Denver songs, along with those of Peter, Paul and Mary, Gordon Lightfoot, James Taylor, Jim Croce and the more "folky" songs by the Beatles, like "Blackbird," "Mother Nature's Son,"

"I've Just Seen a Face," and "Two of Us." "Send Us Your Spirit" is very Denver-esque, influenced by his chord progressions and singable melodies, as well as an his outlook that always seemed to me to be very optimistic and packed with a sense of lift. The chord progression on the refrain of "Send Us Your Spirit" is exactly the same as the opening pattern in "Rocky Mountain High," with the same open D-tuning and Capo 2. Also, the first two chords of the verses were inspired from the chords John Foley utilized in his "Take Lord, Receive," one of the many songs of the St. Louis Jesuits that we played and sang at campus liturgies at the University of St. Thomas. While at St. Thomas, I used to sing for a lot coffee-house types of gigs on campus, so this song resonates with the kind of music I was making when I was not studying classical voice and theology.

This song echoes my own sense of renewal and spiritual search during this time. I was trying to discern whether or not to remain in the seminary and pursue that course, or whether I was called to something else, to focus more on a vocation as a liturgical musician. It was becoming more and more evident that the ordained priesthood was not what I was being called to. But I was sure that I wanted to be in ministry in some fashion, to and for the service of the Church. At that time, more and more parishes were hiring people to serve as pastoral musicians and liturgists as full-time ministers, so that began to appeal to me as I was finishing up most of my theology study.

This song, together with another song I wrote during this period ("To Be Your Bread") was utilized a lot during this time on campus, because of Rob Strusinski, who was the director of liturgical music for campus ministry and conductor of the St. Thomas Liturgical Choir. The very first recording of this song (and of "To Be Your Bread") was actually part of a recorded LP titled *In Song* that Rob coordinated with the Liturgical Choir, featuring composers (other students, faculty and alumni) who had a connection with the campus community during that time, like Michael Joncas, Dan Kantor, James Callahan, Ron Noecker, Michael Rumpza, Jay McHale, Paul Rysavy, and myself—recorded in the beautiful acoustically friendly St. Mary's Chapel at the St. Paul Seminary School of Divinity.

The LP used to be available from the Liturgical Press, but now you probably can only find it on E-Bay. I have a couple of copies, thank goodness. Rob was such an advocate for so many of us young composers in our first attempts at liturgical composition; he became a great colleague and a good personal friend, and has continued to be so over the years. The song is dedicated to him.

The song probably should have been titled "Come, Lord Jesus," because many people have continued to name it so for a long time, since this is the opening lyric of the refrain. It has worked best as a gathering song for Pentecost, celebrations of Confirmation, and other liturgies that focus on the Holy Spirit.

"Send Us Your Spirit" was always one of the usual opening songs for concerts that I did over the years with Michael Joncas and Marty Haugen, and is one of the featured songs on the *Come and Journey* live concert recording, where you can hear us singing the third verse, a la Crosby, Stills and Nash. That was always fun to do. I still like using it as an opening song for concerts that I present alone, and I always love hearing the people sing the refrain as a round. Children seem to like it as well.

My favorite part of the song is in the third verse: "Send us the wings of new birth; fill all the earth with the love you have taught us. Let all creation now be shaken with love…"

Come, Holy Spirit…shake us up. (11.14.17)

CD

MP3
Music

Throughout All Time;
God Has Done Marvelous Things;
Glory Day: David Haas and Friends in Concert;
Without Seeing You: The Best of David Haas, Vol. 3
X-80513
G-4734

SHARE YOUR BREAD WITH THE HUNGRY

Music:
David Haas
Text:
Isaiah 58:7-10
(alt. DH)

Clothe the naked and take them to your care;
do not turn your back on your own.
Then your light shall break forth like the dawn,
and your wounds will be bound and healed.

If you share your bread with the hungry,
if you welcome the poor to your home,
then your light will shine, your light will shine,
and the sun will rise once more.

And your dignity shall go forth before you,
and the glory of God shall keep you safe.
Then you shall call and God will answer,
you will cry and God will be there.

If you remove all oppression from your midst,
and the shame of those who do you harm.
If you offer your bread to the hungry,
your God will dwell with you.

This song was highly influenced, both musically and in terms of message, by the music and ministry of my brother in the Lord, Tom Franzak—particularly his marvelous song-prayer, "Unless a Grain" (the keyboard accompaniment on these verses is very reminiscent of Tom's song). "Share Your Bread with the Hungry" is a setting of Isaiah 58: 7-10, a passage that gets to the heart of the matter without any lack of clarity.

Isaiah is arguably the most known and read of the Hebrew prophetic writers from the Old Testament scriptures. We may have to do some "un-learning" with regard to how we think of prophets in the biblical tradition. The ancients who wrote these texts and, those who first read and heard them, understood that a "prophet" was not someone who could predict the future, nor were they people to label as fortune tellers. In the biblical understanding, a prophet is a "spokesperson for God." Through them, we are hearing and witnessing God's presence and God's vision for our lives.

These prophets are not only known in the scriptures—we have them all around us. We can identify who they are in our lives, these people whom we often claim to be "prophetic" in both and large and small ways. We certainly can say this in regards to many of the saints for whom we might have a strong devotion. Even today, such prophets are among us. For myself the prophetic people who have most certainly been "spokespersons for God" would include people like John XXIII, Thomas Merton, Henri Nouwen, Dorothy Day, Oscar Romero, Peter Maurin, Bishop Kenneth Untener, Martin Luther King Jr., Christianne Brusselmans, Fr. Jim Dunning, Marcus Borg, Sr. Dorothy Stang, Ceasar Chavez, Harvey Milk, and living saints (they are in my humble and correct opinion) such as Sr. Helen Prejean, Fr. Richard Rohr, Sr. Joan Chittister, Fr. Ron Rohlheiser, Bill Huebsch, Jim Wallis, Sr. Elizabeth Johnson, Fr. Greg Boyle, Megan McKenna, Leonardo Boff, Fr. Jim Martin, Bishop Remi de Roo … Everyone reading this has people whom they have found to be "spokespersons for God" in their life. Among them are also people who may not have achieved any sort of celebrity, but who, most powerfully, have witnessed and spoken on God's behalf.

There are two different recordings of this song, included on *God Has Done Marvelous Things,* and *Glory Day.* I love them both because they feature some of my favorite singers who I have worked with over the years. On the *Glory Day* version, of course I love hearing Tom sing the first verse. Lori True brings an amazing power and skill not only vocally, but in communicating the message of the second verse. And then there is David Fischer (who sings the third verse on both versions) and Larry Hylton (featured on the *Marvelous Things* version), who embody true "Tenor-power" on the final and concluding verse and refrain. Great singing on these tracks, and then you add Bobby Fisher's truly "prophetic" guitar solo on both performances … well, I have no words. Love it.

In plain English, this passage contains a core "curriculum" for those of us who want to discover and explore God's will. Isaiah is our professor here. Isaiah's words here are God's words. The question might be, what does God's reign look like? Well, it looks like what we hear and sing in this most holy scripture: the naked are taken care of and not left alone, wounds are healed, the poor are lifted up; prayers are answered, dignity to those disdained is restored, those without food are hungry no longer; oppression is defeated, all shame is driven away—and we are to become God's instruments, God's "spokespersons," who illuminate the light that will shine. This song attempts to "sing" Isaiah's announcement and is intended to be an anthem that awakens our inaction, leading us to become this shining sun, a sun producing a blinding light that can never turn into darkness. (11.19.17)

CD
MP3
Music

Where the River Flows
X-34903
G–4338

SONG FOR THE JOURNEY

Music:
FAREWELL TO
NOVA SCOTIA
(Canadian Traditional,
adapt. DH)
Text:
David Haas

We stand with hopeful eyes facing to the sun,
with our hands and hearts, we will work and pray,
and together we will sing as we travel on our way:
we will walk in the light of our God today!

We stumble while blind, groping in the dark
and we come to wash in the pool of life!
Anointed by God, may the Spirit take flight,
as we seek to serve all people
    with the gift of light!

When trapped by our bondage
    and the grip of our fear
a voice within comes to bring us home!
And may we be free with the prize of new birth,
for our God comes to the rescue
    and renews the earth!

With hearts filled with hope
    and our eyes charged with fire,
we will live as saints, and be born again!
Looking forward, never back,
    with our heads held high,
we will dance and dream
    the reign of God and never die!

Music & Stories SONG FOR THE JOURNEY

The melody for this song is the well-known folk anthem for Canadians, "Farewell to Nova Scotia." Here are the words from the popular refrain:

Farewell to Nova Scotia and your sea bound coast;
Let your mountains dark and dreary be.
When I am far away on the briny oceans tossed,
will you ever have a sigh or a wish for me?

While the lyrics for the majority of these folk tunes are anything but religious, there is something about the intrinsic magic of their melodies that just cries out to be sung. The genius of "anonymous," that great tune writer who has written literally thousands of the most engaging melodies, has been a true gift for composers and text writers of sacred song. To my thinking, this tune is another example of this genius, and so, I could not help myself.

"Song for the Journey" was originally intended as a song to be sung during the season of Lent, in the midst of the celebrations of the scrutinies that occur on the third, fourth, and fifth Sundays during this time. The refrain has an optimistic tone, one of journey and hope, centered in the Lenten practices of prayer, fasting, and almsgiving: "… with our hands and hearts we will work and pray." The verses blend together the Gospel themes and images found in the Year A readings for this season: the story of the Samaritan woman: "… we come to wash in the pool of life"; the passage sharing the journey of the man born blind: "… we stumble while blind groping in the dark … we seek to serve all people with the gift of life"; and the dramatic story of the raising of Lazarus (a name which some scholars have translated as "*God to the rescue*"): "When trapped by our bondage and the grip of our fear, a voice within comes to bring us home … for our God comes to the rescue to renew the earth."

However, while this song may be "initiation focused," I hope that it can be seen as a song of renewal and hope for all of us. That is the intention of the scrutinies. The initiation rites —as well as all sacramental celebrations—are for the entire Body of Christ. *The Rite of Christian Initiation of Adults* makes this clear throughout the ritual text, and in the case of the season of Lent, it is concrete: "For both the elect and the local community … the Lenten season is a time for spiritual recollection in preparation of the paschal mystery" (From the RCIA, n. 138). When speaking about the Scrutinies themselves, the ritual text underlines their importance and centrality during this season, again, not only for the candidates for initiation, but for the church as a body: "… the scrutinies are meant to uncover, then heal, all that is weak, defective, or sinful … to bring out, then strengthen all that is upright, strong, and good" (RCIA, n. 141).

This initiation journey is the journey for all of us, all leading toward a deeper conversion: "Looking forward, never back, with our heads held high, we will dance and dream the reign of God and never die!" This is what Lent, ultimately is to do—it is not merely a season of self-examination as an end in itself. Its mission is to lead us all toward Easter. May this song and all of our sung prayer, seek to do the same. (12.12.17)

CD
MP3
Music

Living Spirit, Holy Fire, Vol. 1
X-71601
G-7664

SONG OF THE ANOINTED

Music:
David Haas
Text:
David Haas;
inspired by
Isaiah 61:1-3 and
The Liturgy
of the Hours

Come, Holy Spirit, fill the hearts of your faithful;
enkindle in them the fire of your love.
Send forth your Spirit, they are created,
you shall renew the face of the earth.

The Spirit of God is deep within me,
for the hand of the Lord has anointed me!

To bring forth to all the lowly and poor
sweet tidings of joy to heal the broken of heart!

To sing liberty for all those in chains,
release from their pain; a year of favor is here!

To comfort and raise from ashes to life,
anointing with joy,
    proclaiming gladness and hope!

A mantle of praise: our spirit renewed;
the glory of God blooming
    with justice and peace!

One of my heroes in the early days of sung prayer that came on the heels of Vatican II was the French priest, Fr. Lucien Deiss (1921-2007). I was so blest to have met and talked with him a few times before he died. He was a joyful man, and he was most affirming of my early compositions. For a young liturgical composer, it is difficult to articulate how important such support means, especially when coming from a true pioneer. I remember well the beautiful sung prayers of his that were included in two ground breaking volumes that he pioneered, *Biblical Hymns and Psalms.*

There was—and is— something so bold in Fr. Deiss' music, and together with his fellow countryman Fr. Joseph Gelineau (1920-2008), he brought forth a "French revolution" that put the scriptures, especially the psalms, on the lips of congregations trying to get their sea legs as a singing people. Think of some of the other pieces from this ground-breaking resource: "Priestly People," "Keep in Mind" (still wondrously popular), "All You Nations," "There is One Lord," "Yes, I Shall Arise," "Like Olive Branches," "Sion Sing," and so many more. These are classics that, in my estimation, still hold up to this day after being made known to us in the late 1960's and early 1970's. Long before we were to discover the scripture-based music of the St. Louis Jesuits, the efforts of Fr. Deiss and Fr. Gelineau, for me, were not only my first experiences of singing the scriptures—they were in many ways, my introduction to the Bible itself!

One of the many treasured memories I have of the music from Fr. Deiss, was singing this gorgeous refrain, grounded in Isaiah 61:1-3:

The Spirit of God rests upon me.
The Spirit of God consecrates me.
The Spirit of God bids me go forth
to proclaim, his peace, his joy.

I continue to be taken in by the strong announcement of the work of the Spirit that is contained in the wedding of music and text in this setting, especially when one considers that these words are translations of the original composition (as is the case with all of Fr. Deiss' music) in French!

When I was faced with the attempt to create my own setting of this text, I knew I wanted to achieve this same sense of proclamation, albeit using contemporary instrumentation that would include guitars, keyboard, bass, and percussion. I did not want the assembly to have to have their eyes buried in a hymnal or worship aid; I wanted it to be able to be sung by heart, so heads could be lifted high while singing. Because this text is a proclamation, and because the role of the cantor is to lead the community in its praise, I chose to employ a "call and response" approach to the structure of not only the refrain, but for the verses as well. I was hoping to honor the "speaker and subject" nature of these passages from Isaiah, so the phrases of the text had to be clear, short, while still remaining faithful to the message. Because the melody was going to be simple enough to be immediately remembered, I wanted to somehow create an energy in the accompaniment that would attempt to suggest the stirrings of God's Spirit.

So I went to work, and "Song of the Anointed" was the result. As I was in the process of writing this piece, I kept hearing this traditional "Spirit" prayer in my head, which is a compilation of liturgical texts drawn from the Mass and the Liturgy of the Hours for Pentecost:

V. Come, Holy Spirit, fill the hearts of your faithful.
R. And kindle in them the fire of your love.

V. Send forth your Spirit and they shall be created.
R. And you will renew the face of the earth.

Let us pray
O God, who by the light of the Holy Spirit,
did instruct the hearts of your faithful,
grant that by that same Holy Spirit,
we may be truly wise, and ever rejoice in your consolation,
through Christ our Lord. Amen.

I decided to bookend the beginning and end of the piece with a simple ostinato contemporary chant of the opening dialogue of this prayer.

While the melody of both the refrain and verses of this song is very simple, it does require that the cantor lead the refrain with courage and strength. So in addition to myself, I asked Lori True and Jesse Manibusan to be the other cantors when I recorded the piece. I have to tell you that to this day when I hear them singing the second and third verses, I still get chills. They totally got the sense of what I was looking for. For the ostinato chant, Tom Franzak and I spent about 45 minutes overdubbing our two voices over and over to achieve a tight blend and landscape for the eruption of the melody at the beginning, and bringing it back again, concluding the song with this mantra as well.

The text comes from what scholars refer to as "Third Isaiah," the verses contained in chapters 56-66 serve as historical context for the dashed hopes of the earliest returnees from the Babylonian Exile. The yearnings of this section reveal that what they had hoped for in their return did not come to bear as they imagined and hoped it would. While a Hebrew Scripture text, it is impossible to not see the obvious messianic overtones contained here. In Luke's gospel (4: 16-30) we have Jesus reading this particular section from the scroll while speaking about himself in the synagogue. Following liturgical practice, Jesus rolls up the scroll, returns it by way on an attendant to its proper place, sits down, and preaches. He begins, "Today this scripture has been fulfilled in your hearing." Jesus is the completion of Isaiah's prophecy.

So what does this have to do with us? I seems to me that we can distill in this proclamation some very clear and pointed directives for the mission of Jesus (which I tried to illustrate musically in the melodic and rhythmic nature of the song). For me, it is a distinct outline:

> 1—*We are all God's servants, appointed by God's Spirit to proclaim God's message.* We are anointed by God, and with that comes the call to proclaim good news.
>
> 2—*This proclamation of God's word is transformative for us who believe.* And what is our message of good news to our sisters and brothers, hopefully heard in our words and more importantly through our actions? The message is that there is good news and hope for the hopeless; that there is good news for those held in bondage, that liberty is God's promise for us; that there is good news that all debts will be responded to with God's grace. The good news is that for those who are steeped in sorrow, joy is breaking forth in their midst.
>
> 3—*This announcement of redemption is the starting point for ministry and service.* This is proclaimed by Isaiah, revealed through Jesus—but ultimately, embodied in the witness of God's people. God's gift of reconciliation is a blessing that leads us all to be a reign of service; and for that we have every reason to offer praise to God.

This "good news" is a message that cries out to be heard—and to be sung! May we all keep singing it, relentlessly, as a litanic examination of conscience for justice, peace, hope and victory for God's people. The people of the Hebrew Scriptures, as well as the early Christian community, were in need of such hope. Nothing has changed for us in our present age. We too, now more than ever it would seem at times, need to cry out and be consoled with this same promise of good news: "Come Holy Spirit, fill the hearts of your faithful … renew the face of the earth." (12.12.17)

CD

MP3 Music

Creating God;
Glory Day: David Haas and Friends in Concert;
Table Songs, Vol. 1 & 2;
You Are Mine: The Best of David Haas, Vol. 2
X-21301
G-3360

SONG OF THE BODY OF CHRIST

Music:
NO KE ANO AHI AHI
(Traditional
Hawaiian song)
Text: David Haas

We come to share our story.
We come to break the bread.
We come to know our rising from the dead.

We come as your people, we come as your own,
united with each other, love finds a home.

We are called to heal the broken,
    to be hope for the poor,
we are called to feed the hungry at our door.

Bread of life and cup of promise,
    in this meal we all are one.
In our dying and our rising,
    may your kingdom come.

You will lead and we shall follow,
    you will be the breath of life;
living water, we are thirsting for your light.

We will live and sing: "Aloha,"
    "Alleluia" is our song.
May we live in love and peace
    our whole life long

I have shared elsewhere in this book about my love for the people of the Malia Puka O Kalani parish community in Hilo, Hawaii, and the marvelous "Big

I WILL BRING YOU HOME

Island Liturgy and Arts Conference" that they inaugurated many years ago. During one of the early years of these conferences that I attended, during one of the evening prayer celebrations they sang a haunting song in their native language that was very simple and at the same time absolutely intoxicating. I asked Joe Camacho, my good friend from Malia, to tell me more about the song. The song is titled "No Ke Ano Ahi Ahi," and it was not a religious song per se, but a family song sung at evening time, that basically speaks about families (that they name as "Ohana") gathering together to share the events, occurrences, and stories of the day. Hearing this explanation, it helped me to have a deeper understanding of the Hawaiians speaking about "talking story." To "talk story" means to not only get together and share what is going on in our lives, but to do so, in order that deeper connections are made and relationships become nurtured.

I began to think more about this wonderful energy of "talking story" and the haunting melody of the song, and so after I returned home to Minnesota, it came to me that this is exactly what we do when we gather for Eucharist. We "talk story" (Liturgy of the Word) and then, respond to each other in love, in sharing the Lord's meal (Liturgy of the Eucharist). It is that simple, really. I came up with a simple refrain text to bind together with the melody of this song: "We come to share our story; we come to break the bread; we come to know our rising from the dead."

The following year when I returned to Malia for the next BILAC conference, I shared the song with Joe and some of the others from the community. I was really nervous, because I was not sure how they would react to someone from a different culture (Haole) taking one of their treasured melodies and changing it by adding completely new words and arrangement. When Joe and others heard it, they broke down and cried. They shared with me how they felt so honored that something from their culture and land would touch the heart of someone from a distant land. That meant the world to me, and I am so amazed as to how this song has spread among so many over the years. I mean, it is so simple—a repeated simple melody accompanied by three chords. It most certainly has been a gift from the Spirit, that is for sure.

I wanted the song to be as inclusive as possible, and so eventually I asked Donna Peña (who was one of the other guest speakers at BILAC that same year) to do a Spanish translation. Donna sang one of the Spanish verses on the recording, and as a way of honoring the host culture, Joe and I sang one of the verses with the original Hawaiian words, "No Ke Ano Ahi Ahi." David Barrickman, a good friend and gifted pianist who also was at the conference that year and who also fell in love with the original Hawaiian song, unknown to me, wrote a piano instrumental piece based on the tune after he got home. So, when I heard it—I had David not only play piano on the track, but the introductory piano part that you hear is excerpted from his treatment of the song. It was also so great to have Marty Haugen and Jeanne Cotter sing on the track as well, since they were also part of the experience that year at BILAC, and for many of the conferences that followed.

I am very pleased by the many ways people have been creative and adapted this piece, especially the refrain, for various liturgical celebrations and other events over the years. A few years ago, Tony Alonso contacted me asking me to create some texts for new verses that could be utilized for each of the celebrations of Triduum - as he wanted to have a unified communion song for all three days. I offer these verses here if you so wish to use this piece for Triduum (these verses are under copyright, so please be sure to include the copyright notice if you print these words in any worship aid):

Holy Thursday:

1. We embrace the cross of glory;
our salvation and our light.
Jesus Christ, our resurrection and our life.

2. We come now with tow'l and basin,
to wash each other's feet,
we will follow your example; make love complete.

3. You give a new commandment,
to follow and explore:
"Love each other as I have loved you, forevermore."

4. Let these gifts now endure among us:
our faith, our hope; our love.
May we now and always remember, the greatest is love.

5. We will share the cup of blessing,
our communion with the Lord,
We will sing of our thanksgiving: love outpoured.

I WILL BRING YOU HOME

6. You proclaim, "this is my body;
my blood—all given for you;
take and drink, and feast in my memory, this you must do."

7. We proclaim your death and rising,
until you come again.
Jesus Christ, our hope and endless great "Amen."

Good Friday:

1. In the suff'ring of our Lord Jesus,
we are saved from the power of sin.
May we all be now made holy, deep within.

2. Like Christ, in our hands we surrender
to our God, our spirit and breath.
May our faith become our vict'ry over death.

3. Christ our Lord became obedient
to his death upon the tree.
By the life that he surrendered, we are now free.

4. Through this cross, we find our glory,
Through this cross, joy is brought to the earth.
Through this cross, we find our promise of new birth.

5. Holy is our God almighty,
Our God is holy and strong!
God's mercy and compassion is our song.

6. In the hope of resurrection,
grant us pardon, comfort and peace.
In our call as your disciples, may love increase.

7. We hold the death of Jesus,
in the hope of rising again.
With the cross as our companion, we sing "Amen."

Easter Vigil/Easter:

1. We are here as friends of Jesus,
on this blest and holy night;
For here the Christ who was dead, now rises to life.

2. Christ now, before, and always,
our beginning and our end.
Our Alpha and Omega; savior and friend.

3. This day, is the day that God made:
be glad, rejoice and sing!
We will weep no more, so let the song of life now ring.

4. Living water, fountain of new life,
flowing forth now in this place.
We are holy sons and daughters, filled with God's grace.

5. Anointed with God's Spirit;
confirmed not to die, but to live;
Bound together as disciples, our lives we give.

6. We dine here at this table,
food and drink for the greatest and least.
Resurrection, life-everlasting; this is our feast.

7. We are now your Easter people.
"Alleluia" is our song.
May we sing as risen people, our whole life long.

I guess what tickles me the most about this piece on so many levels, is the song's utter simplicity. Sometimes, probably most of the time, less is most certainly—more. It provides an opportunity for us to connect more clearly and directly. You know—"talk story." (11.25.17)

CD
MP3
Music

Throughout All Time;
Glory to God: The Best of David Haas, Vol. 4
X-80315
G-4682

SONG OF THE LORD'S COMMAND

Music:
David Haas
Text:
John 13:1-15
(alt. DH)

Do you know what I have done for you,
you who call me your teacher and your Lord?
If I have washed your feet,
so you must do as I have done for you.

What I am doing now you do not know,
but after a time has gone by, you will understand.

Don't you understand what I must do?
If you would be mine,
    then I must bend to wash your feet.

I have given to you an example;
what I have done for you,
    you must do for one another.

"Song of the Lord's Command" is a song to accompany the ritual washing of the feet for the Evening Mass of the Lord's Supper on Holy Thursday, originally composed for this liturgy at St. Thomas the Apostle in Minneapolis in 1996. I was involved as a volunteer for the parish music ministry under the direction of my close friend, Mary Werner. At St. Thomas, everyone in the community is invited to come forward at this Mass to have their feet washed, and the response is almost total. Mary, a fine liturgist as well as a pastoral musician, was looking for a single piece of music that the people could sing throughout the time of this communal ritual action. Far too often in parishes that have communal washing of the feet, the ministers of music will line up several songs to do back-to-back, to help fill up the time. While not intentional and an understandable parish practice, when music for this ritual becomes just a series of songs, the ritual can become cheapened, depriving the worshipping community of a deeper experience. Like other ritual moments that involve processions with lots of people (such as the sharing of communion on a typical Sunday or Veneration of the Cross on Good Friday) the pastoral challenge for music ministers is to provide music that can truly capture and embody the action that is taking place. Some communities have implemented some of the Taizé ostinato chants for such moments, and in those resources there are lots of riches to choose from.

I wanted to create a piece of ritual music in "song form," employing a refrain for the assembly (that could be easily memorized) with verses for the cantor or choir—one that would hopefully not become tedious after being sung for a longer period of time. I chose to craft a refrain that would hopefully hold some substance, and I composed seven verses and two options for instrumental interludes—to help expand and give movement during this time, but to have it be one song, one prayer for this one, very rich, ritual action.

More and more parishes are implementing this pastoral practice of inviting the assembly to have their feet washed; to not have it limited to, as it is worded in the Roman Missal, "The men who have been chosen ..." In parishes where the washing of the feet takes place in a more inclusive and expanded way, additional ministers (most often lay members of the community) assist in the washing of the feet; in many parishes, such as the parish where I worship (St. Cecilia's in St. Paul) the community washes the feet of anyone who wants to come forward. Sadly, many parishes still shy away from attempting this kind of broadening of the ritual, on the grounds that a wide invitation for everyone to come forward would be too complicated and would take far too long…but beautiful, prayerful, life-changing experiences of liturgy never come by watching a clock.

This debate cannot be settled here in this reflection, but I would assert that when our ritual moments are able to be expanded more fully, the result almost always becomes a richer experience for the community. When we do not rush these actions and do them with a sense of care and dignity, accompanying them with song-prayers to illuminate their deeper meaning, then the liturgy comes closer to being a true "sanctifying of the faithful." Part of what makes this ritual so rich and powerful is that it is a unique proclamation of what the Eucharist is, of what true discipleship means. In the synoptic Gospels (Matthew, Mark and Luke), the Last Supper is the scene with the "words of institution" front and center. Not so here, with John's account, which singularly replaces the Last Supper meal with this action of Jesus washing the feet of his disciples. When the community takes part in this ritual, they proclaim the Gospel through the action that they share in. This song puts the very words of the mandatum ("command" or "mandate") in the mouths and hearts of the entire assembly, who are called to be and "put on Christ" with the servant's tools of a towel and basin.

This song is dedicated to my friend and master catechist and author, Bill Huebsch. For so many years, Bill has been the towel and basin for so many who want to deepen their understanding of what it means to be a disciple. Through his writing, teaching and intentional service to the materially poor, Bill has certainly understood the teaching of Jesus: "I have given to you an example; what I have done for you, you must do for one another." The apostles and the early church certainly took up Jesus' call. So has Bill. So must all of us, "for one another." (11.22.17)

CD
MP3
Music

Who Calls You by Name, Vol. 1;
Alive in Christ Jesus; Give Me Jesus
X-34103
G-3337

SONG OF THE RISEN ONE

Music:
David Haas
Text:
Luke 24:5-6;
Matthew 11:4-5,
28:6-7, 19;
Revelation 21:4-5;
David Haas

Why do you look for the living among the dead?
He is not here: he has been raised to new life!
Alleluia! Alleluia!

Come and see!
  The one who you seek is no longer here:
who is risen among you,
  who goes now before you alive!
Alleluia! Alleluia!

Every tear will be driven away; no more pain!
No more weeping and mourning,
  "Behold I make all things new!"
Alleluia! Alleluia!

Strength to the weak!
  New sight for the blind: Jesus alive!
Go and tell all the nations
  the wondrous deeds of our God!
Alleluia! Alleluia!

While the resurrection and the image of the empty tomb most certainly celebrates the glory of Easter, I cannot help but think about when the disciples, after seeing the empty tomb, ran— "half overjoyed and half fearful." Along with the immediate joy of the moment, the disciples must have been feeling some unnerving emotions about the experience, and that same intensity is there for us as well. Along with rejoicing, with the gift of new life comes a certain sense of anxiety. It is a little scary—it realigns our center and our usual way of doing things, the very familiar patterns of how we live.

With the empty tomb comes a new and fierce turning around of our lives, and this is what I wanted to somehow capture in this musical setting of the Easter account. I wanted to create a musical tidal wave of all of these mixed emotions around the amazing event of the risen Christ, right from the beginning notes of the introduction all the way through to the end. I wanted to musically express the rising from the dead as earth-shaking. A spiritual thunder accompanies true conversion, true liberation—a true turning around in one's life. "Jesus alive!" is and should be, the ongoing centerpiece of the many ways we "preach" and give unhesitating witness to the good news.

We need to stimulate a sense of intensity in our liturgical formation, for all of the ministries and, yes, for the gathered assembly. Passion and intensity does *not* mean that things have to be loud and edgy. But they do require deeper preparation, by bringing ourselves totally to what we are doing in our various liturgical ministries. Things can get in the way of this happening, however—often because we are afraid. We are afraid to "put ourselves out there"; we are afraid of "performing" or "drawing attention to ourselves." This is all understandable. The liturgy is not an opportunity for us to call attention to ourselves and our talents—not a time to perform. But this necessary humility sometimes can lead to a sense of apathy. The liturgy that is on paper, that is "in the books" so to speak, is not the problem. Yes, issues of translations that do not speak and engage are realities, as one example. But the liturgy, as we have it, could speak more vividly and effectively if we could just raise the bar and challenge ourselves to bring our very best to the ministries of reading/proclamation, of preaching—to celebrate with lavish and intentional hospitality and inclusivity, and to lead the music with a sense of urgency and excitement.

The *intent* of liturgical celebration should never be to help us to feel good. Its purpose is certainly not to have us feel bad, to engage in the parsing out of guilt and shame—no. But the liturgy, like the experience of the empty tomb, should bring about this interesting tension of being both joyful and a bit fearful. The liturgy should an event of prayer that brings about joy, healing and comfort—but it also needs to pull the rug out from under us, meaning it should make us squirm a bit; it should make us both comfortable and uncomfortable at the same time. Because when we are uncomfortable and somewhat afflicted, change happens. And that is what the liturgy ultimately does; it sends us forth to love and serve the Lord, to "glorify the Lord" with our very lives.

This was most certainly the challenge that the disciples must have faced at that first Easter. Their lives were turned upside down. They went to observe what they thought would be dead—and their expectations were not only reversed, they were decimated. The message "he is not here" provokes us to inquire, well, if he is "not here," then where is he? He is "raised to new life"—and so are we. We are raised in order to live differently; we are raised so that the promise of new life can be announced and proclaimed to the world. We are raised so that our tears and sadness can be freed; we are raised so that our weakness, our blindness, and our apathy can be opened wide and become strengthened and illuminated. This is not just the "Song of the Risen *One*", meaning Jesus Christ alone. It is also the song of the risen "ones"—you and I; the Body of Christ. If we get this, our "Alleluia!" can no longer be apathetic and low-energy. It will demand of us to sing, not only a passionate alleluia that celebrates the good news of this astonishing and awesome event in history, but a glorious alleluia that will continue to open tombs—a relentless musical reminder that what was once dead is "no longer here." (11.11.17)

CD

MP3
Music

To Be Your Bread; Singing Assembly; Winter Grace;
Star Child; I Will Bring You Home
X-1041d
G-2888

SONG OF THE STABLE

Music:
David Haas
Text:
Timothy Dudley-Smith
("Chill of the
Nightfall")

Chill of the nightfall, lamps in the windows,
letting their light fall clear on the snow;
bitter December bids us remember
Christ in the stable long, long ago.

Silence of midnight, voices of angels,
singing to bid night yield to the dawn;
darkness is ended, sinners befriended,
where in the stable Jesus is born.

Splendor of starlight high in the hillside,
faint is the far light burning below;
kneeling before him shepherds adore him,
Christ in the stable long, long ago.

Glory of daybreak! Sorrows and shadows,
suddenly they break forth into morn;
sing out and tell now all shall be well now;
for in the stable Jesus is born!

I composed this piece in 1984, and it was my first serious attempt to compose a Christmas song. It was challenging to find a unique Christmas message, because everyone has their favorite Christmas songs—especially carols, in the religious tradition.

I came across a wonderful collection of hymn texts by Timothy Dudley-Smith (who also wrote the text, "As Water to the Thirsty," that I set to music a couple of years later). In the pages I came across this hymn text/poem, "Chill of the Nightfall." I fell in love with it immediately. It had the feel of a carol, but some of the fresh images just grabbed me instantly: "bitter December bids us remember," "darkness is ended, sinners befriended," and "sorrows and shadows, suddenly they break forth into morn ..." Because the words are so thick and rich, I wanted both the melody and the arrangement to be very accessible, with a certain musical intimacy, which led me to think more "guitar" than piano. I also hoped that the song could be both a congregational hymn, and a possible solo piece at the same time. So, by looking at the almost litanic nature of the beginning of each stanza, I created a repeatable musical motif (E-E-G-B-C) that would occur three times in a row, but building each time by underlining each repetition with a different chordal pattern.

One of the things that I came to love the most about this text, is how it blends together the traditional and sometimes sentimental imagery that we associate with Christmas (with the references of the stable, shepherds and so forth) together with the contemporary human struggles of wandering in the cold, dwelling in darkness, and addressing our sinfulness in the midst of a season that really should not be seen as penitential. Creating this tension musically was an important goal for me.

The result of all of this then became "Song of the Stable." Over the years I have recorded five different versions: the original was recorded on the *To Be Your Bread* recording with Michael Joncas and Marty Haugen, and after that it appears on the *Singing Assembly* CD where Michael, Marty and I sing it live. It also later appears on the *Winter Grace* recording that I did with Jeanne Cotter, preceded by her beautiful piano prelude of "Silent Night," and then, again, on my favorite Advent/Christmas recording, *Star Child*, with David Fischer, Kate Cuddy, and Jim Waldo offering their vocal talents. On the CD that accompanies this book, I have, perhaps selfishly, recorded it again, all by myself.

All of the Christmas songs that I have attempted to create since have had "Song of the Stable" as the standard. A treasured memory for me, is when a couple of years after it was composed, I received a beautiful hand-written note from the poet, all the way from England, thanking me, and sharing with me that it was his favorite musical version of the poem among many other settings. Wow. Thank you Bishop Dudley-Smith, for allowing the muse to pull this beautiful text out of you, giving me the opportunity and privilege to bring it to song. (11.21.17)

CD
MP3
Music

No Longer Strangers;
Without Seeing You: The Best of David Haas, Vol. 3
X-29802
G-3948

STAND UP, FRIENDS

Music:
David Haas
Text:
Brian Wren

Praise the God who changes places,
    leaves the lofty seat,
welcomes us with warm embraces,
    stoops to wash our feet.

Stand up, friends! Hold your heads high!
Freedom is our song! Alleluia!
Freedom is our song! Alleluia!

Praise the Rabbi, speaking,
    doing all that God intends,
dying, rising, faith renewing, calling us his friends.

Praise the Breath of Love,
    whose freedom spreads our waking wings,
lifting every blight and burden till the spirit sings:

Praise, until we join the singing far beyond our sight,
with the Ending—and—Beginning,
    dancing in the light.

This is the third song, chronologically, that I have composed attempting to pray and celebrate a *doctrine*, namely the mystery of the Holy Trinity (the other two being "Alleluia Sing" and "You Are the Presence"—both of which I reflect upon in this book as well).

    This text by Brian Wren sees the doctrine and mystery of the Trinity as holy actions splashed upon us. I absolutely love (and am a little envious) of the images of the three persons that Brian brought to life: God the Father/Creator being seen as "the God who changes places, leaves the lofty seat," The Son, the "Rabbi, speaking, doing all that God intends," and the Spirit—"the Breath of Love, whose freedom spreads our waking wings."

Desiring a buoyant mood, I approached it as contemporary folk song that could also, hopefully, be a bodily act of praise. That certainly has become true through the various gestures that have been created by various groups to embody this spirit, especially a set of gestures created by my friend from Hawaii, Joe Camacho—that invites the worshipping assembly to join in.

To me, every word and image is perfect in this song, and I hope that the music that I found for it elevates this text. Whenever I sing it, it helps me to invest more deeply in the guidance of the Trinity in my life, not as a theology that places God in a narrow box, but a presence that brings about a freedom celebrating the sacred, that is expressed in the refrain—one that results and is completed with "Alleluia!" (11.21.17)

CD
MP3
Music

Throughout All Time; Give Me Jesus
X-80327
G-4693

STEAL AWAY

African-American Spiritual, arr. by David Haas

Steal away, steal away, steal away to Jesus!
Steal away, steal away home,
   I ain't got long to stay here.

My Lord, he calls me, he calls me by the thunder;
The trumpet sounds within my soul;
   I ain't got long to stay here.

Green trees are bending,
   poor sinners stand a trembling;
The trumpet sounds within my soul;
   I ain't got long to stay here.

My Lord, he calls me,
   he calls me by the lightning;
The trumpet sounds within my soul;
   I aint got long to stay here!

I have always loved the African-American Spirituals. I got this from my mother. In addition to being my Mom, she was also my high school choral music teacher, and she often programmed spirituals into our curriculum and our public concerts. I have wonderful memories of singing "Every Time I Feel the Spirit," "Give Me Jesus" (both of which I would eventually create my own arrangements for), "Soon-a Will Be Done," "Go Down Moses," "I Couldn't Hear Nobody Pray," "Ride On, King Jesus," and "Lord, I Want to Be a Christian" (be sure to check out Lori True's wonderful arrangement/adaptation of this song, available from GIA: G-7832).

My mother would always add some "catechesis" (though we did not call it that at the time obviously) when we would learn these songs—and this was at a public school! She would be sure that it was not lost on us that these songs rose from great suffering, and that for the slaves of the south, such songs were rocks of safety that they would cling to, and become the source of hope and rejoicing in a God that they knew and believed was with them in their struggles.

I discovered "Steal Away" many years later, and came to learn from people like Fr. Ray East that when the slaves sang this song, they had in mind "getting" to Jesus—not just the historical Jesus of our memory, but rather, a journey to the real, active, and "alive" Jesus—seen as a promise of a land (moving north) that brought freedom; a new region of justice and dignity. Such songs were a "code" for the slave workers who wanted to lift each other up without the slave masters knowing what they were singing about. In this case, to "steal away" spoke of the literal geographical journey that they would one day make to freedom, where Jesus' care and love for all people would be real. For them the road was hazardous and often ominous and life-threatening, but they sang it just the same. The journey for all of us is similar when we confront fear and the terror of life. What is it that we need to "steal away" from and "steal away" to? We need to "steal away" from advantage to justice, from rage to respect, from self-hatred to self-love, from jealousy to acceptance and gratitude, from the darkness of death to the light of new life.

Whenever I sing and pray this song, I of course think of my Mom, but also those who have taught me much about its roots and heritage, and the power of its sung-prayer, especially Fr. Ray and Lynné Gray; also Leon Roberts, Derek Campbell, and Valerie Battles (may these blessed three all rest in peace), and the people who have been a part of "Robert's Revival" over the years: Tommie, Nova, Larry, Stephen, Eugene, Dion, Juliette, Terita, Robert, and J.T.

Over the years I have chosen to do this arrangement to conclude many of my parish concerts, and I will never forget the privilege and honor to have led people in this prayer at the funerals of both of my parents, and for my mentor, Sr. Roberta Kolasa, SJ. This power-packed spiritual reminds us all, that we "ain't got long to stay here." (11.21.17)

CD
MP3
Music

A Changed Heart
X-82206
G-7726

SUMMER SUN OR WINTER SKIES

Music:
David Haas
Text:
Shirley Erena Murray

Summer sun or winter skies,
Christmas comes—shepherds, angels, lullabies,
words recorded by the wise:
read it in the book—take another look.

Shadows track the hawk in flight
Christmas now—children born in fire and fight,
silent night a violent night,
hawks are in control of a nation's soul.

There where terror plies its trade
Christmas now—children learn to be afraid,
minefields of mistrust are laid,
evil is in force on a winning course.

Child of peace, God's human face,
Christmas now—come to plead war's counter-case,
bring the dove a nesting place,
though her wings are torn, though her blood is drawn.

Winter skies or summer sun
Christmas comes—still the threads of hope are spun,
goodness will outclass the gun,
evil has no tooth that can kill the truth.

This contemporary carol confronts us with an obvious counterpoint to the typical proclamation of the mystery of Christmas. We have so many assumptions about the Incarnation and the many rituals, attitudes, and values that this season presents. One of these values is the "winter-only" way in how Christmas is seen, both in terms of weather and mood. The author of this text, Shirley Erena Murray, lives in New Zealand, where Christmas is celebrated in the heat of summer.

This season, in another such assumption, often embraces a sentimental piety that ignores the realities of our world. Lurking in and around the messages of joy, gladness, and cheer that this season should indeed celebrate is the reality of loneliness and war, violence and genocide, greed and selfishness, racism and deep sadness.

We are taught over and over again that the season of Advent celebrates *two* comings: the historical birth of Jesus Christ into our history, and the advent of God in the final times, the in-breaking of the Reign of God. But there is a third coming that we also tend to forget. We also call to mind the coming of Christ into our own existence, right here, right now, in our time. And what is the state of the world in which our beloved Christ enters and is made known?

This carol reveals a broken, war-torn, and violent world. The text was written soon after the events of September 11, 2001, and graphically presents the world in which Christmas arrives. It pokes holes in the sentimental attitudes that accompany our understandings and sometimes shallow beliefs about Christmas. Christmas is not only about the birth of the Baby Jesus: it is about a promise made in a time when promises are shabby and empty. Ultimately, it is about Love, born into a frenzy of hatred and fear, and about a Christ whose power can and will truly "outclass the gun."

Christmas is about the truth—the truth of how things really are, and our faith in our greatest and most treasured truth: Jesus, the Christ, born into the center of our stories and providing hope for us all. (12.12.17)

CD

MP3
Music

Who Calls You by Name, Vol. 2;
Table Songs, Vol. 1;
Glory to God: The Best of David Haas, Vol. 4
X-26501
G-3694

TABLE SONG

**Music and Text:
David Haas;
Inspired by
Psalms 34, Psalm116,
John 12:24;
1 Corinthians 10:16
(alt. DH)**

We are the Body of Christ.
Broken and poured out; promise of life from death.
We are the Body of Christ.

Is not the bread of life we break,
   a sharing in the life of God?
Is not the cup of peace outpoured,
   the blood of Christ?

How shall we make a return to God,
   for goodness unsurpassing?
This saving cup we shall hold high,
   and call out God's name!

Come taste and see the goodness,
   the wonders of the risen one!
Come bless our God in all things,
   let praise be our song!

Copyright © 1991 GIA Publications, Inc.

While the psalms are at the spiritual center for liturgical composers, crafting songs for the assembly to sing during the sharing of communion at Eucharist stands right alongside. Over the years I have composed dozens of communion songs, but this one is special to me because of it intentionally expressing and naming Christ's presence in the community, as the living embodiment, the most critical Eucharistic, "element."

I composed this song after being inspired (and also jealous) of the wonderful communion song written by Rory Cooney, "Bread of Life," with those remarkable opening phrases: "I myself am the bread of life. You and I are the bread of life." It might have been the very first time that I discovered a communion song that named the assembly as holy, and as a participant in the "real presence." So that was the "inspiration" so to speak, that lured me to write "Table Song," and to have the courage to put these words on the lips of the assembly right at the get-go: "We are the Body of Christ." Originally intended as a communion song to be sung at the Easter Vigil, keeping in mind the newly initiated coming to the table for the very first time, over the years it has been utilized for celebrations throughout the entire liturgical year.

The title, "Table Song" was influenced by my mentor, Sue Seid-Martin, who never referred to this musical moment in the liturgy as the "communion song." She chose to use the image of it being the "Table Song." That stuck with me for a long time, and so, this became the title of this song, and it also morphed into two complete volumes of music for the sharing of communion, called—yes, you guessed it—*Table Songs*.

For the verses, I chose to utilize some of the paschal images of thanksgiving and self-giving from sections of Psalm 34, Psalm 116, as well as John 12:24, and 1 Corinthians 10:16, so that the refrain coming back each time, would be the assembly's convicted response to these proclamations. A friend of mine brought to my attention—several years after I composed this song—that the opening two measures of the refrain was reminiscent of Barry Manilow's "Weekend in New England." Well, I guess it is. All I can say is, that there are only so many notes possible to arrange into a melody, and so, this does happen from time to time. But when comparing the two, I happen to like my lyrics better.

Some have told me that this is their favorite communion song. That means a lot. It is one of my favorites too. (11.12.17)

CD

MP3 Music

Take All the Lost Home;
Most Requested: Music for the Spirit, Vol. 1;
How Can I Keep from Singing; I Will Bring You Home
X-1041o
G-5882

TAKE ALL THE LOST HOME

**Music and Text:
Joe Wise**

Take all the lost home.
Remember their names, all.
Their journey is yours, friend.
Their faces are grey 'til you call.

Walk close by the children
and learn their refrains
and leave your umbrellas
while you learn to walk in the rain.

Remember the one cup
you share in my name.
The wine and the water are one and the same,
all the same.

Comfort the old ones.
Be tender and strong.
Rekindle their tired dreams
and sing them your song,
sing your song.

The bread that is broken
won't be one again
unless in your healing
you gather each one and each grain.

Take all the lost home.
Walk close by the children,
and comfort the old ones
'til I come again, come again.

When I was a young boy growing up in the midst of the joyous light of Vatican II and who eventually would pick up a guitar and become involved in the "guitar/folk mass" movement—I was influenced and inspired (as many were) by the music of such pioneers as Ray Repp, The Dameans, Clarence Rivers, Sebastian Temple, and my good friend, Joe Wise. This was the music that opened up the doors for the people to sing—the congregation, not just the choir alone.

While I was a classically trained young musician (piano being my primary instrument), I loved learning the guitar, and I just soaked in all of this new repertoire. Songs like "Here We Are," "Shout from the Highest Mountain," "Forevermore," "Of My Hands," and "To Be Alive" (all by Ray Repp); "The New Creation," "Yes, Lord," "Look Beyond," "Without Clouds," "The Love of God Will Rise Before the Sun" (just a few of the many early songs of the Dameans), "God Is Love" (Fr. Rivers), "The Prayer of St. Francis" and "The Mass Is Ended" (by Sebastian Temple), and the wonderful early song-prayers composed by Joe Wise: "Take Our Bread," "Lord, Teach Us to Pray," "Glory," "We Are Your Bread," "We Will Hear Your Word," and my personal favorite of his back then, "Gonna Sing My Lord." When I learned "Gonna Sing" I remember just playing it over and over till the calluses on my fingers couldn't take it anymore.

As was the case with all of those saints mentioned above, it was wonderful to see how Joe's music and message evolved and matured over the years through his expanding output of songs, such as personal favorites "Watch With Me" (which Jo Infante and I would sing together back in the day on Good Friday), "This is My Gift," "Here Is My Life," "The Lord Is My Shepherd" (Michael, Marty and I included our rendition of this song on the *Come and Journey* recording), "Song of Blessing," and "Jesus, In Our Hands" (very controversial at the time, as some saw it as an "agenda" piece to promote the practice of receiving communion in the hand).

Right around the time that I was discerning entering the seminary and began composing my own simple liturgical songs, my mentor during this period, Sr. Roberta Kolasa, SJ, sat me down in her office, and put a record on the turntable and out came "Take All the Lost Home" (Sr. Roberta was also the one—and she was not a musician—who introduced me to the "Earthen Vessels" recording and music, and the other early contributions of the St. Louis Jesuits).

This was also around the time that I first came to know Joe personally. Joe was the very first established liturgical composer who heard my earliest song attempts and encouraged me to keep on writing.

"Take All the Lost Home" touched on something that has stayed with me all of these years. It speaks so amazingly in such a simple yet direct way—to what discipleship "looks like." Later on, I found out that Marty Haugen fell in love with this song as well, so not only in my solo concerts, but also in the concerts that I used to present with Marty over the years, this song has been an important inclusion. I always loved singing it with Marty, and you can hear Marty and I, together with Jeanne Cotter, singing it on the live concert recording we did years back, *How Can I Keep from Singing*? I also was able to sing it once with Joe himself. What an honor that was.

I heard once that this song was originally composed when Joe was asked by a diocesan vocation office to write a song to help promote vocations. When the song was played for the people in charge, they rejected it. It seems as though there was nothing in the lyrics for them that spoke directly about becoming a priest or a nun, which to them meant it was not about vocations. I think they missed the point entirely.

Well…I, and so many who have heard the song over the years, very much *do* get it. The song does not get old for me at all. After I sing it at various concerts and retreats, I get asked what CD of mine has me singing it alone. So in response, finally after all of these years, I have included my "cover" of the song on the CD that accompanies this book. Also, my friend Kathy Jellison has published a beautiful choral rendition of the song, available from GIA (G-5882).

Joe has not been involved with music for many years now, but we stay in touch. He and his wife Maleita have been engaged in painting, writing poetry, and other kinds of creative pursuits (check out their website, www.joeandmaletiawise.com) for several years now. Thanks Joe, for helping to get us singing again in church, and for the most important gift of all that you have shared with us over the years—you. (11.21.17)

CD
MP3
Music

Echo of Faith; Do Not Be Afraid, I Am With You
X-50704
G-5660

TAKE ME HOME

**Music and Text:
David Haas**

Take me home,
to your dwelling place,
in your sweet embrace,
ready to hold me in your arms.
Take me home,
to your loving eyes,
with you alone I'll rise,
singing forever,
in your arms, take me home.

O my God, you've led me through it all,
through all the hurt and my shame.
O my God, I have traveled far to meet you,
to see your face and call upon your name!

With you all pain is left behind,
no sorrow or death, on that day.
O my God, how I've longed to know your love,
Come wipe my tears, and take my fear away!

O my God, the road is long and hard,
open your heart, come to me.
God, with you, my sorrow turns to dancing,
reach out your hand and set my spirit free!

I WILL BRING YOU HOME

When my dear friend and fellow composer Leon Roberts died from stomach cancer in 1999, I was absolutely devastated. It happened not long after we collaborated together on a liturgical music project, *God Has Done Marvelous Things*, and we had already begun talking about doing another similar project that would bring together the much needed integration of race and faith. He had become an important and precious friend, a true brother in the Lord. His musical companions, "Robert's Revival," had become family not only for me, but for many in my liturgical music family in Minnesota. Leon—for those of you who did not know him or are not aware of his incredible music—was a major force in liturgical music, presenting a fresh style highly influenced by gospel and urban music from his African American culture. For many years he was Director of Music at St. Augustine Parish in Washington DC, and his creative muse and prolific output was amazing. He was a major contributor for the very first Catholic African American hymnal, *Lead Me, Guide Me* (GIA), and his original music is recorded and published by both GIA and OCP Publications. Our collaboration on *Marvelous Things* (with GIA) continues to be, for me, a true highlight of my work in ministry over the years.

When the news came that he died, I completely lost it. I knew that he was sick but I was not aware of how serious it was. So Helen and I were joined by a contingent from Minnesota and Michigan (which included Kate Cuddy, Fr. Jim Bessert, Lori True, and Jim Waldo) as we made the pilgrimage to St. Augustine's in Washington DC for the funeral celebration. The night before going to the airport I sat at the piano and in the midst of my tears wrote "Take Me Home," and was humbled that together with my companions and Fr. Ray East, I was invited to share it at the funeral the very next day.

I remember the funeral mass very clearly—it probably was the most intense celebration and wedding of both sorrow and joy that I have ever experienced, with a truly spirit-filled homily preached by Fr. Ray Kemp, a good friend and Leon's former pastor. He announced an ongoing refrain, challenging us all from the gospel story of the multiplication of the loaves and fishes, "you give them something to eat." Leon, most certainly, gave us much food through his music, his person, and his love of God.

As pastoral musicians, sharing our gifts at funeral celebrations is so very important, perhaps the most important thing we do. This is the thing that we all share as people: one day we will die. And for Christians, we believe that this is where the rubber hits the road, where we return to where we come from at our birth—Signed with the cross, soaked in the waters of our baptism, and held up to God in prayer and faith. While it is hard to sing at funerals—especially when we are doing so for someone we know and love—it is so important that we do. When it seems as though the last thing we want to do is sing—these are the times and occasions where we need to sing the most. Desperately so. At these most vulnerable times we need to respond as Leon did, with the entirety of his life, to the Lord's call: "you give them something to eat," which I would add and paraphrase, "you—pastoral musicians—give them something to sing."

When my Dad died, my mother asked that this be the gathering song for the funeral mass. Mom also requested it for her own funeral celebration, and we were able to sing it then as well. For both occasions, the two singers who were the soloists for this song when it was first shared, and also on the original recording—Lori True and Fr. Ray—were the cantors when it was sung and prayed.

About a week before Leon died he was visited by a good priest-friend. When he asked Leon how he was holding up, Leon responded, "well, I have bad news and I have good news. The bad news is that I am not going to be able to beat this. It has me by the throat, the pain is immense; and I am not going to survive this much longer." Then his friend asked, "well, what is the good news?" Leon than replied: "Christ reigns." (11.21.17)

CD
MP3
Music

Echo of Faith; Give Me Jesus
X-80313
G-5667

TAKE UP YOUR CROSS

Music:
David Haas
Text:
Matthew 16:24-28;
(alt. DH)

If you lose your life for my sake, you will find it;
if you want to save your life, let it go.
Take up your cross, deny yourself;
Come, follow me; follow me.

How will you profit by gaining the world,
while you forfeit all of your life?
What will you give in return?
What will you give in return?

Before I return in glory,
I will give you the gift of my love.
You will never taste death.
You will never taste death.

This song was composed in thanksgiving for the priesthood of Fr. Paul Jaroszeski, a priest of the Archdiocese of St. Paul and Minneapolis. He was the former pastor at the parish that we currently belong to, St. Cecilia's in St. Paul. I love that the parish is named after the patron saint for musicians, but that is not the primary reason why this community has always been so special. First of all, these people *sing* at liturgy! Quality preaching has also been an important value for this community as well. Another dynamic that makes this community tick is that the parish is small—only about 350 families—and we pray together in what many might think is a rural country church. This size, this enthusiasm for the liturgy and song, and their commitment to one another and service, has made this community a wonderful place for prayer and connection. All of the staff members—including the pastor—are part-time, so everyone really steps up and makes this parish work and thrive. I also love the fact that I am able to sit in the pew and be, primarily, a member of the praying assembly. I have nothing to do with the leadership of the music ministry, as we have a very competent Director of Music, Jeanne Dold. I am on the cantor schedule from time to time, and I love being able to stand in front and with hardly any effort at all, empower this singing congregation to take on their role of being the primary minister of the liturgy.

Fr. Paul's witness to ministry and service under the shadow of the cross was, and continues to be, at the center of his vocation. This song is for him and for all who accept the invitation to take up their cross. (11.25.17)

| CD
MP3
Music | Creating God; Pslams for the Church Year, Vol. 3
X-21306
G-3325 |

THEY WHO DO JUSTICE

Music:
David Haas
Text:
Psalm 15
(alt. DH)

They who do justice will live in the presence of God!
They who do justice will live in the presence of God!

Those who walk blamelessly
    and live their lives doing justice,
who keep the truth in their heart,
    and slander not with their tongue!

Who harm not another,
    nor take up reproach to their neighbor,
who hate the sight of the wicked,
    but honor the people of God!

Who show no condition
    in sharing the gifts of their treasure,
who live not off the poor:
    they shall stand firm forever!

This psalm, with its "reality check" refrain text, has always been a favorite. Psalm 15 holds a directness and no-nonsense message of what it means to be a disciple and to work not for a "retributive" justice (one that exacts punishment) but for a "restorative" justice, that will "honor the people of God" by showing "no condition in sharing," celebrating the dignity of all.

It is a psalm of victory, so for some crazy reason, I called to mind one of my favorite Broadway shows, *Les Misérables*. For this setting I wanted to capture the same passion of "Do You Hear the People Sing" and "Red and Black" that soars in that marvelous production, and create a sense of urgency to the call for all to be a people who "live their lives doing justice." This is why the setting has such a dramatic presentation, and why the cantor actually interrupts the refrain, because the urgency for justice-making should make us impatient—it cannot wait. This is the "feel" that I was looking for when it was recorded, and I love how the instrumentalists on this track—including Bobby Fisher on guitar, David Barrickman on synthesizer, and Gordy Knudtson on drums, bring this fierceness to the fore.

It is sad that there are still people who believe that the liturgy should not be "political"; that it should avoid talking about social justice, and just promote the attitude of charity. Both are needed. When we see a hungry child, the dynamic of *charity* urges us to feed the child, now. But it cannot end there. The dynamic of *justice* asks this question: why is this child hungry in the first place? What are the systems or conditions in our society that cause this to remain? After a celebration of the liturgy one Sunday, a parishioner once lamented to me, "you know, I really love our pastor, but I just wish that he would not talk so much about social justice—I just wish he would stick to preaching the gospel." I could not find any words at the time adequate to express my amazement at such a statement, so I did not say anything. Well, this setting of Psalm 15 is my rebuttal that I wish I had remembered at that moment. (11.21.17)

CD
MP3
Music

Throughout All Time
X-39203
G-4683

THIS CHILD OF OURS

Music:
David Haas
Text:
Jaroslav J. Vajda

This child of ours—this miracle—
You have a dream and plan for it;
You wash it clean, You cradle it,
You bless it and You call it Yours:
this child of ours, this child of Yours,
this child of ours, this child of Yours.

This child of Yours—this miracle—
reborn of Water and the Word;
the Book of Life records its name,
You smile and angels celebrate:
this child of Yours, this child of ours,
this child of Yours, this child of ours.

This child of ours—this miracle—
whom Christ would die for, we may love,
and train and raise, and teach and praise,
and watch the Spirit mold a life:
this child of ours, this child of Yours,
this child of ours, this child of Yours.

This is a wonderful baptismal text created by Jaroslav Vajda, who also authored the words for my Christmas piece, "The Encounter." This particular song was composed for the occasion of the baptism of Alicia Petrunak, daughter of my good friend and colleague, Stephen Petrunak.

Again, as is the case with all of his texts, Vajda's words just bubble up, and each verse builds and celebrates the partnership of people and the God who creates us, in this case with the birth of a child. While a child may "belong" to the parents, the child also belongs to God, and the ongoing dialogue that speaks about "this child of *ours*" and "this child of *Yours*," is not only charming, but also theologically rich. There are so many phrases here that I love, especially in the second verse: we celebrate the child being born of water and word, and "the Book of Life records its name, You smile and angels celebrate." Then the third verse calls us to that which is not only the responsibility of the parents, but that of *all* of us, to "train and raise, and teach and praise, and watch the Spirit mold a life." Such powerful words that I could have never come up with.

Because Stephen is a master guitarist, I wanted to bring to these words to a more "folky-style"; this is a piece really does not work well on the piano (although a simple piano arrangement is provided in the printed edition). On the recording, Stephen happens to be the guitarist, and Lori True and Kate Cuddy join me on the vocals and we were able to take part in a "Crosby, Stills and Nash" arrangement on the final verse (or might it be "Winston Phillips"?). It was great fun, indeed.

Alicia is all grown up now and has become an amazing young woman. God bless her. I hope she realizes, however, that she will always be seen by her parents—and by so many who have known her over the years—as this little "miracle" from God. Every child, at their birth, and when they grow into adulthood, should always be seen this way. (11.25.17)

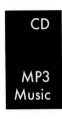

CD

**MP3
Music**

Throughout All Time;
Psalms for the Church Year, Vol. 8;
Without Seeing You: The Best of David Haas, Vol. 3
X-39211
G-4690

THROUGHOUT ALL TIME

Music:
David Haas
Text:
Psalm 89
(alt. DH)

I will sing forever to you my God,
throughout all time I will sing to you;
throughout all time I will sing to you.

I will sing of your love all my days, O God,
your happiness is forever.
You are love everlasting
and compassion stronger than the sky.

The heavens proclaim your wonders;
the skies above tell of your love.
Where is there an equal?
What god can compare with you?

O God, how your people rejoice in you!
You call us forth to share your light.
In your name we find our joy
and your justice will be our song,

All will sing and proclaim to me:
"My God, my rock, my safety."
I will honor my promise;
my love will always be with you.

Psalm 89 is a psalm of gratitude and thanksgiving, and the usual refrain translation that we hear, "Forever I will sing the goodness of the Lord," seemed to call for a fresh paraphrase or "re-set." So that is why my text adaptation came out the way it did. It was originally composed for the ordination liturgy for my dear friend Anita Bradshaw, for her service for the United Church of Christ, at the Yale University Chapel in Hartford, Connecticut, on September 17, 1995.

I was given free rein as to what psalm I could compose for the occasion, so I chose Psalm 89—in thanksgiving for Anita's witness and her many gifts. While this psalm is a complex poem, with references to David (not David Haas, but rather, the David of the Hebrew Scriptures) and the royal and messianic line, I felt as though the overall expression that it offers regarding God's unconditional love could prevail for this celebration. This promise of love that God pours upon us can be trusted because God is like no other—God's word, God's love, never fails. This psalm teaches us to stand firm in hope and to always remember God's amazing fidelity. For me, such a joyful event—Anita's ordination—cried out for a joyful psalm. Its joyfulness has also lent it to be sung and prayed at wedding celebrations for many, and I have experienced it accompanied by liturgical dance—an additional joy-filled blessing.

I remember well the ordination liturgy. I was honored to conduct and lead an amazing choir of women's voices, many of them clergy themselves, and the blend of their voices and hearts is a memory I hold close. That day, I was truly "blessed among women." I continue to be blessed by the friendship I have with faith-filled women who serve the people of God with a joy that many of us who are men could stand to emulate more.

At the center of it all, this is a psalm and song of gratitude and thanksgiving. I have found that when I am joyful, thankful and grateful, the best part of myself comes to the surface. "Throughout All Time" stands right next to my setting of Psalm 116, "The Name of God," as among those psalm settings that bring me the most joy. (11.21.17)

CD
MP3
Music

Before I Was Born; Give Me Jesus;
Glory to God: The Best of David Haas, Vol. 4
X440805
G-5185

TO BE A SERVANT

Music:
David Haas
Text:
Mark 10:35-45
(alt. DH)

For I have come not to be served,
but to serve; to give my life.
If you wish to be the first
you must seek to be a servant,
to be a servant of all.

Can you drink the cup that I must drink;
are you willing?
Can you be baptized like I have been baptized?
Are you able? Are you able?

For to sit at my right hand or at my left,
is not for me to give.
But for those for whom it has been prepared,
it will be given. It will be given.

This song was composed years ago in response to a celebration of the Eucharist with the people of St. Patrick's Church in Milford, New Hampshire. This was the parish where Lori True served as Director of Music for many years before she moved to Minnesota and later became a liturgical composer herself. One Sunday when I visited, we heard the gospel passage from Mark chapter 10, the passage I then used in this song. It is interesting—and I am sure that many people can relate to this—how we can hear certain Bible passages many, many times, over and over throughout the years, and then, for some reason, one Sunday it feels like we are hearing it for the first time. That was certainly the case this at this liturgy.

The message is a challenging one, so perhaps that was the reason why I tuned it out so many times before. But not this time. I could not stop thinking about the call to ministry and the cost, the consequences that accompany such a call. This passage (which also appears in Matthew and Luke) challenges our notions of power and authority in the church. In the case of serving the Body of Christ, these verses invite us to embrace a movement that, paradoxically, leads us also to embrace the cross. It is a clarion call to recognize that our discipleship is a vocation among equals, not one of power over others. No such structure of power that holds an elitist stance can be tolerated in Jesus' vision of leadership. Ministry is rooted in the service of others, where we as leaders decrease so that others, may increase.

I do not have any memory of a struggle to write this piece; it seemed to flow well when I was working on it. I guess the word of God was really doing its work on me, and I am glad I surrendered to it and allowed the song to emerge. I am grateful. This is a favorite of mine.

When the piece was finished, my friend (and eternal pastor) Fr. Ray East came to mind. He has to be, for me, one of the closest human manifestations of light and goodness that I have ever come to know. Those of you who have experienced and spent time with Fr. Ray can certainly resonate with my description. When Fr. Ray cries out: "God is good, all the time! All the time, God is good!" he really means it, and lives it—in the best of times and in the darkest of times. "To Be a Servant" is dedicated to him. Sort of a no-brainer. (11.21.17)

CD
MP3
Music

To Be Your Bread
X-17209
G-2887

TO BE YOUR BREAD

**Music and Text:
David Haas**

To be your bread now, be your wine now,
Lord, come and change us to be a sign of your love.
Blest and broken, poured and flowing;
gift that you gave us, to be your body once again.

We come to your table
with our lives as they are.
Heal us Lord, for we are broken;
make us one again.

Lord, we stumble through
the darkness of night.
Lead us now, O Lord, we follow,
bring us home to you.

Give us the bread and wine
that bring us to life.
Feed us, and we'll never hunger,
never thirst again.

"To Be Your Bread" is another song that is included among some of my earliest compositional efforts, written in the fall of 1979 while I was a student at St. John Vianney Seminary in St. Paul, at what was then the College of St. Thomas (it is now a university). I remember taking a course in Liturgy and Sacraments, and I remember the many informal discussions that I was beginning to have with Fr. Michael Joncas about all things theology. This song was born out of the wonderful learning environment that I was in at the time.

I shared it with Michael and Marty Haugen soon after I wrote it, and Marty liked it and wanted to use it as his parish, so on his own—and I am glad he did—he arranged it for SATB choir. Rob Strusinski, who was the Director of the College of St. Thomas Liturgical Choir back then and for many years afterwards, loved the song as well, and Marty's arrangement, so it became a favorite communion song for many campus liturgies. I was not published by anyone at this point, but the song got around to lots of people around the area and beyond. Rob eventually included it on a recording featuring the Liturgical Choir, titled *In Song*, alongside compositions of others who were closely associated with St. Thomas, such as Michael and Dan Kantor.

"To Be Your Bread" remained in limbo for a while, and eventually OCP Publications came across it, via a short-time life with an organization called Cooperative Ministries, and to this day it is part of many of the assembly publications with OCP. OCP has made it available as a choral octavo edition as well, utilizing Marty's original SATB refrain setting. When I put together my second full collection with GIA, I included it as the title song for that project. It also was the inauguration for many songs to follow, where I seem to be captivated with using the word, "now" (such as "Now We Remain," "Jesus, Heal Us," "Jesus, Be with Us Now," "At Evening," among others). I have been teased a lot about that over the years. I guess I am very impatient. I want everything *now*.

While the song has no designated dedication, whenever I hear it or think about it, my mind goes back to those three years as a seminarian back in Saginaw, and at St. John Vianney Seminary. What an experience that was. Back then, SJV was a completely different kind of center of formation than it is presently. I am thankful for the priest-guides and spiritual directors that walked with me during this time: Fr. Ken Pierre (Rector); Fr. Jerry Kaiser; Sr. Marie Fujan, OSB; and Fr. Ralph Goman. I also remember some of my classmates: Bruce Kaatz, John Hartel, Fr. Tom Fleming, Fr. Dale Korogi, Jeff McLeod, Rev. Vince Schwann, Fr. Tony Stubeda, Joel Bean, Fr. Tom Kaup, Bishop Peter Christiansen, and too many more to remember. I also remember my fellow seminarians back home in Saginaw, Michigan—people like Fr. Jim Bessert and Chris Lauckner; my priest mentors during that time, Fr. Bob DeLand, Fr. Bill Taylor, Fr. Joe Schabel; and my bishop back then, Bishop Francis Reh.

During all of this, I began to see that my calling was not to the ordained priesthood, but rather an invitation to serve God's people through my gifts as a pastoral musician, and eventually, a liturgical composer. As I have already shared, seminaries were different then; at least SJV and the leadership of the Saginaw Diocese were at the time. The issue then was not whether or not I would become a priest. The central message of care that I received, from all of these people, was that I was discerning God's call in my life, regardless of what particular direction that would take. How blest I was. How thankful I am to this day, for the Diocese of Saginaw, and for my time during 1978-1980 at SJV. So, almost 40 years later, I want to dedicate "To Be Your Bread" to all of these wonderful humans named here. (11.21.17)

CD
MP3
Music

Reach Toward Heaven
X-80337
G-6158

THE TOMB IS EMPTY

Music:
David Haas
Text:
Sylvia Dunstan,
vs. 5 by David Haas

The tomb is empty, is empty!
Come and see where once the body lay.
Can it be true, be true
that Jesus Christ is raised to life today?
Sing Alleluia! Sing Alleluia!

The tomb is empty, is empty!
Come and hear these words of life and peace:
"He is not here, not here.
He lives again in all your Galilees."
Sing Alleluia! Sing Alleluia!

The tomb is empty, is empty!
Come and touch the stone and folded shroud.
Christ lives indeed, indeed,
Alleluia! Believers, shout aloud.
Sing Alleluia! Sing Alleluia!

The tomb is empty, is empty!
Come and meet the risen Christ our Lord
in whom we have, we have our victory,
in whom is life restored.
Sing Alleluia! Sing Alleluia!

The tomb is empty, is empty!
Go and serve all people who long to be free!
Raise those who sleep, who sleep,
in tombs of fear, and give them eyes to see!
Sing Alleluia! Sing Alleluia!

I WILL BRING YOU HOME

Easter is not something to watch. It is not a paranormal event to observe in awe. As amazing as that Easter morning must have been at the empty tomb, those who discovered it knew that they could not just stay there and stare. There was an announcement to make, news to share, and a story to continue to keep on sharing. Yes, "the tomb is empty." But what does that mean? What are we to do with this new reality?

This marvelous text by the late Sylvia Dunstan gets at this in her marvelous text, "The Tomb Is Empty." The words of this hymn explode with not only the power and joy of the resurrection, but also the promise that it holds, that while death and suffering will always be with us, these forces will not, in the end, rule the day. There is a power greater than ourselves, and that power is this Jesus Christ who "is raised to life today," as one who "lives again in all your Galilees."

When I was working on the musical landscape for this piece, the line from the text that kept ringing in my heart was the call to us all who embrace resurrection-faith: "Believers, shout aloud." This challenge was the *cantus firmus*, so to speak, for this musical setting.

When I finished the piece, I felt that something was missing. As fantastic as Sylvia's text is, I believed that it needed an additional stanza that would send the praying Church on mission, so I crafted the fifth stanza, with its call to "go and serve." This comes from my stubborn belief (and sometimes ongoing rant) that we need to take on and "put on Christ" with all of his attributes, well beyond the historical story of that amazing day. We are to be the representatives of the empty tomb—ambassadors for the risen Christ, whom we have come to know in the big and small events of our lives. We are the ones who answer with a resounding "yes" to the question posed in an earlier stanza, "can it be true?" Yes, it can. It *is* true. But we have to step up, and become, ourselves, both the answer and the promise. (11.21.17)

CD

MP3
Music

I Shall See God;
With You By My Side, Vol. 1: The Journey of Life;
Blest Are They: The Best of David Haas, Vol. 1
X-22612
G-3397

VOICES THAT CHALLENGE

**Music and Text:
David Haas**

Call us to hear the voices that challenge,
deep in the hearts of all people.
By serving your world as lovers and dreamers,
we become voices that challenge;
for we are the voice of God!

Voices that challenge:
The children who long
  to be heard and respected!
The lowly and broken destroyed by oppression!
The old and the fearful
  who hope for a new day!

Voices that challenge:
The lives and the cries
  of the poor and the silenced!
The young ones who dream
  of a world free of hatred!
The sick and the dying
  who cry for compassion!

Voices that challenge:
The ones who seek peace
  by their witness and courage!
The women who suffer the pain of injustice!
The people with AIDS
  and those plagued with addiction!
The prophets and heroes
  who call us to question!

I WILL BRING YOU HOME

> The healers who teach
> us forgiveness and mercy!
> The victims of violent abuse and aggression!
> The Christ who gave his life that we might live!

One of the most amazing and hope-filled events that takes place in the Church in the United States is the Los Angeles Religious Education Congress, held each year in Anaheim, California, sponsored by the Archdiocese of Los Angeles. Each year, well over 20,000 participants (preceded by an amazing "Youth Day" the day before, attended by over 10,000 young people) come together to celebrate being Church. And I mean, *Church!* It is quite remarkable. At this gathering it seems that (with the exception of a handful of protesters outside the convention center doors) people who represent nearly every cultural group and corner of the Church come together to celebrate. They come to give thanks to God, and to immerse themselves in liturgical celebrations, plenum talks, and literally hundreds of workshops that speak to the many issues in the church and in the world. At this event, diversity is celebrated—people whom we might easily label as "conservative" and "liberal" are here; young and old, professional ecclesial ministers and volunteers, families and friends, and all of the rich diversity of cultures: Hispanic, Vietnamese, Native American, African American, Portuguese, Filipino, Korean, Hawaiian, Japanese, and all of the people from the Pacific Rim—Guam, Tonga, American Samoa, Fiji, and Australia; the Irish and the British—you name the group—and they are here! I have taken part in this Congress for thirty-some years, and it truly has impacted my life and pastoral work.

While it is a conference that is titled as a "religious education" event, liturgy and music are at the center of it all, and the celebrations are rich in diversity. It seems like every well-known contemporary liturgical composer is there, and each year, one of us is invited to compose a song to focus on the "theme" given for that particular year. In 1990, I was asked.

It was a daunting task. First of all, the song composed needs to be simple enough yet engaging enough for everyone to be able to sing, almost instantly, in the main arena space, which holds over 10,000 people. Secondly, the conference is almost always held during the Lenten season (February or March), but the song needs to have a sense of celebration and "lift." So the usual restraint of

Lent, in a way, goes away—because the expectation is that the song needs to be celebrative in nature, and include lavish instrumentation and splash. Finally—one of the most difficult challenges of all—the title of the theme chosen for that year (the composer is not part of the discerning process for what the theme will be), *must* be the actual title of the song, and appear somehow in the sung refrain—regardless of what it is.

The themes for the two previous years were "Send Us as Your Blessing" and "We Are God's Work of Art." Christopher Walker and Marty Haugen composed those two fabulous pieces. But I would add, that they had it easy (in my opinion) because both of those theme titles just cry out for music and singing. What was the theme that was chosen for me in 1990? "Voices that Challenge." I was curious as to where it came from, and I was nervous that this title just didn't seem to immediately sing itself or flow easily in the mouth. I remember calling the Director of the Office of Religious Education at the time—the amazing Sr. Edith Prendergast—and asking her out of curiosity: what inspired the theme? She responded that one of the readings that gave life to it came from the Sermon on the Mount, the *Beatitudes* from the Gospel of Matthew. My instant response to her was, "I have already composed it—it is called 'Blest Are They!'" She giggled on the phone, but said that no, I had to compose something new and it had to be called "Voices That Challenge."

So I had to get to work.

After some time in prayer asking God for help, I began to finally see a strong connection between the Sermon on the Mount and this theme title. On the first level, it seemed to me that this title was calling us to honor and call upon the communion of saints; those who have witnessed and acted upon the true spirit of the Beatitudes. But in contrast to "Blest Are They," it seemed to me that this piece had to be a bit more edgy, and hold a certain fierceness. It had to, in some way, and through the music, compel all who would sing it to respond to the inspiration and challenge put before us by those very saints—not necessarily the saints of our spiritual history, but rather the living saints who right here and right now are living the call to be "voices that challenge."

Before I even had a melody or words, I remember going to the piano and attempting to come up with a piano part, something with a driving rhythmic pulse—It needed to be relentless and never let up. I put that aside then for a while and began to write down as many of the raging issues of concern and social action as I could: some timeless, others more vibrant for that particular time, but all critically important. The list became far too long, and I had to find a way to condense it, because I certainly could not create a verse for each of the issues that I wanted to address. I began to think: "litany." The obvious text to keep punching in on this litany was the title of the song, "Voices That Challenge"; what would follow would be the naming of the kinds of disciples and witnesses that have responded and served those suffering from all of the far-too many sources of concern. It would address care for the broken and hopeless, children, the aging, the hopeless, the poor, those silenced and kept at the margins, the young ones, the rising of hatred, the sick and the dying, and those working for peace and justice. At that time the AIDS crisis was beginning to become more and more present and in our minds; the demons of addiction and abuse were beginning to be spoken of in terms of the need for healing, forgiveness and mercy they engender in every aspect of our lives. All of these became a part of this litany that filled out the verses—coming back to a refrain that calls us to listen and truly hear these voices, responding in love and action.

I was of course, nervous as to whether or not the conference organizers would like it, and whether it would "work" in the context of the three full days of the conference. I guess it did. Even more surprising was the life it took on beyond that event, given how tightly wound to the theme I had thought it was.

I have continually been surprised how well people still sing this piece, how it still seems to stir people. It has appeared in many hymnals, and there are many times when people come up to me and share their experiences with using this piece for celebrations focusing on the call to discipleship. It still blows me away, but I am grateful. Of course, there are many more issues that such a song needs to cry out to, in regards to racism, intolerance, homelessness … so much more. People using and adapting this piece should feel free to be creative, and add their own prophecy to the litany on the verses.

My only real regret in looking back is that I wish I'd had someone create a Spanish translation, so it could have been done in a bilingual fashion at the Congress. Since then, each year the theme song has this as an expectation. I wish I had thought of it then. Maybe, someday, someone will attempt a translation (since I do not have any skills to do this myself). Or other languages as well. Anyone want to give it a try? (11.06.17)

CD

MP3 Music

Who Calls You by Name, Vol. 1;
With You By My Side, Vol. 1: The Journey of Life;
God Will Delight; Glory Day: David Haas and
Friends in Concert
X-89711
G-3292

WE ARE CALLED

Music and Text:
David Haas;
Inspired by
Micah 6:8

Come! Live in the light!
Shine with the joy and the love of the Lord!
We are called to be light for the kingdom,
to live in the freedom of the city of God!

We are called to act with justice,
we are called to love tenderly,
we are called to serve one another,
to walk humbly with God!

Come! Open your heart!
Show your mercy to all those in fear!
We are called to be hope for the hopeless,
so all hatred and blindness will be no more!

Sing! Sing a new song!
Sing of that great day when all will be one!
God will reign, and we'll walk with each other,
as sisters and brothers, united in love!

I have always loved this passage from the prophet Micah:

Listen here, people:
God has already made abundantly clear
what "good" is, and what is being asked of you:
simply, do justice,
love with tenderness,
and walk humbly with your God. (Micah 6: 8)

I WILL BRING YOU HOME

I remember it being the first reading chosen for the ordination for my good friend, Fr. Jim Bessert, a priest of my home diocese of Saginaw (Michigan) in 1980. We were both seminarians around this time. He crossed the finish line; obviously, I did not, as God had other plans for me. After that wonderful celebration I always had in the back of my mind that I would love to compose a setting of this someday. It was also a favorite passage of one of the most important mentors I had while discerning my life direction, from when I was still in college up until the day she died only a few years ago: Sr. Roberta Kolasa, SJ. (Note: the "SJ" after her name might lead one to think that she was trying to be a Jesuit— no, it stands for "The Servants of Jesus," the name of her religious community).

Time went on and many other songs came to life over the years, with this text still lingering in my mind and heart. While serving as Director of Music and Liturgy at St. Thomas Aquinas in St. Paul Park, Minnesota (during the years 1982-1985), I was asked by Jan Viktora from our parish staff to compose a refrain for an upcoming service of healing that we were having at the parish. She wanted the service to make the connection between healing and service, to celebrate that when we experience any kind of deep physical or spiritual healing, the loving response of gratitude back to God is to go forth and serve, and to be missionaries of God's covenant. Micah 6:8 came back into my brain, and rather quickly I came up with the refrain for this song. We used this refrain for the service; those attending found it be moving, and I remember everyone singing it very well, right from the start, with no prior rehearsal. It was a wonderful service (except I remember we had a container with sand where we all placed candles, and we nearly burned the place down!).

So I had this refrain, and soon after I tried to finish the piece with some verses, but everything I came up with seemed forced, and it just did not seem to connect well with the refrain. I put it in a drawer for a while. I even remember giving it to Marty Haugen to see if he might be able to come up with some verses. He had some ideas—but between the two of us, nothing really congealed. So, time went on, and nothing happened with the piece.

After I left St. Thomas Aquinas, I began to travel more presenting workshops and concerts and began a new pastoral ministry serving as Composer-in-Residence at the St. Paul Seminary School of Divinity in St. Paul. I also became involved with the North American Forum on the Catechumenate, and discovered an exciting new connection between the sacraments of initiation and the mission of the Church. I started working with amazing prophetic people like Fr. Jim Dunning, Christianne Brusselmans, Fr. Ron Lewinski, Vicky Tufano, Fr. Ron Oakham, Kathy Brown, Fr. Bob Duggan, Karen Hinman-Powell, Fr. Don

Neumann, and many more. It was Fr. Ron Lewinski who first encouraged me to develop some musical resources for these rites, and people like Fr. Jim, Sue Seid-Martin and Vicky provided much guidance. The result became the first volume of *Who Calls You by Name*. Finally, the completed "We Are Called" became the concluding song for this collection.

The song is dedicated to Sr. Roberta. It also became a big favorite of the Saginaw Diocese Lay Ministry Program (they claimed it as their special theme song after a time), and it quickly also became a favorite of the late Bishop Ken Untener. A few years after the song was published, I remember being back in Saginaw for an RCIA institute, walking by one of the workshop rooms during one of the break times. Bishop Ken was playing the piano (he loved to play) and he was practicing "We Are Called." He saw me through the window and waved me in. I ended up giving him a private lesson, helping him to master the triplet-pattern in the piano part on the introduction. I will never forget that.

In recent years I have had some concerns about the piece and its popularity (as I age, my self-doubt rages within more and more). Whenever I lead it or experience it being sung, I often see people clapping, hanging on to each other and swaying, with big smiles on their faces, singing it full throated. Now, that certainly is not a bad thing—but I become worried that perhaps, maybe, the music might be overwhelming the text and its missionary message. As I read and pray over these words from Micah (and the other calls for discipleship that occur in the verses of the song), I am wondering: "should we really be swaying back and forth? Should we be happily clapping and 'feeling good' while pondering such a message?" Maybe I am taking this all too seriously, but lately, for me—when I ponder these words, they are making me squirm and they are challenging my complacency and my lack of acting with justice; of my forgetting to love with a tenderness full of mercy; of my being humble with God.

I am becoming less and less concerned about whether or not the piece "rocks" or not. I am much more concerned as to whether or not Micah's prophecy and message to us is breaking through and taking hold. Maybe next time you and I sing this ... we need to take a bit more time just reflecting upon and "breaking open" with each other, what this song should be asking of us. (11.06.17)

CD
MP3
Music

We Are Not Alone
X-89602
G-8327

WE ARE NOT ALONE

Music:
David Haas
Text:
refrain based on the writings
of Dorothy Day,
1897-1980 (alt. DH)
verses inspired by
Luke 24:13-35

We are not alone any more,
for we know him,
we know each other in the breaking of the bread.
We are not alone anymore.

As we journey on the way,
    Jesus shows us how to pray.
We belong, we belong to the Lord.

In the stories we are told,
    we find faith along the road.
We belong, we belong to the Lord.

Wisdom flowing from the Word,
    our hearts burn from what we've heard.
We belong, we belong to the Lord.

At this table we are fed,
    sharing stories, breaking bread.
We belong, we belong to the Lord.

Whenever I ponder the Easter story and honestly confront my doubts as to whether or not resurrection is really true, questions like this come to mind: What are some of the things that seem to dash my own hopes and dreams? What are the signs that surround me that can help me recognize that Jesus is alive and real? How do the various circles and communities in my life nurture in me the sense of connection that I need? What are the realities in my life that can hopefully penetrate my loneliness?

Music & Stories WE ARE NOT ALONE

The famous story of the disciples on the road to Emmaus begins to open up answers—or more accurately, *responses* to these questions that are common to all of us. This story is so wonderful because it is so profoundly human. We all can relate to the disciples' feelings of fear and discouragement, when events in our lives seem to drown out our hopes. The fear and sense of abandonment that the disciples experience in this story from Luke is very real; there is the lurking fear that this Jesus was not who and what he said he was, and that their hopes and faith were misguided at best, devastated at worst. We too—at least I know I do—feel a similar sense of discouragement in the many setbacks that shake us to our foundation; they call into question the values and things that we hold close. It can be a very lonely existence at times, and understandably so. Like the disciples in this story, we can feel locked out of a promise to which we gave a total commitment, a promise that seems to be untrue and without integrity.

Jesus provides the disciples on the road a most unexpected gift. He chooses to not reveal his true identity at first, being seen as just another pilgrim along the road. But he gradually discloses himself as one who knows and lives their story, sharing in their humanity and struggles. In this encounter, the most profound divine presence is revealed through stories, conversations and simple teachings. Redemption becomes real. No thunder claps. No bright, shining lights. Rather, a simple "walking with" (that Pope Francis would name as "accompaniment") that brings healing and restoration. When Jesus suddenly disappears from their sight, the disciples may have experienced a relapse, a feeling of being alone again, but they soon recognize that they are anything but alone, because they begin to realize that they belong to the Lord.

The same is true for us. We are not alone. We find our "faith along the road." We come to experience the wisdom of God's story so beautifully fulfilled in our own stories. The result? We find that our hearts burn and that our lives are continually being broken open through a recurring meal that brings us closer and closer to God. Now we "know him." And because of this, we come to "know each other." We are not alone anymore. (12.12.17)

CD
MP3 Music

Who Calls You by Name, Vol. 2;
Alive in Christ Jesus;
Glory Day: David Haas and Friends in Concert;
Glory to God: The Best of David Haas, Vol. 4
X-80602
G-4747

WE ARE ONE IN THE LORD

Music:
David Haas
Text:
Galatians 3:28;
Ephesians 2:19; 2
Timothy 1:9-10,
2:10-11
(alt. DH)

God alone has saved us: We are one in the Lord!
Calling us to be holy: We are one in the Lord!
Death now has been shattered,
    we are risen to new life:
One in the Body of Christ!

Neither Jew nor Greek, neither slave nor free,
    but one in the love of the Lord!
Neither woman nor man,
    but children all are we,
    one in the Body of Christ!

Called as your sons and daughters:
    We are one in the Lord!
Builders of the kingdom: We are one in the Lord!
Light to all the nations, bound together by our love:
One in the Body of Christ!

We are no longer strangers: We are one in the Lord!
Members of the body: We are one in the Lord!
Alien no longer, we are one with the saints:
One in the Body of Christ!

We will now follow Jesus: We are one in the Lord!
Chosen for salvation: We are one in the Lord!
If we die we shall live, if we endure we will reign
    as one in the Body of Christ!

Copyright © 1991 GIA Publications, Inc.

340

Unity among Christians—actually, any effort at unity in general—is difficult to achieve. We live in such divided times—both in the world and, sadly, in our failed attempts to be Church. Over the years, I have heard my good friend and mentor Fr. George DeCosta preach that we are good at *going* to church, but we are not always so good at *being* Church. Paul and the other early authors in the New Testament are relentless (and often very frustrated) in preaching the unity of what it means to be "one in the Lord."

I wanted to compose a piece that would echo these themes of unity found in the New Testament letters, a song that would attempt to present some sense of urgency—a song to compel those who would sing and pray it to be transformed and share this challenge of unity with others. I did not want to write something soothing and sentimental, a gentle song about holding hands and being "one in Christ"; I thought at the time (and I still do now) that what we needed was a song-prayer to push us forward a bit, one that would help us to welcome the reality of unity in an urgent and passionate way. This is why I chose to have a relentless litany response in the verses, as sort of a mantra: "we are one in the Lord." I wanted the entire musical landscape to be have a driving nature, a force that would not let up on those who sing it, or let them get lazy in their conviction—thus the intense rock and roll feel and accented nature of the arrangement.

There are to be no distinctions in our relationship with God; there are to be no divisions for those who claim to put on Christ. The central mission statement of the Sisters of St. Joseph of Carondelet, near where I live in St. Paul, is to "always be moving toward the love of God and the dear neighbor, without distinction." All are God's children, because of our unity. This unity is not a lock-step sort of spiritual adherence to a singularly rigid doctrine or mindset about all things holy. The unity that we seek is an honoring of *all*, of all of the many different ways, languages, expressions and colors that find their joy in Christ. This is why the refrain of this song-prayer was intended to be an explosive reminder that we are called to radical inclusion if we are really going to live as the Body of Christ.

"We Are One in the Lord" was composed around 1990, during a period when I was meeting somewhat regularly with my friend and fellow composer and pastoral musician, Kate Cuddy—a natural "harmonizer." Kate cannot help herself from harmonizing everything she hears, usually right on the spot during the first time she hears a piece. That was the case here—right there as I first played the draft for her, we carved out the vocal arrangement. It is dedicated to her, and the energy and commitment that she brings to not only her music making, but her drive to serve lavishly, especially with young people.

This piece continues to be very important to me; when I sing it I am reminded that I cannot remain complacent in my commitment to intentional hospitality without distinction, and again, in being an instrument of radical inclusion of all into the Body of Christ. (11.07.17)

CD
MP3
Music

We Give You Thanks; Table Songs, Vol. 2
X-80506
G-4973

WE GIVE YOU THANKS

**Music and Text:
David Haas**

For the bread and wine we share here,
    for the friends that we embrace,
for the peace we find in healing,
    for all who gather in this place,
for the faith of those around us,
    for the dead and all those here,
for the hope we find in mem'ry,
    for the love that draws us near:

We give you thanks,
we give you thanks for the grace to receive,
in you we believe.
We give you thanks,
We give you thanks.
With faith and hope
    and love we give you thanks.

For the movement deep within us,
    for the stories that we bring,
for the signs of God's compassion,
    for the journey that we sing,
for the Word that holds our promise,
    for the gifts that we can claim,
for the wonders that surround us,
    for the song that sings our name:

For the water bringing new life,
    for the fragrance of release,
for the fire that blazes forward,
    for the call to bring forth peace,

I WILL BRING YOU HOME

> for the blindness now enlightened,
>   for the bound that are now free,
> for the brightness of your new day,
>   for the kingdom we will be:

Copyright © 1998 GIA Publications, Inc.

"We Give You Thanks" was composed in 1995 specifically for the 100th Anniversary Centennial Mass at St. Patrick's Church in Milford, New Hampshire. It was requested by my blessed friend and partner in ministry, Lori True, who was Director of Music and Liturgy there during that time. For such a vital community of faith, and because thanksgiving and gratitude are such key parts to every parish anniversary celebration, I knew that a song of thanksgiving like this was needed for this special celebration. Over the years, Lori and I have returned to St. Patrick's to offer concerts there, and whenever I sing this piece, I think of these people, and how the beginnings of Lori's ministry were formed and nurtured there. I most certainly give thanks over and over again for the witness of Lori's ministry and heart. Over the years, "We Give You Thanks" has become a favorite for parishes when they celebrate Thanksgiving. I am grateful, and yes, thankful for that blessing.

When we talk about the "holy sacrifice of the Mass," there is the risk of losing an understanding of authentic Eucharist—which is about thanksgiving. We have so much to be thankful for—It may sound child-like to say so, but we really do—if we take the time to be intentional in calling our lives to mind. This is what I was attempting to announce in this piece. We give thanks for the gift of the Eucharist, the gift of being able to go to Mass each Sunday and for other celebrations—especially when more and more, due to the priest shortage and for other reasons, it is becoming difficult or even impossible for some to find a parish or community where they can do so. The celebration of the Lord's Day is the supreme communal act of thanksgiving, when we gather together around word and table, and we share in the bread and wine—the meal that sustains, heals, forgives, and holds our faith to be precious indeed. We give thanks for the lives and the memory of those who have gone before us, and for the hope-filled promise of love overflowing.

We give thanks for the Word—certainly the word proclaimed at every liturgical celebration, but also for the stories of faith that are our own personal tales of the journey. We give thanks for the gifts of everyone gathered on either side of us, in front and in back of us, and the opportunity and privilege to raise our voices in song and offer our gratitude.

We give thanks for the truly sacramental moments in our lives: for the moments of initiation as daughters and sons of the Lord, for God's relentless mercy and forgiveness given so freely without condition, for the moments of conversion that happen all around us. We give thanks when hope is restored and a new day is desired, welcomed, and made real.

We can never, ever, be *too* generous or *too* lavish in our giving thanks to God. Even when it seems as though God is absent, when sadness seems to surround us, the difficult and yet essential call and attitude is to be thankful, to be a living witness of gratitude. When we are thankful, we are our best selves. So let us give to God—always—our deepest thanks. (11.07.17)

CD	We Have Been Told;
	You Are Mine: The Best of David Haas, Vol. 2;
	When Love is Found
MP3	X-80309
Music	G-2662

WE HAVE BEEN TOLD

Music and Text:
David Haas;
Inspired by
John 15:5, 9, 12-15

We have been told, we've seen his face,
and heard his voice alive in our hearts:
"Live in my love with all your heart;
as the Father has loved me, so I have loved you.

"I am the vine, you are the branches,
and all who live in me will bear great fruit."

"You are my friends if you keep my commands.
No longer slaves, I call you friends."

"No greater love is there than this:
to lay down one's life for a friend."

This was the first liturgical composition of mine that became a choral octavo with GIA Publications, back in 1983.

After leaving the seminary, I took a bit of time off to discern what my next vocational step was going to be, and I began to explore finding a parish position as a music and liturgy director. After a few interviews, I took up the challenge to be the first ever Director of Music, Liturgy and Youth Ministry (which included coordinating the parish confirmation program) at Our Lady's Immaculate Heart parish in Ankeny, Iowa (just a bit north of Des Moines, and about 4 hours south of the twin cities) in the fall of 1981. I was 24. While I was nervous to make a move outside of my comfort zone of friends and colleagues in Minnesota, I thought this would be a good thing, to establish myself (in hindsight, a terrible motivation for ministry) in a fresh new place and environment. At the same time that I made this move, I began to receive more invitations to present concerts and workshops at various places. (This was a time when I had a lot of youthful energy I guess, and I was eager to serve and succeed.)

I had no idea at the time—neither did the people of my new parish—that I was totally out of my league and unprepared for what I was being asked to do there. First of all, while I loved working with young people (and it was a love that became nurtured more and more over the years), I had no real skill or competencies in running a parish youth program, in helping to start up a youth group and lead retreats, finding and training catechists to teach religious education classes, and designing and directing a confirmation program for a huge parish with hundreds of kids—O my goodness. I was a disaster. Seriously, I am not kidding or being humble. It was a catastrophic failure. That, along with the fact that I was trying to coordinate a couple of choirs, plan and lead music, and work with the other liturgical ministries—well, the result was (without going into the details) that I lasted only 5 months. Since I had a lease on an apartment in the area, I remained there in the Diocese of Des Moines for another 6 months, did some workshops from time to time, and took time to compose.

But during those five months at the parish in Ankeny, there were many things that I learned, and I made some wonderful friendships—people who I have continued to see from time to time over the years. Among the members of the parish staff was Sr. Rita Connell, a Sister of Mercy, who was the director of adult catechesis, and who also coordinated the RCIA (The Rite of Christian Initiation of Adults) for the many inquirers and their sponsors. Sr. Rita asked me from time to time while I was there to come and help lead prayer and share music for the sessions and programs for these seekers, and in the midst of it all, this became my first practical, hands-on introduction into the ministry of the catechumenate. This was most certainly a blessing, and Sr. Rita and I and her team became fast friends. We had great discussions about theology and spirituality, and we bounced around lots of creative ideas during the short time I was there. During that fall she shared that she was soon to be celebrating her 5th anniversary of her vows and commitment to the Sisters of Mercy, and I was excited to hear about her upcoming celebration.

Excited after one of our many conversations in her office at the parish one day, I had the urge to go into the worship space and compose. Sitting on the piano bench, I think I may have had my first real experience of composing out of a true sense of gratitude and thanksgiving (even though I was struggling very much in my work there at the parish). About 15 minutes later, I had finished "We Have Been Told" (including the arrangement of the introduction featuring the ascending eighth-note pattern on the piano). All I could think of while writing the piece and when I concluded it, was thinking about just "how cool" Sr. Rita was! I decided right then and there that I would dedicate the song to her.

While I was nervous, I was also excited to share the song with her. So right then I walked back into her office and asked her, "do you have a few minutes? I have something I want to share with you." So together we went back into the worship space, and I sat her down next to me at the piano, and I played "We Have Been Told" for the very first time for someone other than myself (I mean, I had only finished composing it a few minutes earlier!). After I finished singing and playing it for her, I said: "This is for you. I am dedicating it to you, and would like to give it to you as your anniversary present." I remember well her first response was, "David, this is really lovely." Then she paused for a few moments (it seemed like an eternity), and said, "you are not going to believe this, but this section of John's gospel that you have set to music here [John 15: 5, 9, 12-15] was the actual gospel reading at the liturgy for the celebration of my first vows five years ago." O my goodness. Well, we both had a good cry for this real "God moment." Just a few weeks later, we sang and prayed this at our own liturgy of thanksgiving for Sr. Rita's anniversary and for her ministry at the parish.

Every once in a while someone will ask me what brought to life the first two lines: we have been told, we've seen his face, and heard his voice alive in our hearts." To be honest, I cannot precisely remember. I would like to think that the Spirit was stirring in me the need to share that the command from Jesus to "live in my love" is something that we have heard, seen, tasted and experienced time and time again, and that we need to recognize it, name it and celebrate it in faith. Works for me.

After I left Iowa and returned to the twin-city area, I began a new ministry in the fall of 1982 as Director of Liturgy and Music at St. Thomas Aquinas Church in St. Paul Park, Minnesota, where I served for three years. The experience in Iowa helped me to prepare for this new adventure, and more songs and psalm settings came to life out of the pastoral need that I discovered there. My vocation as a liturgical composer began in earnest, after composing "We Have Been Told," which for me was a breakthrough. I remember playing it for Marty Haugen, who liked it a lot, and he offered to arrange the choral parts (SAB), that are part of the published edition. The part for the male voices has a big stretch. When the basses in particular, have complained to me over the years about the high tessitura that they have to sing, I tell them not to blame me, but Marty! One time when Marty, Michael and I sang the piece at a parish concert, before we sang it, Michael made a joke about the bass clef part—to which I responded, "well, I didn't write it, Marty did." Marty, with his quick wit, then retorted: "Well, it wasn't my piece, so I didn't care." Big laugh. Good one, Marty.

Among some of my friends and pastoral musician colleagues in Minnesota, "We Have Been Told" has become an anthem for some of us who serve in our sometimes sub-zero climate: "We have been cold; can't feel my face …"

Sr. Rita moved on to other ministry pursuits in the Omaha area and is still there serving with integrity and great spirit. I run into her from time to time, and we always reminisce back to that day. I remain grateful for what I learned from her during that first professional ministry experience for myself, and mostly, for the love she continues to pour out in her life of service.

I have been back to the parish in Ankeny a few times over the years—most thankfully, I was invited to compose a piece and be with them for their 50th anniversary as a parish. It was a great reunion. Sr. Rita was there. Just like the reunion that we have with God, every time we receive and share the amazing goodness of God's love. Yes, we have been told. And we continually see God's face in the witness of those who inspire us, the ones who hear this voice stirring in their hearts. And ours. Over and over again. (11.07.17)

CD
MP3
Music

With You By My Side, Vol. 1: The Journey of Life
X-80518
G-5814

WE PRAISE YOU

Music and Text:
David Haas

For the sun that brightens the day:
We praise you, Lord!
For your moon that guides the night:
We praise you, Lord!
For your source of light and breath:
We praise you, Lord!
For your song of death to life:
We praise you, Lord!

We praise you, Lord! You hear our cry!
We praise you, Lord! You are the answer!
We praise you, Lord! You are always near!
With all our being we praise you, Lord!

For the glory of all creation:
We praise you, Lord!
For all creatures great and small:
We praise you, Lord!
For the seas, the hills and valleys:
We praise you, Lord!
For the mountains strong and tall:
We praise you, Lord!

For your love that greets the morning:
We praise you, Lord!
For your faithfulness through night:
We praise you, Lord!
For your voice that sings in all of us:
We praise you, Lord!
For your call to love and serve:
We praise you, Lord!

For the treasure of joy and laughter:
    We praise you, Lord!
For the myst'ry of sorrow and tears:
    We praise you, Lord!
For the gift of love and healing:
    We praise you, Lord!
For the awesome pow'r of prayer:
    We praise you, Lord!

For your Word, your Holy Wisdom:
    We praise you, Lord!
For the bread, the work of our hands:
    We praise you, Lord!
For the wine, the cup of blessing:
    We praise you, Lord!
For us all, your sacred presence:
    We praise you, Lord!

This is a "praise-song" that I wrote with young people in mind. "We Praise You" was composed originally for morning prayer with the *Music Ministry Alive!* community in mind, and the recording of this song features three MMA "alums" from its earliest days: Michael Mahler (a published liturgical composer himself), Janene Dold, and Melissa Cuddy (daughter of Kate).

While working on this piece, I was reminiscent of the beauty expressed in the "Canticle of Brother Sun and Sister Moon" by St. Francis, so I composed a litany of morning joy in the verses, followed a very simple refrain that could be easily memorized. Sometimes, we are called to just offer our praise to God, without reserve. That is what I wanted to do with this song; I wanted to provide a musical outlet for worshippers to let their feelings go and just offer praise. I recall when I was in Rome years ago as part of a faculty team, leading an institute on Christian Initaition at the North American College in Rome, which is the seminary for American candidates for the priesthood. After one of our liturgical celebrations, a seminarian who was going to be ordained a deacon soon after said aloud during one of the group sessions: "I am not sure about all of this music. It is making me *feel things*." In the years since then, I hope and pray that this young man, who is probably a priest by now, has learned to not only be more comfortable but even to enjoy *feeling* the things that music can bring out in us. (11.25.17)

CD
MP3
Music

When We Are Weak, We Are Strong
X-101110
G-9469

WE RECEIVE, WE BELIEVE

Music:
David Haas
Text:
Refrain inspired
from the words
of Bishop
Kenneth Untener;
Text for verses:
Psalms 145:15-16;
116:12-13; 78:23-24;
34:2-3, 9
(alt. DH)

Amen! Amen!
Yes, we receive! Yes, we believe!

All eyes look to you,
    and you give them food in due season.
You open your hand, you open your hand,
and the desire of every living thing is satisfied.

How can I repay,
    how can I repay to you, O God,
for all the good you've shown to me?
The cup of salvation I will raise;
I will call out your name, O God!

God commanded the clouds above,
and opened the gates of heaven,
raining down manna,
giving us bread, giving us bread from heaven.

I will bless the Lord,
    I will bless the Lord at all times;
God's praise is always on my lips.
In the Lord my soul will make its boast;
the humble will hear and be glad, and be glad!

Taste and see, taste and see the goodness,
the goodness of the Lord.
Blessed are they, blessed are they
who seek refuge, refuge in God!

353

I WILL BRING YOU HOME

This is a musical "ostinato," a refrain or musical phrase that is repeated over and over, like a mantra. This musical form has become more and more popular in liturgical worship, largely due to the tremendous influence of the music from the Taizé Community in southern France. Many of the pieces from Taizé have become a common part of our sung prayer repertoire, with pieces like "Jesus Remember Me," "Ubi Caritas," "Wait for the Lord," "Laudate Dominum," and "Veni Sancte Spiritus."

I am one among many contemporary composers who has employed this approach in our liturgical compositions, and "We Receive, We Believe" is among them. One of the reasons I chose to utilize a repeated ostinato for this piece is that it is intended to be sung during the sharing of communion, and I wanted it to be easily memorized for people while coming forward to receive. I also wanted it to be versatile in terms of its length during the communion sharing. Finally, I had stumbled onto a wonderful quote from the late Bishop Ken Untener, who was bishop of my home diocese of Saginaw, Michigan for many years—and I wanted to have this be the sentiment of the song, echoing our response to sharing in the bread and cup, over and over again: "Amen! Amen! Yes, we receive! Yes, we believe!"

I dedicated this song to David Anderson, who is on the editorial staff at GIA, because in recent years he has become affectionately known as "Mr. Taizé," as he presents workshops on Taizé all across the country and beyond.

I hope that this song can help nurture and refresh our on-going commitment to becoming the Body of Christ, always responding in both the liturgy and in life with strength and courage, "yes, we believe." (11.25.17)

CD
MP3
Music

Who Calls You by Name, Vol. 2;
You Are Mine: The Best of David Haas, Vol. 2
X-25729
G-3662

WE WILL DRINK THE CUP

Music and Text:
David Haas;
Inspired by
2 Timothy 4: 7

We will drink the cup, we will win the fight;
we will stand against the darkness of the night!
We will run the race, and see God's face,
and build the Kingdom of love!

Do not fear, for I am with you,
be still and know that I am God!

You will run, and not grow weary,
for I, your God, will be your strength!

Rejoice and know you are my people;
and know that I am your God!

We are the Church, we are the body;
we are God's great work of art!

While I had already by this time composed many songs inspired and influenced as a result of my several visits to Hawaii, in 1989 I was asked specifically to compose the theme song for the annual Big Island Liturgy and Arts Conference that year, "Can You Drink the Cup?"

Knowing that Sue Seid-Martin was going to be one of the keynote speakers, and that Kate Cuddy was also going to be there as a fellow presenter, and also fully aware of how the people attending this conference each year loved to sing, I decided to compose something in a gospel-style. So I wrote "We Will Drink the Cup?" I wanted to make Jesus' invitation question to have a musical response that moved toward "we," not "me." This is a fundamental aspect of liturgy that is still lacking—we come to liturgy not to take care of ourselves as individuals, but to communally and collectively discover and celebrate the presence of Christ in our midst—as a *people*. This is why the verses of this song are abundantly filled with references such as "you are my people" and "we are the Church, we are the body; we are God's great work of art!" It is only when we embrace and nurture community as the Body of Christ that we can bring about transformation in the church, and in the world—something I rant about a lot through my songs.

Fr. George DeCosta, the pastor of Malia Puka O Kalani parish in Hilo for many years and the founder of the BILAC conference, always preached this, and the people of Malia not only listened, but they drank the cup. They chose to be light, often during times of darkness:

I have fought the good fight,
I have finished the race,
I have kept the faith. (2 Timothy 4:7)

There are times when we need songs that give us courage. Ultimately, that is why I created this song. (11.25.17)

CD
MP3
Music

You Are Mine: The Best of David Haas, Vol. 2;
I Will Bring You Home
X-34108
G-3454

WE WILL RISE AGAIN

Music:
David Haas
Text:
Isaiah 40:11, 26,
2-30; 41:10
(alt. DH)

Like a shepherd I will feed you;
    I will gather you with care.
I will lead you and hold you close to my heart.

We will run and not grow weary,
    for our God will be our strength,
    and we will fly like the eagle,
    we will rise again.

I am strength to the weary;
    to the weak I am new life.
Though the young may grow weary,
    I will be their hope.

Lift up your eyes, and see who made the stars.
I lead you, and I know you,
    I call you each by name.

Fear not, I am with you; I am your God.
I will strengthen you and help you;
    uphold you with my hand.

For many years, at Mercy Hospital in Pittsburgh, Pennsylvania, an integral part of the hospital's mission was caught up in what was named at the time "The Ministry of Healing." Joanne Andiorio, who was President of the hospital for many years, deeply believed that an integral part of the ministry and mission of medicine, especially at a Catholic hospital, had to include prayer, spirituality, and—yes—the liturgy, at the very center of its direction. So together with pastoral musician and liturgist Karen Clarke and others, the Ministry of Healing began, and touched the lives of so many—patients, families, doctors, nurses and the entire staff community—and those beyond the confines of the Pittsburgh area.

In addition to a beautiful chapel which contained a small but excellent tracker pipe organ and a gorgeous ambry for the Oil of the Sick (designed by the liturgical architect and artist John Buscemi), the Ministry of Healing transformed into a regular Sunday worshipping community that was blest by my now good friend, David Dreher, as their excellent and pastoral cantor-in-residence. (Think about that—a hospital having a "cantor-in-residence"!) In addition to their chapel space, the lobby of the hospital and surrounding areas were always adorned with the colors and symbols of the liturgical seasons!

The Ministry of Healing held many special events there in the chapel, and they (a hospital chapel ministry, mind you) sponsored liturgical and musical workshops for people in the Diocese of Pittsburgh. People like Fr. Eugene Walsh, John Buscemi, and others came to share their gifts. I was fortunate to be a part of several such events there over the years, along with colleagues Marty Haugen, Bob Hurd, Bobby Fisher, Jeanne Cotter, Rob Glover, Kate Cuddy, and many others. Every visit there was transformative, and to this day, David Dreher continues to be a very close friend and colleague (he left that ministry at the hospital a number of years ago; he is now a full-time parish music director in the Diocese of Pittsburgh).

This song was then, and continues to be now, dedicated to Karen Clarke and the memory of the Ministry of Healing at Mercy Hospital. "We Will Rise Again" was used often over the years for many of their celebrations, and it has served parishes as well, for services of the Anointing of the Sick, for funerals, and during the season of Lent. Sadly, this powerful ministry no longer exists at Mercy Hospital…but during the years they put faith into action, they touched countless lives with healing and love. (11.07.17)

CD
MP3
Music

I Will Bring You Home
X-1041n
G-9619

WHAT CAN I LEAVE BEHIND

Music:
David Haas
Text:
Adam Tice

What can I leave behind,
    what old and weary ways
that weigh upon my mind
    and strain my song of praise?
God, grant release from binding pain
and let me gain your hope and peace.

What can I claim once more?
    Can life return from loss?
What future lies in store if I take up my cross?
My burden raised, Christ bears it, too.
In all I do may God be praised.

What can I take to share a neighbor's crushing load?
What burdens can we bear together on the road?
We walk and pray, with Christ our guide,
who, by our side, will show the way.

I composed this hymn not long before I began writing this book. The text is by Adam M. L. Tice, and I composed this setting for the occasion of the installation of Kristen Kuempel as Bishop of the Eastern Washington-Idaho Synod of the Evangelical Lutheran Church of America (ELCA) in September of 2017.

When discerning what kind of piece to compose as a gift to her for this occasion, I went to visit her Facebook page, and the banner at the top of her page had this marvelous quote from Martin Luther: "The cross alone is our theology." That provided a lens for me, and so I began to probe some of the work of my favorite hymn text authors. After some searching, I came upon this

I WILL BRING YOU HOME

text by Adam (I have utilized many of his texts in other compositions), and it seemed perfect. I originally conceived it be a congregational hymn, but after she received the score, Kristen asked me to arrange it for choir, as for the "premiere" at her installation, they wanted to present it as an anthem for the choir to sing. So I did. It would work well as either a congregational hymn or as a choral piece.

Because the text is so rich and contemporary, I wanted to encase it with some atypical melodic and harmonic moves, and it was fun to explore some different directions in that regard. The result has been that some people have been surprised to learn that this is a "Haas" piece, as it sounds so atypical for me. I guess that is a compliment. Regardless, I am happy that I was able to offer this hymn as a gift for Kristen's new adventure as Bishop, and hope that the journey that Adam speaks of will be able to prayed and sung by Kristen, the people of her synod, and for all of God's people who come in contact with bearing the cross in their life. (11.21.17)

CD

MP3
Music

I Shall See God;
With You by My Side, Vol. 1: The Journey of Life
X-22608
G-3452

WHAT IS YOUR NAME?

**Music and Text:
David Haas**

Who are you, God? Where you do you live?
High in the mountains,
    deep in the ocean? Are you the wind?

Are you the rain, or the roar of the sea?
Spinner of chaos,
    breathing and stirring deep within?

Fire of love, healer of tears;
friend of the lonely,
    bread for the hungry; hope for the poor!

Dancer of life, mystery of death;
giver and taker, loving creator; guiding light!

You, our desire; maker of dreams;
voice of the trumpet;
    author of silence; blossom of truth!

Wonder of strength; compassion and calm;
Singer of mercy;
    source of our safety; justice and peace!

All of your ways are here in our midst:
presence and absence,
    laughter and anger; life and death!

What is your name? How are you known?
Mother or Father? Sister or Brother?
You are God—beyond our words!

I WILL BRING YOU HOME

Sometimes I have no idea where the songs come from. But this one I remember.

Over the years I have been a part of many discussions, debates and arguments regarding the issue of inclusive language; not only in our liturgical celebrations, but also, in our conversations, discourse, and theological discussions. This formerly hot topic seems in recent years to have faded from our collective screens, both in our musical compositions and in our liturgical books, much to my consternation.

The origins of this song go back to the beginnings of my being sensitized to this concern. There are so many different levels and layers when we have discussions about the importance of language and images, and when we dialogue about liturgical language, we have to separate out the issues: How do we refer to *ourselves* as the people of God? How is *God* to be named and taught? What are the *images and symbols* of our worship and faith that perhaps (not intentionally) project sexist or exclusionary messages? Does this mean that any reference to God as "father" needs to be done away with? Do we recognize the power and influence that language holds for us, from the time we are children well into adulthood? Why is it so difficult for some to even discuss this, or worse yet, why do so many dismiss it—both men *and* women? There are so many diverse and passionate feelings and opinions about these and other related questions.

There is not enough space here to address all of these questions in any kind of detail, but for me, this continues to be important and it is something that for years, I have tried to be very conscious about it when I create texts or adapt biblical verses as well in my compositions.

I remember being at a conference years ago and having dinner one evening with my friends Michael Joncas, Betsey Beckman (a world-renowned liturgical dancer and story-teller), and a few other folks. In our "talking shop" during the meal, this issue of language came up, and we were bantering back and forth about how composers, text writers, poets and authors could come up with more inclusive and more expansive images—especially in how we address God in our prayer. During the conversation we came up with lots of examples that we could try to work with, and the back and forth went on for some time. Finally, Michael concluded that it is impossible to come up with an adequate image that could possibly contain or hold all that is present in the mystery of God. Every effort is in the end, futile.

Michael was so right on this. While we need to continue to try and be creative in all of these issues around language, we need also to realize that God cannot be contained by our language, because God springs up like a fountain from a place infinitely deeper than any word or phrase can reach. We will always fall short in this exercise, and we should celebrate and give thanks for this beautiful truth. (This does not mean however, that we should abandon our search for more inclusive language).

This song was born of that wonderful dinner that we shared. I remembered many of the images that were thrown about during our conversation, and I wrote down a whole bunch more, and this song came to be. It begins with asking the questions about who God is. It continues on to name and celebrate the many ways God breaks open our lives. It then concludes coming to the realization (and celebrating) that God is God—well "beyond our words."

I guess it would be difficult to see what liturgical season or feast this could be used for—maybe Trinity Sunday? That is probably one of the reasons that I do not hear many people speak about it much. It might also be because the topic is too controversial, or maybe still, it is because people just don't like the song!

But while I was composing, it and when I completed it, all I could think about was Betsey, and her marvelous gift and charism for dance and movement; and for her being an inexhaustible source of newness and exploration in her own spiritual journey. She is tireless in her efforts to activate that same journey for so many of us who have been in her presence and experienced her creativity. So it is dedicated to Betsey. After all these years, I have yet to ever see her dance to this piece. So Betsey, how about it? (11.07.17)

When Love Is Found;
Glory to God: The Best of David Haas, Vol. 4
X-80619
G-4079

WHEREVER YOU GO

Music:
David Haas
Text:
Ruth 1:16-17;
Song of Songs
2:10-12, 7:6-7
(alt. DH)

Come, set me like a seal upon your heart;
a seal protecting your arm.
Deep waters cannot quench this love;
the oceans will not sweep it away.

Wherever you go, I will go;
wherever you live, I'll be with you.
Wherever you lie, I'll be there beside you.
Wherever you go, I'll be there.

Arise my beloved, come to me;
the rains are gone; the winter is past.
The flowers appear, the vines are pruned,
and the dove's song is heard in our land.

Wherever you stay, I will stay;
your people will be my people.
Wherever you die,
so will I die with you in the arms of God!

As has already been mentioned, I was born and raised in Bridgeport, Michigan in the Diocese of Saginaw. If you want to know where Bridgeport is located, it is the town right next door to Frankenmuth, a village town known for its German Lutheran history, for the best chicken dinners you could ask for (at either Zehnder's or the Bavarian Inn), and probably most of all for its year 'round Christmas mega-store, "Bronners." Frankenmuth also happens the home of Blessed Trinity Parish, where my dear friend Alissa Hetzner serves as music director.

Frankenmuth was central to my Dad's growing up, and growing up alongside the Haas family was the Brown family. Jan and Bill Brown grew up with my Dad as kids, and they took piano lessons from the same teacher, Zola Rudd. She was quite the character, and there are far too many stories to tell about her, but she had an amazing gift and way as a teacher, and my Dad, my uncle Bill, and Jan and Bill Brown all studied piano with her. Among the many stories about her is that she loved to intervene in the lives of her students (she would not be able to get away with that now), and she played matchmaker for Bill and Jan. Under her tutelage, they eventually became a well-known two-piano team in the area and beyond. They eventually married and had two children—Tim (a year younger than me and a good buddy) and Kathryn, lovingly known as "Shotzi" (again, too long of a story).

Moving to the next generation, Tim, Shotzi, my brother Jeffrey, my sister Colleen, and I, also began our serious piano study with "Aunt Zola." She was a like a member of the family, and because she never had any children of her own, our two families were her family. I grew up through my grade school years performing in many recitals that Zola convened. While we all had a certain level of talent, we found out early on that Shotzi was a child prodigy, and her life flowered over the years in her career as a concert pianist with major orchestras, including being a two-time finalist at the International Van Cliburn Piano competition in Texas. She has been a professor of piano at the Curtis Institute in Cleveland now for many years.

Our two families have remained close ever since those early years. Bill and his son Tim have passed away, but Jan is still going strong, and Shotzi is still active as a pianist, singer, and teacher. When Shotzi married Bob, they asked me to help them plan their wedding liturgy and lead the music with my singing-partner friend of years back, Jo Infante. I offered to compose a song for the liturgy, and "Wherever You Go" was what came forth. As I often do when I compose a piece for a commission or other special event, I ask what the musical forces are going to be for the occasion. They were married at Blessed Trinity parish, but at the time, they did not have much of a piano in the sanctuary. In addition to Jo and me, there was to be another soloist (her college voice teacher) and a very gifted harpist. Knowing that, I thought it would be cool to compose something that could be accompanied on both the harp and the guitar (that would be me playing the guitar—nowhere near as gifted as the harpist, but I thought what the heck, the wonderful harp playing would cover up any mistakes I might commit).

So, I knew what the instrumentation would be, and I knew that Jo and

I WILL BRING YOU HOME

I would be singing it. While most of the music for the celebration was more classical in nature, Shotzi was far from a musical snob, and so I wrote something ala John Denver (sort of my version of "Annie's Song" which served as a kernel of inspiration), and *voilà*, this song, "Wherever You Go" popped out. I chose for the refrain the beloved verses from Ruth 1:16-17, and yoked it together with sections of the love poems found in the Song of Songs. When we sang it at the actual celebration, it was intended as a duet (Jo and I), but because the congregation was filled with trained musicians, we had a lot of spontaneous harmony surrounding the bride and groom. It was very cool. Later the song became part of a wedding liturgy and music resource that I collaborated on with Jeanne Cotter, *When Love is Found*, and soon after it came into its own, and it can still be found in various hymnals and other resources for weddings.

I have not been able to sing it with a harpist since that wonderful day, but I still lug my guitar around and sing it quite often for concerts that I lead. I remain close with Shotzi and Bob, and of course, Jan. I do not see them as much as I would like—but when we do get together, we step right back into the marvelous familial relationship that we have had since we were kids. Along with the Browns and my family, I am now thinking again of Aunt Zola...what a character she was. She married twice, the second time when she was well into her seventies. As I have already shared, she never had any children of her own. But she had us. By the way, Aunt Zola was never happy with how I cut or kept my hair—or anyone else for that matter. She was always obsessed with how we all styled our hair. I wonder what she would think now, being that I do not have hardly any left. (11.21.17)

CD	Who Calls You by Name, Vol. 1;
	Alive in Christ Jesus;
MP3	Glory to God: The Best of David Haas, Vol. 4
Music	X-41601
	G-4865

WHO CALLS YOU BY NAME

Music and Text: David Haas

Blessed be God!
Who calls you by name!
Holy and chosen one!

Come, and return to the Lord!
Live by the Word of God,
who calls you by name!
Who calls you by name!

Seek to be children of light!
Live in the love of God,
who calls you by name!
Who calls you by name!

Sing now with all your heart!
Praise and glory be to our God,
who calls you by name!
Who calls you by name!

One of the most invigorating avenues of ministry that I have been able to be involved with over the years on both the parish level, and in national circles and events, has been working with the ongoing renewal and implementation of the Rite of Christian Initiation of Adults, otherwise known as the RCIA. (Some people have thought over the years that this acronym stands for the "Roman Catholic Intelligence Agency," or "Roman Catholics in Agony.")

The Second Vatican Council called for a rigorous renewal and restoration of the adult catechumenate. I began to become involved with this rite when it was still a provisional text, under the auspices of the *North American Forum on the Catechumenate*, a network of catechists, liturgists, mystagogues, musicians and RCIA teams founded by the prophetic Belgian catechist Christianne Brusselmans and Fr. James Dunning. In 1985 I was invited for the first time to serve on a leadership team for one of their now famous "Beginnings and Beyond" institutes, which have influenced the renewal of the RCIA in North America and yes, "beyond." I was blessed to have served on the team for dozens of institutes from the mid 1980's well into the 1990's, being able to work with people like Jim as well as Vicky Tufano (who first got me involved with Forum), Fr. Ron Lewinski, Karen Hinman-Powell, Fr. Don Neumann, Fr. Richard Fragomeni, Fr. Ray Kemp, Fr. Bob Duggan, Kathy Brown, Maureen Kelly, Thom Morris, Jim Lopresti, Tom Conry, Fr. Ron Oakham, Fr. Jerry Ryle, Jerry Galipeau, Fr. Michael Clay, and a host of others. Forum finally had to close its doors just a few years ago, but its influence is still deeply felt for those still passionate about the RCIA.

Those institutes provided an environment for creativity and a forum for evaluating how our pastoral practices could best work with the rite. They deepened in me an already piqued interest in composing what I would call "ritual music," a term first planted in me by my mentor Sue Seid-Martin and further developed by the prodding of Fr. Ron Lewinski, Vicky Tufano, and of course, Fr. Jim Dunning. It was actually in the midst of those weeks that I composed many ritual acclamations, litanies, psalms, dialogues, and songs for the various rites (Rite of Acceptance and Welcome, the Rite of Election/Sending, the Scrutinies, and the ritual sacraments of Baptism, Confirmation and Eucharist). As a result of these being created at these institutes, followed by evaluation and critique and further implementation on the parish level, I compiled what was the first ever liturgical music resource for Initiation, *Who Calls You by Name*, in 1988.

Composing this kind of "ritual music" requires from liturgical composers an in-depth sensitivity as to the anthropology of ritual activity, which is part and parcel of the human fabric, common to all of us, often celebrating and intensifying the most elemental situations of human activity.

The following story of a typical ritual event by a visitor to America I believe helps to bring the point home:

> You find yourself inside a home. The family is seated around a table. There are four children. It's hard to tell the difference between the boys and the girls; they dress in similar clothes and their hair is about the same length, though the boys' hair seems to be shorter. You wonder if the length of hair has anything to do with age and

position, because the person seated at the end of the table has the shortest hair and he is the largest person there. He must be the father. The person in the next room with all of the storage cabinets on the walls must be the mother. She is preparing something with a fire on top.

She touches a button at the door and the lights go off. Then she enters, carrying the fire on a platter. You remember from previous reading about this culture that this must be what they call "cake." It is a sweet bread-like mixture with an even sweeter covering.

"Cake" is a special food that they eat at various celebrations. This one, you recall, is a birthday celebration; so they call this a "birthday cake." Every year, families celebrate each person's birthday. The candles of fire stand for the number of years the person has been alive. On the cake is usually written "Happy Birthday" and the person's name. The same sweet mixture is used to write these words as it is used to cover the cake so that all of it can be eaten.

The cake can be round or square, though some people prefer the round shape as it suggests unity and the oneness of life. The square cake is usually prepared when large numbers of people are present; it is flatter and easier to cut than is the taller, round cake.

On such occasions, it is important that everyone eat a piece of cake, even a small bite. This is so even for people who do not especially like the taste of cake, or who have joined certain organizations that follow strict dietary laws (these organizations are not to be confused with religious sects, though the people may pray when they meet. The organizations referred to here are concerned with people's health, such as one called "Weight Watchers" which helps people who have a weight problem. Unlike many other cultures, the weight problem here is one of having eaten too much, rather than too little).

To refuse to eat of the cake is an insult to the person whose birthday is being celebrated. The cake is a sign of the person's life. To refuse the cake is to refuse the person. The birthday celebration is the way that these people say *without words* to someone: "We're happy you were born. You bring brightness and warmth to us as do these candles. The longer you are with us, the brighter our lives glow with yours … as is marked by the growing number of candles, year after year. We find you a pleasant a person; you leave a good taste in our mouths as does this sweet food. We eat this food marked with your name to say we believe in you personally and in your goodness. We share this food to make tangible our belief that we are of one life, one body. We treasure and celebrate being united with you and with each other in human life."

The birthday celebration is also marked by a song which is sung as the cake is being brought in and before the candles are extinguished. *On no other occasion is this song used:*

> Happy birthday to you.
> Happy birthday to you.
> Happy birthday dear [the person's name].
> Happy birthday to you.

After the song ends, the birthday person blows out the candles. But before that happens, the person makes a wish. It is said that if the person blows the candles out in one breath, the wish comes true. Although adults do not believe in any cause-and-effect relationship between blowing out the candles and whether or not the wish comes true, adults still perform the rite. It is an expression of hope in the life to come and, as some who have studied this culture believe, making a birthday wish can be interpreted as a sign of faith in a power greater than themselves.

The birthday person is further honored by being allowed to cut the first piece of cake. Even the very small child who cannot manage the knife will at least be allowed a hand on the knife's handle when the first cut is made. Or sometimes the small child is allowed to simply stick a finger into the carefully decorated cake. It is reported in some studies that should the child do this on any other special-cake occasion, the adult slaps the child's hand and sometimes sends the child to another room usually reserved for sleeping. This only highlights the seriousness in which these people take their special cakes and the keeping of certain rites surrounding the eating of these cakes.

(Gerard Pottebaum, The Rites of People: Exploring the Ritual Character of Human Experience, *rev. ed.; The Pastoral Press, Portland, OR, 1992 / pp. 31-34)*

This delightful story outlines the many elements that make up good ritual. Objects and elements are used for the celebration, including movement and procession, darkness and lighted candles, and the *words and songs that are deeply tied* to the ritual experience. The example of the "Happy Birthday" song illustrates what good ritual music does. This is what I came to learn in working with the ritual and musical forms such as acclamations, litanies, dialogues and so forth. This is the kind of music that the RCIA—and all of our rites—call for, especially in the midst of concrete and specific ritual actions.

This is what I was attempting to do with this first volume of *Who Calls You by Name,* which includes pieces such as "Come, My Children," "Christ Will Be Your Strength," "He Healed the Darkness of My Mind," "You Are God's Work of Art," "Water of Life," and "We Are Called." It also includes a new setting of the Litany of the Saints and acclamations for the scrutinies, and the piece featured here, "Who Calls You by Name," a ritual acclamation (with optional verses) for the signing of the names of the elect for the Rite of Election or Rite of Sending. The text for the refrain was instigated while on one of the B&B institutes with Fr. Jerry Ryle, who helped me understand more deeply of what it means to be the "elect," those stating their intention to receive the Easter sacraments at the Easter Vigil. These "elect" are those "chosen" by God, and at this ritual we are celebrating not their being nice people, but rather, their being "chosen" ones— and the testimony of this ritual includes witness to what that "chosen-ness" looks like. That is what brought the refrain text to life. We give thanks to God ("Blessed be God, O blessed be God"), we acknowledge God's call ("who calls you by name"), and we acclaim and give testimony to their "chosen-ness" ("holy and chosen one"). I chose to utilize a "call and response" form, with the cantor leading and the people responding back, by memory, because I did not want the assembly having their eyes buried in a hymnal or worship aid—in the spirit of all good ritual music, I wanted to make sure that their attention could be on the ritual action taking place.

Composing this kind of music helps us, as Sue would always teach us, not to sing *at* the liturgy, but rather, to actually *sing* the liturgy. This really is not a new concept, for we have been doing this for a long time with other "ritual units" that have been a part of our liturgical prayer, well before Vatican II. Music for the Veneration of the Cross on Good Friday comes to mind, as well as the Litany of the Saints for the Easter Vigil and other occasions. Thinking about the Litany of the Saints—this reminds me of when my older brother Jeffrey and I were leading song at our home parish many years ago for Holy Week (we did not use the term "cantor" then). We were singing the names of the saints during the litany, back and forth, and when Jeffrey got to St. Athanasius, his pronunciation went tilt, and it came out "St. Euthanasia." I am sure anyone reading this has experienced the decimation of the name of at least one saint or the other over the years.

My interest with writing ritual music for the RCIA continued, and this first resource became so successful that a second volume was developed and published in 1991. Crafting this kind of music, music tasked with basically and concretely serving to enhance ritual action, began in earnest for me with this resource, and my writing has been forever changed since its publication. It requires that the composer "fall in love" with the liturgy. It also has convinced me that the greatest and most effective "teacher" of the liturgy is not a class, but the ritual itself. Working with the Forum, aided by such incredible guides, and in the concrete pastoral experience of working with these rituals and music, has me utterly convinced that this is true—and that the ritual does not happen to just an individual going through the process, but to all of us. We are all called "by name" for the work of mission, a mission that is activated in us when we do the rites well, and celebrate them with passion. Amen? Amen. (11.21.17)

CD
MP3
Music

When We Are Weak, We Are Strong
X-101111
G-9475

WHY, O GOD?

Music:
David Haas
Text:
Adam M. L. Tice
("For Those Who
Cannot Find a Way")

For those who cannot find
    a way through bitter pain;
for those who cannot see a day they'll sing again;
we pray, we weep, we cry,
and why, O God? Why?

When nothing seems to heal the mind
    or calm our grief;
when chains of suff'ring choke
    and bind and test belief;
we groan, we shake, we cry,
and why, O God? Why?

Half confident, we pray and shout
    through loss and fear;
we hope despite our honest doubt
    that God will hear
our prayer, our song, our cry:
our "Why, O God? Why?"

This is a lament. We tend to shy away from singing laments in our churches. We are, I believe, afraid to do so because it stirs up our emotions and our vulnerability, and this raises the reality of darkness, anxiety, anger, and even rage—toward God. It might be interesting to note that over two-thirds of the poems in the Psalter are either psalms of lament, or penitential psalms. Yet, in our three-year lectionary cycle, we can count the number of lament psalms on one hand.

I WILL BRING YOU HOME

This fear and avoidance of lamenting and crying out to God extends itself to worship services that take place in the midst of the aftermath of extreme horror and violence. Over the years I have watched various funeral services on TV for people who lost their lives in war, from acts of terrorism, and for those who have been victims of gun violence, cancer, and other events that stretch our ability to face the world. I am saddened when I see the faces of the families of these lives who have been lost, ready to explode with anger and rage to God, only to be numbed in doing so, because the music, the preaching, and the readings and poems speak of a sweet and loving God who provides comfort. Certainly, communicating comfort and the message of God's peace is a critical element during such times, not only regarding death, but in all forms of suffering. But the grieving also needs to find release—release of their anger, their confusion, their loss, and their anxiety, and freedom to voice the penetrating question "why?"

With the words of this hymn text, Adam Tice has given us words so we can lament. This moved me to create a melody that would hopefully allow us to sing, pray, and scream our grief. Not the most pleasant piece to compose, but an important one. (11.25.17)

CD
MP3
Music

With Gratitude
X-100608
G-9273

WILL YOU COME AND SEE THE LIGHT?

Music:
David Haas
Text:
Brian Wren

Will you come and see the light
   from the stable door?
It is shining newly bright, though it shone before.
It will be your guiding star,
   it will show you who you are;
will you hide, or decide to meet the light?

Will you step into the light that can free the slave?
It will stand for what is right, it will heal and save.
By the pyramids of greed
   there's a longing to be freed;
will you hide, or decide to meet the light?

Will you tell about the light in the prison cell?
Through it's shackled out of sight, it is shining well.
When the truth is cut and bruised,
   and the innocent abused;
will you hide, or decide to meet the light?

Will you join the hope a-light in a young girl's eyes,
of the mighty put to flight by a baby's cries?
When the lowest and the least
   are the foremost at the feast;
will you hide, or decide to meet the light?

Will you travel by the light of the babe new born?
In the candle lit at night, there's a gleam of dawn,
and the darkness all about is too dim to put it out:
will you hide, or decide to meet the light?

I WILL BRING YOU HOME

Far too often, when we hear and listen to the Gospel stories that are proclaimed each Sunday we tend to keep our distance, as though we are *observing* something that happened "back then." Liturgical music, especially those musical settings of a particular Gospel reading text, or pieces that explore mystagogical reflection upon the proclamation, has the potential to invite us, not to listen or watch, but to actually take part in the story.

With his text "Will You Come and See the Light," Brian Wren has done just this; he has presented the Matthean story proclaimed on Epiphany by putting you and me into the story, so the Magi become *us*. The awesome mystery of the light guiding all of us toward the Incarnation is part of the deeper story of Epiphany, and this hymn text provides provocative questions and challenges. It says of this light, "It will be your guiding star, it will show you who you are"; with such powerful phrases as, "Will you step into the light that can free the slave?" and "Will you tell about the light in a prison cell?" it places the search for the manger into our present situations. And in the powerful conclusion, it gives witness to Epiphany's message that even while we encounter "darkness all about," we can become the light of Christ ourselves—a growing light that renders the darkness "to dim to put it out." This intentional "placing" of you and me into the story is what excites me about this text, and it is what led me to put it to music in this hymn.

This hymn is also special for me because it was among the final songs that Michael Joncas, Marty Haugen and I would ever sing and record together in the studio. We put together three new pieces along with some of our older songs on a CD project, *With Gratitude,* as a way to say thank you to so many who have supported us over the years, as we presented our final concerts together as a trio in 2016-2017. The vocal arrangement found in the printed edition were originally conceived because I knew Michael and Marty would sing the harmonies on the final stanza.

I chose to dedicate this piece to Cameron Cabot, a young "light" from Ohio who, for me, lives and serves as an ambassador for all of the young people that I have been able to walk with over the years, especially in the "Music Ministry Alive" program. Cameron is but one among many young people I have seen travel by the light. I look forward to where they will lead us. (11.26.17)

CD

MP3 Music

Before I Was Born; With You By My Side, Vol. 1:
The Journey of Life; Glory to God: The Best of
David Haas, Vol. 4; God Is Everywhere!
X-95919
G-5008

WITH YOU BY MY SIDE

**Music and Text:
David Haas**

When I'm feeling all alone,
and I'm far away from home,
God, I need you to hear me.
When my friends all turn away,
then I ache to hear you say
that you are with me through it all.

You are the light,
you're the song that I'm singing;
whom should I fear when you are with me?
For you are my God,
and with you there is nothing I can't do,
with you by my side.

When I feel all sick inside,
with no safe place to hide,
God, I need you to listen.
When it seems I can't go on,
then I long to hear the song
reminding me you are my friend.

And as I go through my life,
I will keep you in my sight
to walk with me and be my strength.
God, I know your plan for me:
to help all those in need.
To you alone I give my life!

Copyright © 1998 GIA Publications, Inc.

I WILL BRING YOU HOME

As many know, in my many years in ministry, I have had a passion for young people and I have striven to promote advocacy of their full participation in the life of the Church, particularly the liturgy. I have been involved in parish youth ministry at various parishes throughout the years, but the most rewarding experiences I have had with young people have been the years bringing young people together in St. Paul for *Music Ministry Alive!* and my experiences in working part time at two different Catholic high schools in the Archdiocese of St. Paul and Minneapolis, Benilde-St. Margaret's School in St. Louis Park, and Cretin-Derham Hall in St. Paul.

It was at BSM where "With You by My Side" came to life. I served part time there for 13 years as campus minister and artist in residence, and this song was composed for the graduating class of 2000; it was sung for the first time at the final spring choral concert that year, under the direction of my friend and fellow composer Kate Cuddy. (Kate was choral music teacher there and basically my boss during my tenure at BSM.)

While it has been used, I have been told, for liturgical celebrations, and has been included in various hymnals, I really did not intend it for liturgical use, though it is meant to be a song that people can sing along with on the refrain. While I do like its sentiment (I mean, I wrote it after all), I really do not believe it fits in with the principles of liturgical music and ritual actions. While it is a prayer, it really is not *liturgical* prayer, as I see it as a song for concerts, rallies, retreats, graduation celebrations, and other kinds of events.

The lyrics for the piece came out of what I have experienced to be at the core of the basic cries of young people, especially teenagers: the vulnerable feelings of poor self-esteem, loneliness, and isolation; the experiences of abandonment by friends and others; the rising feelings of this age group of deep anxiety and worry about their future; and the way they feel paralyzed emotionally and unable to move forward in the midst of dark times in their lives. But more than just naming these human aches, I wanted to help lift their experience to realize that they are not alone, that there is a God who is real, walking with them, and who offers hope when all might seem hopeless.

I also chose to take the message even a step further. I believe that even during a time when young people are naturally and developmentally very self-absorbed, there is a way for them to rise above the painful and fear-filled parts of their journey—and that path is through service and self-giving. God is the source of strength for this move beyond themselves: "God, I know your plan for me, to help all those in need ..."

Musically, it is composed and arranged, unabashedly, as a pop song, with an instrumental bridge, largely influenced by the music that pulled me in when I was their age: The Beatles, Elton John, Chicago, Billy Joel, and the Moody Blues. After I finished "With You By My Side," I was not sure that the style would appeal to the young people I was working with, as they were not part of the generation that produced the music of these artists that were popular when I was their age. Well, come to find out—young people love *all* kinds of music. In fact, they love a lot of the music that was created long before they were even born. I remember a young man, one of my students, coming up to me one day very excited to share something wonderful that happened to him: "Mr. Haas, the other day I heard this really cool song—have you ever heard it? It's called 'Strawberry Fields Forever.'" I said, "uh … yeah… I kinda do know that song." He continued: "yeah, it is by this really great band called 'The Beatles.' You gotta check it out." He walked away as though he had come upon a new discovery. Me? I just felt old. (11.22.17)

Mass for the Light of the World;
Glory Day: David Haas and Friends In Concert;
Without Seeing You: The Best of David Haas, Vol. 3
X-80509
G-3928

WITHOUT SEEING YOU

Music and Text:
David Haas;
Inspired by
1 Peter 1:8; Psalm 84
and Psalm 23

Without seeing you, we love you;
without touching you, we embrace;
without knowing you, we follow;
without seeing you, we believe.

We return to you deep within,
    leave the past to the dust;
turn to you with tears and fasting;
    you are ready to forgive.

The sparrow will find a home,
    near to you, O God;
how happy, we who dwell with you,
    forever in your house.

For you are our shepherd,
    there is nothing that we need;
in green pastures we will find our rest,
    near the waters of peace.

"Without Seeing You" was composed for my brother-in-law at the time, Richard Cotter, Jr., who died on May 20, 1992 after a long struggle with AIDS. Ritchie was a wonderful person and a blessing and gift to all who knew him. Like his younger sisters, Jeanne and Anne Marie, he was a gifted pianist, and he was a source of joy and redemption for his family and for so many. Before he died, he and Jeanne were able to record a piano collection together with GIA, titled *Coming Home*. When they recorded the album, Ritchie was already quite sick, and had all but completely lost his eyesight. Experiencing his passionate playing and creativity in the midst of his blindness, I was reminded of this verse, 1 Peter 1:8: "without seeing him, we love him."

In the early evening on that very day, May 20, 1992, Jeanne and I, together with many of our singer friends, were recording this very piece at Paisley Park Studios in Chanhassen, Minnesota—about 45 minutes away from the home of Jeanne's mother where Ritchie lived during the final months of his life. Not long after we finished recording the song, Jeanne got an emergency phone call telling her that Ritchie was in the final stages of his life, and that we better get to her Mom's house right away. The two of us jumped in the car and sped all the way to St. Paul and joined Ritchie, along with his parents and other siblings, for those final moments. It was an experience that I have never forgotten, and do not want to, as it was a most holy experience.

We sang and prayed this song during the sharing of communion at the funeral mass a few days later. The words of the refrain, I believe, rang true for everyone who was gathered together that day. And the words ring true still. Whenever I sing "Without Seeing You" I think of Ritchie, and all those who miss their loved ones who have passed away, so very, very much. (11.22.17)

CD

MP3
Music

Who Calls You by Name, Vol. 1;
Alive in Christ Jesus;
You Are Mine: The Best of David Haas, Vol. 2
X-19524
G-3193

WONDER OF WONDERS

**Music:
David Haas
Text: Brian Wren**

Wonder of wonders, life is beginning,
fragile as blossom, strong as the earth.
Shaped in a person love has new meaning.
Parents and people sing at their birth.

Now with rejoicing, make celebration;
joy full of promise, laughter through tears.
Naming and blessing bring dedication
humble in purpose over the years.

Wisdom of ages, new every morning,
Mother and Father, partner and Friend.
freeing, forgiving, lift all our loving
into your presence, joy without end.

I was asked to compose a piece for Infant Baptism. I could not seem to come up with a message that did not sound hokey, but that would have a simple, child-like manner in both the words and with the melody. Surprisingly, the basic outline of melody came to me before I found the right words. Then I discovered this text from Brian Wren. I love the sentiment expressed here in these words—loving, intimate, and warm, yet partnered with mission and service for all present. In such a celebration, we see the possibility of renewal embodied in the newly born: "shaped in a person, love has new meaning .... joy full of promise ... Lover of children, lift all our loving into your kingdom..." These are the kinds of promises that we adults are called to make as this young new Christian is now among us. (11.25.17)

CD
MP3
Music

Who Calls You by Name, Vol. 2;
Alive in Christ Jesus
X-41607
G-4867

YOU ALONE ARE THE WORD

Music and Text:
David Haas
Inspired by John 6:68

Lord, to whom shall we go?
You alone have the word,
you alone are the Word that saves us.

Deep in our longing, you know our searching,
then why do you hide your face?
Come be our answer,
God, give us an answer
    to all of our crying and tears!

Here in our desert, terror surrounds us,
in anguish we call on your name!
Hear us and listen,
O God, do you listen to questions
    we cannot bear?

Fearful, uncertain, feeble and trembling,
we reach for your hand to heal!
Come, be Messiah,
are you Messiah to all our broken dreams?

I believe that "You Alone are the Word" was my first attempt to compose a true and honest lament. I have always believed that Peter's famous response to Jesus, "Lord, to whom shall we go? You have the words of eternal life" was just that—a lament, an admission of desperation when all else has failed for him and his companions. The same is true for us. When we attempt to white-knuckle our way through the darkest of times, we often eventually hit a wall, realizing that we cannot navigate and survive such challenges under our own power. We need to first lay before God our anxiety, worry and fear (as expressed in the verses of this song); then, and only then, can we surrender ourselves over to the divine guide: "Lord, to whom shall we go?" We cannot save ourselves. We need to surrender ourselves over to the care of God. (11.25.17)

CD

MP3
Music

Who Calls You by Name, Vol. 2;
You Are Mine: The Best of David Haas, Vol. 2;
Glory Day: David Haas and Friends in Concert;
Do Not Be Afraid, I Am With You;
God Will Delight; I Will Bring You Home
X-39201
G-3656

YOU ARE MINE

**Music and Text:
David Haas**

I will come to you in the silence,
I will lift you from all your fear.
You will hear my voice,
I claim you as my choice,
be still and know I am here.

I am hope for all who are hopeless,
I am eyes for all who long to see.
In the shadows of the night
I will be your light,
Come and rest in me.

Do not be afraid, I am with you.
I have called you each by name.
Come and follow me,
I will bring you home;
I love you and you are mine.

I am strength for all the despairing,
healing for the ones who dwell in shame.
All the blind will see,
the lame will all run free,
and all will know my name.

I am the Word that leads all to freedom,
I am the peace the world cannot give.
I will call your name,
embracing all your pain,
stand up, now walk, and live!

I WILL BRING YOU HOME

This song is dedicated to a dear friend, Frank Brownstead. Frank was a mentor for me years ago, as he was for many pastoral musicians whose lives he touched over the years. Whenever I think of Frank, the song by Elton John and Bernie Taupin comes to mind: "Someone Saved My Life Tonight." Those of you who have known Frank—you know what I am talking about.

Over the entirety of these past forty years, no other liturgical composition of mine has aroused more interest, or been a source of so many diverse stories, than "You Are Mine." At every event where I present—whether it be a concert, workshop or retreat—there is at least one person who comes up to me with a story to share about "You Are Mine" and how it has touched their life in some powerful way.

And yet, when I wrote it, I never intended for anyone to hear it.

I remember the circumstances well. Without going into any specifics, it came to be during a very dark, vulnerable, and fearful time when I felt very much alone, when I felt I really did not belong to anyone, and most especially, did not feel loved at all or at home with myself. I was having one of those chapters in my life when it seemed as though God was very far away, almost absent.

One day during this period I was at the piano trying to compose, but nothing at all was coming forth, at least not anything worthwhile. Feeling lost and angry, out of nowhere—in about ten minutes—the refrain just fell out of me. All of it—both the words and the music. I scribbled it out, but I was shaking afterwards and feeling very strange. The verses came moments later. But I packed it away. The song kind of scared me, and so I kept it to myself for a very long time.

About a year and a half later, I was sitting down at the piano with Kate Cuddy in the sanctuary of St. Thomas the Apostle Church in Minneapolis, and the two of us, as we would do from time to time (like I used to with Michael and Marty), were sharing some of our new songs with one another. She had a few songs, and I had a binder full. When we were almost through plowing through my binder, when I turned the page and this song was there, I quickly passed over to the next song. I remember Kate saying, "aren't you going to play that last one for me?" I brushed it off, saying to her that it was nothing, and then played three or four more pieces. As I was beginning to pack up my music, Kate persisted. She wanted to hear that song that I passed over. Again, I resisted. I just felt too close to the song. I thought the song—get ready for this—would not be able to be understood by anyone else but me, because it was so attached to a very vulnerable and difficult time in my life. I felt that it was just too personal, that it contained too much of my searching and struggles and the memory of how shaken I was after I composed it. I also thought that it might be too "sappy." I certainly did not think a song like that should be sung at liturgy, being that liturgical prayer is *communal*, not personal. But she finally persuaded me to play it for her. So I did. Kate was the first person who I shared the song with.

After I played through and sang the song for her, with my hands shaking and heart pounding, we just sat there for a few moments and said nothing. Then Kate finally broke the silence, in a way that only she could do, as the blunt and "to the point" person that she was: "Uh … David …. I think you need to bring this song out of hiding." She had me play it again, and a couple more times after that, while she slowly added some harmony to the refrain each time. We cried and hugged it out. And she made me promise her that I would record and publish it. I meekly agreed. I tested the refrain out at a workshop I presented in New York a while later, and was stunned as to how the people responded.

Go figure. Who would have thought? I sure didn't. It has awakened in me how narcissistic I was being during all that time before playing it for Kate, and how crazy I was for thinking that there was no way that anyone else could go through or understand the pain that I went through—that my feelings of darkness and loneliness were not universal. While I did share it at a couple of concerts before then, it was deliberately sung and prayed in public for the first time (and released as a recording and choral octavo—with Kate's wonderful harmony part) at the 1991 convention of the National Association of Pastoral Musicians in Pittsburgh, for an opening night communal celebration of the Anointing of the Sick. As the years have gone by, this song has somehow penetrated the hearts of many. It has been translated into numerous languages and recorded and arranged by many artists; one only has to surf on YouTube to see how many different "covers" of this song have come to the surface. It has become the most requested song for me to share wherever I go, and it seems to have found its way into dozens of hymnals of numerous Christian denominations.

Many have also sent to me various instrumental versions of the piece, and numerous choral music publishers have published their own arrangements of the song. What was and continues to be a huge surprise to me, have been the numerous recordings I have received from solo Christian artists (of every denominational stripe and of varied levels of talent) who have recorded it as a solo performance piece. This still is difficult and uncomfortable for me, as it was never, ever my intent that this be anything but a piece sung by the people. Sometimes the performances are quite good, while other vocal performances are painful and extremely stylized (badly)—and such renderings, to be honest, make me shudder. Sorry.

I WILL BRING YOU HOME

However, I have been in the congregation when this song is used, and I have enjoyed—and have been able to pray with—some very interesting interpretations. One year, when I was in an arena with 12,000 teenagers (at "Youth Day" during the annual Los Angeles Religious Education Congress), the young singers and instrumentalists on the stage chose this as the opening song for their final liturgy. They arranged and adapted it as a slamming rock and roll song, with a big and aggressive back beat, and power chords coming forth from the electric guitars. I have to say, it was *wonderful*. It really worked. It seemed as though everyone in the arena grabbed on to it, and offered it as a passionate prayer.

This is an important lesson for all liturgical composers. While I certainly have heard some questionable interpretations of "You Are Mine" and other pieces of mine, I have also been happily presented with interpretations and arrangements where someone who is not so close to the piece has discovered a nuance or insight into the song, and been able to present it to a wider audience in a beautiful way. As I learned the lesson from my own self-absorbed feelings about sharing this song when I first wrote it, I have come to know that once you compose and publish something, you have to set it free. The song does not belong to the composer—as I very dramatically found out. It belongs to the church, most prominently in the celebration of liturgy, but also to those who find such music meaningful in significant times of their lives. When I first composed "You Are Mine," it was totally mine. Not anymore.

Beyond all of the many interpretations and versions, I have to say that I am most touched and moved when someone comes up to me and shares with me that "You Are Mine" was sung at the funeral of a loved one, or when I hear stories about how the song has gotten someone through a difficult and painful time; when I have heard from chaplains that the song has been a life-line for offenders who have been incarcerated, and when young people thank me for writing for them a song of comfort when they have been battling with poor self-esteem or contemplating suicide. These are the instances where I know that the song was from the beginning, and continues to be, a gift and a reminder that I have merely been the vehicle, not the source, of the comfort and solace that this song has been for so many. God is so good.

I have nothing more to say except—thanks, Kate! (11.27.17)

CD
MP3
Music

As Water to the Thirsty; Singing Assembly;
You Are Mine: The Best of David Haas, Vol. 2;
Glory Day: David Haas and Friends In Concert
X-17713
G-3506

YOU ARE THE PRESENCE

Music and Text:
David Haas

You are the presence, breath of all passion and fire!
Filling the earth, splashing the heavens with light!
Wind and the ocean, maker of earth and the skies!
Color and sound, seeking and singing the song!

You are the healing, hope for all people in fear!
Comfort and peace, tenderness is your embrace!
Word and the silence, strength to the broken and weak!
Laughter from tears, promise of life from death!

You are the thunder, power and voice of the just!
Holy and strong, fountain of wonder and might!
Father and mother, lover and dreamer for all!
Joy of our lives, returning, renewing the earth!

God's activity in the midst of the natural wonders of creation is an awesome thing, indeed. "You Are the Presence" is my response to such an encounter.

In the early 1980's I had been hearing much about a conference that was held each year in Hilo, Hawaii, called, The Big Island Liturgy and Arts Conference, held at a very small native Hawaiian village just outside the city limits, at a parish named "Malia Puka O Kalani" (which translates, "Mary, Gate of Heaven"). Joe Wise had presented there in past years, and so had Marty and Linda Haugen. I was invited to attend and present there for the first time at their fall 1985 gathering. I found out later that the conference organizers—Fr. George DeCosta, Joe Camacho, Paul Neves and Clayton Kua—were "checking me out" for some time, to see if I would be a good fit for this very unique event that brought together people from throughout the Islands to be formed, nurtured, and affirmed in their ministry of liturgy and music.

I WILL BRING YOU HOME

I had no idea how profound an experience it would be to be a part of this event, nor could I have predicted the level of impact that this community, this conference, and these wonderful people would have on me throughout my life. There is not enough space here to share how powerful the experience was, other than to say it was transformative. The blending together of powerful music, dance, preaching, storytelling, all through the lens of the indigenous Hawaiian culture and their people, brought about a seismic shift in how I saw the possibility of passionate liturgical celebration and the pastoral care of God's people.

I have been invited back almost every year since 1985, for many conferences at Malia and other locations including (in recent years) Chaminade University in Honolulu. In particular, Fr. George and Joe Camacho have been a part of numerous projects and events that I have been involved with here on the continent; Joe has sung on many of my recordings, and Fr. George has been a most attentive mentor and friend. Others from Malia and other parts of Hawaii are now an intimate part of the fabric of my life, such as Kathy and Glenn Baybayan, Fr. Alapaki Kim, Paulette Ching, Dean Pakele, Sr. Yoo Soo Kim, Bro. Dennis Schmitz and the entire Marianist community at Chaminade, and Joe and Peggy Farias and their two children: Sr. Louis Bullis, MM and Doreen Baptiste and her family. It was at one of the BILAC conferences where I first met Helen while she was pursuing graduate studies at the University of Hawaii. I have made many pilgrimages there with my parents and other close friends and colleagues, and it was here where I came to meet for the first time and develop close friendships with people like Betsey Beckman, Fr. Michael Sparough, Graziano and Nancy Marcheschi, and Waldemar Perez.

At that first conference in 1985 I was part of a team of presenters that included Marty and Linda, Bobby Fisher, Waldemar, Elaine Rendler, Fr. Don Osuna, and Ron Griffen. After the three-day conference and a few more days of play, fun and sight-seeing, it was time for me to return home to Minnesota. I was one of the last artists to leave the Hilo airport to return home that day, so Fr. George and I had a wonderful and friendship-deepening dinner, just the two of us, at a Japanese restaurant nearby. In the middle of the dinner, Fr. George received a phone call telling him that the still active volcano, *Kilauea*, had erupted in a major way, and we needed to come to where they lived so we could get a good view. So off we went, and I do not think I have ever seen anything quite like it. It was a geyser of fire and lava leaping into the sky (it happens to have been the last time it has had an eruption of this size), and I was totally transfixed in silence, starring at it for about 20 minutes. Then I had to get to the airport.

Music & Stories YOU ARE THE PRESENCE

After being seen off by about 30 people from the parish, I got on the plane. After we left the ground, the pilot flew as close as he could for us to see an even more fantastic view of what was for me, a wonder of the world.

Once we got farther away from the Hilo airport, I took a pen to paper, and on the plane, right then there, created a poem, the words that you see above. It came screaming out of me just like the volcano was erupting. No music, just the words. It was a lasting memory that will always remain holy for me.

It was a couple of weeks later that the music arrived to give life to the words. All I could think of was the movement and energy of the volcano, which is why the rhythmic piano part was created. I remember when I played it for Fr. George for the first time. He liked it so much he had me share it at the conference the following year, accompanied by a video of *Kilauea* doing its magic. I recorded it in 1987, calling upon Bobby Fisher (electric guitar) and Marty Haugen (synthesizer) to assist me in creating an instrumental interlude between the second and final verse. The other instrumentalists, like Patrice Pakiz on oboe, and the amazing drummer, Gordy Kundtson, filled out our "volcanic" ensemble. I have no way to describe it. You just have to hear it.

This was during the time when Marty, Michael Joncas and I were active in presenting concerts and workshops together across the country, and so I called upon them to sing it with me on the recording, along with some extra male "beef" from our bass-singer friend Jim Waldo (who to this day, still sings on all of my recordings). In addition, the amazingly powerful and laser-singing of Robin Medrud on the final descant ... amazing.

It was not until the recording was finished (appearing for the first time on *As Water to the Thirsty*), that I realized that the song is Trinitarian, but expressed—not consciously at the time—through the core elements of nature. The first verse begins: "You are the presence ..." (the Father Creator), followed by "You are the healing" (Jesus, the incarnation of God to the world), and "You are the thunder" (the movement and work of the Spirit).

The video performance of *Glory Day* which took place in 1996 provides both an aural and a visual experience of the song, featuring clips from the volcano erupting, Joe Camacho beginning the song with a Hawaiian chant, and incredible dance and movement by Joe, Donna Anderle, Jean Bross-Judge, and Bob Piercy.

I love my annual visits to Hawaii, as each one calls to mind that first conference experience, this song, and the deepening of such important friendships. The song is dedicated to Fr. George; his passionate preaching, teaching, and witness of ministry is like the fire of the volcano—always stirring, never tiring, always convicted. I love every opportunity I have to be there. When I am not able to do so, I have to resort to watching the episodes of "Hawaii-Five-O" to keep me connected. Mahalo! (11.22.17)

CD
MP3
Music

We Have Been Told;
Without Seeing You: The Best of David Haas: Vol. 3
X-80501
G-2705

YOU ARE THE VOICE

Music and Text:
David Haas

You are the voice of the living God,
calling us now to live in your love,
to be children of God once again!

Praise for the light
  that shines through the night,
from darkness to light, from death to new life,
and praise to the morning
  that brings forth the sun,
to open our eyes to the Lord!
  To open our eyes to the Lord!

Praise for the water that springs from the sea,
the seed that gives live to all who believe,
God's love overflowing,
  our hearts know the joy
to be daughters and sons of the Lord!
To be daughters and sons of the Lord!

Praise for the singing and praise for the dance,
with new heart and voice, all raise the song
of praise to creation; all heaven and earth,
come sing of the glory of God!
Come sing of the glory of God!

Copyright © 1983 GIA Publications, Inc.

I WILL BRING YOU HOME

It has been brought to my attention over the years by several people, that this refrain reflects the way I often talk and how I can be in social situations—this long refrain is one sentence with no place to breathe! Many years ago, one of the parish organists I worked with bumped into Marty Haugen at a store, introduced herself and shared that she worked with me at her parish. Marty then replied, "you must be exhausted."

This song is an example of how true it is that hope often springs eternal when we are in the darkest and most hopeless of places. I had left my first parish job, and I was living in the basement of some friends of mine during the year I lived in Iowa (1981-1982). I had no money, no job, and because I did not know how to cook (I still don't), I often would make soup out of a can in my cold and damp environment. A few months earlier I had composed "We Have Been Told," but after that I remained for some time in the midst of a major musical and creative drought, in uncertain transition, not knowing where I would end up and what I would find myself doing.

Then, one evening while eating my chicken noodle soup, out of nowhere came the refrain for this song, totally, with no punctuation (a couple of commas finally came later). I don't know why or how it came to the surface, but I do remember it providing me a bit of hope that maybe I still had some more things to say and to share. The refrain remained in my briefcase for quite a while. Three months later, I moved back to the twin cities, and was hired as Director of Music and Liturgy at St. Thomas Aquinas in St. Paul Park. Soon after, I finished this piece, and then more hymns, psalms, and (hopefully!), inspired songs began to emerge, leading this song to be a part of my first recorded collection with GIA, "We Have Been Told." I guess good things come to those who are cold, poor, and anxious while eating their soup. (11.25.17)

CD
MP3
Music

Before I Was Born; Living Spirit, Holy Fire, Vol. 2
X-44801
G-5181

YOU MAKE ALL THINGS NEW

Music:
David Haas
Text:
Ezekiel 36:24-28
(alt. DH)

God, you make all things new.
Wash us, renew us.
Breathe your Spirit into us.

I will draw you from the nations,
gather all from exile
and bring you home, bring you home.
I will cleanse you in fresh water,
free you from all the filth of idols
and make you clean again.

A new heart I will give to you,
breathe into you my own Spirit
and remove your heart of stone
and give to you a heart of flesh.
I will give you my Spirit
to lead you in my way,
faithful to all my commands.

Breathe your Spirit into us:
Then you will live in the land,
a land that I gave your ancestors.
You will be my people,
and I will be your God;
and I will be your God.

I WILL BRING YOU HOME

In the final months of 1999, with the beginning of the new millennium close at hand, I was reflecting and meditating quite a bit as to what my new resolve would be when this event came upon us. I was thinking about my vocation and ministry in particular, and I vowed at the time that I wanted to make a new start, a new beginning—not just as a minister, but in every aspect of my life. In doing this examination of conscience, this song came to life. New things. Renewal. Accepting the breath and work of the Spirit in my life. It made sense to me then when I composed this. It still makes sense to me now. When and if you get the chance, listen to the recording of this piece. I sang the verses with Lori True. All that I will say here is that I think it is very cool. (11.25.17)

CD
MP3
Music

As Water to the Thirsty;
You Are Mine: The Best of David Haas, Vol. 2
X-17707
G-3501

YOU'VE SEARCHED ME

Music:
David Haas
Text:
Psalm 139
(alt. DH)

You've searched me, Lord.
You know me when I sit and when I stand.
You know me. You know me.

Where can I escape you?
  Your presence surrounds me.
When I climb to the heavens, you find me.

If I fly to the sunrise, or westward to the sea,
your right hand would guide me, holding me.

I have two musical settings of Psalm 139, and "You've Searched Me" was the first attempt, composed back in 1987 (the later setting was composed in 2000, "Before I Was Born"). This psalm is often referred to as revealing God as the "Hound of Heaven," due to its showing us a God who knows everything we do, everything that we think, everything we are about to say before we say it, everywhere we are. We cannot escape God's presence, attentiveness and activity in our lives.

The strongest remembrance for me about this psalm setting was that it came about as I was coming to grips with the reality that to have a God who knows us this well is not always a comforting thing. Sometimes it is downright terrifying. To be that *known*, to know that there can be no secrets with God, that God knows absolutely everything—is an intense and very vulnerable thing. It can be scary. It often is. I know I felt that when I wrote this setting, and to this very day I have moments or periods of time, when this comes piercing through.

At the same time, however, if I—if we—believe in a God who loves us beyond our imagination, who never desires punishment or shame toward us, who forgives and heals and never gives up on us—then, to be this *known*, to be totally "found out" by God, offers the gift of freedom. I think about the story of the Samaritan Woman (John 4: 5-42): the gift she is given in this encounter with Jesus is that he offers her an astonishing example of this love of God, that while naming and revealing to her the darkest demons of her life, he not only still loves her, but he loves her even more.

This is God's way and attitude toward us. God knows all of the things we keep secret from others, and even the things we keep secret from ourselves. And that love keeps coming. Being "searched" is an action of an unconditional love. It is in that total transparency that God sees before we see—and the love of God pours out upon us beyond our wildest dreams. When I sing and pray, "you know me," my fear can turn to serenity. God certainly wants this kind of deep peace for us, and desires that we hold nothing back, but put it all out there. If I can get in touch with that, I do not need to run, I do not need to escape. I can be right here, just as I am. (11.22.17)

GOSPEL KINDRED

Traditional Shaker song, adapted and arranged by Michael Joncas and David Haas

Gospel kindred, how I love thee.
Tongue nor pen can never say
the very feelings of affection
growing stronger day by day.
Together we travel with the gospel,
and we bow down to what is true,
and tell the world that Christ our savior
is creating things anew!

Arrangement Copyright © 2017 GIA Publications, Inc.

I conclude this book as I often conclude many of my concerts, with this song—an adaptation of a song from the Shaker tradition. Michael Joncas first shared this piece and other songs from the Shakers with me, many years ago. Another favorite is "O, the Blessed Gospel" (that I included on my CD, *Living Spirit, Holy Fire, Volume 1*):

O, the blessed Gospel!
O, the blessed Gospel—it shall be mine!
I will labor for it;
I will labor for it—it shall be mine!

After learning and singing "Gospel Kindred" with Michael from time to time, I took a few of the notes of the melody and changed it a bit. After all of these years of sharing what I call this spiritual "love note of gratitude"—I have finally recorded it and it is part of the CD that accompanies this book.

It says it all. It gets to the heart of the matter regarding the vocation of the pastoral musician and those who are engaged as liturgical composers—at least for me. The ministry of liturgical music, which I have been a very small participant in over the past forty years, speaks to the heart of the mission of my life, and all of our lives: to live, breathe, and sing in relationship with God and in relationship with the people of God—yes, in the liturgy that we celebrate in our communities of faith, but also in the midst of the liturgy of life that we are called to bring to birth. The result, hopefully, is that we will always be able to participate in the holy announcement of Christ's rising, and our rising with him, "creating all things new."

So, my dear sisters and brothers—my "Gospel kindred"—know of my affection for you and deep gratitude for your entering into the song-prayers of my life.

Soli Deo Gloria! (11.22.17)

POSTLUDES

APPENDIX 1:
REFERENCE GUIDES
#1: Chronology of Recordings, Printed Music Collections, & Liturgical Music Resources

Unless otherwise noted, all of the recordings, collections, and resources listed here are available from GIA Publications, Inc.

1979	**I Am Yours Today** (LP: Self-produced – out of print)
1981	**In Song** (with various composers, The Liturgical Press; LP, cassette, - out of print)
1982	**Psalms for the Church Year** (with Marty Haugen: LP, CD, cassette, music editions)
1983	**We Have Been Told** (LP, cassette, CD, music book)
	I Am Yours Today: Second Edition (Cooperative Music; LP, cassette, song book—all out of print)
1985	**Come and Journey** (with Marty Haugen and Michael Joncas; LP, cassette, song book; VHS video-out of print)
	To Be Your Bread (LP, cassette, CD, music book)
1986	**Light and Peace** (LP, cassette, CD, music book, various prayer editions)
1987	**Lead Me, O Lord** (with Christopher Walker, Paul Inwood, & Jeanne Cotter. OCP Publications; LP, cassette and music book—all out of print)
	As Water to the Thirsty (LP, cassette, CD, music book)
	I Am Yours Today: A New Recording (OCP Publications; LP, cassette, music book—out of print)
	Singing Assembly (with Marty Haugen and Michael Joncas; CD, cassette)
1988	**Winter Grace** (with Jeanne Cotter; CD, cassette, music book)
	Who Calls You by Name, Vol. 1 (Double CD, cassette, music editions)
1989	**Creating God** (Including *Mass of Light*; CD, cassette, music book)
	Mass of Light (Music editions)
	I Shall See God (CD, cassette, music book, octavo packet)
	Psalms for the Church Year, Vol. 3 (with Jeanne Cotter; CD, cassette, music editions)
1991	**Who Calls You by Name, Vol. 2** (Double CD, cassette, music editions)
	Gospel Proclamations for the Scrutinies (with Vicky Tufano; proclamation book for Lectors)
	Table Songs, Vol. 1 (CD, cassette, music book, octavo packet)
	How Excellent, Vol. 1 & 2: Music for Teens (various composers; CD, music edition)

I WILL BRING YOU HOME

1992	**Mass for the Life of the World / Misa Par La Vida del Mundo** (CD, cassette, music editions, octavo packet)
1993	**When Love Is Found** (with Jeanne Cotter, CD—Selections; cassettes, several music editions, liturgy planning book)
	How Can I Keep from Singing? (with Marty Haugen and Jeanne Cotter; CD, cassette)
1995	**Blest Are They: The Best of David Haas, Vol. 1** (CD, cassette)
	You Are Mine: The Best of David Haas, Vol. 2 (CD, cassette)
	No Longer Strangers (CD, cassette, music book, octavo packet)
	Come and Journey (with Marty Haugen and Michael Joncas; re-release; CD, cassette)
	With Every Note I Sing (Prayer book for pastoral musicians)
1996	**Where the River Flows** (CD, cassette, music book, octavo packet)
	Psalms for the Church Year, Vol. 8 (CD, cassette, music editions)
	Ritual Song (Hymnal; several editions)
	I Will Call God's Name: The Ministry of the Cantor (with Bonnie Faber; VHS video)
1997	**Glory Day: David Haas and Friends in Concert** (CD, cassette, octavo packet, VHS video)
	Throughout All Time (CD, cassette, octavo packet)
	God Has Done Marvelous Things (with Leon Roberts, CD, cassette, octavo packet)
	Walking by Faith (with Robert Piercy, CD, cassette, music book and ancillary editions)
1998	**Alive in Christ Jesus** (CD, cassette, octavo packet)
	We Give You Thanks (CD, cassette, octavo packet)
	Mass: Jesus, the Compassion of God (Various printed editions)
	Music and the Mass (Book; LTP Publications)
	Psalms for the Church Year, Vol. 9 (CD, cassette, music editions)
1999	**Teach Us to Pray: Praying the Psalms** (Video program; St. Anthony Messenger Press)
	Spirit of Malia (with various composers; CD)
	Give Your Gifts: The Songs (with various composers; CD, music editions)
	We Are Fire! Companion Songs for the Catholic Youth Bible (with various composers; CD; Saint Mary's Press)
	First Annual "*Music Ministry Alive!*" Institute (St. Paul, MN)
2000	**Before I Was Born** (CD, cassette, octavo packet)
	Star Child (CD, cassette, octavo packet)
2001	**I Will Sing Forever** (Prayer book for pastoral musicians)

Echo of Faith (CD, cassette, octavo packet)

With You by My Side, Vol. 1: The Journey of Life (CD, cassette,
   music book)

With You by My Side, Vol. 2: Confirmation (CD, cassette, music book)

To Worship in Spirit and Truth (Booklet)

Singing Our Faith (Children's Hymnal; several editions)

Give Your Gifts: The New Songs (with various composers; CD, music editions)

2002 **The Ministry and Mission of Sung Prayer** (Book, St. Anthony Messenger Press)

2003 **Reach Toward Heaven** (CD, cassette, octavo packet)

Do This in Memory of Me: Holy Communion (CD, cassette, octavo packet,
   liturgical editions)

Psalms for the Seasons (Music book)

2004 **Table Songs, Vol. 2** (CD, cassette, octavo packet)

Blest Are We (Catechetical Resource; with other composers, 8-CD set, various editions)

2005 **God Is Here** (CD, cassette, octavo packet)

Come to the Table: Music for First Communion (with various composers;
   CD, choral packet)

Biblical Way of the Cross (CD, prayer book)

A Time to Pray: With the Old Testament (CD, prayer book)

A Time to Pray: With the New Testament (CD, prayer book)

Increase Our Faith (CD, prayer book)

2006 **A Time to Pray: For Justice and Peace** (CD, prayer book)

2007 **Living Spirit, Holy Fire, Vol. 1** (CD, octavo packet)

Living Spirit, Holy Fire, Vol. 2 (CD, octavo packet)

2008 **Companion Songs for "Called to Holiness"** (various composers, CD;
   (GIA & St. Anthony Messenger Press)

2009 **Without Seeing You: The Best of David Haas, Vol. 3** (CD)

Glory to God: The Best of David Haas, Vol. 4 (CD)

Give Me Jesus (CD, octavo packet, prayer book)

2010 **A Changed Heart** (CD, octavo packet, prayer book)

2011 **Mass for a New World** (Revised Order of Mass 2010; CD, music editions)

Mass of Light (Revised Order of Mass 2010; CD, music editions)

Mass for the Life of the World / Misa Par La Vida del Mundo
   (Revised Order of Mass 2010; CD, music editions)

Instruments at Prayer, Vol. 1 (CD)

Instruments at Prayer, Vol. 2 (CD)

2013 **We Are Not Alone** (CD, octavo packet, prayer book)

Music and the Mass: Second Edition (Book, LTP Publications)

Cry Out with Joy: Year A (with Lori True, Paul Tate, Stephen Pishner, and Kathleen Harmon, SNDden; CD, music editions)

Cry Out with Joy: Christmas, Triduum, Solemnities and other Celebrations (with Lori True, Paul Tate, Stephen Pishner, and Kathleen Harmon, SNDden; CD, music editions)

2014 **Mass of Christ, Our Hope** (Revised Order of Mass 2010; CD, music editions)

Do Not Be Afraid, I Am with You (CD, octavo packet, prayer book)

God Will Delight (with Lori True; CD, octavo packet)

God Is Everywhere! (CD, octavo packet)

Cry Out with Joy: Year B (with Lori True, Paul Tate, Stephen Pishner, and Kathleen Harmon, SNDden: CD, music editions)

2015 **The Rosary with St. James** (CD; music and various prayer editions)

I Will Live On (CD; music and various prayer editions)

Cry Out with Joy: Year C (with Lori True, Paul Tate, Stephen Pishner, and Kathleen Harmon, SNDden; CD, music editions)

Glory Day: David Haas and Friends in Concert (Video re-release on DVD; Fransican Media)

On Eagle's Wings: Minnesota's Sacred Music (Television Documentary: KMSQ Public Television, Austin, MN; with Michael Joncas, Marty Haugen, Dan Kantor, Lynn Trapp, and Sr. Delores Dufner, OSB)

The Beloved of God (Digital download)

Praying and Singing as the Beloved of God (Digital download; Clear Faith Publishing)

2016 **With Gratitude** (with Marty Haugen and Michael Joncas; CD, octavo packet)

Ritual Song: Second Edition (Hymnal; several editions)

2017 **When We Are Weak, We Are Strong** (CD, octavo packet)

With Gratitude: An Evening Celebrating the Music of David Haas, Marty Haugen, and Michael Joncas (with Marty Haugen and Michael Joncas; Livestream Video, GIA, available on YouTube)

An Interview with David Haas: Music, Ministry and Life (Livestream Video, GIA, available on YouTube)

That You Might Have Life (Digital CD Download)

God Never Tires (with Zack Stachowski; CD, octavo packet)

2018 **I Will Bring You Home: Songs of Prayer, Stories of Faith** (Book with CD featuring musical selections)

#2: Hymnals, Missalettes, and Congregational Supplements

The hymnals, missalette programs and supplements listed below all contain numerous compositions of David Haas. This is not a complete listing.

GIA PUBLICATIONS
Catholic Community Hymnal
Cross Generation
Gather
Gather Australia
Gather: Second Edition
Gather Comprehensive
Gather Comprehensive: Second Edition
Gather: Third Edition
Gather to Remember
Hymnal Supplement 1991
Lead Me, Guide Me: Second Edition
Oramos Cantando / We Pray in Song
Our Growing Years
Revised Order of Mass Supplement (2010)
Ritual Song
Ritual Song: Second Edition
Singing Our Faith
Singing Our Faith: Second Edition
Worship: Third Edition
Worship: Fourth Edition

OTHER PUBLISHERS
Breaking Bread (OCP Publications, various editions)
Catholic Book of Worship III (Canadian Conference of Catholic Bishops)
Catholic Worship Book II (The Australian Catholic Bishop's Conference)
Celebrating Grace (Celebrating Grace, Inc)
Chalice Hymnal (Disciples of Christ / Chalice Press)
Common Praise (Anglican Church of Canada)
Evangelical Lutheran Worship (Augsburg Fortress)
Glory and Praise (OCP Publications, various editions)
Glory to God: The Presbyterian Hymnal (Westminster John Knox Press)
In Caelo: Songs for a Pilgrim People (Ireland/Veritas)
JourneySongs: Second Edition (OCP Publications)
The Laudate Hymnal (England, Decani Music)

I WILL BRING YOU HOME

One Voice (Australia / Willow Publishing, Ltd., various editions)

People's Mass Book: Second Edition (WLP Publications)

Psalms for All Seasons (Faith Alive Christian Resources)

Lift Up Your Hearts (Faith Alive Christian Resources)

Sacred Song (The Liturgical Press, various editions)

Sing the Journey (Mennonite; Faith & Life Resources)

Spirit & Song (OCP Publications, various editions)

Today's Missal (OCP Publications, various editions)

This is Our Faith (Silver Burdett)

Voices as One (WLP Publications, various editions)

We Celebrate (WLP Publications, various editions)

Wonder, Love, and Praise (The Church Pension Fund)

Word and Song (WLP Publications, various editions)

Worship & Praise (Augsburg Fortress)

Worship & Rejoice (Hope Publishing Company)

Worship Together (Mennonite Brethren Churches / Christian Press)

APPENDIX 2:
PROFESSIONAL / EDUCATION CHRONOLOGY

1975—2018

1975	Graduated from Bridgeport High School *(Bridgeport, MI)*
1975—1977	Studies in Vocal Music Performance at Central Michigan University *(Mt. Pleasant, MI)*
1977—1978	Ministry at Parish and School Communities, Diocese of Saginaw, MI *(St. Christopher's, Bridgeport; St. Casimir's School, Saginaw; Sacred Heart, Bad Axe; St. Roch's, Caseville; St. Helen's School, Saginaw; St. Josaphat's, Saginaw)*
1978—1980	St. John Vianney Seminary / College of St. Thomas *(St. Paul, MN*
1978—Present	Member and Presenter for the National Association of Pastoral Musicians
1979	Release of first recording, *I Am Yours Today (Self-produced)*
1980—1981	Pastoral Musician, Blessed Sacrament Parish *(St. Paul, MN)*
1981—1982	Director of Music and Youth Ministry, Our Lady's Immaculate Heart Parish *(Ankeny, IA)*
	Consultant for the Diocesan Office for Liturgy *(Des Moines, IA)*
1982—1985	Director of Music/Liturgy, St. Thomas Aquinas Parish *(St. Paul Park, MN)*
1982	Release of first published original collection of liturgical music with GIA Publications, *Psalms for the Church Year (with Marty Haugen)*
1983	Release of first solo recorded/published original collection of liturgical music with GIA Publications, *We Have Been Told*
1984	"Come and Journey" concert with Michael Joncas and Marty Haugen for the Archdiocese of St. Paul and Minneapolis "Faith Gathering" *(Minneapolis, MN)*
1985—1996	Faculty/Team Member for Institutes with the North American Forum on the Catechumenate
1985—1987	Member of the Steering Committee for the Association of Liturgical Ministers, Archdiocese of St. Paul and Minneapolis
1985—1988	Composer-in-Residence/Adjunct Instructor, St. Paul Seminary School of Divinity. *(St. Paul, MN)*
1985—2015	Presenter at the annual Big Island Liturgy and Arts Conference *(Hilo & Honolulu, HI)*
1986—Present	Presenter for the Los Angeles Religious Education Congress *(Anaheim, CA)*
1987—1988	Member of the Editorial Committee for the first edition of the *Gather* Hymnal with GIA Publications
1991	Grammy Award Nomination, *I Shall See God (GIA)*

I WILL BRING YOU HOME

1991—1994	Composer-in-Residence / Pastoral Musician, St. Thomas the Apostle Parish *(Minneapolis, MN)*
1991	Completion of Bachelor of Arts Degree in Theology and Vocal Music Performance, The University of St. Thomas *(St. Paul, MN)*
1991—1992	Participant at the Milwaukee Symposia for Church Composers
1992	Team member for *Beginnings and Beyond Institute* in Italy *(The North American College, Rome)*
1992—Present	Director, The Emmaus Center for Music, Prayer and Ministry
1993	Presenter at the National Liturgical Music Convention *(Melbourne, Australia)*
1994	Distinguished Alumnus Award / The University of St. Thomas *(with Michael Joncas and Marty Haugen; St. Paul, MN)*
1995	Leader; First Biblical and Musical Pilgrimage to Israel *(with Art Zannoni)*
1996	Leader; Second Biblical and Musical Pilgrimage to Israel *(with Art Zannoni)*
1997	Leader; Third Biblical and Musical Pilgrimage to Israel *(with Art Zannoni)*
1997—2011	Campus Minister & Artist-in-Residence, Benilde-St Margaret's High School *(St Louis Park, MN)*
1998	Faculty, Annual Conference of the Irish Church Music Association *(Maynooth, Ireland)*
1999—2002	Member of the Advisory Council for the National Association of Pastoral Musicians
1999—Present	Founder and Executive Director, *Music Ministry Alive!* *(St. Paul, MN)*
2000	United Catholic & Video Association Unity Award *(with Marty Haugen and Michael Joncas)*
2002	Faculty Presenter at the Knockadoon Folk Liturgy Course *(with Lori True; Knockadoon, Ireland)*
	United Catholic & Video Association Unity Award
2003	Catholic Press Association Book Award for *The Ministry and Mission of Sung Prayer*
2004—2005	Member of the National Advisory Board for Harcourt Religion Publishers *(Orlando, FL)*
2004	Pastoral Musician of the Year; The National Association of Pastoral Musicians
	Crosier Award for Outstanding Service in Ministry / Crosier Fathers and Brothers *(St. Paul, MN)*
	"To Serve as Jesus Did" Award; Servants of Jesus *(Saginaw, MI)*
2005	Leader; Biblical and Musical Pilgrimage to Turkey and Greece: In the Footsteps of St. Paul *(with Marty Haugen, Michael Joncas, Bob Batastini)*

2007	Public Television Program/Video: *Glory Day: David Haas and Friends in Concert (Cincinnati, OH)*
2011—2015	Campus Minister, Cretin-Derham Hall High School *(St. Paul, MN)*
2011—Present	Animator; Cretin-Derham Hall Taize' Prayer Community in St. Paul
2013—2015	Member of the Steering Committee for the St. Louis Liturgical Composers Forum *(St. Louis, Missouri)*
2014	Emmaus Award for Excellence in Catechesis; National Catholic Education Association /National Association of Parish Catechetical Directors *(Pittsburgh, PA)*
2015	Honorary Doctorate in Humane Letters, *HONORIS CAUSA*; University of Portland *(Portland, OR)*
	Association of Catholic Publisher's Book Award for *Welcome, Faithful Presence*
2016	"Lumen Pacifica" Concert and Workshop Tour to Guam, The Philippines, and Singapore
2017	Fourth Biblical and Musical Pilgrimage to Israel *(with Art Zannoni)*
	Association of Catholic Publisher's Book Award for *My Heart Is Ready*
	Final Joint Concert with Marty Haugen and Michael Joncas: Los Angeles Religious Education Congress *(Anaheim, CA)*
	Catholic Press Association Book Award for *My Heart Is Ready*
	2017 Pax Christi Award / St. John's Abbey and University *(with Michael Joncas and Marty Haugen; Collegeville, MN)*
	Plenum, Keynote, and Workshop Presenter/for the Australian Pastoral Musician's Network National Conference *(Perth, Australia)*
	Concerts and Workshops, New Zealand *(Dunedin, Wellington, Auckland)*

APPENDIX 3:
INFORMATION ABOUT ACCOMPANYING CD:
I Will Bring You Home

Listed here are the songs in order that are included on the companion CD (CD-1041).

All of the others songs, hymns, psalms and other titles featured this book, are available in recorded versions, on various CD's and as individual MP3 downloads.

1—I Will Walk with You

2—I Am Yours Today

3—Now We Remain

4—Song of the Stable

5— My Only Desire

6—Piano Improvisation no. 1 *(Arranged and performed by Gregory Papesh)*

7—My Lord and My God

8—Table Song

9—Mimi's Song

10—The Name of God

11—As Water to the Thirsty

12—We Will Rise Again

13—Piano Improvisation no. 2 *(Arranged and performed by Gregory Papesh)*

14—What Can I Leave Behind?

15—Take All the Lost Home *(Joe Wise)*

16—You Are Mine

17—Gospel Kindred *(Traditional Shaker Song)*

APPENDIX 4:
PHOTO GALLERY COMMENTARY

1—Mom and Dad met in college, and made music together from the start, including here on their wedding day.

2—This was around Christmas time, I think.

3—Always eager for some good cake.

4—When we were young through our high school years, the three of us performed together often for local events in the Saginaw, Michigan area and for Mass at church of course. Mom and Dad loved posing us together at the keyboard.

5—This was the parish where I grew up, right across the field from our house. A lot of forward looking things happened at this parish during those years. In recent years St. Christopher's and another parish clustered together, and while this remains the primary worship site, the parish was renamed as St. Francis de Sales. It will always be St. Christopher's to me.

6—This was on July 4, about a year before he died.

7—Taken with my Mom a couple of years before she passed away.

8—I just love this picture of them both.

9—This is when we were together in June 2017, to celebrate my belated 60th birthday.

10—This photo was taken in the fall of 2017 when I presented some workshops and concerts in Australia in New Zealand.

11—My mother was our high school choir director at Bridgeport High School, and my freshman class had many good young male singers—so she formed us into a group, originally named "The Freshmen," and later throughout our high school years we were dubbed, "The Gentlemen of Song." What a riot.

12—Some people call this my "Jerry Lewis" look—I still have it from time to time.

13—I was a member of what was in the 1970's, the award-winning Bridgeport High School Bearcat Marching Band. These very hot double-knit uniforms reminded people of employees at the local Burger King.

14—I was very involved in musical theatre and opera throughout my high school and college days—this is during my sophomore year at Central Michigan University, where I landed the lead role of "El Capitan the Bloodthirsty" in this rarely-performed comic opera by John Phillip Sousa.

15—These songbooks contained the repertoire of my earliest experiences of contemporary liturgical music: "The Hymnal for Young Christians" (FEL Publications), included those early classics by Ray Repp, Fr. Peter Scholtes, Paul Quinlan, Robert Blue, and Fr. Clarence Rivers; "Biblical Hymns and Psalms" (World Library) by Fr. Lucien Deiss contained some of the first musical settings of biblical texts, including "Keep in Mind," which is still sung widely today; and the very first published volume by Joe Wise, "Gonna Sing My Lord" (World Library Publications, now available from GIA) that included the title song and "Take Our Bread."

16—Here I am during my junior high years, in Florida with my very first piano teacher (who was also my Dad's first piano teacher, believe it or not), "Aunt" Zola Rudd Patrick. She was quite the influence on my life both musically and personally. While she was not a blood relative, she was truly a part of our family. She never liked how I had my hair. She never liked how ANY of us had our hair. Don't know why. I do not have hardly any at all now. She would probably complain about that too.

17—This is Maria "Mimi" Infante, who when she received her first communion in 1972—I wrote my very first song (that is addressed here in the book), "Mimi's Song." Here she is during Christmas 2017. For some reason, for many years now, she calls me "Chuck."

18—Jimmy and I were in the seminary during the same years; he was ordained in 1980, and has served as a priest for the Diocese of Saginaw, MI, ever since. We remain dear friends to this day. He was my very first liturgical mentor.

19—There is not enough space to adequately express the influence that Roberta had on my life—and she still does to this day. I really miss her, especially in my times of self-doubt.

20—I learned from my parents, since the early days of my youth, the joy of sing-alongs. Here I am leading one.

21—A true hero.

22—The Dameans, from L to R: A very young Gary Daigle, with Darryl Ducote, Mike Balhoff, Gary Ault, and Paul "Buddy" Ceasar.

23—A picture of a very young Sr. Suzanne Toolan, taken back in the 1960's. Sr. Suzanne composed the iconic song "I Am the Bread of Life" in the 1960's and it was published in 1970. This song still holds up and prays beautifully to this day. At the time of my writing this, she is well into her 90's, and still leading a regular Taizé prayer gathering regularly at the Mercy Center in San Francisco. A true inspiration and model for us all.

24—This is the cover of my self-produced LP that was released in 1979 (3 songs from this are featured in this book, "I Am Yours Today," "Mimi's Song," and

"My Lord and My God"). The illustration of me (from a winter ski photo) is by my sister Colleen, and the overall design was created by my seminary classmate, Peter Christiansen, who is now the Bishop of the Diocese of Boise, Idaho.

25— I guess this was my very first "publicity" photo, taken by my good friend David Gilmour, back in 1978. It appeared originally on the back cover of my first LP (self-produced), *I Am Yours Today.*

26—I still have this, and the edges are pretty crinkled. To this day, I still have not learned Finale or any music notation software. I still write my scores out by hand, much to the consternation of many of my colleagues. My response? If it was good enough for Mozart, it is good enough for me. I am old school. God bless GIA for making the music look so good!

27—This was a project under the direction of Rob Strusinski, an early mentor of mine, and for many years the Director of Chapel Music at the College of St. Thomas/University of St. Thomas in St. Paul. St. Thomas self-produced this record (1981) that features pieces by students, faculty and alums and sung by the campus Liturgical Choir. Back row, from L to R: Michael Joncas (this was very soon after he was ordained), myself, Paul Rysavy, Jay McHale, Dr. Jim Callahan (my music theory professor), and Rob. Kneeling, from L to R: Mike Rumpza (who played guitar on my "I Am Yours Today" LP), Ron Noecker, and Dan Kantor. This was the very first recording of two of my pieces: "Send Us Your Spirit" and "To Be Your Bread." It is also the premiere recording for Michael's "No Greater Love." It is very difficult to find a copy of this after all these years.

28—Michael Cymbala is really the one - along with Bob Batastini - who brought me in to the doors of GIA. There are no words to express how grateful I am to him, for his early advocacy, his humor, and his support over the years.

29—I was Director of Music and Liturgy here from 1982-1985. This was the community that gave life to many of my first published songs from GIA: "Now We Remain," "You Are the Voice," "The Harvest of Justice," "We Are God's People," "We Will Rise Again," "Alleluia Sing!," "You are God's Work of Art," "Jesus, Wine of Peace," "Song of the Stable," "If Today You Hear God's Voice," "The Lord is My Light," "Be Light for Our Eyes," "Blest Are They," the Mass of Light "Glory to God," "Jesus, Heal Us," and far too many more to mention.

30—This collection not only started the psalm series, but also ignited the well-known "Celebration Series" from GIA that is still going strong.

31—No comment. Getting old. Hate it.

32—This photo shows what is happening in the control room of what was then, Cookhouse Studios (and now, Creation Audio). This was my first full recording with GIA, with "a little help from my friends": Marty was the producer, Jerry engineered, and Sue conducted the choir with gusto.

33—This recorded collection of liturgical music, in my opinion, revolutionized contemporary liturgical music. The music of Roc, Tim, Bob, Dan and John, and their impact on contemporary liturgical music cannot be overstated. "Neither Silver nor Gold," "Earthen Vessels" and "A Dwelling Place" were some of my earliest influences when I began composing liturgical music. These guys were the first "contemporary/folk" composers that truly delved into the scriptures and they re-invented, in my opinion, the role of the choir not as a performance group, but as leaders of prayer. I was (and continue to be) so honored to have been invited to be one of the soloists on their last "group effort" recording, *The Steadfast Love*.

34—Here is the earliest score of the song. If you take a close look at third line of the refrain, you notice that on the word "glad," it is a C minor chord. My friend Jim Waldo heard that and suggested I change it to F minor. I did. It made all the difference.

35—This photo was taken during the rehearsal before the *Come and Journey* concert in 1984 at the old Minneapolis Auditorium.

36—Bobby Fisher is one of the most amazing musicians I have ever worked with, and in addition to playing on dozens and dozens of my recordings, he also has played on many of the recordings of Joe Wise, the St. Louis Jesuits, Ed Gutfruend, Marty Haugen, Jack Miffleton, Bob Hurd, Fran O'Brien, Liam Lawton, Lori True, Tony Alonso, Grayson Warren Brown, Tim Schoenbachler, Michael Joncas, Rob Glover, Paul Tate, Ian Callanan, and many others. Anything with strings—guitars of every kind, mandolin, banjo, ukulele, and even the fiddle—he brings magic to the music.

37—Ed Harris came from a long family line of people working for Carl Fischer in Chicago. In 1967 he bought GIA (which then stood for "The Gregorian Institute of America," founded in 1941), which was for the most part a correspondence training course for Gregorian Chant; the company had recently acquired the US rights for the Gelineau Psalms. After he met Bob, Ed bought the company, and the two of them began this amazing adventure. The story is that after Ed signed the deal, founder of GIA Clifton Bennett said," well, good luck. I have tried everything and have taken this company about as far it could go." To learn more about the GIA story, get a copy of the *GIA Diamond Jubilee Collection: Celebrating 75 Years of Music for the Church* (G-9275). The opening chapters tell the marvelous tale.

38—Bonnie is about to sing solo on two of the pieces for the *Light and Peace* project: "In the Shadow of Your Wings" and "God Is My Light" (addressed in this book). The very next day, she gave birth to her son Jonathan.

39—To learn more about the birth of this song, consult the reflection/story presented in this book.

40—One of my earliest advocates during my days at St. John Vianney Seminary/College of St. Thomas. "Send Us Your Spirit" is dedicated to him.

41—Truly a visionary, and another one of my "pastors" and mentors throughout my life. Fr. George was pastor of Malia Puka O Kalani Church (Mary, Gate of Heaven) in Hilo, Hawaii for many years, and was the founder and primary mover and shaker of the prophetic "Big Island Liturgy and Arts Conference." This gathering not only touched the lives of people throughout the Hawaiian Island, but far beyond, including many composers who have been able to tap in the special charism of both Malia and BILAC: Marty Haugen, Michael Joncas, Lori True, Rory Cooney, Gary Daigle, Donna Peña, Bob Hurd, Bobby Fisher, Michael Mahler, Tony Alonso, Jeanne Cotter, Rob Glover, Marc Anderson, Jesse Manibusan, Christopher Walker, Tom Conry, Paul Tate, Leon Roberts, Derek Campbell, Lynné Gray, Pedro Rubalcalva, and so many others.

42—This is the little parish that gave birth to the Big Island Liturgy and Arts Conference under the leadership of their pastor, Fr. George DeCosta.

43—A recent picture of Bob. What a blessing he has been to the praying church.

44—This collection by the Dameans had a great impact on the development of contemporary music, with its focus on contemporary musical settings of the psalms. This was the first recording/project after Gary Daigle came aboard with the Dameans.

45—Dear friends going back many years.

46—Tom is the engineer who taught me most of what I know today about recording. May he rest in peace.

47—Jim was the founder and first president of the North American Forum on the Catechumenate, which for many years was the single most profound source of formation for the implementation of the Rite of Christian Initiation of Adults (RCIA) in North America and beyond (and much of the music I was to create for the catechumenate). One of the honors of my life was being able to help coordinate and lead the music for his funeral with Tom Conry in 1995.

48—My good friend Bob and I recorded (via many vocal overdubs) the male chant that you hear on the original recording of "Prayer for Peace." One of the most positive people I know.

49—Two very important people in my life who were taken from us way too soon. I was a member of the parish staff with Michael Grimes when I was at St. Thomas Aquinas (1982-1985), and he is the one that planted in my brain the passage from Philippians that led to my composing the song, "The Harvest of Justice." Sue Seid-Martin taught for many years at Notre Dame, then later at St. Catherine University and the St. Paul Seminary School of Divinity in St. Paul. She was an important friend to me, and a mentor for so many of us in liturgical music. In addition to being a masterful organist and choral director, she influenced many composers, beginning with David Clark Isele (his famous "Holy Cross Mass Lamb of God" was a result of Sue's initiative), as well as myself, Marty, and so many others.

50—Thanks Jeanne, for all of the great years of music making and shared concerts and workshops. An amazingly talented woman.

51—At one of the early BILAC conferences (Big Island Liturgy and Arts Conference), around 1998 or so. Standing on the front steps of Malia Puka O Kalani Church. We all were VERY young in this picture.

52—Ed was one of the very first composers to publish and record with North American Liturgy Resources (NALR), with many folk-influenced liturgical songs like "In the Day of the Lord" and "Good Morning, Zachary" (the first contemporary version of the Canticle of Zachary I ever heard). Ed also brought to my attention (and to others as well) treasured traditional songs like "How Can I Keep from Singing" and "The Lights of the City" through his wonderful arrangements. Bobby was often his right-hand man for his recordings and concerts, and while I do not remember when and where this picture was taken, it is a treasure for me.

53—Donna has been an amazingly passionate presence with her commitment to issues of social justice and in exploring the depths of her own culture as well as the traditions of other cultures. People really began to stand up and take notice when they came to know "I Say, Yes, Lord" ("*Digo Si, Señor*").

54—The first collection of its kind, of ritual music for the RCIA.

55—Archbishop Rembert Weakland and Sr. Theophane Hytrek convened several gatherings of the "Milwaukee Symposia for Church Composers" years back in Milwaukee (I was fortunate to have been invited to participate in some of these gatherings), resulting in a ten-year report often referred to as *The Milwaukee Statement for Church Composers*. I remember most of the people in this picture, so here are they are, beginning with the front row, from L to R: Sr. Theophane; Archbishop Weakland; and Omer Westendorf. Second row, from L to R: Paul Inwood; Bob Hurd; Nathan Mitchell; Fr. Andrew Ciferni, O.Praem; and Peter Finn. Third row, from L to R: Marty Haugen; Becket Senchur; Bro. Howard Hughes, SM; Don Saliers; and Fr. Ed Foley, OFM Cap. Fourth row, from L to R: Bernadette Farrell; Fr. Jim Chepponis; yours truly; Fr. Michael Joncas; and

David Clark Isele. Fifth row, from L to R: Gabe Huck; the next two women's names elude me, so very sorry; Eugene Englert, and Fr. Bill Bauman. Top row, from L to R: Fr. Frank Quinn, OP; Bob Twynham; Richard Hillert; Dr. Michael Connolly; and Fr. Charles Conley.

56—The longest my hair has ever been. Not sure it was a good idea at the time. O well.

57—This picture was taken in 1987 at Metro Studios in Minneapolis, during the *As Water to the Thirsty* vocal sessions.

58—We are sharing music at an NPM convention showcase here, from the *Echo of Faith* recording/collection, which had just been released in 2000.

59—Fr. Ray has been a presence of light for all who have come to know him. You can hear him sing on several of my recordings, on songs like "Take Me Home," "God Has Done Marvelous Things," "The Blue Green Hills of Earth," and many others. One of the MMA students a few years back referred to him as "love on legs."

60—This was when Lori was still Director of Music there. In the front row, seated in a chair toward the right, you will see her daughter, Elizabeth.

61—Kathy and Glenn are "Ohana" for Helen and I – our Hawaiian family.

62—If you are thankful for "You Are Mine," thank Kate. She is the one who convinced me to pull it out of hiding. When I met her, she was a professional jingle singer—you can still hear her from time to time on many commercials. She also is addicted to harmonies. Any piece she hears, she just has to add an alto part. They are all really good.

63—This song is dedicated to Frank Brownstead (former Director of Music at the Los Angeles Cathedral and mentor for many). To all who know Frank, I bet they would know why.

64—I have been blest to lead several pilgrimages to Israel over the years. This is always a favorite spot.

65—My Advent/Christmas record *Star Child* is probably one of my favorite recordings for pure listening purposes. In addition to original songs and adaptations of traditional Christmas pieces, there are songs on this collection by Lori True, Dan Kantor, Grayson Brown, and John Foley. To promote the release of the recording, several dear friends of mine (all who are heard on the recording) joined me on a 6-city tour during the Incarnation season in 2000. Back row, from L to R: Tom Franzak, Lori True, Eileen Bird, Kate Cuddy, Dave Hanzel, and Jim Waldo. Middle row, from L to R: Dik Hedlund, David Fischer, a young Sarah Hudetz (the title song is dedicated to her), and Stephen Petrunak. I am kneeling in front with Bobby Fisher.

66—For many years prior to being involved in ministry, Joe was a professional entertainer, singer, dancer, and story-teller who travelled many corners of the world. I met him while he was part of the team at Malia Puka O Kalani in Hilo, HI. He has been an important part of my music through his singing, his dancing, and his spirituality.

67—I think this picture of us was taken at one of the conferences in Hawaii; my choice of shirt gives it away. Lori has been the most significant singing partner from the very beginning, she always "gets" what I am trying to say in my music, and has helped to make it better.

68—Leon was an amazing force. The sheer amount of his body of work is immense. Most of his music has still yet to be published or discovered. One of the most creative composers I have ever known and worked with. Collaborating with him and his musical compatriots ("Robert's Revival") on the *God Has Done Marvelous Things* project stands out as some of the most rewarding moments of music ministry for me.

69—If I were pressed, I would have to say that Marty is among the very best of liturgical composers since Vatican II. He has always challenged himself, and asked important questions about what he is writing and why; always seeking out the important issues that affect sung prayer, especially around the issues of social justice.

70—I have known Richard for many years, and it has been just the last few years where I have gotten to work and collaborate with him. A true prophet.

71—Stephen and I go way back, since he brought me to his parish (St. Blaise in Sterling Heights, MI) in 1984 for a workshop. We have been fast friends ever since, and he has played guitar on many of my recordings over the years. We nickname him "the machine" because of his amazing sense of time and precision. After 40-plus years at St. Blaise, he is now the President of the National Association of Pastoral Musicians. Who would have thought? God bless him.

72—One of the most gorgeous voices ever. We all miss him so very much.

73—How do you like my hair?

74—Here I am with Pearl and Remi at a dinner held at the home of Bonnie Faber and Michael Griffin. Having these two amazing people as part of my life has been quite the gift. As of this writing Remi is well into his nineties—being one of the very few surviving bishops who participated in all four sessions of the Second Vatican Council.

75—At one of the gatherings of the Liturgical Composers Forum in St. Louis.

76—Virgil was the founding president of the National Association of Pastoral Musicians, and always a most supportive presence in my life.

77—My good friend Art was my Hebrew Scriptures professor in college; together we have led several pilgrimages to Israel and collaborated on so many other events and projects. My primary "go-to" guy for anything to do with the Bible. Arthur, *sarò sempre grato per la tua conoscenza, passione, amicizia e amore per le sacre scritture.*

78—MMA is the best thing I have done with my life; better than any musical composition I have created.

79—Here is Bonnie at Corpus Christi Parish in Roseville, Minnesota, one of several communities she has served at over the years. She and I have been close friends since 1982. Bonnie has sung on almost all of my recordings; we taught together at the St. Paul Seminary School of Divinity in the 1980's, and she continues to be the most amazing voice teacher and vocal pedagogue for cantors everywhere. Those who have experienced her in her workshops know exactly what I am talking about.

80—One of my true "sons in the Lord." In my opinion, Zack represents the best of the next generation of liturgical composers. I was so excited to collaborate with him on the *God Never Tires* project. I could say so much more. Not enough room. I look forward to seeing what the future holds for him and for the singing Church who will come to know his music.

81—Especially in the last few years, Lori was the mastermind behind just about every aspect of MMA; Zack came on board in leadership the last year, but he is an alum and been one of our most valuable teachers over the years; Jes is an alum who has a strong business background (she works for TARGET and we are positive that she will run the place some day) and has brought so much hard work in recent years to the program; Fr. Ray has been our MMA pastor from the very beginning; Bill has been a recent addition to the team, but for 2016 and 2017 he has been the primary choral leader for the week (he is chairman of the music department at the University of the Incarnate Word in San Antonio); and Matt is also an alum, who has brought a diversity of gifts to MMA for so many years.

82—I love working with young people so much.

83—This is the beautiful campus at St. Kate's—that has been the sacred space for MMA every year since its beginnings in 1999.

84—While at Cretin-Derham Hall as campus minister (2011-2015) I began the CDH Liturgical Choir. Pure joy.

85—Steve has been the primary engineer for all of my recording projects since *Where the River Flows* in 1996. A true partner in helping my music come to life in the studio.

86—One of the last concerts we presented together, at St. Catherine University in St. Paul.

87—Showing Jesse some love. Sure wish I had written "Open My Eyes."

88—Jim and I go way back to 1982 when I began working at St. Thomas Aquinas. He remains my first call bass singer whenever I put any kind of choir together, and even though he had to endure being my roommate many years ago, I think he still likes me. Dear friend.

89—Marty always brings his unique charism to everything.

90—A true hero. A true saint.

91—One of my favorite pictures of the three of us.

92—This was done many years ago … somewhere in Texas, that is all I can remember.

93—These three goons are just a few among so many wonderful liturgical composer colleagues.

94—To me, Bill continues to be a prophetic voice in all matters regarding catechesis, and in helping to bring the spirituality and wisdom of Pope Francis to life. He also knows more about Vatican II than anyone I know, and has always been so supportive and a joy to collaborate with.

95—Still blown away that this happened. Here I am with some of the friends who came to support and celebrate with me: Virgil Funk, Jimmy Bessert, Bonnie Faber, and Dr. Michael Connolly (from UP).

96—With dear friends and blessed composer colleagues—during one of the meals we had while working together in the midst of the *Cry Out with Joy* project.

97—A most wonderful evening that I will never forget.

98—With one of my very best friends from over the years, Rob Glover.

99—In the fall of 2016 I had an incredible experience doing a concert/workshop tour to Guam, the Philippines, and Singapore. While in Manila, I came to know well this amazing group of young pastoral musicians, named "Hangad" (which means "desire"). "My Only Desire" was composed especially for them.

100—Larry, Derek, and Steve were all members of "Robert's Revival" and collaborators with me on the *God Has Done Marvelous Things* project. Derek was an accomplished choral director, and also one of the featured singers as part of the *Glory Day* concert recording/video. A true humble servant of God. We miss him very much Both Larry and Steve live in New York City, enjoying very successful singing careers. And of course, Joe—what a blessing he is. Some amazing men here in this picture.

101—All I can say, is that I had a blast at this event. We all did.

102—Another highlight of my life, to visit the final resting place of a friend who I never met, but a friend just the same in the midst of my spiritual walk.

103—This is the conference that Fr. Richard Rohr leads every year, sponsored by the Center for Action and Contemplation in Albuquerque.

104 - Every year we had a composer track at MMA. At the very first year (1999) Tony was a participant in this track, and that very week he composed some of his earliest music that eventually was recorded and published by GIA. In addition to Tony, Marty and Ricky, other composer teachers at MMA over the years have included Bobby Fisher, Paul Inwood, Tom Kendzia, Gary Daigle, Zack Stachowski, Fran O'Brien, Michael Joncas, and myself. The young men in this picture are Dale Gray and Michael Ellman.

105—I served here as part of the campus ministry team from 2011-2015. A most marvelous school. I still am connected, as I presently serve as the animator for the monthly gathering of the Cretin-Derham Hall Taizé Prayer Community.

106—I have been blest by so many wonderful singers who have made up the choirs and soloists on my recordings over the years. This picture was taken during a break of the *I Will Live On* vocal sessions. Front row, kneeling, from L to R: Lisa Habeck, Jes Garceau, Katherine True, and Brad Runyan. Second row, from L to R: David Livingston, Bonnie Faber, Angie Flake, Erin Keefe, Lisa Cressy, Zack Stachowski, Lori True, Paul Tate, Stephen Petrunak and yours truly. Back row, from L to R: Eileen Bird, Matt Maus, Joel Fischer, Dave Berget, Jim Waldo and Matt Reichert.

107—Retired priest of the Archdiocese of St. Paul and Minneapolis, and chaplain at Cretin-Derham Hall in St. Paul while I served there. He is the one who first shared with me about Mama D and "putting the love into the food," and who inspired the song, "Be a Blessing."

108—One of many concerts that I have been a part of in the Mystical Rose Oratory on the campus of Chaminade University in Honolulu.

109—A most precious moment for me.

110—What a blessed friend Bonnie has been and continues to be.

111—Masada is an amazing place, truly a wonder of the world. This was taken during the 2016-2017 pilgrimage there, which I led with Art Zannoni and Fr. Ray East.

112—Well, time will tell …

113—Here I am, singing the solo vocals for my lament, "Why, O God?" while wearing the T-shirt proclaiming: "There's no crying in baseball."

114—Conducting in my usual reserved style.

115—This was taken with Michael just before we were to go out and present our final concert together with Marty, at the 2017 Los Angeles Religious Education Congress. I have no words to adequately express what a foundational font of friendship, love, support and insight Michael has been for me throughout my adult life. He has "saved my life" more than once, I can tell you.

116—Preaching on the steps of the Church there, just before we are about to go inside and sing "Blest are They."

117—Fooling around.

118—Truly my brother. My most recent composition "I Will Walk with You" is dedicated to him.

119—Matt and Zack co-host the now already popular podcast, "Open Your Hymnal." Be sure to check it out. Both are MMA alums, and they have been so good to me over the years.

120—Rehearsing before a take of one of the tracks for our *With Gratitude* CD.

121—I have nicknamed him "Baboo," and it seems to have stuck. Another MMA alum who has been there for me in so many ways.

122—There is no one I enjoy leading sung prayer with more, and I have been so excited to see her own liturgical compositions make their way into the prayer life of so many parishes.

123—A more recent photo with Jo, back during a visit to Saginaw. She continues to be a source of joy and faith that has resulted in a friendship that never tires.

124—A typical scenario.

125—A very special part of God's creation.

126—Another MMA alum and blessed "son" of mine, Greg is from Indianapolis. A monster pianist and musician, he is the one performing the improvisations that you hear on the CD that accompanies this book.

127—Bob was the one who opened the door for me at GIA; connected me to many of the hymn text writers that I have come to love over the years, and nurtured my love of hymnody. I will always be grateful.

128—While we have become good friends only in recent years, Anna has been singing with and on the recordings of many liturgical composers for many years, and is now becoming a composer in her own right.

129—*Gather* has held a huge influence for the contemporary liturgical music repertoire since the late 1980's. I was fortunate to have been on the original hymnal committee for the first edition (the one on the far left), along with Michael, Marty, Bob Batastini and Michael Cymbala.

130—Dan drives me crazy. He is 10 years older than me, but he looks like he just graduated from high school.

131—Not only are they great singers and cantors—they are also a lot of fun. Kate is holding one of my many rabbits ("Haas" in German, means "the Rabbit.").

132—Still to this day. And they only cost about 90 bucks.

133—Back row, L to R: Kenni Holmen (an amazing sax player!), Steve Petrunak and Bobby Fisher on guitars. Front row, L to R, singers Derek Campbell, David Fischer, Kate Cuddy and Lori True.

134—I was Lisa's confirmation sponsor back in 1985. In spite of that, she has turned out to be quite the marvelous person. You hear her singing solos on several of my recordings. I am so proud of her. She is married with fully grown children, and she presently serves as Director of Liturgy at St. Ambrose in Woodbury, Minnesota.

135—Dan of course is the composer of the iconic, "Night of Silence." An amazing musician, pianist, composer, graphic artist, all around master of the humanities, and dedicated friend. Dan designed the CD covers for many of my recordings, including *No Longer Strangers, We Give You Thanks, Glory Day,* the first two "Best of" CD's; *Before I Was Born, Echo of Faith, Reach Toward Heaven, Star Child, Living Spirit, Holy Fire,* and many more.

136—I composed "Dedicate Yourselves" for their special celebration.

137—One of my good friends from back home in Michigan, Alissa can sight-read just about anything and has been a tremendous coach and advocate for young people both in liturgical music and in musical theatre.

138—Truly, my brother and companion in the Lord. We are constantly trying to come up with new nick-names for each other—I call him the "Tominator!" When he sings, I feel God's spirit moving in him.

139—I was so nervous because Henri's younger brother, Laurent, was in the audience.

140—The inspiration behind "What Is Your Name?," Betsey is one of the most passionate dancers, actors, and storytellers that I have ever known. She has danced and proclaimed at many important moments in my life.

141—They are so patient, tolerant, enduring—and supportive—of me.

142—The MMA vocal faculty, in the summer of 2017, from L to R: Anna Betancourt, Kate Cuddy, Bonnie Faber, Bill Gokelman (standing in the back), Lisa Habeck, George Miller, and Lynné Gray. Awesome teachers. Awesome people.

143—This was a homily that I gave for the Feast of St. Blaise (Blessing of the Throats), at Corpus Christi Church in Roseville in 2016, now an annual celebration that I have been leading - especially for cantors - in the Archdiocese of St. Paul and Minneapolis.

144—Ready to go, I guess.

145—Jim is the Publisher/CEO of Clear Faith Publishing, who have published several of my books on prayer and spirituality. He has been an important advisor to me in recent years.

146—Kate continues to inspire me, and her love of teenagers as a teacher and mentor is truly her legacy.

147—With my former pastor (I think he will ALWAYS be my pastor) from my teenage years at St. Christopher's in Bridgeport, Michigan—Fr. Bill Taylor, at the festival mass celebrating his 50th anniversary as a priest, at St. Dominic's Church in Saginaw, Pentecost 2017. I composed the responsorial psalm for this celebration and served as the cantor.

148—Lori and I made the marquee at this concert in New Hampshire. Thanks Lisa Boucher!

149—A special day.

150—The Liturgical Composers Forum was begun by John Foley many years ago, and we meet every January in St. Louis for a week of learning, support and deepening of friendships. This is what happens when there is free time in the schedule.

151—A most happy memory.

152—I miss Sue so much. I hope that she would have been proud of me. I owe her so much.

153—Teaching the adult participants at one of the *Music Ministry Alive!* institutes. Over the 19 years of the summer program, we have had close to 700 adults take part.

154—A bit messy, but most assuredly, a busy spot for me.

155—Lori has been a most valued and trusted colleague, friend, and I am continually amazed at her creativity as both a composer, master cantor, workshop leader and liturgist. She served in parish ministry for many years back in New Hampshire and also in Minnesota; and for 14 years was Campus Minister for Liturgy and Music at St. Catherine University (begun and still sponsored by the Sisters of St. Joseph of Carondelet, St. Paul Province); and now works for the sisters as their Director of Ritual and Liturgy Services. As I have said elsewhere in these pages, no one has been a better interpreter of my music, and serving with her for so many years has been at the top of the list of the many blessings I have had as a minister.

156—David and Dan played on the accompanying CD for this book.

157—During my tour of Australia and New Zealand in the fall of 2017. Michael and his wife Anne, have now become very dear friends.

158—At dinner in Cincinnati during the NPM convention in the summer of

2017. Some of my favorite people on the planet.

159—Teaching at MMA2016

160—This is one of my favorite icons, "Christ and the Believer." This depicts Christ walking alongside us, not in front or in behind us. This icon helps me in my times of prayer, to always remember that I am not alone.

160—Yup.

The many photos found in this book come from a wide variety of sources, known and unknown. Thanks to the following people and organizations who were the source of many of the photos, or who discovered them and contributed them to this book: Pat Gallery, David Gilmour, Helen Haas, Maria Infante, Bill Rustic, John Kascht, Gary Eittreim, Kathy Baybayan, Bonnie Faber, the people of GIA Publications, Rita Martin, Bob Gordon, Barb Conley Waldmiller, The Catholic Spirit/Archdiocese of St. Paul and Minneapolis, The North American Forum on the Catechumenate, Joe and Pat Hudetz, Sharie Bowman, Jim and Teresa Knipper, Maureen Briare, Miles Hanson, Steve Wiese, Scott Malchow, Jay and Aui Tamayo, Kenneth Dacanay, Janet Lim and the Archdiocese of Singapore, Eydie Stephanie, Suzanne Orland, The Servants of Jesus in Saginaw, Michigan, Peter Gleich, Chrissy Fritzen, Tom Hoerl, The Archdiocese of Milwaukee, Dawne Mechlinski, Pearl Gervais, Greg Papesh, Eileen Bird, Fr. Alapaki Kim, Mary Reimann, The Archdiocese of Wellington in New Zealand, Michael Mangan, Stephanie Braley, Matt Reichert, and also, the author. Apologies and regrets, but also deep thanks to those who are unable to identify and not named here, but who captured some of these people and events on camera.

GRATITUDE

There are so many people who I feel compelled to thank for their having played a significant role in the birthing of these "hymns, psalms" and hopefully, "inspired songs" over the span of the last 40 years. It is not lost on me that to serve as a composer of liturgical music is a very high calling. Knowing this, I believe that whatever good I may have accomplished in my life through this vocation is the outcome of a life touched and formed by so many blessed mentors, teachers, friends, guides, heroes ... and all of them in my mind—saints.

I give thanks to God for my mother and father who, beyond being awesome parents and role models, were also outstanding musicians. My Dad was a pianist, organist, and piano teacher, and he worked in music retail for many years. My Mom was my very first piano teacher (I started when I was four), but she was primarily a singer who also taught music in the public school system (elementary and secondary) most of her adult life. This was the environment that I, as well as my brother and sister were born into. Jeffrey and Colleen are very fine musicians, artists and teachers in their own right who share their artistic gifts and love of teaching in many different environments. I remember that when my brother and I were young, we both were not allowed to have breakfast until we practiced piano for an hour when we first got up in the morning. We also had to put in an hour after we got home from school, and another half-hour before we went to bed. Jeffrey studied vocal music and theatre in college, and Colleen studied art and music and holds a doctorate in Ethnomusicology and Folklore from Indiana University.

As a family, we often made music together and entertained as a family for various civic occasions and events in the greater Saginaw area in Michigan, where we grew up. I will never forget the piles of recitals that we presented in our home, the numerous musical theatre productions that we were a part of, hours upon hours of choir and band practice at school and at church, and most of all—the many family sing-alongs we had, often at parties that we hosted in our home. Mom— who as young college student used to teach music to the cloistered Carmelite nuns in Traverse City Michigan— was the choir director and Dad—who was an organist and chaplain's assistant in the army during the

I WILL BRING YOU HOME

Korean Conflict—was the organist at our home parish; with Jeffrey, Colleen and I, always a part of the ensembles. Jeffrey and I were also altar boys when we were young, and my church singing "career" began when I would often, after communion, walk over to the organ (wearing my altar boy cassock and surplice), to sing in my boy soprano voice the Ave Maria, or at Christmas time, "The Birthday of a King." I miss my parents so very much. Jeffrey, Colleen remain very precious to me, as well as other members of my extended family, and of course, Helen.

My goodness, how blessed I was to have so many amazing music teachers, mentors and other musical friends over the years! There is not enough room to elaborate regarding all that I learned and gleaned from them, but I must name them here, those who were teachers from my earliest years as a boy, and throughout college and beyond. Piano teachers, voice teachers, trumpet and French horn teachers, guitar teachers, and more. Some have passed away, and all played an integral role during the many chapters of my musical education: My very first piano teacher Zola Rudd Patrick, who nurtured the ingredient of "delight" in music making; DeVere Fader, who was the first to put a baton in my hand and instill in me the confidence to be a musical leader and teacher; Bill and Janet Brown, Bob Klump, John Leaman, Bob Brown, Bob Pepera; John Gilmour, who taught me more than the mere chords on the guitar and led me to explore folk music and indigenous songs; Gwen Wilder, who made me learn the Mozart Piano Concerto in A Major—it is still my favorite. I was very much involved in theatre while in high school, a highlight being my being cast as Motel the Tailor in *Fidder on the Roof.* I also had very unique national opportunities while in high school, being able to tour with a national vocal ensemble under the direction of Fred Waring, and as a member of the trumpet section with the United States Collegiate Wind Band during a summer European tour in 1975.

I am thankful for my best friend in high school, David Gilmour, who shared with me a common passion for music of great diversity and styles. He and I created our own summer program for young junior high and high school students in my home town of Bridgeport to build awareness of music appreciation, diversity and culture, long before we had ever heard terms like "pedagogy" and "ethnomusicology."

During my years at Central Michigan University as a music major, I continued to be blest with wonderful teachers and guides like Jeffrey Foote, who was the voice teacher who truly unlocked my singing voice and helped me to keep finding it, as well as my opera director Tim Caldwell, and other professors such as Moonyeen Albrecht, Stephen Hobson, John Irwin, and Steve Egler.

I continued to be active in musical theatre, and then opera, while at CMU, culminating with the wonderful experience of singing the lead in John Phillip Sousa's comic opera, "El Capitan." This led me to being offered to tour with a national Broadway production of "West Side Story" (in the role of Tony—now remember, this was when I was skinny, had hair, and I also had breath control!). I turned that opportunity down when I discerned that I was not called to a performance career in musical theatre, but rather, to serve in some fashion in ministry.

All of these teachers, companions, and music opportunities that I was able to have way back then have informed how I compose and how I have tried to teach over the years.

In addition to the witness of my parents and other extended family members, I was fortunate be formed and encouraged by many wonderful mentors and guides from my home Diocese of Saginaw, Michigan. I want to recognize Fr. Bert Gohm, who as a young seminarian would come over to our catechism classes when I was of elementary age at St. Christopher's in Bridgeport, and lead us in the first "guitar-church songs" that were composed for the liturgy in the aftermath of the Vatican II explosion; songs by people like Ray Repp, Joe Wise and Clarence Rivers. I was more fortunate than many, to have grown up in a parish with such wonderful priest models like Fr. Joseph Favara, Fr. Fritz Loos, Fr. Chet Pilarski, Gerry Banister, Fr. Tom Sutton, and Fr. Bill Taylor, who I claim to be my life long pastor. While I did not attend Catholic school, I was formed in faith by many of the Dominican Sisters from Grand Rapids; the Felician Sisters from Detroit, the Fransiscans and Capuchins in the Saginaw area, and, later, the Servants of Jesus, who always had a very strong presence in the Saginaw Diocese.

When I returned home in 1977 after two years of college at Central Michigan University to discern what God wanted me to do next, I was led to deeper connections with people like Fr. Bob DeLand, my good friend Fr. Jim Bessert, Fr. Ray Oswald, Chris Lauckner, Fr. Joe Schabel, Bud and Donna McCormick, Bill and Dee Rustic, Vince and Olympia DeAgostino, Rudy and Rachel Barnes, Mel and Theresa Harvey, and especially Sr. Roberta Kolasa, SJ—who, from the summer 1977 all the way through until her death in 2013, continued to be my ongoing cornerstone in faith and point of reference and support during the many different ministry adventures that I was to become a part of. In addition to St. Christopher's in Bridgeport, I was fortunate to have wonderful pastoral experiences at other parishes and schools in the Diocese: St. Roch's in Caseville, Sacred Heart in Bad Axe, St. Casimir's and St. Helen's

I WILL BRING YOU HOME

in Saginaw, and St. Josaphat's in Carrollton. I celebrate my friendship with Jo Infante. We were cantors and sang in the folk group together at St. Christopher's during my later teens and during this transition year. And I can say without any reserve, that Jo is the one who was the first to model for me what it means to *pray* when you sing. We led music together for many different liturgical celebrations and concerts in the area and beyond, and we remain very close to this day—and I am so thankful. It was during this year when I began to compose liturgical music more intentionally and met Joe Wise for the first time. He heard a couple of my songs and encouraged me to keep writing. I will never forget that.

In the fall of 1978 my adventure in Minnesota began, and I have lived here ever since (with the exception of one year in Iowa). I remember the two years at St. John Vianney Seminary and my studies at what was then the College of St. Thomas in St. Paul, in theology as well as vocal music performance. Very soon I came connected to other students who had a similar passion for music and ministry; who helped me make my very first recording, *I Am Yours Today*, in January of 1979. God bless Bruce Kaatz, Jeff McLeod, Mary Quigley, Mary Beth King, Vince Schwann, Dale Korogi, Greg Tolaas (may he rest in peace), Jeanne Dold, and Vince Therrien in particular for being such wonderful companions on that exciting maiden voyage. I had great teachers and mentors during this time—thank God for Fr. Ken Pierre; Fr. Ed Foley, OFM Cap; Fr. Jerry Kaiser; Fr. Ralph Goman; Fr. Thomas Conroy; Sr. Rosalie Ryan, CSJ; Fr. (now Bishop) Arthur Kennedy; Sr. Gertrude Foley, SC; Maurice Jones; and Sr. Catherine Litecky, CSJ—just to name a few.

It was during this time at the seminary that I met both Michael Joncas and Marty Haugen. That association changed my life forever, and I have no need to elaborate, other than to give thanks to God for our collaborations, mutual support, and friendship that remains so precious to this day.

I was fortunate to hold two full time positions in parish ministry, first as the Director of Music and Youth at Our Lady's Immaculate Heart parish in Ankeny, Iowa (I was only there five months, but it is where and when I composed "We Have Been Told"), and for three years as Director of Music and Liturgy at St. Thomas Aquinas parish in St. Paul Park, Minnesota (1982-1985). I am especially grateful to the community at STA, and to my pastor during those days, Fr. John Fitzpatrick, for providing rich soil for me as I began to mature as a liturgical composer and pastoral minister. I also served as composer-in-residence and adjunct instructor at the Saint Paul Seminary School of Divinity (1985-1988) and also as a pastoral musician and composer-in-residence at St. Thomas the Apostle parish in Minneapolis for four years (God bless you, Mary

Werner). While I have not served in a leadership position at a parish for many years, I am thankful for being a member of the faith community at St. Cecelia's in St. Paul, where I have served as a cantor. I also had some unique experiences as part time campus minister at two Catholic high schools in the Archdiocese, Benilde-St. Margaret's School in St. Louis Park, and at Cretin-Derham Hall in St. Paul. I could go on and on about these parish and school experiences, and how they became additional birthing places for liturgical composition and for my pastoral work in ministry.

I am also thankful to Jeanne Cotter for all of the years of music making and ministry together; for her various piano arrangements that helped some of my compositions take flight, and for all of the trips we made together to spread the "good liturgical music news"; to Fr. Virgil Funk and the early formative years of my involvement with National Association of Pastoral Musicians (NPM); and for the creative pastoral work that I was able to explore and develop as a team member for many years with the North American Forum on the Catechumenate, with such marvelous colleagues and friends as Vicky Tufano, Fr. Jim Dunning and Fr. Ron Lewinski (may they both rest in peace), Fr. Bob Duggan, Thom Morris, Maureen Kelly, Fr. Don Neumann, and Fr. Ray Kemp. Thanks need to go out to the various non-music publishers that I have worked with, such as St. Anthony Messenger Press, which is now Fransiscan Media (God bless you, Lisa Biedenbach, Ron Riegler, and Fr. Greg Friedman, OFM), Liturgy Training Publications, Saint Mary's Press, Brown-ROA, Harcourt Religion Publisher, Crossroad, Twenty-Third Publications, The Pastoral Center, and especially Jim Knipper and everyone involved at Clear Faith Publishing. I need to thank Sr. Edith Prendergast, RC for her years of leadership and inviting me to be part of the annual Los Angeles Religious Education Congress for the past 30-some years. As a workshop leader, concert performer, and conference speaker I have been fortunate and blest to have travelled to all 50 states, Washington DC and Guam, as well as to Canada, England, Ireland, Germany, Italy, The Bahamas, Israel, Greece, Turkey, the Philippines, Singapore, Australia and New Zealand. The ministry of sung prayer has literally brought me to places where I would never have dreamed of visiting, and to be before so many wonderful people.

For the last 20 some years, Lori True has been by my side in numerous ministry and faith endeavors, and like Michael and Marty, she been a very honest and forthright source of feedback and critique in regards to my liturgical music as well as all of my ventures in ministry. We began *Music Ministry Alive!* together, and working on that experience has brought about blessing upon blessing. Our ministry together in presenting workshops, retreats and concerts has brought about some of my most treasured experiences in serving God's people. Thanks beyond thanks goes to Lori.

Probably the best "composition" that I ever came up with, was the *Music Ministry Alive!* program that, with Lori by my side, began in 1999. For the past 20 years, over 2500 young people have been a part of this experience every summer.; it brought together high school and early college age students from all across the country and well beyond—many of whom are still continuing and deepening their commitment to ministry. Along with Lori, my deepest thanks go to those original team members who took the risk with me during that first effort in July 1999: Kate Cuddy, Fr. Ray East, Stephen Petrunak, Leisa Anslinger, Tom Franzak, Bobby Fisher, Eileen Bird, David Fischer, my sister Colleen, Bonnie Faber, Robin Medrud, Art Zannoni, Bill Huebsch, Greg Weinand (may he rest in peace), and Laurie Delgatto—God bless them always, as well as those who served with Lori and me in leadership so lavishly in more recent years, especially Tim Westerhaus, Jes Garceau, Matt Reichert, Zack Stachowski, Katherine True, Sarah Wente, Ellen Larson (all MMA alums!), and Carmen Grace Poppert. All of the youth and adult participants, team members, and others who supported us, especially Sr. Andrea Lee, IHM—I believe that they are among the most beautiful stars in the sky.

I think of all of the recording projects that I have been able to produce over the years with GIA; and the dozens and dozens and dozens of talented singers, instrumentalists and engineers—far too many to name here— who helped to bring my music to life, and I thank God for all of them. The memories of making beautiful music together at Cookhouse and Metro Studios in Minneapolis, Paisley Park in Chanhassen, and in recent years, Creation Audio in Minneapolis are sacred for me.

While some of these people have been mentioned already, I am in need of naming some of them again, and I am also grateful to other friends, composer colleagues, former students and "encouragers" who have inspired and held me up in my creative work and in my darkest of days: Gary Daigle; Rory Cooney; Fr. George DeCosta; Joe Camacho; Barb Conley-Waldmiller; Sr. Kathleen Harmon, SNDden; Fred Moleck; Stephen Petrunak; Fr. Ricky Manalo, CSP; Tom Kendzia; Bob Hurd; Rob Strusinski; Alissa Hetzner; Greg Papesh; Sr. Helen Prejean, CSJ; Lynné Gray; Mary Jane and Jim Moore; Sr. Bridget Waldorf, SSND; Pam Cole; Fr. Peter Damian Massengill, OFM Conv.; Kathy and Glenn Baybayan; Jeff and Jean Bross Judge; Bro. Dennis Schmitz, SM; Kathryn Brown; George Miller; Tom Backen; Kristen Wenzel; Paulette Ching; Fr. Alapaki Kim; Becky Gaunt; Cameron Cabot; Abbey Scherrer; Fr. John Forliti;

Gratitude

Dan Schutte; Jim Moudry and Carole Kastigar; Robin Medrud; Lisa Habeck; Roc O'Connor, SJ; Sharon and Mark Nicpon; Barbara Colliander; Maureen Riedl and her family; Sr. Kate Kuenstler, PHJC; Joel Loecken; Danielle and Madeline Peterson; David Feily; Fr. Ron Rohlheiser, OMI; Abbie Rivard; Fr. Mike Byron; Sr. Andrea Lee, IHM; Steve Kron; Chrissy Fritzen; Rev. Anita Bradshaw; Jes Garceau; Mary Frances Reza; Bob Harvey; Sandy Homb; Fr. Bob DeLand; Jeff and Julie Koval; David Gilmour and Judith Martin; Doug and Brenna Starkebaum; Lindsey Rebber; John Angotti; Fr. Anthony Ruff, OSB; Lisa Ersilla; Mary Kay Werner; Jaimé Cortez; Mary Reimann; Anna Betancourt; Bro. Mickey McGrath, OSFS; Jo Greene; Eileen Bird; Marc Anderson; Rev. Dana and Michael Strande; Steve Wiese; Miles Hanson; Lisa Boucher; Archbishop Rembert Weakland; Bill Gokelman; Owen Alstott; Peter Kolar; Jerry Galipeau; Carol Porter; Scott Malchow; Vicky Tufano; Sr. Sue Mosteller, CSJ; Amy Barnes; Olympia DeAgostino; Robert Jonas; Roldolfo Lopez and Stella Garcia; Lisa Driscoll; and Maria "Mimi" Infante. I also want to offer a special blessing of gratitude to my dear uncle, Bill Haas, who has always been a very important presence in my life, especially in recent years.

I believe that I must give a holy shout out to these companions who alongside Michael, Marty, and Lori, continue to make up a core and vital circle of life in ministry for me: Rob and Mary Glover; Bill Huebsch; Matt Reichert; Zack Stachowski; Lou Anne Tighe; Dan Kantor; Sr. Kathleen Storms, SSND; Kate Cuddy; Mary Werner; Fr. Bill Taylor; Jo Infante; Fr. Joe Kempf; Betsey Beckman; Leisa Anslinger; Matt Maus; Jim Waldo; Bishop Remi de Roo; Pearl Gervais; Paul Tate; Fr. Ray Kemp; Andrea Goodrich; Fr. Jim Bessert; Lisa Cressy; Sr. Gertrude Foley, SC; my "brothers in the Lord": Tom Franzak, Gary Daigle, Stephen Pishner, and Jim Knipper; my dear friend in faith and in laughter, Bonnie Faber; and my ongoing and "go to Scripture-guru," friend, and fellow Israel pilgrim, Art Zannoni. What a wonderful community of believers these people have been and continue to be!

As I write these words, I am remembering those saints who graced my life who are no longer with us. I remember again Sr. Roberta Kolasa, SJ; who was a profound presence and friend throughout the many chapters of discernment in my life. I also remember Sue-Seid Martin, who was a mentor beyond description, a formidable force that pulled important music out of me for ritual prayer. I am also remembering other mentors, colleagues, collaborators, heroes and friends like Leon Roberts; Fr. Jim Dunning; Mike Hay; Derek Campbell; Bob Piercy; Michael Grimes; Valerie Battles; Fr. Ron Lewinski; Dee Rustic; Sr. Rosalyn Nowak, SJ; Bill and Tim Brown; Vince DeAgostino; Bishop Francis

I WILL BRING YOU HOME

Reh; Fr. Mike Bell; Jeffrey Johnson; Marty Coffman; Bishop Ken Untener; Ralph Kiefer; Christianne Brusselmans; Sr. Maria de la Cruz of the Society of Helpers; Larry Gully; Fr. Eugene Walsh, SS; Fr. Jeffrey Donner; Sr. Anne Bryan Smollin, CSJ; M.D. Ridge; Fr. Lucien Deiss; John Riedl; Marcy Weckler Barr; Sharon Maurer; Fr. Joseph Gelineau; Shirley Gilmour; Rudy Barnes; and Fr. Eugene LaVerdiere, SSS. The earth was truly holy ground while they were with us, and that holiness continues to rise up. I also hold up to the angels and communion of saints—my parents and grandparents, my aunts and uncles Ann Haas, Glenn and Colleen Purvis, and other aunts, uncles, and cousins who have passed away. Thank God that all of these people were in my life. I want to give thanks to God for Fr. Henri Nouwen, who I was never able to meet personally before he died suddenly in 1996 (we came close a couple of times), but whose impact on my life spiritually has been nothing less than profound.

Finally, I want to share my deep gratitude for the wonderful people who are and who have been a part of GIA Publications. I remember the first time I visited them around 1982 or so, and played some of my music for the first time for Bob Batastini and Michael Cymbala. I also remember being absolutely terrified. I thought I was going to explode with excitement when Bob told me that very day that they wanted to publish my music. I left that day planning for my first full collection with them, "We Have Been Told." I will always be grateful to Bob for taking that chance with me, and to Michael for advocating for me, my ideas, projects, and my talents—especially in those early years. Praise be to God for Alec and Ed Harris. Thanks to all of the others who have been a part of the GIA family over the years and who are there now: Michael Silhavy, Tom Hawley, Kelly Dobbs and Jeff Mickus, David Anderson, Suzanne Orland, Andrew Schultz, Tony Franchetti, Victoria Zibell, Kyle Cothern, Gladys Guerrero, Gregg Sewell, Brian Streem, Phil Roberts, Neil Borgstrom, Michael Boschert, and to Brenna Cronin, who manages with class the wild beast that is "One License." Thanks beyond words to Jennifer Kerr Budziak for her courage in editing and guiding this project to completion, and to everyone else at GIA for their tireless energy and support. These are the people who have made it possible for my music to get into the hands of music directors and into the hearts of worshippers who gather together to pray and celebrate. It has been a privilege and honor to create music with them all these years and to be a part of their ongoing mission, to serve and sing with the people of God with gladness.

What an extraordinary, at times exhausting, and usually, exhilarating journey I have been a part of! I want to thank all of you who sung and prayed with this music in your celebration of the liturgy over time, and also in the many varied ways that many of you have shared with me as to how this music has been important in your patterns of prayer that have hopefully, helped to lead you to a deeper discipleship. Thanks for being a part of the many chapters of the last 40 years. To any of you who I may have hurt, caused pain, or disappointed at times, know of my deep regret and sorrow for doing so. All of you who have walked with me have been partners and co-creators in these compositions for sung prayer. God has gifted my life beyond words, and so have all of you who have been singing and praying these hymns, songs, mass settings, and psalms. My prayer continues to be that through whatever gifts I have been given, God is being announced more boldly with courage through my efforts over these years.

I could go on and on (as many of you who know me could attest) with more expressions of gratitude, but as my Italian ancestors would say: "Basta!" (Enough!) I have no idea what God has in store for the future, and I have no way of knowing if there are many—if any—more song prayers to compose. We will have to see what God has in mind. Mimi—this is all your fault, you know! All I can call to mind now, are the words that Dag Hammarskjold once shared: "For all that has been—thanks. For all that will be—yes." DH

ABOUT DAVID HAAS

David Haas is from Eagan, Minnesota, where he is the director of The Emmaus Center for Music, Prayer and Ministry, in addition to serving as the animator for the Cretin-Derham Hall Taizé Prayer Community in St. Paul. Highly regarded as one of the preeminent composers of liturgical music in the English-speaking world, he has produced well over 50 collections and recordings of original liturgical music with GIA Publications. His music has been translated into many languages, appearing in hymnals and resources of various Christian denominations throughout the world.

David was the founder and executive director for *Music Ministry Alive!*, an international liturgical music formation program and movement that has reached out for almost 20 years to high school and college-age youth. He has travelled extensively as a workshop presenter, retreat leader, and concert performer throughout the United States, Washington DC and Guam, as well as in Canada, England, Ireland, Germany, Italy, the Bahamas, Israel, Greece, Turkey, The Philippines, Singapore, Australia and New Zealand. A former Grammy Award nominee, he is also the author of numerous books in the areas of liturgy and music, prayer and spirituality, religious education and youth ministry. In 2015 David was the recipient of an Honorary Doctorate in Humane Letters from the University of Portland in Oregon, and together with Michael Joncas and Marty Haugen, the 2017 Pax Christi Award from St. John's Abbey and University in Collegeville, Minnesota. Visit his website: www.DavidHaas.us

David's mission is embodied as follows:

SERVANT
Ministry grounded in the Spirit of Jesus

COMPOSER
Sung prayer for the Body of Christ

I WILL BRING YOU HOME

TEACHER
Workshops & programs for formation & renewal

ARTIST
Concerts, events & recordings to nurture prayer, faith & mission

MENTOR
Leadership & advocacy to empower the young church

HARBINGER
Brightening the light of others who witness "Good News"

AUTHOR
Resources for pastoral ministry & spirituality

HERALD
Commitment to God's movement, reign & justice in the world

May my voice be
the voice of a servant,
as you are:
washing feet
healing wounds,
and leading praise.

1) Mom and Dad
   on their wedding day (June 28, 1952)

2) The family Haas making music (1961)

4) With sister Colleen
   and brother Jeffrey (1964)

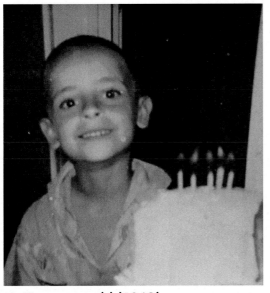

3) Five years old (1962)

5) St. Christopher's Church,
   Bridgeport, MI

6) With Dad

7) With Mom

8) Joan and Robert Haas

9) With Colleen and Jeffrey (2017)

11) First year of high school, 9th grade (1971)

10) With Helen in New Zealand (2017)

13) Senior year (1975)

12) 11th grade (1974)

14) Holding the lead role in "El Capitan" (1977)

15) David's earliest liturgical music influences

16) With his very first piano teacher, Zola Rudd Patrick

17) Maria "Mimi" Infante (2017)

18) With Fr. James Bessert

19) Sr. Roberta Kolasa, SJ; David's primary mentor over the years

20) Sing-along (1979)

21) David with Joe Wise

23) A very young Suzanne Toolan, RSM

22) The Dameans

I Am Yours Today

SONGS OF PRAYER AND CELEBRATION
By DAVID HAAS

25) 1978

24) David's first LP, "I Am Yours Today" (1979)

26) The first rough score of "Send Us Your Spirit"

27) College of St. Thomas composers on "In Song"

29) Saint Thomas Aquinas Church, St. Paul Park, MN

28) Michael Cymbala

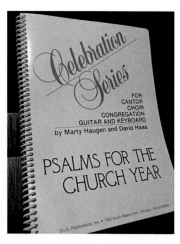

30) Psalms for the Church Year (1982)

31) 1983: Young, skinny, and he has hair

32) Recording "We Have Been Told" (1983): with Marty Haugen, Jerry Steckling, and Sue Seid-Martin

33) Earthen Vessels (St. Louis Jesuits)

34) First draft of "Blest Are They" (1984)

35) With Marty Haugen & Michael Joncas, before the "Come and Journey" concert (Minneapolis, 1984)

36) Bobby Fisher

37) The founders of GIA:
    Ed Harris and Bob Batastini

38) Recording with Bonnie Faber
    ("Light and Peace," 1986)

40) Rob Strusinski

39) Barbara Colliander,
    the inspiration for "Blest Are They"

41) Fr. George DeCosta

42) Malia Puka O Kalani Church
    (Mary, Gate of Heaven), Hilo, HI

43) Bob Hurd

44) Remember Your Love,
one of David's all-time favorites
(The Dameans)

45) With Barb Conley Waldmiller
and Thom Morris

46) With engineer Tom Tucker;
Metro Studios, Minneapolis (1987)

47) Fr. James Dunning

48) Recording "Prayer for Peace"
with Bob Harvey (1987)

49) Michael Grimes
and Sue Seid-Martin (1987)

50) With Jeanne Cotter (1990)

51) With Fr. George DeCosta,
Mary Werner,
& Sue Seid-Martin

52) With Ed Gutfruend
and Bobby Fisher (1987)

53) Donna Pena

54) "Who Calls You By Name" (1988)

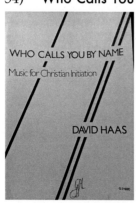

55) The Milwaukee Symposium
for Liturgical Composers;
with Archbishop Rembert Weakland (1988)

56) 1992

57) Robin Medrud, Bonnie Faber
& Mary Werner
("As Water to the Thirsty,"1987)

58) With Lori True (2000)

59) Monsignor Ray East

60) With Lori True
and the St. Patrick's (Milford, NH) Children's Choir

61) Glenn and
Kathy Baybayan.

62) With Kate Cuddy,
who encouraged David to bring
"You Are Mine" out of hiding (1990)

64) At the Western Wall in Jerusalem

63) Published score for "You Are Mine"

65) The "Star Child" tour
(December, 2000)

67) With Lori True

66) Joe Camacho

68) Leon C. Roberts,
   "God Has Done Marvelous Things"

69) Fun with Marty

70) With Richard Rohr, OFM

71) Stephen Petrunak

72) Mike Hay

73) The "Glory Day" concert
   (Cincinnati, 1997)

74) With Pearl Gervais & Bishop Remi de Roo

75) With Tom Kendzia, John Foley, & Marty Haugen

76) With Fr. Virgil Funk

77) With Art Zannoni (Caesarea by the Sea, 2016)

78) Music Ministry Alive! (2017)

80) With Zack Stachowski

79) Bonnie Faber

81) With Lori True, Zack, Jes Garceau, Fr. Ray East, Bill Gokelman, & Matt Reichert (MMA 2017)

82) Coaching young cantors at MMA

83) St. Catherine University, St. Paul, MN; home of Music Ministry Alive!

85) With engineer Steve Wiese

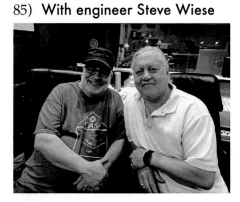

84) The Cretin-Derham Hall Liturgical Choir, St. Paul, MN (2014)

86) At St. Catherine University

87) Giving Jesse Manibusan some love

88) With Jim Waldo

89) With—guess who?

90) With friend and heroine,
Sr. Helen Prejean, CSJ

91) At the Los Angeles Religious
Education Congress (2016)

92) An artist's rendering

93) With Jaime Cortez, Rory Cooney, and Gary Daigle

94) With Bill Huebsch

95) Receiving his Honorary Doctorate in Humane Letters (University of Portland, 2015)

96) Stephen Pishner, Paul Tate, & Sr. Kathleen Harmon, SNDden

97) With choirs at Ateneo University, Manila, the Philippines (2016)

98) With dear friend Rob Glover

99) The members of "Hangad,"
Manila (2016)

100) Larry Hylton, Derek Campbell,
Joe Camacho, & Steve Herring

101) Concluding his concert in Singapore (2016)

102) At Henri Nouwen's grave,
Richmond, Ontario (2016)

103) At the "Conspire" Conference, Albuquerque (2016)

104) With Tony Alonso,
Marty,
Ricky Manalo, CSP;
& young composers
at MMA 2016

105) Cretin-Derham Hall,
St. Paul, MN

106) Choir recording session for
"I Will Live On" (Creation Audio, 2015)

107) Fr. John Forliti

108) With Lori True, Kate Cuddy,
Paulette Ching, Michael Joncas
& Tony Alonso; Chaminade University,
Honolulu (2015)

110) With Bonnie Faber

109) Renewing Baptismal Promises
with Fr. Ray at the Jordan River
(2017)

111) Singing "You Are Mine" with
Nora Strande at Masada (2017)

112) David's revised and new mass settings

113) Recording lead vocals
and not crying in baseball (2016)

114) Conducting at MMA (2017)

116) Preaching at the
Mount of the Beatitudes,
Israel (2017)

115) With Michael Joncas

117) Being goofy; Los Angeles Religious Education Congress (2017)

118) In Hawaii with Gary Daigle

119) With Zack Stachowski & Matt Reichert

120) Their last recording session together (2016)

121) Matt Maus, David's right hand man

122) With Lori after one of their concerts

123) With Jo Infante (2017)

124) Lori is in charge, Zack is rolling his eyes, David looks confused

126) With Greg Papesh

125) Bob Piercy

127) With Bob Batastini

128) With Anna Betancourt

129) The many incarnations of the "Gather" hymnal (GIA)

130) With Dan Schutte

131) Three of David's favorite cantors:
Kate, Lori, and Bonnie

132) He loves his SM-58 microphone

133) "Glory Day" concert
(Cincinnati, 1996)

134) With Lisa Cressy

135) Dan Kantor

136) Wedding Day!
Zack Stachowski
& Natalie Spehar (2015)

137) With Alissa Hetzner

138) With "brother in the Lord,"
Tom Franzak

140) Betsey Beckman

139) The "Spirituality of Henri Nouwen"
Conference (San Antonio, 2017)

141) With GIA Leadership:
Tom Hawley & Alec Harris

142) Voice teachers at MMA 2017

143) Preaching

144) Waiting for his solo
spot at Creation Audio (2016)

145) With Deacon Jim Knipper;
CEO, Clear Faith Publishing

146) Kate Cuddy

147) With former pastor,
Fr. Bill Taylor
(Diocese of Saginaw, 2017)

148) Lori and David
making the marquee!

149) The 2017 Pax Christi Award
(St. John's, Collegeville; 2017)

150) Liturgical composer antics
with Rob Glover, Gary Daigle,
John Angotti & Stephen Lay

151) At Emmaus (2017)

152) One of David's
key mentors,
Sue Seid-Martin

153) Teaching at MMA 2017

154) Where David works

155) Lori True

156) Recording with former students,
David Feily & Dan Gershgol

157) With Michael Mangan (Wellington, New Zealand; 2017)

158) With dear friends: Natalie, Zack, Matt, Lori and Bonnie

159) Teaching at MMA 2016

160) David's favorite icon: Christ and the Believer (7th century)

161) Tired. But grateful. God is good.